Innovation in the Digital Economy

The rapidly changing world requires constant revisions and adaptations to existing business strategies and models. The emerging industry 5.0 reality is forcing companies to transition to a more sustainable, human-centric, and resilient industry through innovation. This book presents concrete business models and practical frameworks to assist managers in developing and implementing innovative and robust businesses, both globally and locally.

This edited collection compiles an experienced team of contributing authors with diverse academic backgrounds who cover a range of topics on different aspects of innovation, from exploring the challenges associated with industry 5.0 to incorporating artificial intelligence in modeling consumer behavior. Based on the experiences and challenges posed by recent economic developments and recovery from the COVID-19 pandemic, the book offers the reader a chance to read case studies from global companies that have successfully implemented new innovations. Thanks to a rigorous research methodology in accordance with principles and standards recognized by the DAC Network, the book provides an actionable road map on how to change one's innovation strategy techniques in light of changing business conditions.

Innovation in the Digital Economy will be of direct interest to scholars and subject matter experts in the field of innovation management. Business leaders and reflective practitioners will find the content relevant and accessible.

Agnieszka Rzepka is a Professor at Lublin University of Technology in the Faculty of Management in the Department of Economics and Economic Management. She specializes in inter-organizational management, intellectual capital, self-management, and SMEs. Her current research is focused on teal organizations. In addition to 140 papers, she has written 7 proprietary and collective monographs such *as Inter-Organizational Relations and Intellectual Capital as Factors for the Development of Micro and Small Enterprises: A Study of Polish and Georgian Enterprises* (Difin, 2018). She is also the co-author of *Self-Management, Entrepreneurial Culture, and Economy 4.0: A Contemporary Approach to Organizational Theory Development* (Routledge, 2022) and *Inter-organizational Management in Agile Enterprises* (Texter, 2017).

Routledge Studies in Innovation, Organizations and Technology

RIOT!

Organizational Change, Innovation and Business Development
The Impact of Non-Technological Innovations
Edited by Magdalena Popowska and Julita E. Wasilczuk

Public Innovation and Digital Transformation
Edited by Hannele Väyrynen, Nina Helander and Harri Jalonen

Innovation and Leadership in the Public Sector
The Australian Experience
Mahmoud Moussa, Leonie Newnham, Adela McMurray and Nuttawuth Muenjohn

Advancing Big Data Analytics for Healthcare Service Delivery
Tiko Iyamu

Open Labs and Innovation Management
The Dynamics of Communities and Ecosystems
Edited by Valérie Mérindol and David W. Versailles

Technology Brands in the Digital Economy
Edited by Wioleta Kucharska and Ewa Lechman

Business Models for Industry 4.0
Concepts and Challenges in SME Organizations
Sandra Grabowska and Sebastian Saniuk

Innovation in the Digital Economy
New Approaches to Management for Industry 5.0
Edited by Agnieszka Rzepka

For more information about this series, please visit: www.routledge.com/Routledge-Studies-in-Innovation-Organizations-and-Technology/book-series/RIOT

Innovation in the Digital Economy

New Approaches to Management for Industry 5.0

Edited by
Agnieszka Rzepka
***Translated by* Jakub Prachowski**

Routledge
Taylor & Francis Group
LONDON AND NEW YORK

First published 2023
by Routledge
4 Park Square, Milton Park, Abingdon, Oxon OX14 4RN

and by Routledge
605 Third Avenue, New York, NY 10158

Routledge is an imprint of the Taylor & Francis Group, an informa business

British Library Cataloguing-in-Publication Data
A catalogue record for this book is available from the British Library

ISBN: 978-1-032-46993-5 (hbk)
ISBN: 978-1-032-47035-1 (pbk)
ISBN: 978-1-003-38431-1 (ebk)

DOI: 10.4324/9781003384311

Typeset in Bembo
by KnowledgeWorks Global Ltd.

Innovation in the Digital Economy

New Approaches to Management for Industry 5.0

Edited by
Agnieszka Rzepka
***Translated by* Jakub Prachowski**

Routledge
Taylor & Francis Group
LONDON AND NEW YORK

First published 2023
by Routledge
4 Park Square, Milton Park, Abingdon, Oxon OX14 4RN

and by Routledge
605 Third Avenue, New York, NY 10158

Routledge is an imprint of the Taylor & Francis Group, an informa business

British Library Cataloguing-in-Publication Data
A catalogue record for this book is available from the British Library

ISBN: 978-1-032-46993-5 (hbk)
ISBN: 978-1-032-47035-1 (pbk)
ISBN: 978-1-003-38431-1 (ebk)

DOI: 10.4324/9781003384311

Typeset in Bembo
by KnowledgeWorks Global Ltd.

Contents

Contributors

Przemysław Adamkiewicz, Ph.D., is a Lecturer at the University of Economics and Innovation in Lublin. For seven years, he has been professionally involved in implementing research and development projects in the field of industrial tomography and measurement systems, including managing projects in the field of device-free localization. Przemysław Adamkiewicz is the author of 80 scientific publications on new technologies. His scientific interests include the Internet of Things, Indoor Localization and Navigation Systems, Radio Tomography, Distributed Measurement Systems, and Beacons.

Jakub Bis, Ph.D., since 2004, employed in the Department of Economics and Management of Economy at the Lublin University of Technology. In his research work, he concentrated mainly on startups, business models, and foreign direct investments. He is the author or co-author of 50 scientific books, articles, or chapters in monographs.

Sylwester Bogacki, Ph.D. Prof. WSEI, is the Dean of the Faculty of Administration and Social Sciences at Lublin's School of Economics and Innovation. He specializes in financial management and the design of investment processes. His scientific output includes about 50 scientific articles. A member of management and control bodies of commercial companies in the development industry. Associated with the university for over 15 years.

Agnieszka Bojanowska is a Lecturer at Lublin University of Technology since 2004. She is a member of the Management Faculty Council of the Lublin University of Technology. She is the author of approximately 50 published articles and reviews and the author/editor/co-editor of a few books, including *Managing Customer Relationships at Banks That Grant Mortgage Loans* (2012). Her teaching and research interests include customer relationship management, neuromarketing, green marketing, marketing, marketing communication, and consumer behavior, among others.

Ewa Bojar, Ph.D., is a retired Professor at the Lublin University of Technology. During 50 years of her professional career, she was Deputy Rector for Scientific Affairs, the Dean and Deputy Dean of Management

Faculty. Her scientific and research interests are centered on regional issues. Currently on: creation of networks, clusters, and startups as economic and social organizational forms activity; sustainable development and leadership. Author and co-author of over 140 scientific publications in this area.

Matylda Bojar, Ph.D., is an employee of the Faculty of Management at Lublin University of Technology. Her scientific and research interest is focused on problems of management in the regions, innovational aspects of regional development, startups, clusters and clustering processes, leadership, regional aspects of business, and implementation of CSR norms in Polish enterprises. Author and co-author of over 70 scientific publications.

Ryszard Borowiecki is a Professor at Krakow University of Economics, where he served as a Rector from 2002 to 2008. He is also a researcher with 54 years of experience and is the author, co-author, and/or scientific editor of more than 600 works in the fields of corporate management, economic analysis and diagnostics, and corporate development.

Borys Burkynskyi is a Doctor of Economics, Professor, Academician of the NAS of Ukraine, and Director of the Institute of Market Problems and Economic&Ecological Research of the National Academy of Sciences of Ukraine. His research interests include economics and management, market mechanisms, investments in commodity markets, entrepreneurship development, and sustainable development.

Tomasz Cieplak, Ph.D., is an Assistant Professor at the Lublin University of Technology and a specialist in distributed systems at Netrix Group sp. z o.o. Professional activity in the field of computer science for over 25 years. He is the author of about 95 scientific articles. The current scientific activity covers basic and applied research focusing on machine learning methods and artificial intelligence. The work is implemented in distributed information systems developed by the author to support the activities of modern enterprises.

Magdalena Czerwińska is an Assistant Professor at the Lublin University of Technology and head of the Department of Economics and Economic Management. She is an active member of scientific societies (Polish Economic Society, Scientific Society of Economic Informatics, Scientific Society of Organization and Management). She is the author of over 50 papers. She specializes in knowledge management, health, information technology acceptance models, and health information.

Zdzisława Dacko-Pikiewicz is a Professor of Applied Sciences and Rector at WSB University, Poland.

Joanna Dzieńdziora has Ph.D. in economics, specialization in human resource management. She is an Assistant Professor in the Department of

Management, Coordinator of the Doctoral Seminar at WSB University. She is an author of numerous articles and essays concerning the management of enterprises and human resources management; long-term employee of public administration. The research interest of the author concentrates on the subjects concerning human resources management of small and medium enterprises and on the role of women in management.

Łukasz Gołąbek, M.Sc., is the vice-president of Netrix Group sp. z o.o. and Netrix Venture sp. z o.o. He participated in and managed several scientific and research projects, investment and consulting projects. He is the author of several articles. His scientific interests focus on applications of computational intelligence in commercial systems, data analysis, and enterprise and investment capital management.

Valeriy Goryachuk is a Doctor of Economics, Senior Researcher at the Institute of Market Problems and Economic & Ecological Research of the National Academy of Sciences of Ukraine. His research interests include mathematical modeling of socio-economic and ecological systems, state regulation of the regional economy, competitiveness and capitalization of economy, and international strategies of economic cooperation.

Elwira Gross-Gołacka, Ph.D., is an Associate Professor and a researcher at the Faculty of the Management University of Warsaw, member of the Board of Directors of the University of Warsaw Foundation. She has many years of experience in managing projects. She has many years of experience in business management (Director General of the Ministry of Economic Affairs, Director Department). She is the author of many publications in the field of organization management, diversity management, CSR, wellbeing, sustainability, and quality management. She is a lecturer and trainer, member of supervisory boards, scientific committees, and program boards.

Adam Kiersztyn is an Assistant Professor at Lublin University of Technology. His teaching and research interests include data analysis, data mining, in particular, the detection of anomalies and outliers. He is the author of approximately 50 published articles. Among the numerous publications in the field of anomaly detection and outlier data, it is worth mentioning: Karczmarek, P., Kiersztyn, A., Pedrycz, W., & Al, E. (2020). K-Means-based isolation forest. *Knowledge-Based Systems, 195*, 105659.

Krzysztof Król, M.Sc., is an employee of R&D department in the Research and Development Centre of Netrix S.A. and an assistant at the Higher School of Economics and Innovation in Lublin. Professional activity in the field of computer science for over 14 years. He conducts scientific research in the field of process tomography, IoT, and sensor networks. He is the author of 17 scientific articles. He conducts scientific research in the field of process tomography, IoT, and sensor networks.

Monika Kulisz is an Assistant Professor who has been conducting classes and research at Lublin University of Technology since 2013. Her teaching and research interests include the area of logistics as well as modeling and prediction of phenomena and processes with the use of machine learning methods. She is the author of numerous expert opinions and opinions for the production and service environment, co-author of 39 publications, and a contractor/manager in research projects.

Teresa Kupczyk is a Professor of Economics and Management at General Tadeusz Kościuszko Military University of Land Forces and the University of Business in Wroclaw. She teaches HRM, Project Management, Advanced Leadership in a project team, CSR, Sustainable Development, and GS. Her major fields of interest are managerial competencies, leadership, HRM, military recruitment, and education and training of armed and security forces personnel. She has many years of experience in business management (vice-Rector for Scientific Research, director of post-graduate studies). She is a scientist, and author of books and publications.

Tomasz Kusio is the Assistant Professor in the Economic Policy and Development Programming Department at the Cracow University of Economics. His research interests focus on innovation and development of profit and non-profit organizations as well as inter-organizational relations and the role of stakeholders in relations building. Apart from his research interests, he is also engaged in EU-funded project coordination and realization. He authored or co-authored more than a hundred publications including manuscripts in highly ranked international journals.

Oleksandr Laiko is a Doctor of Economics, Senior Researcher, and Vice-Director for scientific work of Institute of Market Problems and Economic&Ecological Research of the National Academy of Sciences of Ukraine, Odesa, Ukraine. His research interests include investments, capital flows regulation, regional and spatial development, mechanisms of interregional economic cooperation, and entrepreneurship development.

Magdalena Maciaszczyk is an Assistant Professor at the Lublin University of Technology, where she held the position of Deputy Dean for Student Affairs. She is the author of approximately 50 published articles and reviews and the author/editor/co-editor of a number of books, including *Consumer Behaviour of Motor Disabled: A Report from the Research*. Her teaching and research interests include marketing, marketing communication, advertising, consumer behavior, and organizations in a turbulent market, among others.

Michał Maj is an employee of the R&D department at the system architect position in the Research and Development Centre of Netrix S.A. and an assistant at the Higher School of Economics and Innovation in Lublin.

He has been professionally active in IT for over ten years. Main areas of scientific interest: image reconstruction, computer vision, and deep learning. As part of his research work, he published 17 articles in scientific journals.

Zbigniew Makieła is a Professor at the oldest Polish university, Jagiellonian University, and is the Head of the Organisation and Management Department. A member of the Polish Economic Society and the Polish Academy of Sciences of Kraków, he is a Polish economist specializing in innovation management and entrepreneurship.

Barbara Mazur (Prof.) is a researcher at the Lublin University of Technology since 2014, specializing in cultural aspects of management, corporate social responsibility (CSR), and international business. She is the author and co-author of over 170 original research works, including 7 scientific monographs published in Polish and English. She has been a member of the Praxeology Scientific Society and three international organizations: the European Business Ethics Network (EBEN), the Consumer Citizenship Network (CCN), and the Partnership for Education and Research about Responsible Living (PERL).

Radosław Miśkiewicz is a Professor at the Silesian University of Technology. He professionally combines business and research activities; hence, his scientific interests pertain to the organizational structures of metallurgical enterprises, knowledge transfer and management, and the integration of metallurgical enterprises in terms of the transfer of innovative technologies. He has an impressive academic achievement that comprises more than 140 papers. He is also an expert, consultant, and scientific patron on numerous projects. Experienced in implementing research grants, he has received numerous awards for his publications.

Zbigniew Olesiński is a Full Professor at Vistula University in Warsaw who specializes in inter-organizational management, inter-organizational networks, clusters, and globalization problems. He has participated in or managed 11 research programs and 13 EU research grants. He is also the author or co-author of 206 publications, including 14 books such as *Inter-Organizational Relationship Management* (2010) and *Regional management; Poland – Europe-World* (2005). In addition, he was the scientific editor of *Components of Teal Organizations* (2020).

Artur Paździor is a University Professor and Head of the Department of Finance and Accounting at the Faculty of Management of the Lublin University of Technology. The scientific activity of professor Paździor includes over 100 publications in peer-reviewed monographs and scientific journals of national and international scope. Professor Paździor has 20 years of experience in cooperation with businesses in the field of preparation and verification about 100 economic and financial analyzes, recovery programs, restructuring and development projects, and company valuations.

Damian Pliszczuk, M.Sc., is a Data Scientist/Data Engineer in Netrix S.A. Professional activity in the field of computer science for three years. He is the author of two articles on machine learning. His scientific interests are based on the application of mathematics in AI issues – Machine Learning, Deep Learning, and NLP. In his work, he creates complete solutions for a given system – from identifying the issue to implementing algorithms and building the appropriate data flow, up to implementing an IT system.

Jakub Pizoń is an Assistant Professor at the Lublin University of Technology. He is an experienced business professional (over eight years of experience) with integrated computer systems offered to the commercial markets and public sector. His teaching and research interests include manufacturing data analysis, project management, and management application of modern information technologies related to the fourth and fifth industrial revolutions. He is the author of over 20 publications in the areas of his scientific interest.

Aleksander Prokopiuk is the Doctor of Economics, Rector of the Bialystok School of Economics. His research interests include regional economic development, structural modernization of the regional economy, and models of regional development.

Tomasz Rymarczyk, Ph.D., D.Sc., Eng., is the director of the R&D Center in Netrix S.A. and the Institute of Computer Science and Innovative Technologies director at the University of Economics and Innovation, Lublin. He has worked for 29 years in many companies and institutes, developing innovative projects. His research on applying non-invasive imaging techniques, electrical tomography, image reconstruction, numerical modeling, image processing and analysis, process tomography, artificial intelligence, and computer measurement systems. Author of over 400 scientific publications.

Barbara Siuta-Tokarska, Ph.D., an employee of the Department of Economics and Organization of Enterprises at the Cracow University of Economics. Her scientific and research activity with educational and popularizing work in respect of science and knowledge about small and medium-sized enterprises in Poland and in the European Union countries, sustainable and durable development, innovations, the evolution of management sciences, digitalization processes, and development management is widely recognized. She is the author and co-author of over 150 scientific works, including 6 monographs.

Łukasz Skowron is an Associate Professor at the Lublin University of Technology, where he held the position of the chairman of the management and quality scientific council. His teaching and research interests include marketing, business and marketing research, and business performance management. He is the author of approximately 80 published articles and reviews and the author or co-author of 4 books.

Stanisław Skowron is a Professor of Management at the Lublin University of Technology, where he was the Dean of the Faculty and Vice-Rector for student affairs. He deals with the issues of using the strategic potential of enterprises, designing business models, analyzing human capital, analyzing customer market behavior, marketing communication processes, and changes in network organizations. He is the author and co-author of over 150 scientific publications. He participates as an expert in many domestic and foreign research projects.

Sylwia Skrzypek-Ahmed, Ph.D., is the Director of the Office of English Studies and an Assistant Professor at the Faculty of Administration and Social Sciences at the School of Economics and Innovation in Lublin. She has been working at the university for 21 years. She specializes in the field of innovation, entrepreneurship, and project management. Business practitioner, running his own business. Her scientific output includes over 40 scientific articles and monographs.

Jolanta Słoniec is a Professor at the Lublin University of Technology, where she held the position of Head of the Department of Enterprise Organization. She was a visiting professor in Spanish, Kazakh, Russian, and Ukrainian universities and cooperated with some foreign universities conducting joint scientific research and projects and co-authorship of scientific publications. She is the author of approximately 70 published articles and reviews and the author/editor/co-editor of a number of books, including *IT Outsourcing in the Big Polish Companies* (2018).

Małgorzata Smolarek is a Doctor of Economics in the field of management studies, specialty: enterprise and management of small and medium-sized businesses. Assistant Professor of Humanitas University in Sosnowiec. A member of Scientific Committee of the journal *Humanitas University's Research Papers*. An author of many articles and papers in the field of business management, strategy, and human resources management. Her research interests focus on the issues connected with small and medium-sized business management.

Katarzyna Szczepańska-Woszczyna, Associate Professor, Ph.D., Vice-Rector for Research and Education of WSB University. She is a Member of the board "Excellent Science" at the Ministry of Education and Science (Poland). She has conducted research that contributes to the achievements and development of HRM, competencies management, corporate culture, innovation management, and family business. She has organized ventures that inspired the cooperation between science and business aimed at the development of the region. The result of the author's scientific activity is over 100 scientific works published.

Barbara Szymoniuk is an Associate Professor at the Faculty of Management of the Lublin University of Technology. Her teaching and research interests include international marketing and integrated marketing communications.

For 20 years, she has also been conducting research on business clusters. She is the author of over 40 publications on the management and marketing of these organizations, including *Marketing Communication in Clusters and the Conditions for Its Effectiveness* (2019).

Agnieszka Thier is an Assistant Professor in Department of Economics and Organization of Enterprises, Institute of Management, College of Management and Quality Sciences, Cracow University of Economics, Poland.

Anna Walczyna is a doctor of humanities who lectures and conducts research studies at the Lublin University of Technology. She is the author of 40 published articles and reviews and the co-author of a research book on the effectiveness of management. Her teaching and research interests include stress at work, security climate, determinants of entrepreneurial attitudes, CSR, and sustainable management of human resources (SHRM).

Jacek Witkowski is a Doctor of Economic Sciences. Since 1996, he has been teaching and conducting research at the Lublin University of Technology, being employed at the local Faculty of Management as an assistant professor. He deals with the issues of environmental management at the local level and the development of entrepreneurship based on the pro-ecological use of natural resources. He is the author of over 40 scientific publications.

Tomasz Wołowiec, Ph.D., D.Sc., Prof. WSEI is the Director of the Institute of Public Administration and Business at the Higher School of Economics and Innovation in Lublin. He has been associated with the university since 2013. His academic output includes over 250 publications in economics, management, local and regional development, and entrepreneurship.

Joanna Wyrwisz, Ph.D. (Eng.), is an Assistant Professor at Lublin University of Technology, Faculty of Marketing, Department of Management. Her teaching and research interests include marketing, modern instrument of marketing communications, content marketing, and new media technologies. She is the author of approximately 65 published articles and reviews and the author/editor/co-editor of a number of books, including *The Relationship between Consumers' Characteristics and the Expectations towards a Brand's Value* (2021).

Dawid Żebrak is a Ph.D. student at the Doctoral School of WSB University. Master of Arts in the social communication and national security field; an effective manager in the area of the strategic and operational decision-making process, with many years of experience in institutions with highly organized structures; an effective negotiator with building long-term relationship capacity dealing with many private and public actors in the international environment, and an experienced employee in public administration. The author's research interests are focused on management in small and medium-sized enterprises.

Anna Żelazna has a Ph.D. in economics, employed since 2004 at the Lublin University of Technology in the Department of Economics and Economic Management. Her teaching and research interests include microeconomics, contemporary forms of corporate finance, sustainable development, and ethical aspects of business. She is the author and co-author of over 40 published articles and book chapters.

Leszek Zelek is a Doctor of Social Sciences in the field of management and quality sciences. He is the Lecturer at the University of Social Sciences and the WSB University. He is an expert and manager of national and international projects in the field of social, health, and energy policy. He is an advisor to SMEs, local government organizations, social welfare organizations, and health organizations. He is the President of the Institute of Socio-Economic Development since 2019. His teaching and research interests include management in SME, theory of organization, and public management.

1 Boundaries of the social and the planetary

New approaches to management in the 21st century

Agnieszka Rzepka, Zbigniew Olesiński, Ryszard Borowiecki

Introduction

The thesis of the chapter is the idea that innovative management will play a fundamental role in the emerging Economy 5.0 (Hypothesis 1). To prove this assumption, we have proposed several hypotheses, such as that the functioning of society and the economy will be determined by the requirements of sustainable development (ecological ceiling) and the requirements for access to basic resources to meet our human needs (social foundations). Respecting these requirements should draw attention to the importance of soft management factors such as (1) knowledge, (2) human capital, (3) social capital, (4) intra-organizational relations, (5) inter-organizational relations, (6) trust, and (7) intercultural conditions.

The very emergence and development of soft management factors do not affect either of the two boundaries; therefore, the increase in the value of a product or service caused by the increase in the value of the soft factors that make up that product or service does not pose a threat to either the ecological ceiling or the social foundation (Raworth, 2021). What is more, the increase in the role and importance of soft factors, especially knowledge, human capital, or social capital, leads to innovation that reduces the pollution caused by the production of goods and services by using new technologies and reduces the use of hard factors, such as raw materials, resources, energy, etc. Hence, the consideration of increased use of soft factors is conducive to environmental protection and a decreased use of raw materials and resources (Hypothesis 2), and in order to increase the effectiveness of developing innovations, it is advisable to use inter-organizational cooperation, develop inter-organization networks, and transform one's organization into a teal organization (Hypothesis 3) (Laloux, 2016; Olesiński, 2020; Wade, 1996; Wilber, 2008).

A safe and fair space for humanity

In Europe, the summer of 2021 was unusual; a significant number of hot days above the statistical average resulted in fires in Turkey, Greece, and beyond, while significant amounts of rainfall caused flooding in Germany, Belgium,

DOI: 10.4324/9781003384311-1

and elsewhere. While the greenhouse effect may not be the only cause, to a large extent, these anomalies were caused by it. There are fewer and fewer people who doubt that the greenhouse effect poses a threat over the next few decades or so; it is, therefore, important to draw attention to attempts to scientifically conceptualize this phenomenon.

In 2021, Kate Raworth's published a monograph entitled *Doughnut Economics: Seven Ways to Think like a 21st-Century Economist*. It is our understanding that the word *doughnut,* which is entirely original for a scientific text, comes from the shape of the diagram the author used in her book, which depicts two concentric circles that correspond to the cross-sectional scheme of the globe, with the upper circle representing the ecological ceiling and the lower circle representing the social foundations (Raworth, 2021).

The diagram is presented by the author in the monograph a number of times in its various modifications and is an inspiration and a starting point for formulating the seven ways of thinking about the economics of the 21st century. In her book, she recalls going to Oxford University to get the skills that she thought would prepare her for the job. The economic theory she encountered, however, left her frustrated as it ignored the very issues she was passionate about while making awkward assumptions about how the world worked. She found the tutors to be too constrained by the syllabus they were required to teach and the students to master, despite being inspirational and open-minded (Raworth, 2021).

The author defines the "ecological ceiling" as a whole consisting of climate change, ocean acidification, chemical pollution, nitrogen and phosphorus loading of water, freshwater withdrawal, land conversion, loss of biodiversity, air pollution, and damage to the ozone layer. According to Raworth, the social foundations encompass access to energy, clean water to drink, food availability, access to healthcare and education, minimum income, work, peace, and justice, political voice, social equity, gender equality, livable housing, and networks (Raworth, 2021).

Given the limited resources of the earth and the inevitable pollution of land, air, and water during their processing and consumption, a specific correction to the economy is necessary.

Kate Raworth offers seven ways of thinking like a 21st-century economist – (1) change the goal, (2) see the full picture, (3) nurture human nature, (4) get savvy with systems, (5) design to distribute, (6) create to regenerate, and (7) be agnostic about growth (Raworth, 2021).

A first approach proposes that instead of chasing endless GDP growth, it's time to discover a way to live well in balance. The second indicates a need for stronger integration of the economy into society. The third way is a continuation of the idea behind the second way of thinking and proposes to integrate the economy with social processes more closely. The fourth postulates to see the economy as an ever-evolving, complex system and reject the mechanisms that control it. The fifth is a way to redistribute wealth, especially the wealth that controls the land, entrepreneurship, technology, and knowledge of how to create money.

The sixth way says that the current century needs economic thinking that will promote a circular – not linear – economy. Finally, the seventh way is to point out that GDP growth does not always have to be pursued as an economic goal or achieved (Raworth, 2021).

As can be seen above, Kate Raworth draws attention to the need to take a different perspective on GDP growth (we can live with or without it, which corresponds to the first and seventh ways of thinking), to control the redistribution of earth's resources and the pursuit of their regeneration (which corresponds to the fifth and sixth ways), and, finally, to establish a strong connection between economic and social processes (the second, third, and fourth ways).

Alternatively, one could formulate it in an even shorter way by referencing Rifkin (2016), who observes that in the 21st century, it is necessary to pay attention to the consensual (social and contractual) establishment of economic rules and especially to normative regard to the rules of land exploitation and environmental protection (Rifkin, 2016). The number of rules governing the market economy (for instance, those governing the consumption market or money) is a separate problem.

Economics and management in the economy of the 21st century

Social conditions have manifested themselves in the economy to a greater extent in the 21st century than has been emphasized in scientific literature. Hence, when considering management in the 21st century, it is imperative to give greater consideration to social conditions than in the 20th century. In particular, it is appropriate to draw attention to such management conditions as the ecological ceiling and the social foundation described above. If we focus on the conditions for obtaining and using earth's resources, it is impossible to continue to overexploit them in the long run. As a result, both economics and management are becoming increasingly concerned with soft factors in management. Their characteristic feature is that as they are utilized, humans produce more and more of them, which is quite contrary to material resources (i.e. hard factors).

Taking the current state of human knowledge into account and trying to predict its further development, it appears that there are no limits to the development of knowledge. Decades ago, Edvinsson and Malone (1999) attempted to bring attention to the role and importance of intellectual capital in the production process. They were also the first to present a universal intellectual capital measurement and reporting system that could be used by any organization. This first attempt to assess the value of the capital gave consideration to the value of the hard factors involved in the production and the market value of the finished product, which often created a fairly significant difference. Edvinsson determined that part of this difference was the value of soft factors (back then, the term they applied was intellectual capital).

Over the years, in the course of empirical research, the increasing importance of these soft factors in the production process, especially in technologically advanced products, has been pointed out. Taking into consideration the two boundaries defined by Raworth (ecological ceiling and social foundations), if soft factors were to be more heavily incorporated into human activity, further economic and social growth would be possible, though it would be different from the current one.

One example of such changes is the advent and development of solar technology, which allows generating power in an almost pollution-free manner and with no or little resource consumption (panels, wires, converters, etc.). Another example is the great opportunities to save the earth's resources and limit pollution of the earth's water and air that have been provided by the development of computer science, which offers ways of communicating without having to travel, thereby resulting in a reduced carbon footprint.

A major challenge in achieving this is to increase the durability of material goods used by man (e.g. apartments, household appliances, cars, clothing, furniture, etc.) and, on the other hand, reduce the number of goods used.

We believe that the above remarks make an important correction to the conclusions drawn by Raworth – we are most certainly for the respect for the boundary of the ecological ceiling and the social foundation as well as for the shift of economic philosophy toward a more social perspective; however, such a change need not be coarse – according to us, such a change should mean that humans improve their adjustment to the surrounding reality. As part of this adjustment, management should play a significant role in guiding human behavior, including, as it currently seems to be true (as of 2021), paying attention to the increasing importance of soft management factors.

Among soft management factors, knowledge is the most well described (Rifkin, 2016). Even the concept of *knowledge management* was conceived. The value of knowledge management can be estimated in a manner similar to that used by Edvinsson to determine the value of intellectual capital. Essentially, it is the difference between the book value of a company and its stock market value. But this difference is also made up of all the soft factors. Currently, the value of human capital (or, according to Edvinsson and Malone (1999), intellectual capital) is defined as the value of an employee's education at all levels, including higher and postgraduate education. When a company employs many people, this amount can significantly exceed the difference between its stock exchange value and its book value.

In companies that employ a small number of employees and offer innovative products, if a portion of this amount remains after subtracting the value of human capital, then, in principle, we can consider it the organization's knowledge value in its entirety. Other soft factors are relatively less valuable than human capital and knowledge.

It is possible that in organizations where intra-organizational relations are important (large companies using state-of-the-art technologies in the field of aeronautics, for example), relationships between research teams can be crucial. The same is true of the value of inter-organizational relationships (see Chapter 4). On the other hand, social capital or trust may have greater value in smaller companies operating in difficult markets which deal with providing assistance for conflict-affected economies or in areas where laws are not sufficiently regulated or enforced.

The last soft factor – intercultural conditions – is also important. Repeated and long-term research in this area indicates that it is of fundamental importance in developing innovative techniques, adapting to new markets, and coping with unusual circumstances. This factor can be considered the third pillar of teal organizations, in addition to self-management and wholeness.

Given this context, it is a good idea to consider whether all seven soft factors cannot be included as teal organizational requirements.

Empirical research shows that currently, the book value of a company and the size of soft factor values differ. In general, for low-tech products, the book value of the company will be higher when hiring employees who are low-skilled. And vice versa, in the case of a company producing high-tech products with the help of technologically advanced machines and with the participation of highly qualified employees, the value of soft factors may be greater or much greater than the book value. For a company providing services that require high qualifications, such as advertising, IT, and expertise, the book value of the company is small, and the rest depends on the talent of its employees and the current situation on the market.

Creating innovative environment

One of the most important effects associated with the functioning of soft management factors and the development of inter-organizational relationships is the development of innovations. Innovation is a complex phenomenon because it is not so much the achievement of an invention or even the patenting of it but the ability to bring the invention to market and achieve economic success. Nowadays, in view of the widespread inclusion of the ecological ceiling and the social foundation, this is of particular importance because, in principle, innovative products should respect the requirements (limits) set by those boundaries. Thanks to inventiveness, these boundaries present themselves not so much as barriers but as guidelines for the right way to proceed in the economy and the functioning of society.

There is rich scientific literature on innovation. Its goal has been to try to identify certain economic, management-related, and social mechanisms that stimulate its development. An example of such a response to this problem is the model for the creation of an innovative environment of enterprises (Laloux, 2016).

This model presents an inter-organizational network designed to increase innovation and effectiveness within oganizations. The assumption of the model is to demonstrate that innovations are more often and faster developed in an environment that is innovative, diverse, and specialized to create innovations.

Generally, organizations that tend to form networks are those with horizontal structures, decentralized, in which self-managing teams of employees are predominant. Their main advantage is that they maintain extensive relationships with other organizations, which facilitates the flow of necessary information. This situation is conducive to reviewing and updating priorities and objectives, i.e. the process of adjusting the direction of activities in response to incoming data (Laloux, 2016). Continual updating, like self-management, is a hallmark of teal organizations. Thus, it can be argued that for innovative organizations which cooperate in inter-organizational networks, it is purposeful to include the organization's evolution toward the teal model (Laloux, 2016).

It is possible for an inventor to come up with an invention at any given moment. Research indicates that this may be a situation that occurs at random. However, the development of such an invention, as well as patenting and manufacturing it, requires significant, often lengthy, and expensive activities.

Practical observation of the invention-making process reveals that inventions are most often created in universities as well as scientific and research institutes. Many of them are developed by students, which is why in many universities there are organizations referred to as spin-offs, i.e. ones that have the nature of an enterprise but allow to develop an initial concept for the implementation of the invention. If these works advance and success in implementing the invention is forecast, it is recommended to transform an existing spin-off into a spin-out, i.e. into an independent company functioning outside the organizational framework of the university. Often, at the beginning of a spin-out's life, institutions such as a business incubator or a technology park prove helpful.

Financial support for spin-outs can be obtained from funding from venture capital or business angels. Buying shares in a spin-out involves some risk for this fund. If successful, the spin-out can transform into an independently operating enterprise; it can also receive assistance from other forms of funding and government grants, such as those for start-ups.

The research aspect

The chapter draws on empirical research carried out by the authors among enterprises operating in Poland. This study determined the extent and intensity of cooperation of these enterprises with external entities in acquiring knowledge and information, as well as the relationships between them (Rzepka, 2019). The assumption was that intensifying cooperation among companies would bring a number of advantages and contribute to strengthening the market position of agile businesses.

Prof. Rzepka conducted the research under two own grants from October 2016 to January 2017 and from September 2020 to January 2021.

A total of 235 respondents were selected from a variety of enterprises in the Podkarpackie Province, Poland, using a purposive basis. A sample of 200 respondents was selected for the study. A statistical analysis of the obtained data was performed using Pearson's χ^2 (chi-square) test of independence. STATISTICA 10 was used to analyze the questionnaire survey data. The types of questions and the categories of answers included in the questionnaire determined the qualitative nature of the variables analyzed. In order to evaluate the interdependencies between the examined features using Pearson's non-parametric test of independence, the interview results were presented as numbers and percentages. The choice was determined by the availability of data. The respondents consisted of executives and managers.

The research revealed that cooperation with outside entities usually takes the form of outsourcing contracts (45%), virtual organizations (24%), strategic alliances (16%), and economic clusters (15%) (Rzepka, 2017), which corresponds to the model presented above. Respondents stated that establishing inter-organizational relations brings numerous advantages, which range from gaining access to know-how and expert knowledge (25% of responses), improvement of the competitive position (25% of responses), increased revenues (25% of responses), acquisition of new skills (15% of responses), and shared risk (5% of responses) (Rzepka et al., 2022).

The research also showed that soft management factors play a crucial role. As can be seen in Table 1.1, cooperation with other enterprises is significantly more frequently undertaken by women who are middle-level managers employed in companies that have been operating between one and three years and are engaged in activities other than those in the three leading trends. The table clearly indicates that the type of activity of a given company influences the direction of cooperation with a given institution.

Rapid changes in the human environment and organization inevitably cause changes in people's living conditions and organizations' performance in that environment. Ongoing changes in the workplace offer opportunities for change and expansion of the scope of services, which in turn creates an opportunity for a change in one's lifestyle.

It is worth mentioning that there are many industries that have benefited from increased automation and robotization as well as the integration of machines with IT systems in the era of Industry 4.0 (Młody, 2017). As indicated in the OECD report, the leading industries that use robots are the automotive and consumer electronics sectors (OECD, 2017). However, the implementation of advanced technologies in other sectors, e.g. in the clothing industry, will reduce the size of the labor force, but, on the other hand, it will be applicable to segments where advanced automation will probably never occur, e.g. in the construction industry.

It can be concluded from the research results that the growing role of cooperation based on soft management factors contributes to the success of many enterprises. As has been shown, the most developed and prevalent dimension in the enterprises surveyed is human capital; therefore, managers should see it

Table 1.1 Collaboration between respondents and organizations according to chosen respondent characteristics (on a scale of 1–7, where 1 represents "never" and 7 represents "always")*

Respondent characteristics		*N*	*Companies*	*Consulting firms*	*Research centers*
Duration of the company's existence	A year or less	7	2.43	1.71	1.14
	1–3 years	29	3.17	2.38	2.55
	4–7 years	33	3.06	2.67	1.88
	8 years or more	133	3.08	1.94*	1.68*
Sector	Industry	60	3.07	2.40	2.03
	Trade	57	3.14	2.07	1.86
	Services	66	2.91	1.85	1.47
	Other	19	3.37	2.26	2.26*
Operational scope	Local	102	3.02	2.04	1.75
	Regional	58	2.88	2.00	1.76
	European	33	3.52	2.45	2.18
	Global	9	3.11	2.44	1.78
Number of employees	10 or fewer	49	3.33	2.16	1.78
	10–49	97	2.94	2.10	1.80
	50–249	29	3.10	2.41	2.03
	250 or more	27	3.00	1.74	1.74
Respondents' positions	Top management	25	3.08	2.84	1.92
	Middle management	33	3.61	2.76	2.27
	Lower management	57	2.89	2.05	1.93
	Other	87	2.97	1.70**	1.55*

Source: Own elaboration based on Stage I of the research.

*Statistically significant variables at: $*p < 0.05$; $**p < 0.01$; $***p < 0.001$.

The Shading Signifies the Most Extreme Results (as Compared to the Other Responses)

as a primary source of their firm's success in the future. Companies that own significant soft factors and want to hold onto their employees' talents that are valuable to their business reward their employees with a variety of incentive remuneration and non-monetary rewards (Hasan & Uddin, 2022).

The results of the research prove that the adoption of agile qualities in inter-organizational relations by organizations translates into the achievement of a better competitive position and a higher level of innovation, especially in the era of Industry 4.0. Not all businesses are capable of adapting to changes, and that can be determined by the country's economic policy, how businesses are managed, and, above all, the way in which collaboration between organizations is handled.

Summary

The analysis carried out above indicates the legitimacy and usefulness of the concepts of the ecological ceiling and social foundation. The problem that we have analyzed in this chapter pertains to the way we ought to understand these concepts and the changes that are taking place in cognitive and innovation-related processes.

Ecological ceilings undoubtedly exist, but the details of what they mean are an entirely different matter. For example, in current times, global warming caused by the greenhouse effect, which is associated with excessive CO_2 emissions, seems to be the most apparent. It is becoming more and more common for an increasingly greater number of social groups and governments to try and minimize emissions of greenhouse gases. The current (as of 2021) estimate is that greenhouse gas emissions from coal combustion are expected to be reduced by 2050.

It is clear that this is not the only element contributing to the ecological ceiling. Another problem that is commonly acknowledged is the widespread use of plastic packaging in our lives. Attempts are being made to eliminate them. In recent years, we have increasingly been phasing out the use of plastic cutlery and packaging. One of the biggest problems is the amount of toxic plastic that goes into landfills. A relatively recent notable example involved Lebanon's health crisis in 2015 that was associated with the closing of a huge landfill site and the government failing to replace it, which resulted in widespread demonstrations (Galer, 2022). Luckily, such situations typically evolve into initiatives and civil movements whose aim is to solve the issue. The world's plastic waste is estimated at 8.3 billion tonnes, and even though we have done our best to combat the problem, there's still that needs to be done about it (Lufkin, 2022).

The evidence presented above suggests that identifying the component elements of the ecological ceiling is a significant scientific challenge, and its understanding will change over time. A separate problem is the translation of scientific findings into legal standards and giving them the status of enforceable law. This requires a fairly widespread acceptance of such norms among nations, the adoption of the legislation by governments, and, what should be presumed to be the most difficult task, ensuring that the legislation is enforced.

Nowadays, social foundations are manifested under similar conditions. There is a relatively good understanding of water resources and the possibilities for their use. Drought and desertification are the results of strenuous exploitation of the earth's resources, which makes it difficult or even impossible for people to live in many areas of the world. Currently, in view of a significant increase in the world's population (nearly 8 billion people), we are nearing the maximum carrying capacity of our planet according to some estimates (Wolchover, 2011). On an ongoing basis, specialists identify threats and propose specific countermeasures, such as the construction of retention reservoirs, maintaining and caring for woodlands, and maintaining green spaces. It is easy to emphasize that these are costly activities, often against the interests of specific social groups (e.g. the construction industry), which are lengthy and only cause slow improvement. The earth, however, may hold much greater riches than we previously thought – for instance, more oil and gas resources. Hence, without questioning the role that understanding the social foundation plays, it is necessary to systematically catalog resources throughout the Earth and impose strict standards for their exploitation.

The above illustrates that both the proper shaping of ecological ceilings and social foundations require specific, constant, and systematic actions on a global scale, which is associated with significant costs.

In this chapter, we have strived to demonstrate that the notions of ecological ceiling and social foundation will be profoundly influenced by scientific progress and innovation.

Attention should be paid to the characteristics of the modern era – the era of services – which is associated with the emergence of organizational structures different from the ones that existed previously, including, in particular, their horizontality, decentralization, employees' increased self-management, and their desire to collaborate or cooperate through networks (Hypothesis 3). An example of creating such networks is the aforementioned model of the creation of an innovative environment in enterprises.

Today, as the network of inter-organizational cooperation develops, innovation-related processes can accelerate, leading to the emergence of innovative solutions that facilitate the functioning of social groups in conditions that are new, attractive to such a group, and that are not harmful to nature (Hypothesis 2).

The boundaries set by ecological ceilings and social foundations should not be viewed in the same way as the floor and ceiling in an apartment. Instead, they should be regarded as a point of reference that is defined by specific criteria that stimulate the processes of social and economic development of humanity, which mark the development path. They do not represent insurmountable barriers to development, which tend to occur in certain circumstances but are generally feasible to be changed through innovation and a change of direction in one's actions. Such an attitude is similar to our capability to maneuver around an obstacle in our path and respect it (Hypothesis 1).

We have demonstrated the validity of Hypotheses 1, 2, and 3, which support the conclusion that innovative management will play a fundamental role in the emerging Economy 5.0.

To sum up, the recognition of the ecological ceiling and the social foundation plays a fundamental role in the modern world. With the help of worldwide human relationships, it is possible, through negotiation and consensus, to formulate rules that are universally binding, enacted by sovereign states as binding legislation, and rigorously enforced by them, ensuring respect for the boundaries defined by the ecological ceiling and the social foundations. In today's innovation-driven world, it is possible to develop innovative solutions made by scientists, experts, and entrepreneurs, which will lead to a systematic improvement of living conditions while observing the standards of ecological ceilings and social foundations.

References

Edvinsson, L., & Malone, M. (1999). *Intellectual capital*. Maxima.

Galer, S. (2022). *Lebanon is drowning in its own waste*. Bbc.com. Retrieved July 25, 2022, from https://www.bbc.com/future/article/20180328-lebanon-is-drowning-in-its-own-waste

Hasan, M. M., & Uddin, M. R. (2022). Do intangibles matter for corporate policies? Evidence from organization capital and corporate payout choices. *Journal of Banking & Finance, 135*, 106395. https://doi.org/10.1016/j.jbankfin.2021.106395

Laloux, F. (2016). *Pracować inaczej*. Wydawnictwo Studio EMKA.

Lufkin, B. (2022). *How will we deal with all of the world's rubbish?* Bbc.com. Retrieved July 25, 2022, from https://www.bbc.com/future/article/20171003-how-will-we-deal-all-of-the-worlds-rubbish

Młody, M. (2017). Przemysł 4.0 – Potencjalne korzyści i wyzwania na poziomie mikro, mezo oraz makro. In A. Lipińska & P. Klimas (Eds.), *Kierunki badań innowacyjnych* (s. 43). Wydawnictwo Uniwersytetu Jagiellońskiego.

OECD. (2017). *OECD Science, Technology and Industry Scoreboard 2017: The digital transformation*. OECD Publishing. http://dx.doi.org/10.1787/9789264268821-en

Olesiński, Z. (2020). *Składniki turkusowych organizacji*. Difin.

Raworth, K. (2021). *Ekonomia obwarzanka. Siedem sposobów myślenia o ekonomii XXI wieku*. Wydawnictwo Krytyki Politycznej.

Rifkin, J. (2016). *Społeczeństwo zerowych kosztów krańcowych*. Wydawnictwo Studio Emka.

Rzepka, A. (2017). Współpraca międzyorganizacyjna i jej wpływ na innowacyjność na podstawie badań empirycznych. In A. Lipińska & P. Klimas (Eds.), *Kierunki badań innowacyjnych* (s. 43). Wydawnictwo Uniwersytetu Jagiellońskiego.

Rzepka, A. (2019). Innovation, inter-organizational relation and cooperation between enterprises in Podkarpacie region in Poland. *Procedia Manufacturing, 30*, 642–649.

Rzepka, A., Olesiński, Z., & Jędrych, E. (2022). *Self-management, entrepreneurial culture, and Economy 4.0: A contemporary approach to organizational theory development*. Routledge.

Wade, J. (1996). *Changes of mind: A holonomic theory of the evolution of consciousness*. State University of New York Press.

Wilber, K. (2008). *Małżeństwo rozumu z duszą*. Jacek Santorski & Co Agencja Wydawnicza.

Wolchover, N. (2011). *How many people can earth support?* NBC News. Retrieved July 25, 2022, from https://www.nbcnews.com/id/wbna44860924

2 Innovation management in SMEs in CEE countries

Łukasz Skowron, Joanna Dzieńdziora, Małgorzata Smolarek, Leszek Zelek, Dawid Żebrak

Introduction

Innovation in small and medium-sized enterprises (SMEs) is influenced by a variety of factors, the most important being external environments within which they operate. These factors can be considered on different levels of subjective and relational activities that result in multidimensional interactions between the company and its environment at various levels. SMEs quite often use innovation to improve their competitive position. However, these innovations are rarely classified as pioneering in nature. They tend to be imitations, which are based on innovations developed by another entity and adopted by the market. Innovative activities in a rapidly changing environment not only provide companies with a competitive edge but are also one of the best ways to remain competitive and succeed in the market.

An important factor for introducing innovation into SMEs is the creation of networks that facilitate access to new markets, new knowledge, and risk-sharing among stakeholders. Networking is a key driving force of innovation in the information technology sector for SMEs. The emergence of information technology has changed competition and innovation strategies among SMEs. Prior to digitalization, many products were strictly mechanical. The value chain was characterized by many activities based on verbal instructions and process instructions. The advent of computers and automation resulted in a rapid increase in productivity. During the 1980s and 1990s, the growth of the Internet led to a significant strengthening of this trend through the coordination and integration of processes.

Due to the development of computing power, wireless networks, and miniaturization, goods, and services today are becoming more intelligent. As sensors, processors, software, and network technologies become increasingly integrated, network products become more and more technically complex. Despite the high level of pressure to innovate, many small and medium-sized companies have difficulty creating strategic management of innovation within their day-to-day operations. In comparison to large corporations, SMEs face challenges that hinder their development, which can have a negative effect on their market position. SMEs often struggle with limited financial and human

DOI: 10.4324/9781003384311-2

resources, meaning that the decisions they make must be more deliberate and systematic.

The aim of this chapter is to evaluate innovation management in SMEs in Central and Eastern European (CEE) countries. It focuses on identifying innovations and factors that influence their use in SMEs and aims to answer the question about the types of innovation and the types of strategies related to innovation used in SMEs. The role of open innovation was also discussed due to its practical importance for the SME sector in terms of building a competitive advantage through collaboration, and thus acquiring and sharing knowledge.

Literature review

Innovation is one of the most effective instruments for achieving, maintaining, and improving a company's position in the market (Vitezić & Vitezić, 2015). It is imperative to integrate innovation into a company's entire management system (Goller & Bessant, 2017). Goffin and Mitchell (2017) see innovation as an activity within a business that generates new ideas. Therefore, the need for flexibility and innovation within an organization is becoming increasingly critical, particularly in the context of Industry 5.0.

Innovation is the process of introducing a new or significantly improved product (goods or services) or process, a new marketing technique, or a new organizational strategy into a company's business practices, workplace, or external relationships (Dossou-Yovo & Keen, 2021, p. 23). It can refer to products, production processes, or organizational practices. A product innovation occurs when a new product is introduced to the market or when one that has been significantly improved is introduced. An SME innovates in a very different way than a large enterprise. The ability to effectively manage innovation processes is especially challenging for small businesses operating in technology-driven industries where innovation is essential to the survival of SMEs (Dossou-Yovo & Keen, 2021, p. 22).

Innovation is the ability to create new things or ideas that are disseminated in practice through the so-called diffusion of innovation. It could mean a new idea or behavior relating to a new product, service, or technology (Beyene et al., 2016). Depending on the scientific disciplines studied, researchers from the social, economic, and technical sciences define innovation differently. It is possible to reduce the cost of production and sales through innovative activities while increasing the quality of manufactured products and increasing revenue.

For Gogołowicz, innovation means introducing a new product (service) onto the market, implementing new processes, or reorganizing business activities (2013, pp. 75–94). Koch, however, takes a slightly different view of innovation (2005, pp. 81–82) by defining innovation as a broad concept encompassing new products, new services, a new management style, new structures and processes in an enterprise, state, or administration. Innovation can originate from the transfer of technologies or from the development of new business concepts and can be organizational or technological in their nature. Innovation is the result of complex relationships between people, organizations, and their environments, thus demonstrating that an innovation strategy cannot solely focus on the relationship between research and innovation.

The theoretical approach to innovation, due to its ambiguity in many areas of socio-economic life, may not explain much. It is important to note that innovation is generally associated with new technologies, which do not always predict success but can suggest significant dynamism in the field of technological change. As such, innovation can be either significant or incremental and can come as a result of discovery or as a result of a process by which a new product is created (Minh & Hjortsø, 2015, pp. 209–228). When it comes to implementing ideas or changes in the intangible realm, we can say we are dealing with soft or social innovations. Pol and Ville (2009, p. 879) examined the existing definitions of social innovation and found them to be very general, unclear, or highly restrictive.

Innovations are ideas incorporated into business practice through deliberate and organized actions, and their effect is an increase in sales or a reduction in costs (Poole et al., 2000). The literature offers several criteria by which innovation strategies are divided. Most commonly, innovative strategies can be classified as internal or external. The internal approaches include improving product appeal, increasing market share, improving the existing marketing strategies, and improving the human capital and capital resources' productivity. The external approaches include offensive, defensive, or counteroffensive strategies (Janasz, 2003, p. 67). When it comes to the level of innovation, the literature on innovative strategies has them divided into imitation strategies and pre-emptive strategies (Janasz, 2003, p. 74). A first strategy involves following the proven paths of the company's development (it can become an overtaking strategy). On the other hand, a second strategy involves great creativity but comes at a high cost in terms of investment and leadership. The use of pre-emptive innovation strategies in SMEs appears to be linked to other practices, such as knowledge management.

Creating value through innovation is unquestionably the best strategy (Halim et al., 2019, p. 18). Nevertheless, some organizations are better positioned to take advantage of new opportunities than others. Small and medium-sized companies face a severe disadvantage in this regard because of their limited resources. Innovation, however, is often limited to certain parts of a product rather than the whole (Zhu et al., 2012), which gives SMEs an opportunity to develop expertise in specific fields and generate new ideas within them. Small and medium-sized businesses can gain an advantage by:

- being highly flexible and able to respond quickly to new technological opportunities,
- working with strong partners who can help them increase the knowledge and financial resources needed to acquire key technological competencies,
- overcoming technological limitations,
- intuitively and quickly recognizing changes in consumer preferences and market trends to identify new opportunities (Keskin, 2006).

As a result of economic transformations in the CEE region, SMEs have been experiencing delays in technological development while their economies transition from centrally planned to market-driven economies. In today's economic climate, resources are used more efficiently and current activities are given more importance, which means innovation that has been strategically planned is not given as much attention. Additionally, the increase in digitalization and the transition into Industry 5.0 mean that we are increasingly dealing with breakthrough innovations.

The goal of Industry 5.0 is to make use of human creativity. It involves experts collaborating with powerful, intelligent, and precise machines. According to many industry experts, Industry 5.0 will restore the human element to manufacturing. A key aspect of Industry 5.0 is its combination of fast and accurate machines and cognitive capabilities. Another important element of Industry 5.0 is personalization, where customers can choose products that are tailored specifically to their needs.

The implementation of Industry 5.0 increases production efficiency and facilitates a range of connections between people and machines, allowing interaction and constant monitoring; after all, the goal of human-machine collaboration should be to increase productivity within a short period of time. Industry 5.0 also aims to improve the quality of production by assigning repetitive and monotonous tasks to machines and robots, and tasks requiring critical thinking to humans (Nahavandi, 2019, p. 4371). With Industry 5.0, breakthrough technologies such as robots, cobots, and 5G will be tailored to the intelligence and innovation of people, which will allow SMEs to meet the demand for personalized products at a faster pace (Li, 2020, pp. 579–592). Continuous technological advances and innovations in SMEs' management are key factors to the success of supply chain management (SCM) in the key concept of Industry 5.0, which is the integration of mass personalization into their production systems.

Materials and methods

This section describes a study that aims to examine innovation management in SMEs in selected CEE countries in the textile and clothing (T&C) industry.

The research project carried out from February to July 2019 focused on the development of SMEs in the CEE region. The data collected were quantitative. The use of a questionnaire as a research tool allowed for a comparison of the percentages of collected responses. A total of 417 companies were selected for the purposes of this study. To conduct further analysis, we narrowed the number down to 295 companies that claimed that they had implemented innovation management in the 3-year period prior to the study. Table 2.1 describes the characteristics of the test sample.

The primary research question posed as part of the study asked whether innovation management took place in small and medium enterprises in the T&C industry. Additional research questions covered such issues as innovation

Table 2.1 Research sample characteristics

Research sample = 295 (100%)		
Respondent characteristics		
Sex	Female	29.5%
	Male	69.5%
Age	Up to 25	12.2%
	26–35	10.8%
	36–45	31.2%
	46–55	36.6%
	Over 55	9.2%
Education	Higher	32.5%
	Secondary	41.4%
	Vocational	26.1%
Seniority	Up to 5 years	12.2%
	5–10 years	16.6%
	11–20 years	43.1%
	21–30 years	19.0%
	Over 30 years	9.2%
Position held	Executive	16.6%
	Managerial	83.4%
Characteristics of businesses surveyed		
Company size by number of employees	Micro-enterprise (0–9)	42.0%
	Small enterprise (10–49)	47.8%
	Medium enterprise (50–249)	10.2%
Country of operation of the company	Poland	32.2%
	Lithuania	19.3%
	Czech Republic	21.4%
	Slovakia	27.1%

Source: Own elaboration.

management in SMEs, the main factors influencing innovation management strategies, and the main barriers to open innovation collaboration in SMEs.

The research hypothesis (H0) stated that as companies' operations grow in size, SME innovation management becomes more important to them. The study also put forward some additional research hypotheses that stated that in SMEs:

1 innovation management is typically focused on products,
2 open innovations are only a small part of innovation management,
3 lack of collaboration in innovation is primarily due to reluctance to partner in the creation and introduction of a new product and a distrust of business partners.

Characteristics of the geographic scope of the study

The countries that are considered to be part of CEE include Bulgaria, Croatia, Czech Republic, Hungary, Poland, Romania, Slovakia, Slovenia, and the three Baltic States – Estonia, Latvia, and Lithuania. CEE's economic growth is a consequence of its market's internal situation. Effective use of EU funding has increased investments in fixed assets. Maintaining high economic growth rates in the CEE region is principally hindered by internal risks such as labor shortages, production delays, and rising wages. Another important factor is a decrease in investments, particularly in the construction sector, due to a decrease in EU funding that supported infrastructure investments heavily in the past. Because of this, it may be impossible to maintain the current growth rate in the CEE region without a suitable increase in efficiency. Furthermore, this risk is aggravated by external forces such as increased protectionism and the COVID-19 pandemic.

SMEs, which are characterized by a small size and an uncomplicated structure, are key to the economy of any country with a market economy. Their potential for growth makes them more dynamic than large firms, which helps create jobs. However, they are also more vulnerable and lack access to finance and capital (Rusu & Roman, 2017, p. 104). The management process of SMEs differs from that of large organizations, and SMEs cannot be viewed as miniaturized versions of large organizations as they follow different rules, focus on different values, and respond differently to external factors (Sipa, 2012, p. 250). In a market economy, these companies determine a country's economic strength.

Figure 2.1 shows the number of SMEs in each CEE country. Nevertheless, when we look at the number of SMEs per 1000 people, we see that there are some differences among the countries. The number of SMEs per 1000 inhabitants (aged 15 or over) in countries such as the Czech Republic, Slovakia, Slovenia, Lithuania, Latvia, Estonia, and Hungary exceeded the EU-28 average of 58 companies per 1000 inhabitants, with more than 80 SMEs per 1000 in the first four countries. This figure was below the EU average in Bulgaria, Poland, Croatia, and Romania (European Commission, 2019, p. 18). Such high fluctuations in the number of SMEs per 1000 inhabitants can be explained by factors such as the industrial structure of the economy, policies that promote self-employment and entrepreneurship (especially

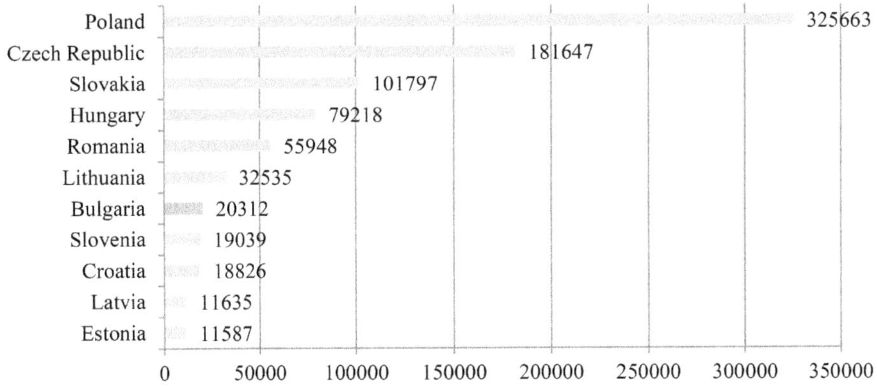

Figure 2.1 The number of SMEs in CEE countries in 2018.

micro-enterprises), the level of entrepreneurship, and the general economic and political climate.

In the surveyed countries, the importance of the SME sector is a consequence of their significant contribution to creating added value and providing employment, but with some differences between individual countries. In this regard, the Czech Republic, Hungary, Slovakia, Poland, and Romania were below the EU-28 average of 56.4%. Estonia, on the other hand, ranked highest. In terms of employment, the EU-28 average was 66.6%, with Romania being the only country below it. For countries like Bulgaria, Estonia, Lithuania, and Latvia, SMEs accounted for more than 75% of employment (European Commission, 2019, p. 19).

As a result of the COVID-19 pandemic, the global economy declined. The SME sector in the EU-27 experienced a sharp drop in economic activity in 2020. The added value (in current prices) generated by SMEs decreased by 7.6%, compared to an increase of 3.8% in 2019. Employment in SMEs fell by 1.7% in 2020 after an increase of 1.4% in 2019. Figure 2.2 shows changes in the contribution of SMEs to added value to the economy in individual CEE countries.

At the same time, it should be noted that SMEs are a heterogeneous sector. In addition to geographical diversity, there is also sector diversity. A high concentration of SMEs is found in industries such as textiles and fibers, which is classified as light industry and includes the production of fabric garments and clothing, underwear, household linen i.e. bedding, kitchen linen, table linen,

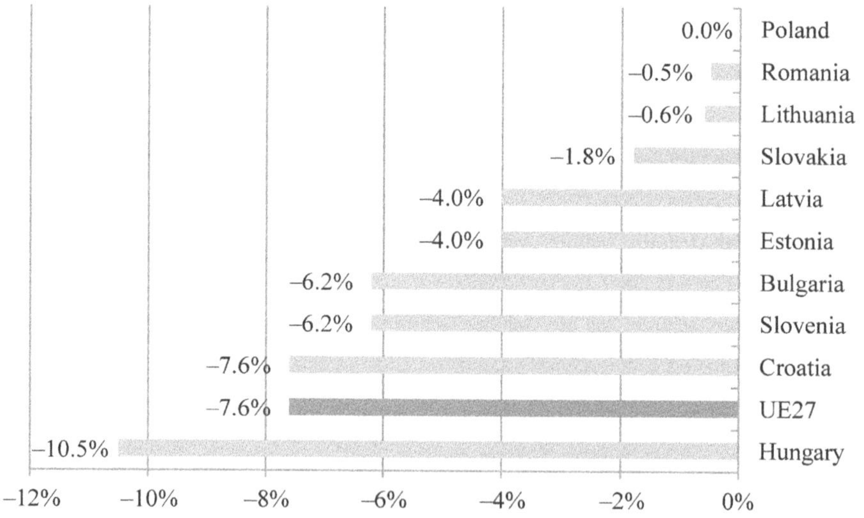

Figure 2.2 Changes in the contribution of SMEs to added value in the economy in 2020, by country.

Source: European Commission (2021). *Annual Report on European SMEs 2020/2021. Digitalisation of SMEs. SME Performance Review 2020/2021,* Brussels, 25.

clothing accessories, leather accessories, fabrics, carpets, rugs, tulles, laces, coats, footwear, and other items using natural fibers (cotton, flax, jute, sisal, hemp, wool, silk) and artificial ones (synthetic fibers supplied by the chemical industry). It covers a wide range of activities from the processing of natural fibers (cotton, flax, wool, etc.) or synthetic (polyester, polyamide, etc.) for the production of yarn and fabrics to a wide range of products such as high-tech synthetic yarns, bedding, industrial filters, and clothing.

The T&C sector is an important part of the European manufacturing industry, playing a key role in the economy and social well-being in many regions of Europe. According to Eurotax data, there are around 160,000 companies in the EU (of which 99.8% are SMEs), employing 1.5 million people and generating a turnover of EUR 162 billion (Eurotax, 2020). At the same time, the textile and textile industries are among the most labor-intensive sectors of the economy and at the same time the least efficient. Currently, this industry is experiencing a clear crisis, a decline in exports, and competition from cheap imported goods (mainly from East Asia). As a result, many textile plants were liquidated. In just the last decade, textiles have contributed to less than 1.6% of the industry's sales. It ought to be noted that what remains of the textile industry must be of relatively high quality. Hence, the proper management of innovation in this sector is of particular importance.

Results

Enterprises in the SME sector largely declare their interest in implementing innovations (87.1%). Of these, 70.7% declared that they had made innovative changes in the last 3 years preceding the survey. Innovations for these 295 companies (those that indicated that in the last 3 years preceding the survey they implemented innovative changes) were most often new on a company scale (63.1%). 17.4% of respondents indicated a novelty in the local market, 13.3% indicated a regional market, only 6.2% on a national scale, and only 1.0% on a foreign market scale. It should be noted, however, that these were only declarations, and in reality, the percentage of companies that implement innovations that are considered novel on the outside of the company could be even lower. A geographic breakdown of the responses is shown in Figure 2.3.

Innovations related to introducing new products that mimic competitors' products (75.3%) dominated among the implemented innovations. During this period, 14.9% of previously known technologies were modernized and implemented in SMEs, but only 9.8% of completely novel solutions were developed. This indicates that companies were more focused on adapting existing solutions rather than creating completely new ones. Figure 2.4 shows the types of innovations introduced depending on the country of operation.

An analysis of the results of the study identified the relationship between the degree of involvement in innovation management and the country of residence ($P = 0.009$). When asked about the company's commitment to innovation management, the Czech respondents came out on top (87.6% said

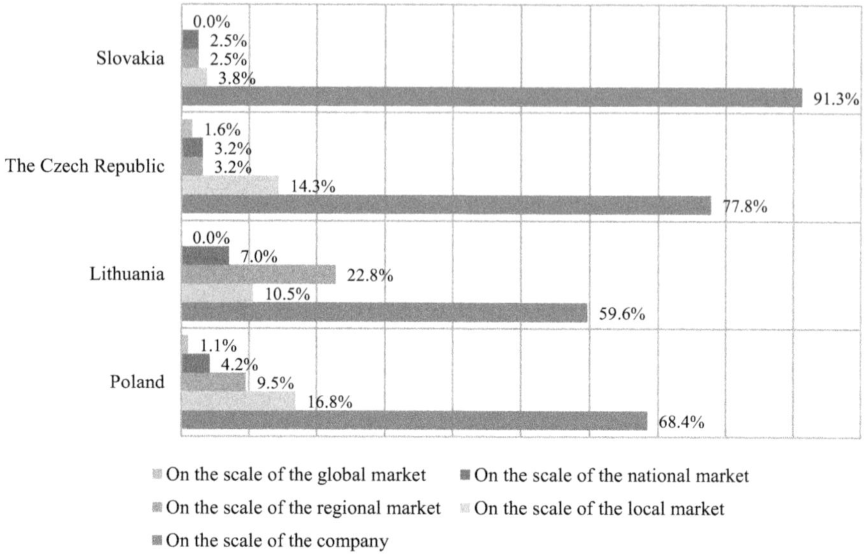

Figure 2.3 The degree of novelty of the implemented innovation in selected countries.

Source: Own elaboration.

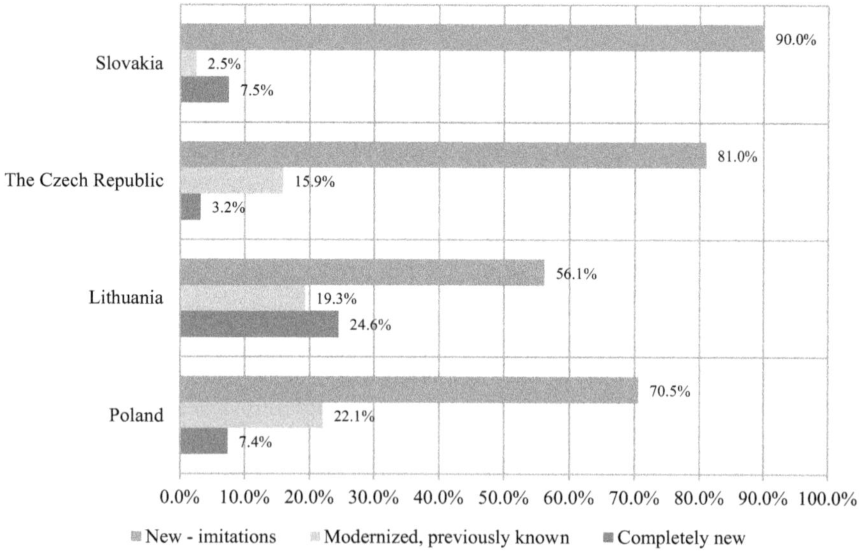

Figure 2.4 The nature of country-specific innovations.

Source: Own elaboration.

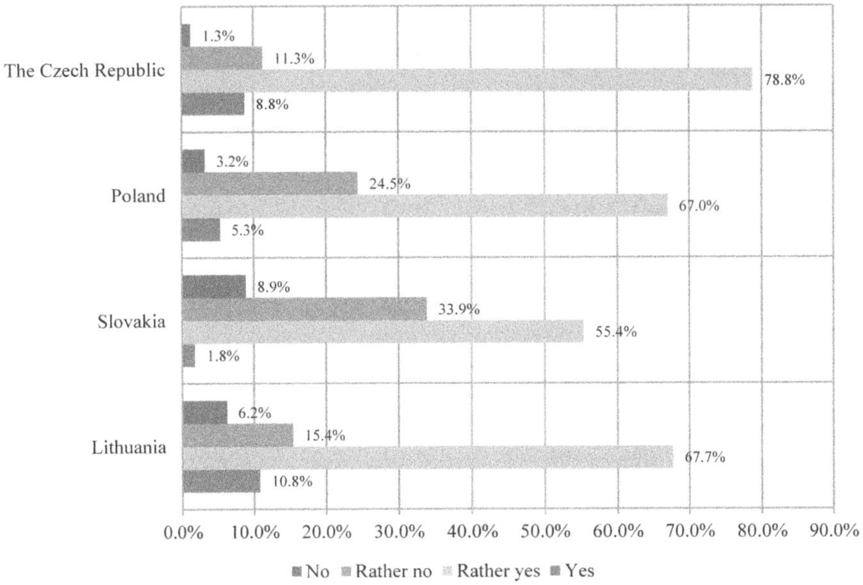

Figure 2.5 Involvement in innovation management in individual countries.

Source: Own elaboration.

"yes" or "rather yes"), while Lithuania came second with 78.5% of affirmative responses. Poland ranked third (72.3%), while Slovakia showed the least interest in innovation management (57.2%). The statistics are shown in Figure 2.5.

The proportion of affirmative responses about the company's involvement in managing innovations at the respondents' workplace also corresponded with the scale of the companies' operations, as evidenced by the results of the selected tests in Table 2.2. Therefore, it can be concluded from the study that the degree to which innovation is managed in the T&C industry is correlated with the scale of the companies' operations, and therefore the H0 hypothesis has been confirmed.

Most of the surveyed companies (42.1%) focused their innovation management on products. They also addressed processes (16.6%), production (12.5%),

Table 2.2 Values of selected tests of the correlation between the country of residence and the scale of operation of companies

Test	*Value*	*df*	*Asymptotic (bilateral) significance*
Pearson's chi-square	46.955	9	0.000
Credibility quotient	50.559	9	0.000
Linear compound test	2.665	1	0.103
N valid observations	295		

Source: Own elaboration.

organization (11.2%), services (8.5%), marketing (5.8%), and management (3.1%). Figure 2.5 illustrates the innovation management areas across different countries.

It is often difficult for SMEs to compete effectively in the race for innovation. Therefore, it is important to effectively use the available solutions and ideas. Especially today, when even large enterprises often prove that skillful use of existing ideas is key to being competitive in the market. Meanwhile, relatively few small and medium-sized companies use the concept of open innovation in innovation management. The results of the study indicate that only 6.4% of all surveyed companies seek to use such solutions. It can also be observed that open innovation strategies were used by companies with a larger scale of activity (see Figure 2.6).

Despite a lack of sufficient resources for research in the area of developing and introducing a new product, SMEs are reluctant to cooperate in this area. According to the survey, 79.3% of the companies do not collaborate or have never collaborated with institutions or other enterprises. 15.3% of companies have collaborated with R&D institutions in the past, and only 5.4% with other companies. This may be an indication of a lack of trust in both research and development institutions and business partners. A collaboration of this kind is likely to increase development opportunities, especially for the implementation

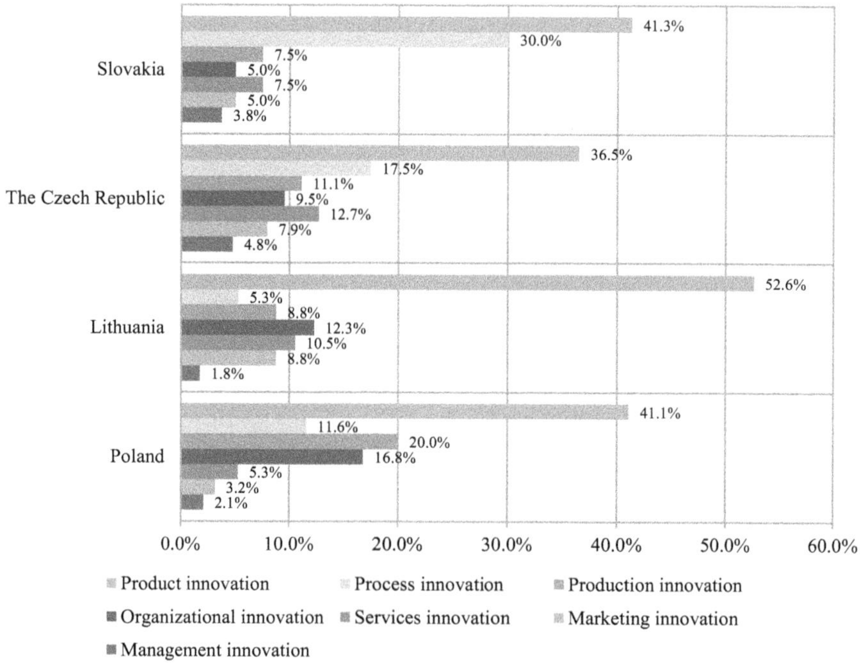

Figure 2.6 Areas of innovation management in SMEs, by country.

Source: Own elaboration.

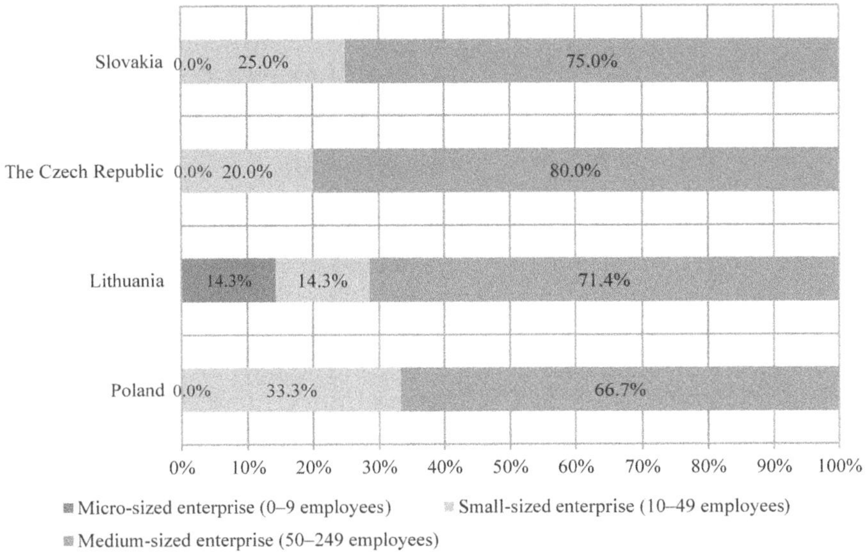

Figure 2.7 The importance of open innovation in innovation management in individual countries based on a company's size.

Source: Own elaboration.

of open innovation and the competitiveness of an organization, especially since collaborations with external sources of knowledge are now considered to be vital (see Figure 2.7) (Avalos-Quispe & Hernández-Simón, 2019).

In the opinion of the respondents, the main barriers to establishing cooperation with other companies are a lack of trust in joint efforts (75.9% of responses) as well as a lack of interest among enterprises to cooperate with others (60.3%). Collaboration is also hindered by a lack of awareness of its potential benefits (51.5%). Interestingly, the inability to collaborate in creating and disseminating innovation can also be ascribed to the lack of institutions in the company's environment that can disseminate knowledge (27.8%) and facilitate entrepreneurs' business connections (33.9%). Based on the country of operation of the SMEs surveyed, Figure 2.8 shows the main impediments to collaboration.

Conclusions and recommendations

Currently, innovation is becoming a necessary condition to achieve and maintain a competitive advantage in the market. SMEs have the potential to innovate, which means that they can play an increasingly important role in creating innovative activities and that they can become significant creators of many new innovations. A significant increase in innovation can only occur when it is not the result of random events but is the result of deliberate management of the innovation process.

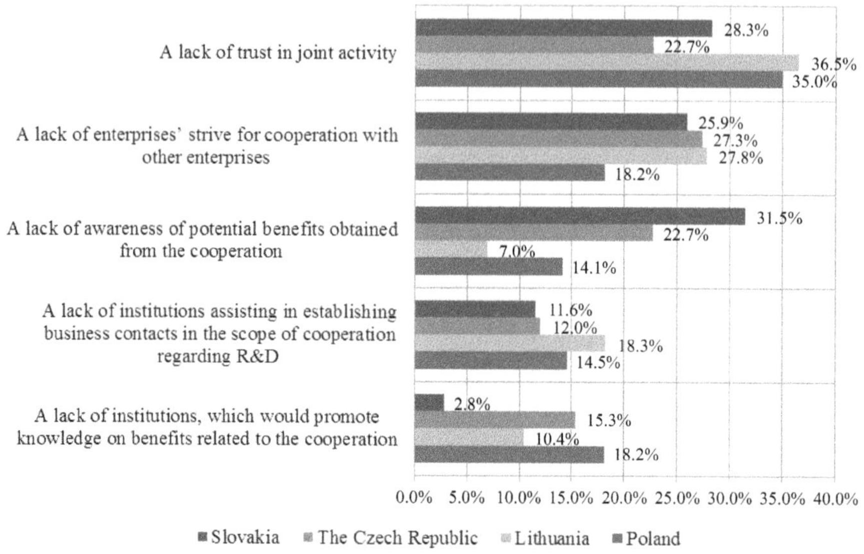

Figure 2.8 The importance of obstacles faced by SMEs to engage in collaboration with business partners and R&D institutions, by country.

Source: Own elaboration.

In this study, the research assumptions were positively validated. At the moment, SMEs are interested in implementing innovations, but numerous barriers are preventing them from doing so. As a result, almost two-thirds of the surveyed enterprises declared that they had implemented innovative changes in the last 3 years. They claimed this was due to their ability to effectively manage the innovation process. Unfortunately, in a significant number of cases, innovations were new only to the company itself. Among T&C companies, there were only 9.8% of completely new solutions. That may indicate that SMEs were focused on adapting existing solutions rather than creating completely new ones. SMEs' reluctance to cooperate in costly R&D research is a significant obstacle to innovation implementation.

The rise of the network economy has forced a redefinition of the concept of innovation, putting emphasis on the ability of organizations to benefit from the process of sharing intellectual capital. Due to the fact that the commercialization of innovative ideas is essential to innovations, and that SMEs lack the resources to commercialize their innovative ideas, a solution can be drawn to expand the practice of open innovation in SMEs. When it comes to the commercialization of innovative solutions, the practice of open innovation that relies on collaboration with others may prove crucial for such firms, provided that they overcome their reluctance to work with other companies. It can be argued that the implementation of innovation will soon become a necessity for SMEs and that the opening of innovation processes will be an inevitable reality in the years to come. A new approach to the development of innovation can be a great opportunity to strengthen SMEs, but it can also pose a challenge to companies that are hesitant to cooperate in R&D, which is extremely important to the Industry 5.0 concept. This concept aims to harmonize the workspaces and performance of people and machines. Management of innovation in SMEs is an essential component of Industry 5.0, which is about increasing production and customer satisfaction. There are many challenges and open issues that SMEs face, such as security, privacy, human-robot collaborations, and a skilled workforce. It is important to treat these factors as areas of exploration for the implementation of Industry 5.0 in the near future with regard to innovation management in SMEs.

References

Avalos-Quispe, G., & Hernández-Simón, L. (2019). Open innovation in SMEs: Potential and realized absorptive capacity for interorganizational learning in dyad collaborations with academia. *Journal of Open Innovation: Technology, Market, and Complexity, 5*(3), 72. https://doi.org/10.3390/joitmc5030072

Beyene, K., Shi, C., & Wu, W. (2016). The impact of innovation strategy on organizational learning and innovation performance: Do firm size and ownership type make a difference? *The South African Journal of Industrial Engineering, 27*(1). https://doi.org/10.7166/27-1-1308

Dossou-Yovo, A., & Keen, C. (2021). SMEs and the innovation management process: A multi-level process conceptual framework. *Technology Innovation Management Review, 11*(1), 22–33. https://doi.org/10.22215/timreview/1414

Euratax (2020). Facts & Key Figures of the European Textile and Clothing Industry, Brussels. Retrieved July 25, 2022, from https://euratex.eu/wp-content/uploads/EURATEX-Facts-Key-Figures-2020-LQ.pdf

European Commission (2019). Annual Report on European SMEs 2018/2019: Research & Development and Innovation by SMEs. SME Performance Review 2018/2019, Brussels. Retrieved July 25, 2022, from https://data.europa.eu/doi/10.2826/603707

European Commission (2021). Annual Report on European SMEs 2020/2021. Digitalisation of SMEs. SME Performance Review 2020/2021, Brussels. Retrieved July 25, 2022, from https://data.europa.eu/doi/10.2826/120209

Goffin, K., & Mitchell, R. (2017). *Innovation management: Effective strategy and implementation*. Palgrave.

Gogołowicz, J. (2013). Innovation and networking as conditions for the development of the enterprise. *Scientific Notebooks Studies and Works of the College of Management and Finance, 133*, 75–94. Retrieved July 25, 2022, from http://yadda.icm.edu.pl/yadda/element/bwmeta1.element.ekon-element-000171275343

Goller, I., & Bessant, J. (2017). *Creativity for innovation management*. Routledge.

Halim, H., Ahmad, N., & Ramayah, T. (2019). Sustaining the innovation culture in SMEs: The importance of organisational culture, organisational learning and market orientation. *Asian Journal of Business Research*. https://doi.org/10.14707/ajbr.190059

Janasz, W. (2003). *Innovations in business models*. Wydawnictwo Naukowe Uniwersytetu Szczecińskiego

Keskin, H. (2006). Market orientation, learning orientation, and innovation capabilities in SMEs. *European Journal of Innovation Management, 9*(4), 396–417.

Koch, J. (2005) *Regional development strategy – a joint work of the lower Silesia community.* Scientific Works of the Lower Silesian University of Entrepreneurship and Technology, Series of Conferences, 1.2005.

Li, L. (2020). Education supply chain in the era of industry 4.0. *Systems Research and Behavioral Science, 37*(4), 579–592.

Minh, T., & Hjortsø, C. (2015). How Institutions influence SME innovation and networking practices: The case of Vietnamese agribusiness. *Journal of Small Business Management, 53*, 209–228. https://doi.org/10.1111/jsbm.12189

Nahavandi, S. (2019). Industry 5.0 – A human-centric solution. *Sustainability, 11*(16), 4371. https://doi.org/10.3390/su11164371

Pol, E., & Ville, S. (2009). Social innovation: Buzz word or enduring term? *The Journal of Socio-Economics, 38*(6), 878–885. https://doi.org/10.1016/j.socec.2009.02.011

Poole, M. S., Van de Ven, A. H., Dooley, K., & Holmes, M. E. (2000). *Organizational Change Processes: Theory and methods for research.* Oxford University Press.

Rusu, V., & Roman, A. (2017). Economic performance of the SME sector in CEE countries: An empirical investigation. *Acta Universtais Danubius, 13*(3), 102–114.

Sipa, M. (2012). Specificity of innovation sources in micro and small enterprises. In S. Hittmár (Ed.), *Theory of management 6. The selected problems for the development support of management knowledge base* (pp. 250–254). University of Zilina.

Vitezić, N., & Vitezić, V. (2015), A conceptual model of linkage between innovation management and controlling in the sustainable environment. *Journal of Applied Business Research. 31*(1). https://doi.org/10.19030/jabr.v31i1.8999

Zhu, Y., Wittmann, X., & Peng, M. (2012). Institution-based barriers to innovation in SMEs in China. *Asia Pacific Journal of Management, 29*(4), 1131–1142.

3 Open innovation and virtualization

Magdalena Czerwińska, Tomasz Kusio, Ryszard Borowiecki

Organizational determinants of open innovation

The paradigm of open innovation has become increasingly important in the context of globalization and technological advancement (Chesbrough & Bogers, 2014; Kusio, 2020). In this sense, it manifests itself in an increased need to identify and establish relationships with public, private, and business partners and to sustain those relationships. Closely related to the paradigm of open innovation is the imperative of change (Borowiecki & Siuta-Tokarska, 2021), where the need to make changes is a necessary condition for the functioning of the modern market economy (Kusio, 2019). Representatives of the sectors of science, business, public administration, and society (triple helix or quadruple helix) participate in the processes of creating developmental changes. The representatives of these sectors are more commonly known as stakeholders, especially when we take into consideration their pursuits. In the context of open innovation, the notion of stakeholders – initially referring to the social responsibility of business – takes on both a personal and institutional dimension because today individuals and institutions from all sectors are participating in innovation processes. Moreover, participation in projects that create new knowledge and value contributes to an organization's intellectual capital, which becomes more dynamic as an organization becomes more open to exchanges of information and views. Dynamic capabilities are influenced by relationality, which in turn facilitates open innovation. (Jantunen et al., 2018) Organizations repurpose existing capabilities while developing and renewing other capabilities through their dynamic potential. An organization's dynamic potential stems from its limitations, and it is correlated with a propensity toward organizational openness in terms of innovation. It can refer to businesses, social or public sector organizations as well as small- and medium-sized businesses to a greater extent because of the need these organizations have for intellectual resources and knowledge.

In a study conducted by EUIPO, whose findings are also confirmed by national studies on the perception of knowledge and the importance of intellectual property in innovation, the low level of this knowledge is evident in the SME sector (Dereń, 2020). An important contributing factor to such a

DOI: 10.4324/9781003384311-3

state of affairs is insufficient inventive activity and low levels of intellectual property protection. In contrast, issues related to the perceived value of stakeholders' contributions to knowledge creation are related to open innovation and its impact on innovation potential (Laursen & Salter, 2004). Increasing the level of dynamic capabilities requires adequate management of open innovation in the organization (Elia et al., 2019), specifically openness to innovative projects, which is a necessity for small organizations.

As part of knowledge exchange projects aimed at developing new, innovative solutions, organizations bring their own skills, knowledge, and intellectual resources but must also protect those resources. Many organizations have fundamental doubts not only about the level of how their own resources are shared but also about the planned tasks that require such resources to be shared, and what areas of their activity can be characterized as directions and degrees of innovation openness in their organization. As a result, the added value that arises from such collaboration may be more significant for one organization than for another, which leads to different perceptions of the value of the solutions. The solutions that are developed, while protected by a contract between the partners, may increase the organization's motivation to put those solutions into practice.

Innovation projects and the role of knowledge in decision-making dynamics

Innovation models have changed over the years ranging from push-and-pull to the current open innovation model (Siuta-Tokarska, 2021). Open innovation has evolved from being understood as good ideas originating within or outside an organization (and then being implemented within or outside the organization) (Chesbrough, 2003) to a method for disseminating innovations that uses deliberately controlled knowledge flows across organizational boundaries using monetary or non-monetary mechanisms according to the business model (Chesbrough & Bogers, 2014). Innovation, however, has always had a conceptual and implementation dimension, which is documented in the literature and is normative in nature.

Knowledge acquired during the implementation of development initiatives and used to create innovation is accumulated, integrated, applied, and transformed (Patrício et al., 2021). Research on dynamic capabilities supports processes that relate to knowledge (Eriksson, 2014), among them gathering, integration, application, and reconfiguration of knowledge. In the context of project implementation, knowledge-related processes are dynamized, which is consistent with the specifics of project implementation, which require time and resource discipline. Development projects are implemented within a specified time frame and within a specified amount of material and intangible resources. It has been shown that dynamic capabilities and their benefits are present in project management (Biesenthal et al., 2019). In the context of project management, the issue of utilizing the skills gained by people participating in the implementation of projects is given special attention. Having this kind of knowledge should facilitate faster decision-making and increase the accumulation of factors impacting management decisions. As part of this accumulation, agility comes into play (Cesarotti et al., 2019). Therefore, innovation projects increase the potential and dynamize it while being closely aligned with the need for efficient decision-making.

While there is an economic openness to innovation processes, globalization processes continue to exert a decisive influence. In an era of globalization, national economic systems are now more interdependent than ever, implying new qualitative connections at the national level and among individual organizations. A number of these connections can be traced to the growing freedom and increasing speed with which transactions are accomplished and concluded (Borowiecki, 2017). Increased globalization increases interpersonal dependencies, as well as the need for developing inter-organizational dependencies (Ferreira, 2018). Open innovation includes a number of factors that practitioners and decision-makers take into account for innovative projects. Among them are innovation networks, collaboration with stakeholders (supply chain participants), innovation eco-systems, and ICT technologies that influence decision-making (Uttama, 2021).

The principle of resource efficiency and the need to achieve greater economic efficiency drive the search for innovative solutions. A natural outcome, one might say, is the need to increase the rationality of resource usage. This results in self-regulation of information and knowledge of a specialized nature. The result of these processes is open-source innovation, which is the result of regulating intensified knowledge needs while delivering it through network collaborations and innovation projects. Today, open innovations are viewed as the current innovation reality (Kusio, 2020).

Virtualization of connections within organizations

The blurring of geographical boundaries in innovation processes confirms the growing importance of globalization. As globalization processes intensify, people are more likely to seek out innovative solutions beyond their own organizations or immediate environments. Thus, increased open innovation is linked to globalization, leading to an increased interest in the possibility of developing initiatives and projects in a virtual setting.

Within the discussion of innovative creativity that results in innovative solutions, there is a thread of innovative geography (Doehne & Rost, 2021) that is strongly tied to cluster formation and effective functioning. When stakeholders work together in a cluster, they gain access to new, creative resources that may not be available individually or may be easier to obtain within the cluster. This is especially true for SMEs. Thus, scientific institutions that hold many creative resources and provide innovative solutions are becoming increasingly important. Moreover, knowledge and technology transfer sectors are also becoming more important as they energize knowledge exchange processes. A number of interesting innovative solutions originating from scientific institutions have been commercialized by academics. This includes academic enterprises, or spin-outs, whose creation and operation seem to satisfy the requirements of implementing developed solutions adequately. Clustering promotes innovation appropriation, i.e. getting the most credible information to the most appropriate audience at the earliest possible. These considerations can be traced to the roots of civilization, namely the civilizations of Athens and Rome, as well as the similarly successful Silicon Valley cluster (Audretsch & Feldman, 2004). The level of openness of the organization and its innovation level (Laursen & Salter, 2004) and, especially, the level of interest in undertaking innovative initiatives have already been established in research on open innovation.

From a global perspective, which increasingly affects the functioning of not only economies (macro-level) but also startups (micro-level), we believe the most effective knowledge should be produced by the best thinkers for the best possible institutions that implement these solutions without regard to geographic, technological, or financial barriers (Kusio, 2021). The specific specialization that is part of innovation appropriation is evident in several socioeconomic sectors and is complementary to the need to establish academic enterprises. A critical element of the theory of innovation appropriation is the importance of appropriate relationships, which are largely peer-to-peer and which, in clusters, take the form of direct contact. At this stage of the development of social networks, the issue of open innovation in relation to creativity has high research potential. The social exchange theory – indicates that social interaction drives mutual communication and facilitates the formation of more lasting relationships. The parties involved in the social dialogue should therefore strive to strengthen this interactional exchange rather than avoid it. The development and creation of social networks attract and expand creative discussion between individuals who have overlapping interests (Sorenson, 2018). Through collaborations based on exchanging ideas and views among people with similar interests, it is easier to develop creative solutions as well as to create or co-create added value. When discussing levels of creativity and the general culture of innovation within an organization, social interactions come into play as part of regulated work (Fried et al., 2007). Networking, which has been associated mainly with the environment of the organization, concerns both the external and internal environment and, as evidenced by observation, the social context of this interconnectedness can affect the level of creativity and perhaps its quality, while certainly it should be seen a positive impact on the processes of innovation appropriation. Moreover, innovation appropriation can be also applied to social interactions, and this is an interesting direction of consideration. As a counterweight to clusters with close geographic proximity, there is the formation of online relationships with no geographic connection but due to the emotional social component can connect people and organizations who seek appropriate solutions that are not only needed but also represent an object of interest for employees and others associated with the organizations.

Virtualization of connections outside organizations

Among the studies conducted for the purpose of learning about the peculiarities of open innovation, there was also an emphasis on virtual teams (Gassmann et al., 2010) that have become more important in light of the current pandemic. Knowledge sharing, generating, and processing is becoming increasingly feasible as a result of progressive technological developments (Bjorkdahl, 2020). Increasing data collection and the subsequent processing of these data that leads to knowledge creation supports decision-making processes and minimizes the risk of uncertainty in decision-making within an organization (del Vecchio et al., 2018). Increasing the volume of data an organization has access to increases the processing capacity and reduces the potential risk of making wrong decisions. When virtual teams work together, *co-worker social interaction* occurs (Metallo et al., 2021), which is a reference to the so-called New Ways of Working. Moreover, as research findings indicate, similar working methods have a positive effect on *intrepreneurial behavior* (Metallo et al., 2021).

Creating interactions can be explained through the ARA model (actors, resources, activities). In this model, there are three variables that interact with one another, i.e. actors (network participants), resources of individual participants, and activities that involve sharing or using resources, among other things (Czaplicka-Kotas et al., 2017). On the other hand, the OECD's approach to networking focuses on the creation and use of internal and external connections (communication, interaction, coordination) between people, teams, and organizations (links) to enhance efficiency. Network relationships within organizations, which are social in nature, either between employees or between employees and their managers, have a positive impact on creativity as well as on the implementation of new economic practices in the organizations where they work (Gerards et al., 2021). Therefore, the social aspect of interactions is beneficial both during the development and implementation of new solutions.

Employees who devise innovative solutions for their companies are often referred to as *intrapreneurial employees* (Blanka, 2018). On a similar note, we can talk about two notions that preceded this concept – knowledge workers (a concept with a similar definition), and the concept of talent, which can be traced back even further (Kopeć, 2018). An intrapreneur is someone who, through their own inventiveness, develops solutions that can be applied to the market within the company they work for. Contrary to this approach, it is also possible to see instances where innovative solutions are developed and not implemented within an organization, which may indicate a lack of openness in the enterprise or a high level of adherence to the data security policy.

There have been assessments and studies on employee characteristics and competencies associated with open innovation (McPhillips & Licznerska, 2021). The studies explore the employee characteristics that contribute to their ability to recognize and apply information from outside the organization. This includes pursuing such knowledge, fostering innovative activities within the organization, and facilitating the application of these ideas across the enterprise. Creativity, organizational abilities (entrepreneurship), and language skills that can refer to communication are found to be among the identified employee characteristics associated with openness to innovation (Hong & Kim, 2020). In the literature, it is confirmed that open innovation requires the right traits (Mahdad et al., 2020). Digitization of work is a progressive trend in nature that has been accelerated by the pandemic. Although originally attributed mostly to non-organizational relationships, the digitalization of work has taken on the meaning of regular work within an organization, as well as to the strength of these relationships and the fact that they are becoming increasingly strong due to socialization.

Intellectual property rights

The issue of intellectual property rights closely accompanies open innovation (Brem et al., 2017). Efficient use of the characteristics of intellectual resources in the process of creating innovation helps organizations obtain more value than their competitors (Dogwood, 2020). For large organizations, intellectual property holds a special significance, since they often devote part of their activities to R&D and generally have more potential than entities that have fewer employees and are primarily engaged in their current activity. Developing their own intellectual resources and self-generating novel solutions plays a significant role in enterprises whose innovation strategies are not geared toward openness and where the *outside-in* model trumps the *inside-out* model. The skills and qualifications of staff assume great significance in such a context (Felin & Zenger, 2014). There is a widening gap in the balance between the beneficiaries of innovation (that is, those who represent intellectual capital, i.e. innovators, investors, shareholders) and those who depend on labor. There will be a growing demand for highly qualified specialists, but the demand for unskilled laborers is expected to decline (Geryk, 2020).

A company's intellectual resources are intangible resources and can be considered inexhaustible, yet the quality represented by its employees can vary greatly. It is often the case that intellectual resources are proprietary in nature, and they can become part of the company's assets through an exchange. Intangible resources such as ambition, value system, and level of involvement, otherwise known as non-economic factors, lead to the development of innovations (Dogwood, 2020) and are directly related to workers and entrepreneurs alike. In its initial stage, innovation aims to develop solutions and ideas that will address current problems and challenges in a more efficient manner. This could be related to new products, services, processes, or ways of working. The benefit is that it is a more effective way to manufacture, organize, sell, and provide services. As creators, humans are crucial at this point in identifying customer needs, and also in generating new ideas. At the same time, entrepreneurship that manifests itself in creative anxiety is the engine of pro-innovation actions. Entrepreneurship is primarily an attribute of human activity, which further confirms that in the early stages of innovation (on a micro-level, i.e. in the organization) the role of the human as an employee is crucial (Kusio & Makieła, 2020).

It seems that the digitization of relationships that has been described in the earlier part of this chapter (and that is gaining acceptance) refers to the creative workforce. Moreover, in the processes of *corporate entrepreneurship* or *intrapreneurship,* new solutions that emerge from innovation initiatives in relationships (whether intra-organizational or with other organizations) are implemented in economic practice. The legal aspect of such solutions is all the more important in this context. Another reason is that many of the solutions developed fail to spark the interest of owners and managers.

As experience has shown, it is possible to encounter situations that are unfavorable or that threaten the positive effects of accessing a limited amount of data, when using such data could cause problems (Dahlander et al., 2021), particularly when it comes to intellectual property rights. However, a similar approach can in large part refer to individuals who, when sharing knowledge, are not aware of what purposes the knowledge they share will serve. In addition to the discussions, there is the question of equivalence, which seems extremely relevant in the context of open innovation.

Summary

Based on the above discussion on open innovation, its current formation, and the observed directions for its development, it can be concluded that:

- It is individuals representing economic and social organizations who take part in creative processes. Participating in the innovation process makes these individuals stakeholders in creating innovative solutions, adding to their importance to the organization;
- Communication is increasingly based on technological solutions, enhancing virtual communication and interaction between individuals and institution stakeholders;
- We are observing an increase in the importance of the social dimension of relationships, especially when it comes to online interactions. This increase promotes the creative nature of solutions by connecting stakeholders with similar emotional characteristics and similar interests;
- The social nature of stakeholder relationships relates both to intra-organizational relationships (which include relationships among representatives at different levels of organizational structure and on different levels of subordination) and relationships outside of an organization. This is also supported by the growing importance of teal organizations and agile structures. It seems that the socialization factor can provide an explanation for the success and effectiveness of work in these types of structures to an extent;
- The interactions include phases during which ideas are formulated or sought but also implemented. According to the open innovation paradigm,

internal and external sources of knowledge and technology may appear at different stages of the project implementation process (Vanhaverbeke et al., 2008), which may include both conceptual and implementation phases;

- As part of the innovation implementation process, the developed solutions can be implemented by knowledge workers within the organization (intrapreneurship) or outside of it (corporate entrepreneurship). However, many of the developed solutions may not be implemented at all, thereby multiplying the organization's intangible resources and intellectual capital;
- As an organization becomes more open, its potential becomes more dynamic. Organizational openness is accompanied by a greater level of inclination toward innovation. Thus, a higher level of dynamic potential leads to a higher likelihood of innovation in the enterprise. There are various features that pertain to the need to increase dynamic potential such as the need for the organization to be much more responsive to changes in its environment as well as to increase its ability to identify those changes (Patrício et al., 2019). A changing environment that affects the identification of opportunities and risks, and the ability to make adaptive decisions requires the organization to have appropriate tools. As an example, such tools may include systems based on digital technologies, customary systems of human communication one-on-one, or multiperson exchange of information. When it comes to identifying changes in the environment where individuals are involved, simplified information exchange systems are possible, such as provider-recipient, client-seller, and applicant-supplier. Communication between them is based on the commodity that is being exchanged or sold. Interpersonal and inter-organizational relationships are a layer of knowledge production, where the end recipient is the source.

The concept of open innovation can be thought of as a means to find a solution to a given problem within an organization, without having a sufficient amount of resources, but most importantly a means to continue existing in the future. This can be achieved by collecting information about existing solutions, despite the fact that real creators and innovators tend not to be the ones implementing their own ideas, or may reap hardly any no benefits from their own innovative contributions (Teece, 2006).

References

Audretsch, D. B., & Feldman, M. P. (2004). Knowledge spillovers and the geography of innovation. *Handbook of Regional and Urban Economics, 4*, 2713–2739.

Biesenthal, C., Gudergan, S., & Ambrosini, V. (2019). The role of ostensive and performative routine aspects in dynamic capability deployment at different organizational levels. *Long Range Planning, 52*, 350–365.

Bjorkdahl, J. (2020). Strategies for digitalization in manufacturing firms. *California Management Review, 62*(4), 17.

Blanka, C. (2018). An individual-level perspective on intrapreneurship: A review and ways forward. *Review of Managerial Science*. https://doi.org/10.1007/s11846-018-0277-0

Borowiecki, R. (2017). The role of change leader in modern enterprise. In E. Bojar (Ed.), *Leaders on leadership* (pp. 20–24).

Borowiecki, R., & Siuta-Tokarska, B. (2021). Management science and the idea of sustainable and sustainable development. In B. Fiedor, M. Gorynia, & Ł. Hardt (Eds.), *Uniformity or pluralism: Reflections on the nature of economic sciences and the economy* (pp. 145–155). Publishing house of the Polish Economic Society.

Brem, A., Nylund, P. A., & Hitchen, E. L. (2017). Open innovation and intellectual property rights: How do SMEs benefit from patents, industrial designs, trademarks and copyrights? *Management Decision*, *55*(6), 1285–1306.

Cesarotti, V., Gubinelli, S., & Introna, V. (2019). The evolution of project management (PM): How Agile, Lean and Six Sigma are changing PM. *The Journal of Modern Project Management*, 7, 1–29.

Chesbrough, H. W. (2003). *Open innovation: The new imperative for creating and profiting from technology*. Harvard Business School Press.

Chesbrough, H., & Bogers, M. (2014). Explicating open innovation: Clarifying an emerging paradigm for understanding innovation. In H. Chesbrough, W. Vanhaverbeke, & J. West (Eds.), *New frontiers in open innovation* (pp. 3–28). Oxford University Press.

Czaplicka-Kotas, A., Kulczycka, J., & Kuźmierz, P. (2017). National and international scientific networks initiator of innovation in economic practice. *Economics and Enterprise Organization*, *3*(806), 52–61.

Dahlander, L., Gann, D. M., & Wallin, M. W. (2021). How open is innovation? A retrospective and ideas forward. *Research Policy*, *50*, 104218. https://doi.org/10.1016/j.respol.2021.104218

del Vecchio, P., Di Minin, A., Petruzzelli, A. M., Panniello, U., & Pirri, S. (2018). Big data for open innovation in SMEs and large corporations: Trends, opportunities, and challenges. *Creativity and Innovation Management*, *27*(1), 6–22.

Dereń, A. M. (2020). Własność intelektualna Jako Kluczowy Zasób Organizacji Innowacyjnej. *Przegląd Organizacji*, *5*, 10–19. https://doi.org/10.33141/po.2020.05.02

Doehne, M., & Rost, K. (2021). Long waves in the geography of innovation: The rise and decline of regional clusters of creativity over time. *Research Policy*, *50*.

Dogwood, A. M. (2020). Intellectual property as a key resource for innovation organization. *Review of the Organization*, *5*(964), 10–19.

Elia, S., Massini, S., & Narula, R. (2019). Disintegration, modularity and entry mode choice: Mirroring technical and organizational architectures in business functions offshoring. *Journal of Business Research*, *103*, 417–431. https://doi.org/10.1016/j.jbusres.2017.11.034

Eriksson, T. (2014). Processes, antecedents and outcomes of dynamic capabilities. *Scandinavian Journal of Management*, *30*, 65–82.

Felin, T., & Zenger, T. R. (2014). Closed or open innovation? Problem solving and the governance choice. *Research Policy*, *43*, 914–925.

Ferreira, C. (2018), *The relationship between globalization and economic growth: A co-integration approach* [Conference session]. Materials from the 4th International Scientific Conference: Globalization and regionalization in the modern world: Competitiveness, development, stability. Cracow University of Economics.

Fried, Y., Levi, S. A., & Laurence, G. (2007). The job characteristics model and LMX-MMX leadership. In G. B. Graen & J. A. Graen (Eds.), *New Multinational Network Sharing* (pp. 157–197). Information Age Publishing.

Gassmann, O., Enkel, E., & Chesbrough, H. (2010). The future of open innovation. *R D Management, 40*(3), 213–221. https://doi.org/10.1111/j.1467-9310.2010.00605.x

Gerards, R., van Wetten, S., & van Sambeek, C. (2021). New ways of working and intrapreneurial behavior: The mediating role of transformational leadership and social interaction. *Review of Managerial Science, 15*, 2075–2110. https://doi.org/10.1007/s11846-020-00412-1

Geryk, M. (2020). Challenges posed for universities. In P. Buła & B. Nogalski (Eds.), *The future of management. Industry 4.0 and digitalization* (pp. 141–148). Wydawnictwo Uniwersytetu Jagiellońskiego.

Hong, K., & Kim, B. (2020). Open innovation competency of Design Enterprises to Outsourcing Service. *Journal of Open Innovation: Technology, Market, and Complexity, 6*(2), 36. https://doi.org/10.3390/joitmc6020036

Jantunen, A., Tarkiainen, A., Chari, S., & Oghazi, P. (2018). Dynamic capabilities, operational changes, and performance outcomes in the media industry. *Journal of Business Research, 89*, 251–257. https://doi.org/10.1016/j.jbusres.2018.01.037

Kopeć, J. (2018). Talent manager for the challenges of the future. *Scientific Works of Wrocław University of Economics, 511*, 114–122.

Kusio, T. (2019). *Więzi relacyjne nauki z biznesem*. AGH Publishing.

Kusio, T. (2020). Open innovation financing. In E. Step & J. Swacha (Eds.), *Innovation and management* (pp. 125–134). SIZ Publishing House.

Kusio, T. (2021). Regional innovation in the example of lesser Poland. In Z. Makieła, Stuss & R. Borowiecki (Eds.), *Sustainability, technology and innovation 4.0* (pp. 103–122). Routledge.

Laursen, K., & Salter, A. J. (2004). Searching high and low: What type of firms are universities as a source of innovation? *Research Policy, 33*(8), 1201–1215. https://doi.org/10.1016/j.respol.2004.07.004

Mahdad, M., Marco, C. E. D., Piccaluga, A., & Minin, A. D. (2020). Harnessing adaptive capacity to close the Pandora's box of open innovation. *Industry and Innovation, 27*, 264–284.

McPhillips, M., & Licznerska, M., (2021). Open innovation competence for a future-proof workforce: A comparative study from four European universities. *Journal of Theoretical & Applied Electronic Commerce Research*, 16, 2442–2457. https://doi.org/10.3390/jtaer16060134

Metallo, C., Agrifoglio, R., Briganti, P., Mercurio, L., & Ferrara, M. (2021). Entrepreneurial behaviour and new venture creation: The Psychoanalytic Perspective. *Journal of Innovation & Knowledge, 6*(1), 35–42. https://doi.org/10.1016/j.jik.2020.02.001

Patrício, V., Lopes da Costa, R., Pereira, L., & António, N. (2021). Project management in the development of dynamic capabilities for an open innovation era. *Journal of Open Innovation Technology Market and Complexity*, 7, 164. https://doi.org/10.3390/joitmc7030164

Patrício, V. S., Pereira, L. F., & Santos, J. P. (2019). *Dynamic Capabilities trends: A brief review of the state of the art* [Conference session]. Proceedings of the 2019 IEEE International Conference on Engineering, Technology and Innovation (ICE/ITMC), Valbonne Sophia-Antipolis, France, June 17–19. https://doi.org/10.3390/joitmc7030164

Siuta-Tokarska, B. (2021). Economics of moderation: Towards sustainable development. *Social Inequality and Economic Growth*, 3(67), 5–15.

Sorenson, O. (2018). Social networks and the geography of entrepreneurship. *Small Business Economics, 51*, 527–537.

Teece, D. J. (2006). Reflections on "profiting from innovation". *Research Policy, 35*(8), 1131–1146.

Uttama, N. P. (2021). Open innovation and business model of health food industry in Asia. *Journal of Open Innovation Technology Market and Complexity*, 7, 174. https://doi.org/10.3390/joitmc7030174

Vanhaverbeke, W., Van de Vrande, V., & Chesbrough, H. (2008). Understanding the advantages of open innovation practices in corporate venturing in terms of real options. *Creativity and Innovation Management*, *17*(4), 251–258. https://doi.org/10.1111/j.1467-8691.2008.00499.x

4 Industry 5.0

New approaches to innovation in the industry

Jakub Pizoń, Monika Kulisz

Introduction

The production sector is a branch of the economy that contributes to society's prosperity and development. With the advent of subsequent technical inventions throughout history, progress would take place and new professions would emerge, along with new needs. These periods of intensive development are known as industrial revolutions. As indicated in the literature (Horváth & Szabó, 2019, pp. 119–132; Nowotarski & Paslawski, 2017), the First Industrial Revolution began at the end of the 18th century and relied on steam and hydropower. The Second Industrial Revolution started at the beginning of the 20th century, with electric power being used to implement mass production. The next industrial revolution began in the 1970s with the use of electronic and computer-based automation. The Fourth Industrial Revolution is currently underway, also known as Industry 4.0, which is characterized by cyber-physical systems (CPS) based on heterogeneous data and knowledge integration (Maddikunta et al., 2022).

A common characteristic of all revolutions is that each one was initiated by some specific change, some form of innovation, which completely altered the way goods had been produced until that point. With each revolution, new means of production were introduced and some were abandoned. These developments inevitably had political, economic, and social consequences. It can be observed that emerging innovations in production gradually reduced the amount of labor directly involved in the manufacturing process. People's work became redundant over time – especially when the work was simple and repetitive. In addition to the opportunity to replace workers with machines, the technology also provided a way to increase labor efficiency, reduce costs, and thus increase the volume of production.

In spite of its economic justification, however, this approach was found to have neglected a very important aspect of development and innovation. History has shown that innovation has always been the gateway to the future and that people have always been the source of innovation. Thus, the focus in the development of production systems again turns to the people involved in the production process. It should be noted that this return has a completely

DOI: 10.4324/9781003384311-4

new character and does not involve eliminating machines but rather involves cooperation. Therefore, it must be emphasized that the development of modern production systems is rooted in the cooperation of people and machines (Mourtzis, 2021).

There are many challenges in this regard, both on a social and a technical level. It is necessary to meet a number of technical, technological, and organizational requirements (Demir et al., 2019, pp. 688–695; European Commission et al., 2020). Models for implementing this cooperation both on a small and a large scale are required. It is also necessary to find ways how to utilize such cooperation to acquire innovations that can be used to create even better solutions that lead to the creation of production systems.

Thus, the purpose of this chapter is to present the concept of a man-machine collaboration environment for innovation acquisition in relation to the Fifth Industrial Revolution. The concept proposed herein for this purpose is a well-thought-out design that can be used as a basis for further research, or as an inspiration for ready-made solutions in production processes.

This chapter begins with a review of the literature and provides the background for the discussion that follows. Following is a description of the available methods for developing the concept. The description of the designed environment for innovation in Industry 5.0 is presented in the fourth part. The chapter concludes with a discussion of the conclusions to be drawn.

Literature review

Industry 4.0

As part of the process of building cooperation and acquiring innovations, modern production systems must be utilized. Here, the solutions of the current industrial revolution prove useful. The concept of Industry 4.0 was originally introduced to the German economy in 2011. Various definitions of Industry 4.0 exist (Hermann et al., 2016, pp. 3928–3937; Humayun, 2021, pp. 2957–2971; Vogel-Heuser & Hess, 2016, pp. 411–413) but for the purposes of this chapter, we will assume that the term Industry 4.0 means a new level of organization and control over the entire value chain of the product, directed at increasingly individualized customer needs (Rüßmann et al., 2015). In Industry 4.0, the primary goal is to meet the individual needs of customers, which impacts areas such as order management, research, and development, including all phases of production, delivery, up to and including the disposal and recycling of products (Vaidya et al., 2018, pp. 233–238). The implementation of a task of this magnitude requires widespread integration within production systems (Salkin et al., 2018).

At the heart of Industry 4.0 is the digitization of products, machines, or entire production processes. Digitalization is carried out by a range of IT systems linked to a technical infrastructure that allows the production data to be obtained and processed. Digitalization enables you to map physical objects in virtual reality as digital models, with a set of accuracy parameters. Based on the acquired data, the model shows changes to the object in real-time. Therefore, the data in the digital system directly reflects the state of a given machine or process. A digital form such as this may be used for monitoring production, as well as to analyze and discover hidden possibilities or predict threats. Advanced data processing algorithms and techniques for aggregating multidimensional data sets are involved in this dimension. For that, Industry 4.0 utilizes the technologies of the industrial internet of things (IIoT), industrial artificial intelligence (IAI), cloud computing (CC), or CPS) (Pizoń et al., 2021).

Industry 5.0

A natural direction for the development of the current Fourth Industrial Revolution is Industry 5.0. This concept restores the role of humans in the production process. The concept of Industry 5.0 is a collaboration between humans and machines, and more specifically, collaborative robots (cobots). This cooperation relies on the machine, by way of observation and interaction, seeking out with the human the most efficient solutions wherever possible. When a solution has been developed, it is implemented throughout the entire production process. As a result, the implemented solution combines the knowledge of people with advanced analysis utilizing artificial intelligence (AI) algorithms. As with previous revolutions, costs are reduced due to this sort of innovation, but the human factor is also taken into account, which often determines consumer preference and is the basis for sustainable development.

Industry 5.0 emphasizes the importance of research and innovation in enabling the industry to provide long-term services to humanity. Researchers are only beginning to formulate and consider the definition of Industry 5.0. For the purposes of this chapter, we shall define Industry 5.0 as a human-centric design in which the ideal human and cobots work together with human resources to enable the personalization of autonomous manufacturing through corporate social networks. This, in turn, is enabled by man-machine collaboration. Cobots are not programmable machines, but they can sense and comprehend human presence. In this context, cobots will be used for repetitive tasks and laborious tasks, and a human will be responsible for personalization and critical thought (Maddikunta et al., 2022, p. 100257).

The three main characteristics of Industry 5.0 are human-centeredness, sustainability, and resilience. A human-centered approach in the industry places basic human needs and interests at the center of the production process. Instead of asking what we can accomplish with new technology, we ask what it can accomplish for us. Instead of expecting industry employees to adapt their skills to the demands of rapidly developing technology, we need to use technology to adapt production processes to the needs of employees, for example, by training or guiding them. In contrast, sustainability involves developing circular processes for repurposing, recycling, and reusing natural resources, so that waste and environmental impacts can be reduced. As for the final characteristic, resilience refers to the need for industrial production to be more resilient so that it can be better protected from disruptions and be able to provide and support critical infrastructure during times of crisis (European Commission et al., 2021).

Industrial revolutions as a source of innovation

In the Fifth Industrial Revolution, workers are given renewed attention, and machines and human minds are paired to further harness the power of human minds and creativity to increase process efficiency by combining workflow with intelligent systems. The focus of Industry 4.0 is mostly on automation, whereas Industry 5.0 emphasizes the synergy between people and autonomous machines. A workforce that is autonomous is perceptive and aware of human intentions and desires. Having robots as co-workers will not only provide peace of mind but also allow people to work together without fear, knowing that the robots understand them and can efficiently work together. Instead of replacing human workers, robots will work with them to increase productivity.

An example of such cooperation would be as follows. At first, the robot observes the human and understands how the work is done. The robot then analyses the human intentions using visual observation (RGB camera) and, for example, functional spectroscopy sensors in the near-infrared. Following that step, the robot begins to move and helps the employee by lifting objects from the worktable. In the next step, the robot picks up an object that the employee wants. It then brings the object to the employee. Robots only deliver objects to employees when they need them and accept them. Implementing such solutions will result in an extremely efficient production process with high added value, a flourishing autonomy based on trust, and a reduction of waste and associated costs (Nahavandi, 2019, pp. 43–71).

This is primarily because robots offer a number of advantages. To begin with, robots create consistency in the quality of services and products, as well as in the flow of the production line, thus meeting the need for high-quality, low-cost products. In addition, they keep employees from performing potentially dangerous tasks at work, and they generate data on the quality of the process so that the company and production processes can be optimized. Industry 5.0 products/services, which are created by combining man and machine, allow people to fulfill a basic human need to express themselves. Personalized products are also referred to as "human touches". Customers demand and pay the most for products that bear the sign of human care and craftsmanship (Ozkeser, 2018, pp. 422–428).

In conclusion, the Fifth Industrial Revolution is groundbreaking in its combination of the two main pillars of Industry 4.0, automation and efficiency, with an individual approach to people (Mourtzis, 2021). This combination provides a favorable environment for the creation and discovery of new innovations in production processes, as well as a source of new solutions.

Materials and methods

To develop a method of acquiring innovations, it is necessary to use the solutions of technology associated with the Fourth Industrial Revolution.

In order to formulate a fully functional solution, these technologies need to be combined. Listed below are the key technologies essential to the development of our concept.

- Industrial internet of things
  The task of the IIoT is to collect data from manufacturing processes in real-time. Internet of Things solutions include sensors that read data, reliable data transfer protocols, and hardware infrastructure that allows for the acquisition of parameters for objects, machines, and electronic systems via technical communication interfaces (Asghari et al., 2019, pp. 241–261).
- Cloud computing and artificial intelligence
  CC provides high computing power without having to invest in computing infrastructure and is part of Industry 4.0. It allows manufacturing companies to purchase computational power on an as-needed basis (for instance, in the case of IAI). IAI focuses on creating models for the production applications needed (Lee et al., 2018).
- Cyber-physical systems
  A CPS is an integration of both computational and physical processes that is essential to Industry 4.0. It integrates imaging and control functions into a relevant system. A key feature of these systems is their ability to respond to feedback. This allows for immediate feedback and management of the process to produce the desired results (Oztemel & Gursev, 2018, pp. 127–182).
- Digital twin
  A digital twin is a comprehensive digital representation of a single object. With models and data, it describes the properties, states, and behavior of the actual object. A digital twin is developed along with a physical twin and remains its virtual counterpart throughout the life cycle of the product (Haag & Anderl, 2018, pp. 64–66). The mapping allows you to monitor the current state of the object in real-time, analyze its current operation, and predict its future behavior (Kenett & Bortman, 2021; Semeraro et al., 2021, p. 103469). Digital twin solutions are also used to enable human-machine collaboration (HRC). The digital space is a three-dimensional representation of a co-existing or collaborating human and a robot, while the physical space is a real production system comprised of people, robots, and other equipment. Each element in a virtual space represents the design and operational behavior of a connected physical object in physical space (Malik & Brem, 2021, p. 102092).

According to the above technology overview, an Industry 5.0 solution is a collaborative robot that utilizes the functionalities provided by subsequent Industry 4.0 technologies, as shown in Figure 4.1.

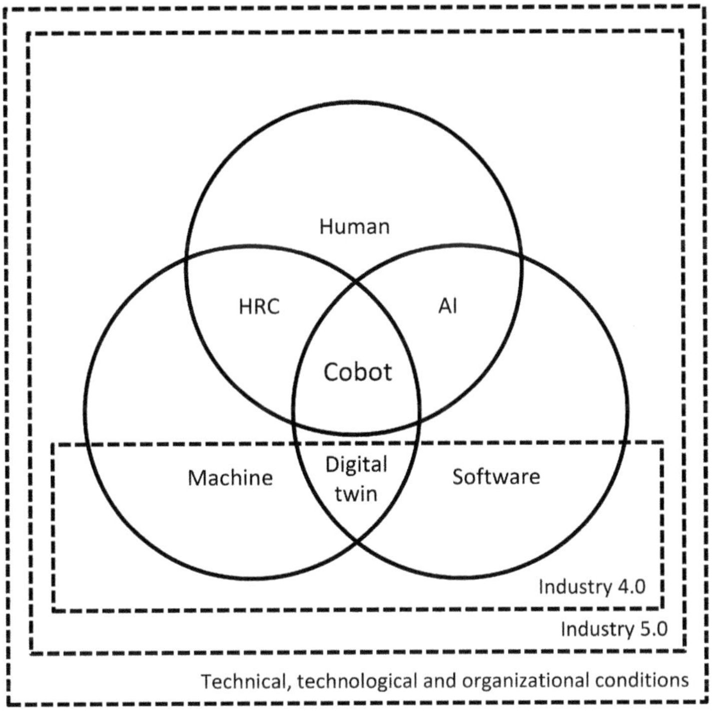

Figure 4.1 Collaborative robot as an Industry 5.0 solution.

Source: Own elaboration.

A cobot uses and implements technological and organizational conditions that support human-machine cooperation. Solutions used in a digital twin allow for awareness of human presence, awareness of the environment (machines, products, materials) in which the robot is located, and as a result, awareness of collaborative work in the production environment. It is possible to discover new optimal ways of performing tasks or even identify new approaches with the help of AI in the area of deep learning or transfer learning. Such a combination of technologies, needs, and collaboration creates an environment that fosters acquiring innovation. The fact that most of the process is digital makes it possible to quickly spread the innovation to other areas of the company. Furthermore, it is possible to tailor the obtained solution to fit the needs of other companies or for similar problems – as described in the next chapter.

Results

From the perspective of the Fifth Industrial Revolution, this chapter presents the idea of a human-machine partnership aimed at innovation acquisition. Below are two examples of such collaborations – the manufacturing process of ready-to-assemble kitchen cabinets with the use of a cobot at the

Figure 4.2 Production process of kitchen cabinets for self-assembly.

Source: Own elaboration.

completion stage, and the production process of windows that can be customized based on the needs of the customer.

The ready-to-assemble kitchen cabinets for self-assembly are made from laminated chipboard measuring 2800 × 2070 × 18 mm. Production is split into six steps, as shown in Figure 4.2.

As soon as the above operations have been completed, the cabinets go to the semi-finished products warehouse to be stored (Kulisz & Pizoń, 2015, pp. 42–48). The next step in the production process is the completion and packaging of the cabinet, and attaching a label. During the completion stage, employees are responsible for retrieving all elements of a given cabinet from the warehouse of semi-finished products and from the warehouse of furniture accessories (e.g. hinges, screws, handles, glass) and packaging boxes. As this stage of production is critical, it is only reasonable to introduce HRC. As part of this process, the packaging employee collects all the materials required to complete the daily plan from the semi-finished product warehouse using a pallet truck. Once all the elements on a pallet truck are in place, the truck is taken to the packaging employee workstation. The employee then organizes and packs the cabinet elements in accordance with the assembly instructions. By analyzing this stage of the process, it can be concluded that the human manual work can be supported by a cobot.

Collaboration with a robot could proceed according to the following scenario. The packaging employee performs tasks that are part of the completion stage while the robot monitors this process through a camera placed on a gimbal (also known as the robot's eye). A brain-computer interface device allows the employee to communicate with external devices through thought processes alone by using near-infrared spectroscopy (NIRS), an optical technique that measures localized cortical brain activity. By analyzing the recorded image and identifying the performed patterns, the cobot processes the received data (deep learning, transfer learning) locally or using CC. By doing so, it can predict the next move or action of the packaging employee in the long run. In the event it reaches a certain level of certainty, it will try to help the employee. In that way, an algorithm will be implemented in the robot on the basis of which appropriate movements will be made. As the robot records images and information from BCI, it will send it to CC. This data will then be used in CC for re-training and updating the robot's algorithms. When the algorithm is modified, it will be sent to the robot and it will be updated.

Such use of a cobot would increase the efficiency of the process because the robot would act as a second employee by repeating the employee's movements during the completion process. With this process, it would be able

Figure 4.3 PVC window production process.

Source: Own elaboration.

to predict the next component of a cabinet that needs to be assembled and hand this component to the packaging employee, which would improve its work. This is one example of dealing with standardized elements during the completion process.

The second process involves the production of windows (Figure 4.3). There is a significant difference between this example and the previous one in that the item of production is fully personalized based on the customer's order. PVC windows are produced by cutting profiles according to previously determined sizes (specified in the order – depending on the customer's order). For this purpose, materials are obtained from a warehouse. This process is performed using CNC machines that are fed with files that contain optimal cutting conditions. In the case of cutting steel, circular saws are used. To properly identify all machined parts on the production line, each element is tagged once it is completed. Those profiles that have been cut correctly are further processed, i.e. technological holes are drilled in them (to later fit handles in them, ensure drainage or decompression). Then the frames and sashes are welded. There are different types of welding machines depending on the type of window, such as traditional shapes (rectangular, square) or unconventional shapes (round). As this process involves high temperatures, weld lines tend to form on the surface, and they are removed during the next step. After this, the assembly of the necessary additional elements takes place (hinges, micro ventilation, anti-burglary hooks, locking mechanisms, key-operated handles) at assembly lines where workers use a number of amenities to match the fittings to the window. A penultimate step involves glazing the windows with assembled glass and sealing them. Employees must take special care during this step, especially when dealing with windows of unusual shapes: the panes must be perfectly aligned. After this is done, windows are subject to quality control and final adjustments. Lastly, they are marked and packaged, then transported to warehouses, from where the final product is delivered to the customer.

HRC can be beneficial at the following stages of the process: installation of the necessary additional window elements, sash and frame fitting, and glazing. In the fitting stage, the employee must first gather all the elements needed for this stage and place them on the sashes and window frames in the proper order. A similar step is required during the glazing stage when the employee must insert the pane of glass into the window sash and seal it. Human work can be assisted by a robot during these operations.

As in the first case, a robot that is equipped with a camera and BCI can identify the patterns performed by the employee by registering and monitoring the process through recognition of objects and through an algorithm based

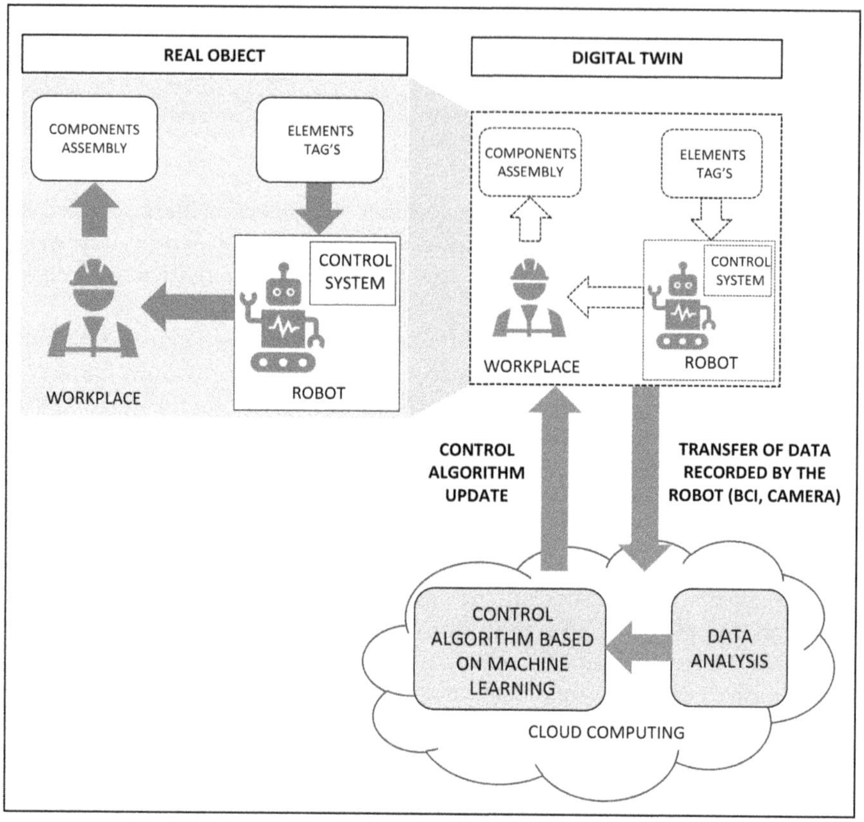

Figure 4.4 Diagram of human-machine collaboration environment.

Source: Own elaboration.

on machine learning methods. As a result of integrating with CC, whereby subsequent recorded data is collected and analyzed, the robot's algorithm is improved, and the robot learns, as shown in Figure 4.4. The presented solutions are based on IIoT, CC, and AI, CPS, digital twin, and cobots.

Once the robot is capable of reproducing human activities concerning handling components required for assembly at a given point in time (e.g. hinges, fittings, or glass), it can assist a person in these activities, which will boost productivity at these workstations. The assistance provided by the robot will consist of either handing the right component at the right time to the employee or mimicking the employee's movements and working simultaneously. The process will thus become more efficient since certain activities can be performed simultaneously.

This concept is the basis for acquiring innovations related to the Fifth Industrial Revolution. While collaborating with the human, the robot constantly monitors the changing situation. The robot records the worker's behavior, his condition, and the tasks he performs based on the tools he uses and the materials, semi-finished products, or objects he uses. Additionally, after the work has been carried out, a quality assessment determines whether it has been done correctly or not. Therefore, not only the completed task's data but also its outcome is available. Data can therefore be aggregated in this way to provide a multidimensional data set. Using such a set, situations that deviate from a particular norm can be analyzed and identified, or the entire process of cooperation can be standardized. Anomalies caused by human activities or resulting from different categories of activities deserve special attention and gain the status of possible innovations. Furthermore, by registering subsequent repetitions of the task and generalizing the results obtained, standardization can be achieved.

An analytical consideration of such circumstances can be used to develop innovations in the form of new solutions, improvements, waste reduction, or making existing norms more realistic. A number of benefits that result from such a collaboration may trigger a change in the way a workstation is organized; it may be that some of the elements of such a workstation tend to distract employees or hinder cooperation with the robot. What's more, it may be possible to find a better way to perform a given activity, or in some cases, inform the operator of an error that occurred, which will improve the training process but also protect the company from incurring additional losses. In addition, due to the digital nature of this solution, it is easy to distribute it to cooperating machines through updates, which shortens the time needed to implement innovation.

Discussion

In the literature, many solutions are described on how to organize such cooperation from the perspective of the Fourth Industrial Revolution. The focus is primarily placed on the technical aspects of such collaboration, while the proposed solutions on how to achieve such collaboration focus on modern information technology. These solutions focus mainly on the development of new algorithms that make it possible to plan the work of the robot more efficiently (Bragança et al., 2019; Schou et al., 2018; Veloso et al., 2012). In their research, Veloso et al. have presented cobots – collaborative robots in multistory office buildings. The robots are equipped with a Microsoft Kinect depth camera, video cameras for telepresence and interaction, a small Hokuyo LIDAR for avoiding obstacles, as well as wireless access and signal processing (Veloso et al., 2012, pp. 5446–5447). Schou et al. presented in their research a task-level programming tool called skill-based system (SBS). Skills-based programming and execution, robot and workstation configuration, navigation configuration, and manual equipment control are among the capabilities of SBS (Schou et al., 2018, pp. 72–80).

Currently, safety conditions related to implementing robots within a production environment are being worked on. In short, topics that may lead to increased efficiency or increased safety (such as enabling industrial robots to avoid obstacles in the workplace using machine learning) are also being addressed (Dröder et al., 2018, pp. 187–192).

However, this chapter draws attention to the topic of innovation that can result from such collaboration. For example, employees on an assembly line may unintentionally notice errors and problems, the detection and correction of which will protect the company from significant losses. Working with a robot will allow us to discover these opportunities. On the other hand, people can do work that an autonomous machine could replace but that would not be worth the cost of its implementation. As a result, the human-machine pair offers a cost-effective solution, from both an economic and sustainable perspective. A collaboration of this kind is a stepping stone to the future both in terms of work organization and the product delivered.

The case studies presented in the chapter show that the result of such collaboration yields inspiration that, once evaluated, can be classified as innovations worth being promoted both internally and externally as either a service or a product that a company offers.

Conclusions

HRC requires intelligence on both sides and all of our collective expertise that has been formalized through successive industrial revolutions. The Fourth Industrial Revolution focuses on automation, minimizing human labor through the use of AI solutions. On the one hand, it is motivated by the desire to reduce costs, and on the other, it is driven by the desire to meet the growing global demand for products. The problem with this approach, however, is that it overlooks the issue of innovation, which is inherent to human endeavors. Thus, this article discusses the concept of an environment that has been digitized to allow both registering and discovering possible innovations. Interaction between humans and robots is used as a source of potential innovations.

We recognize the topic's importance and its potential for development. It is necessary to develop both formal procedures and ways of obtaining and evaluating discovered innovations for such a specific environment. As a result, further research will be conducted on the topic of the Fifth Industrial Revolution and cobots.

References

Asghari, P., Rahmani, A., & Javadi, H. (2019). Internet of things applications: A systematic review. *Computer Networks*, *148*, 241–261. https://doi.org/10.1016/j.comnet.2018.12.008

Bragança, S., Costa, E., Castellucci, I., & Arezes, P. (2019). A brief overview of the use of collaborative robots in Industry 4.0: Human role and safety. *Studies in Systems, Decision and Control*, 641–650. https://doi.org/10.1007/978-3-030-14730-3_68

Demir, K., Döven, G., & Sezen, B. (2019). Industry 5.0 and human-robot co-working. *Procedia Computer Science*, *158*, 688–695. https://doi.org/10.1016/j.procs.2019.09.104

Dröder, K., Bobka, P., Germann, T., Gabriel, F., & Dietrich, F. (2018). A machine learning-enhanced digital twin approach for human-robot-collaboration. *Procedia CIRP, 76*, 187–192. https://doi.org/10.1016/j.procir.2018.02.010

European Commission, Directorate-General for Research and Innovation, Breque, M., De Nul, L., & Petridis, A. (2021). *Industry 5.0: Towards a sustainable, human-centric and resilient European industry*, Publications Office. https://data.europa.eu/doi/10.2777/308407

European Commission, Directorate-General for Research and Innovation, & Müller, J. (2020). *Enabling Technologies for Industry 5.0: Results of a workshop with Europe's technology leaders*, Publications Office. https://data.europa.eu/doi/10.2777/082634

Haag, S., & Anderl, R. (2018). Digital twin – Proof of concept. *Manufacturing Letters, 15*, 64–66. https://doi.org/10.1016/j.mfglet.2018.02.006.

Hermann, M., Pentek, T., & Otto, B. (2016). *Design principles for industrie 4.0 scenarios* [Conference session]. 2016 49Th Hawaii International Conference on System Sciences (HICSS). https://doi.org/10.1109/hicss.2016.488

Horváth, D., & Szabó, R. (2019). Driving forces and barriers of Industry 4.0: Do multinational and small and medium-sized companies have equal opportunities? *Technological Forecasting and Social Change, 146*, 119–132. https://doi.org/10.1016/j.techfore.2019.05.021

Humayun, M. (2021). Industry 4.0 and cyber security issues and challenges. *Turkish Journal of Computer and Mathematics Education Industry, 12*(10), 2957–2971.

Kenett, R., & Bortman, J. (2021). The digital twin in Industry 4.0: A wide-angle perspective. *Quality and Reliability Engineering International, 38*(3), 1357–1366. https://doi.org/10.1002/qre.2948

Kulisz, M., & Pizoń, J. (2015). The application of cloud computing with the internet of things. *Applied Mechanics and Materials, 791*, 42–48. https://doi.org/10.4028/www.scientific.net/amm.791.42

Lee, J., Davari, H., Singh, J., & Pandhare, V. (2018). Industrial artificial intelligence for industry 4.0-based manufacturing systems. *Manufacturing Letters, 18*, 20–23. https://doi.org/10.1016/j.mfglet.2018.09.002

Maddikunta, P., Pham, Q., Prabadevi, B., Deepa, N., Dev, K., Gadekallu, T. et al. (2022). Industry 5.0: A survey on enabling technologies and potential applications. *Journal of Industrial Information Integration, 26*, 100257. https://doi.org/10.1016/j.jii.2021.100257

Malik, A., & Brem, A. (2021). Digital twins for collaborative robots: A case study in human-robot interaction. *Robotics and Computer-Integrated Manufacturing, 68*, 102092. https://doi.org/10.1016/j.rcim.2020.102092

Mourtzis, D. (2021). Towards the 5th Industrial Revolution: A literature review and a framework for process optimization based on big data analytics and semantics. *Journal of Machine Engineering*. https://doi.org/10.36897/jme/141834

Nahavandi, S. (2019). Industry 5.0 – A human-centric solution. *Sustainability, 11*(16), 4371. https://doi.org/10.3390/su11164371

Nowotarski, P., & Paslawski, J. (2017). Industry 4.0 concept introduction into construction SMEs. *IOP Conference Series: Materials Science and Engineering, 245*, 052043. https://doi.org/10.1088/1757-899x/245/5/052043

Ozkeser, B. (2018). Lean Innovation Approach in Industry 5.0. *The Euroasia Proceeding of Science, Technology, Engineering & Mathematics (EPSTEM)*. ISRES Publishing, 422–428.

Oztemel, E., & Gursev, S. (2018). Literature review of Industry 4.0 and related technologies. *Journal of Intelligent Manufacturing, 31*(1), 127–182. https://doi.org/10.1007/s10845-018-1433-8

Pizoń, J., Kulisz, M., & Lipski, J. (2021). Matrix profile implementation perspective in industrial internet of things production maintenance application. *Journal of Physics: Conference Series, 1736*(1), 012036. https://doi.org/10.1088/1742-6596/1736/1/012036

Rüßmann, M., Waldner, M., Lorenz, M., Gerbert, P., Engel, P., & Harnisch, M. (2015). *Industry 4.0: The future of productivity and growth in manufacturing industries*. Retrieved July 28, 2022, from https://www.bcg.com/publications/2015/engineered_products_project_business_industry_4_future_productivity_growth_manufacturing_industries

Salkin, C., Oner, M., Ustundag, A., & Cevikcan, E. (2018). A conceptual framework for Industry 4.0. In A. Untundag, & E. Cevikcan (Eds.), *Industry 4.0: Managing The digital transformation* (3–23). Springer Series in Advanced Manufacturing. https://doi.org/10.1007/978-3-319-57870-5

Schou, C., Andersen, R., Chrysostomou, D., Bøgh, S., & Madsen, O. (2018). Skill-based instruction of collaborative robots in industrial settings. *Robotics and Computer-Integrated Manufacturing, 53*, 72–80. https://doi.org/10.1016/j.rcim.2018.03.008

Semeraro, C., Lezoche, M., Panetto, H., & Dassisti, M. (2021). Digital twin paradigm: A systematic literature review. *Computers in Industry, 130*, 103469. https://doi.org/10.1016/j.compind.2021.103469

Vaidya, S., Ambad, P., & Bhosle, S. (2018). Industry 4.0 – A glimpse. *Procedia Manufacturing, 20*, 233–238. https://doi.org/10.1016/j.promfg.2018.02.034

Veloso, M., Biswas, J., Coltin, B., Rosenthal, S., Kollar, T., & Mericli, C. et al. (2012). *CoBots: Collaborative robots servicing multi-floor buildings* [Conference session]. 2012 IEEE/RSJ International Conference on Intelligent Robots and Systems. https://doi.org/10.1109/iros.2012.6386300

Vogel-Heuser, B., & Hess, D. (2016). Guest editorial Industry 4.0 – Prerequisites and visions. *IEEE Transactions on Automation Science and Engineering, 13*(2), 411–413. https://doi.org/10.1109/tase.2016.2523639

5 Industry 5.0

A new reality, new challenges

Magdalena Maciaszczyk, Zbigniew Makieła, Radosław Miśkiewicz

Introduction

Technological breakthroughs that lead to fundamental changes in production organization or alter the way human factors are incorporated into production are defined as industrial revolutions. What have been the characteristics of each industrial revolution? And what does Industry 5.0 involve?

Today, many companies are still struggling to digitize their operations. It is done by incorporating artificial intelligence (AI) into everyday life, using the internet of things (IoT), processing data and storing it in cloud computing, or by using dynamically developing modern technologies. Advances in digitization and digitalization, globalization, customer orientation, and high agility in business processes, among others, cause business models to undergo relentless transformations and transformations.

The development of technology and the progressive integration of people and AI will bring Industry 5.0 to everyday business activities, where innovation means that business adapts to the evolving environment, anticipates future trends and adapts to them, and recognizes the need to change. Such behaviors not only provide an opportunity to survive in the face of another industrial revolution but they should also be considered a prerequisite for growth and increasing market value.

The concept of Industry 5.0 is therefore considered a new industrial revolution in which human creativity collaborates with efficient, intelligent, and accurate machines to create more user-preferred manufacturing solutions than those in Industry 4.0 (Maddikunta et al., 2021).

The chapter will analyze the business market situation to identify gaps in running a business along with identifying the associated opportunities and risks and making recommendations for how to best transform the business during the next industrial revolution.

From Industry 1.0 to Industry 4.0

The First Industrial Revolution of the 18th century was the time of accelerated development caused by the invention and widespread use of the steam engine.

DOI: 10.4324/9781003384311-5

Steam-powered machinery revolutionized the industry while the switch from manual to mechanical production and the development of transportation methods greatly sped up the process of manufacturing and distributing goods, as well as pushed the industry to undergo further revolutions (Agolla, 2018; Xu et al., 2018). The First Revolution was also the beginning of industrial culture in which small businesses were able to develop into organizations with up to thousands of employees (Loy et al., 2021). A period of industrialization took place during this period, which was marked by a transformation from a traditional society into an industrial society through the introduction of an economy based on the mechanization of production (Bairoch, 1982).

Industrial Revolution 2.0 began in the 1870s when electricity was invented and assembly lines were implemented. This period is also known as an evolution of Industry 1.0, where industrial culture was introduced to management systems. Production management methods that contributed to improving the quality of mass-produced goods and increasing productivity or reducing production costs were implemented (Zhang & Yang, 2020). These methods included labor division and standardization, timely production, and lean manufacturing.

In that period, the workforce was divided into decision-makers (tasked with formulating plans, determining the resources necessary for their implementation, issuing orders and monitoring their implementation) and contractors, or workers, who were only expected to follow strict orders. The result was a high degree of centralization of planning and decision-making. The traditional model of motivation created by F. Taylor assumed that workers acted as Homo economicus and that raising their productivity was triggered by financial incentives rather than working conditions, social relationships, or other non-financial motivations (Coccia, 2019; Locke, 1982; Zafar, 2019). Organizations were seen as well-oiled machines, the management of which consisted merely of shaping appropriate behavioral reflexes in predictable, repetitive, accurate, and reliable subordinates.

During the 1960s, however, the negative effects of distancing planning from executive functions started to manifest themselves, including low employee engagement, a poor synergy between actions, and employee conflict. Over time, the approach to management began to evolve and the significance of planning in managing organizations was redefined. Control and planning systems that coordinated production processes and production management strategies in enterprises began to emerge during this time. These systems included computer-integrated manufacturing (CIM) and later manufacturing execution systems (MES) and provided an organizational orientation, which enhanced the coordination of activities and alignment with business objectives (Benis et al., 2020). The use of digital technologies greatly improved data processing and made it possible to systemically increase the level of efficiency and the precision of information flow in production facilities, as well as facilitate the connection of people and ideas on a global scale. Thus, Industry 3.0 marks the beginning of the digital revolution.

The Third Industrial Revolution began in the 1970s due to the continued development of the industry and the computerization and automation of manufacturing, assembly, and logistics processes. However, robots were increasingly used to perform programmed sequences, and industrial automation became a driving force behind technological unemployment. At the same time, the demand for skilled workers capable of solving problems independently and developing technological solutions increased. Planning began to evolve toward the concept of management by objectives (MBO), in which managers decide what general tasks should be accomplished while employees are given the choice of how to accomplish the objectives (Shamim et al., 2016).

The Fourth Industrial Revolution is a time of increased use of communication and information technologies, and systems integration and networking; it is the age of smart machines, storage systems, and production lines that exchange information independently and carry out activities while controlling one another without human intervention (Shafiq et al., 2015). It is also a time of automation of the planning and decision-making processes. Industry 4.0 provides an effective integration of physical manufacturing processes with the available virtual information technologies, in which intelligent production systems (IPS) technologies are utilized to increase business efficiency. Using these systems, algorithms can optimize the flow of resources, tasks, or people between teams of people and autonomous machines (Gao et al., 2020; Uhlmann et al., 2017). It can be said that Industry 4.0 is aimed at creating smart factories where manufacturing technologies are transformed and modernized via cyber-physical system (CPS), IoT, and cloud computing (Yin et al., 2018; Zhong et al., 2017). A number of other technologies are also used in Industry 4.0, such as virtual reality, augmented reality, (collaborative) robotics, digital twins, and advanced simulations (Aheleroff et al., 2021; Egger & Masood, 2020; Malik & Brem, 2021; Malik et al., 2020; Masood & Sonntag, 2020).

However, in order for a transformation to the form dictated by Industry 4.0 to be successful, three dimensions must be taken into account (Ustundag, 2018). The first dimension is horizontal integration, which involves the creation of value between organizations to increase product lifecycles, effective financial management, efficient real-time data sharing, and accurate planning. The second dimension is vertical integration, where different layers of an organization collaborate through interconnectedness and digitization. End-to-end engineering includes the design and development of products and services that take into account the needs and requests of consumers and incorporate digital technologies.

A key success factor in the highly competitive environment of Industry 4.0 is the subordination of business goals to changing customer needs and expectations (Galletta et al., 2017; Gubán & Kovács, 2017; Kuo et al., 2020; Müller & Däschle, 2018). Flexibility and agility allow organizations to identify opportunities and risks in the market environment and to adapt to changes that are taking place (Akkaya, 2021; Brosseau et al., 2019; Eslami et al., 2021).

Nowadays, consumers looking to buy tend to search for offers that will meet their needs to the fullest extent. For companies, this means they must strive for continuous improvement by enhancing the quality of their products, ensuring their continued availability on the market, and taking care to keep costs low. It is not easy to optimize processes, but Industry 4.0 aims to offer benefits in specific areas such as performance, agility, innovation, customer knowledge, cost reduction, and revenue generation. With fewer employees and more automation, the decision-making process is accelerated and performance is maintained. Additionally, automation tends to maintain product quality at a consistent level and reduces production problems resulting from manual labor. The high standardization of small batches forces companies into high flexibility (agility) in the production process. Considering the fact that the production lines of Industry 4.0 companies are able to handle a wide assortment and small batches, they are ideal for introducing new products and experimenting with the development of new solutions. With the ability to respond quickly to the dynamically changing needs of customers, companies can provide the right products and services in a very short period of time. It is obvious that these activities are costly, but after initial investments in transformation, costs will decrease. As a result, the revenue of Industry 4.0 companies will increase (Paschek et al., 2019).

Industry 5.0 as a new quality for organizations

The concept of Industry 5.0 has been developing simultaneously with the adoption of Industry 4.0 principles since 2016 (Özdemir & Hekim, 2018; Skobelev & Borovik, 2017) and addresses the dehumanization of organizational processes and limitations of the human role in industry 4.0. While the Industry 4.0 paradigm emphasized automation and converting production facilities into IoT-enabled intelligent machines connected by cloud servers, Industry 5.0 focuses more on human collaboration with machines in order to increase efficiency. Industry 5.0 focuses on combining human creativity and craftsmanship with the speed, productivity, and precision of machines (European Economic and Social Committee, 2018), as well as placing people at the center as opposed to previous concepts of industry (Rundle, 2017). Nonetheless, it is not about replacing technology with the human component but only about a complete synergy and integration of human actions with the utility of machines and algorithms (Nahavandi, 2019). In Industry 5.0 we will see a digital intelligent society, virtual and physical space integration, IoT, robots, augmented reality, human-machine interface, and the fact that humans are central to technology. Consequently, Industry 5.0 will increase collaboration between people and smart systems, especially in manufacturing companies. This solution will allow machines to handle unitary, repetitive tasks while allowing people to use their creative talents.

The interaction between humans and technology will not only lead to improved productivity, but will also impact the economy, ecology, and social world (Bednar & Welch, 2020; Østergaard, 2018; Shelzer, 2017), as well as eventually lead to a boom in industrial upcycling with which various types of waste can be associated (Rada, 2018).

Industry 4.0 and Industry 5.0 differ in the fact that consumers show a high demand for customized products (Atwell, 2017). The products that reach customers are significantly more customized than in the past, thanks in part to a greater degree of human involvement in the design process and increased interaction between people and machines (Ozkeser, 2018). There is also some uniformity in this process. Handmade and artisanal products boast constant popularity among the audience, and the demand for them increases as consumers strive to emphasize their individuality through their purchases and use of products. This implies a level of expected personalization and subjective perception of luxury in society with which the industry must contend (Østergaard, 2018).

Results and methodology

This chapter presents the results of a study that examined whether contemporary enterprises exhibited the traits associated with teal organizations in the age of Industry 4.0 and whether they could adapt to the concept of Industry 5.0. The assumption is that modern enterprises exhibit characteristics of teal organizations in their activities and management; however, the degree to which these characteristics are present varies greatly.

During the study, the following work was carried out – desk research, individual in-depth interview (IDI), and questionnaire research involving selected groups using computer-assisted web interview (CAWI) and paper and pencil interview (PAPI) approaches. In this study, the χ^2 test – Pearson's Chi-square independence test – was chosen as the method of statistical analysis. The data obtained from surveys was analyzed with the SPSS STATISTICA 21 computer package.

In total, 75 mid-level representatives of market operators from various industries and backgrounds participated in the study, as illustrated in Table 5.1.

Listed below are several questions pertaining to the issue raised in the chapter, and the issues of organizational agility, adaptation to changing customer needs, and optimization of processes using machine and human input. Responses were collected from respondents using a Likert scale of 1 to 5, with 1 denoting strong disagreement and 5 denoting strong agreement. The average results of the survey are shown in Table 5.2.

Unfortunately, few companies are equipped with tools that make use of modern technologies, making it difficult for them to communicate with customers using ICTs (Information and Communication Technology). The situation reflects the ability of the organization to adapt to changes in the market environment and to adapt the market offer to the evolving needs of customers.

Based on the available literature, there is a relationship between using modern technologies and creating tailored offers (Kiselev & Yakutenko, 2020; Saniuk & Grabowska, 2021), which is one of the key determinants of

Table 5.1 Description of the examined market entities

Geographical scope of activity (%)		*Predominant mode of companies' operation (%)*	
Local	36	Production	8
Regional	56	Commerce	16
National	18	Services	76
Total	110		100

Source: Own elaboration.

the Industry 5.0 paradigm. As noted by Grabowska and Saniuk (2021), the adoption of modern technologies correlates positively with the efficiency and quality of an organization, including a customized offer for customers with varied expectations. Moreover, it turns out that with a lack of activities recognizing changes in customer requirements caused by changes in their environment, customers cannot expect to receive personalized offers (Kucharska, 2021; Południak-Gierz, 2019).

Another negative aspect revealed by the research concerns the utilization of employee creativity. Proper management of the intellectual capital of employees allows a company to maintain a high degree of competitiveness and innovation (Imran et al., 2018; Muthusamy & Rasid, 2018; Venkatesh, 2021). Although the manufacturing sector appears to be in worse shape, all other sectors surveyed struggle to manage human capital fully and rationally. It is important to remember that Industry 5.0 focuses primarily on product quality, so in the face of this new era, companies must ensure that their products are developed with a human touch.

Conclusions

The concept of Industry 1.0 has progressed from Industry 1.0 (mechanization, i.e. the use of steam-powered machinery) to the form in which it exists today under the name Industry 5.0 (personalization, i.e. collaboration between humans and machines using cognitive calculations to produce user-oriented goods and services (Ozkeser, 2018).

Table 5.2 Companies' adaptation to the concept of industry 5.0

Areas of operation	*My company invests in modern technologies that make work easier (IT, automation)*	*My creative potential is fully utilized*	*Our customers influence our offer*	*Tools that use modern technologies and improve processes are at my disposal*	*Our offer is not mass-produced but tailored to the needs of individual customers*
Production	3.16	3.08	2.06	3.45	2.13
Commerce	4.01	3.70	4.02	3.66	4.17
Services	3.86	3.86	4.32	4.04	4.42
Average	3.67	3.54	3.46	3.72	3.57

Source: Own elaboration.

The key benefits of implementing the concept of Industry 5.0 in businesses include reduced costs (Rada, 2018), improved productivity, improved agility, improved readiness to adapt to change, improved adaptability, as well as a responsive work environment (Kurniawan et al., 2019; Rzepka et al., 2021).

Today, many enterprises operate in the 4.0 era in which transitions play a key role in defining the economy. The unpredictable nature of the business environment forces businesses to search for an appropriate strategy to meet the growing demands of an ever-changing reality. Any organization, regardless of its field of operation, must therefore adapt to the changes in its environment by utilizing soft management factors, one of which is the organizational agility that determines the development of relationships with other players in the market, and customers among them.

Nonetheless, some of the market players are still only adjusting to the concept of Industry 4.0, since the level of digitization and digitalization is still relatively low. Moreover, the processes occurring in the surveyed companies are not automated, which means they have a long way to go before they can meet the demands of Industry 5.0.

Recommendations for practical application

A number of recommendations can be formulated using the results of the research and considerations discussed in this chapter. To begin with, it must be kept in mind that the nature of the market activity is changing rapidly and is driven by the new digital technologies that support Industry 5.0, causing a rethink of the extent to which machines automate and aid human labor. However, given the direction in which the modern market is going, the nature of innovation, and the current forecasts on the demand for new digital skills, it would appear that one of the key requirements of the modern market is to train employees to use data science, machine learning, and AI in their everyday work.

In light of the fact that skilled workers in Industry 5.0 are expected to perform tasks that are of high value to production, legal policies and standardization should be implemented to address all the issues related to technology, society, and management. Providing qualified employees involves a number of issues related to management, employees, culture, and infrastructure (Paschek et al., 2019).

The main challenge associated with skill development is the lack of qualified instructors as well as financial barriers to providing adequate coaching to employees who work with machines. By the time the Industry 5.0 assumptions have been fully introduced, the demand for skilled workers will grow since new technologies will continue to emerge and evolve, necessitating proper education provided to both future instructors and those being educated.

Enterprises that are looking to adapt to the new reality of 5.0 must address the challenges posed by the rapidly changing market by developing features that highlight their uniqueness and ability to respond to stimuli from the market environment (Kocot et al., 2022). The ability to adapt to changes in the business environment, or organizational agility, is undoubtedly a key competency any enterprise must prepare its employees for. Such agility can be expressed as a system's resistance to change, its flexibility, and responsiveness in the case of dynamic changes in the system's load. Properly trained employees can further enhance such organizational excellence.

Industry 5.0 aims to increase production and customer satisfaction by using a range of new technologies and applications. Those entering the era and striving to achieve the assumptions of the Industry 5.0 concept will encounter a number of challenges and open issues such as security, privacy, human-robot collaboration, maximizing human potential, scalability, and a skilled workforce.

References

Agolla, J. (2018). Human capital in the smart manufacturing and Industry 4.0 revolution. In A. Petrillo (Ed.) *Digital Transformation in Smart Manufacturing* (pp. 41–58). IntechOpen.

Aheleroff, S., Xu, X., Zhong, R., & Lu, Y. (2021). Digital twin as a service (DTaaS) in industry 4.0: An architecture reference model. *Advanced Engineering Informatics, 47*, 101225.

Akkaya, B. (2021). Leadership 5.0 in Industry 4.0: Leadership in perspective of organizational agility. In M. Khosrow-Pour (Ed.) *Research anthology on cross-industry challenges of Industry 4.0* (pp. 1489–1507). IGI Global.

Atwell, C. (2017). *Yes, Industry 5.0 is already on the horizon*. Retrieved September 21, 2021, from https://www.machinedesign.com/industrial-automation/yes-industry-50-already-horizon

Bairoch, P. (1982). International industrialization levels from 1750 to 1980. *Journal of European Economic History, 11*(2), 269.

Bednar, P., & Welch, C. (2020). Socio-technical perspectives on smart working: Creating meaningful and sustainable systems. *Information Systems Frontiers, 22*(2), 281–298.

Benis, A., Nelke, S., & Winokur, M. (2020). Upgrading industrial engineering and management curriculum to Industry 4.0. In *2020 IEEE International Conference on Industrial Technology (ICIT)* (pp. 355–359). IEEE.

Brosseau, D., Ebrahim, S., Handscomb, C., & Thaker, S. (2019). The journey to an agile organization. *McKinsey & Company*. Retrieved December 21, 2022, from https://www.mckinsey.com/capabilities/people-and-organizational-performance/our-insights/the-journey-to-an-agile-organization

Coccia, M. (2019). Theories of self-determination. *Global Encyclopedia of Public Administration, Public Policy, and Governance, Springer International Publishing AG, Part of Springer Nature, 10*, 978–973.

Egger, J., & Masood, T. (2020). Augmented reality in support of intelligent manufacturing – a systematic literature review. *Computers & Industrial Engineering, 140*, 106195.

Eslami, M., Jafari, H., Achtenhagen, L., Carlbäck, J., & Wong, A. (2021). Financial performance and supply chain dynamic capabilities: The moderating role of Industry 4.0 technologies. *International Journal of Production Research*, 1–18. https://doi.org/10.1080/00207543.2021.1966850

European Economic and Social Committee (2018). Retrieved October 15, 2021, form https://www.eesc.europa.eu/el/agenda/our-events/events/industry-50

Galletta, A., Carnevale, L., Celesti, A., Fazio, M., & Villari, M. (2017). A cloud-based system for improving retention marketing loyalty programs in Industry 4.0: A study on big data storage implications. *IEEE Access, 6*, 5485–5492.

Gao, K., Huang, Y., Sadollah, A., & Wang, L. (2020). A review of energy-efficient scheduling in intelligent production systems. *Complex & Intelligent Systems, 6*(2), 237–249.

Grabowska, S., & Saniuk, S. (2021). *11 modern marketing for customized products under conditions of fourth industrial revolution*. Routledge.

Gubán, M., & Kovács, G. (2017). Industry 4.0 conception. *Acta Technica Corviniensis-Bulletin of Engineering, 10*(1), 19

Imran, M., Ilyas, M., Aslam, U., & Fatima, T. (2018). Knowledge processes and company performance: The mediating effect of employee creativity. *Journal of Organizational Change Management, 31*(3), 512–531. https://doi.org/10.1108/JOCM-10-2016-0202

Kiselev, B., & Yakutenko, V. (2020). An overview of massive open online course platforms: Personalization and semantic web technologies and standards. *Computer Science Procedure, 169*, 373–379.

Kocot, D., Wiench, P., & Maciaszczyk, M. (2022). Inter-organization relationships on virtual level in terms of employee agility as determinant of Industry 4.0 era. In A. Rzepka, Z. Olesiński, & E. Jędrych (Eds.). *Self-management, entrepreneurial culture, and economy 4.0* (pp. 102–117). Routledge.

Kucharska, B. (2021). Innowacje w badaniach zachowań klientów w przestrzeni wewnątrzsklepowej. In K. Mazurek-Łopacińska & M. Sobocińska (Eds.) *Badania marketingowe w gospodarce cyfrowej* (pp. 99–110). Wydawnictwo Uniwersytetu Ekonomicznego we Wrocławiu.

Kuo, C., Chen, W., Tseng, C., & Kao, C. (2020). Developing a smart system with Industry 4.0 for customer dissatisfaction. *Industrial Management & Data Systems, 121*(6), 1353–1374.

Kurniawan, A., Komara, B., & Setiawan, H. (2019). Preparation and challenges of Industry 5.0 for small and medium enterprises in Indonesia. *Muhammadiyah International Journal of Economics and Business, 2*(2), 155–160.

Locke, E. (1982). The ideas of Frederick W. Taylor: An evaluation. *Academy of Management Review*, 7(1), 14–24.

Loy, A. C. M., Chin, B. L. F., & Sankaran, R. (2021). Industrial revolution 1.0 and 2.0. In K. W. Chew, & T. C. Ling (Eds.), *The prospect of Industry 5.0 in biomanufacturing* (pp. 1–14). CRC Press.

Maddikunta, P. K. R., Pham, Q. V., Prabadevi, B., Deepa, N., Dev, K., Gadekallu, T. R., Ruby, R., & Liyanage, M. (2021). Industry 5.0: A survey on enabling technologies and potential applications. *Journal of Industrial Information Integration, 26*(2),100257. https://doi.org/10.1016/j.jii.2021.100257

Malik, A. A., & Brem, A. (2021). Digital twins for collaborative robots: A case study in human-robot interaction. *Robotics and Computer-Integrated Manufacturing, 68*, 102092.

Malik, A. A., Masood, T., & Bilberg, A. (2020). Virtual reality in manufacturing: Immersive and collaborative artificial-reality in design of human-robot workspace. *International Journal of Computer Integrated Manufacturing, 33*(1), 22–37.

Masood, T., & Sonntag, P. (2020). Industry 4.0: Adoption challenges and benefits for SMEs. *Computers in Industry, 121*, 103261.

Muthusamy, V., & Rasid, S. Z. A. (2018). Leveraging human capital development for successful labour mix rationalization and productivity growth. *International Journal of Innovation and Business Strategy (IJIBS), 10*(2), 46–58.

Nahavandi, S. (2019). Industry 5.0 – A human-centric solution. *Sustainability, 11*(16), 4371.

Østergaard, E. H. (2018). Welcome to Industry 5.0, the "human touch" revolution is now under way. Retrieved October 21, 2021, from https://info.universal-robots.com/hubfs/Enablers/White%20papers/Welcome%20to%20Industry%205.0_Esben%20Østergaard.pdf?submissionguid=00c4d11f-80f2-4683-a12a-e821221793e3

Özdemir, V., & Hekim, N. (2018). Birth of industry 5.0: Making sense of big data with artificial intelligence, "the internet of things" and next-generation technology policy. *OMICS Journal of Integrated Biology, 22*, 65–76.

Ozkeser, B. (2018). Lean innovation approach in Industry 5.0. *The Eurasia Proceedings of Science Technology Engineering and Mathematics, 2*, 422–428.

Paschek, D., Mocan, A., & Draghici, A. (2019, May). *Industry 5.0 – The impact expected of next industrial revolution* [Conference session]. Thriving on Future Education, Industry, Business, and Society, Proceedings of the MakeLearn and TIIM International Conference, Piran, Slovenia, pp. 15–17.

Południak-Gierz, K. (2019). Consequences of the use of personalization algorithms in shaping an offer – A private law perspective. *Masaryk University Journal of Law and Technology, 13*(2), 161–188.

Rada, M. (2018). *Industry 5.0. definition.* https://michael-rada.medium.com/industry-5-0-definition-6a2f9922dc48.

Rundle, E. (2017). The 5th industrial revolution: When it will happen and how. Retrieved October 7, 2021, from https://devops.com/5th-industrial-revolution-will-happen

Rzepka, A., Maciaszczyk, M., Wiśniewska, A. M., & Kocot, M. (2021). E-consumers and their agile qualities as creators of eco-innovations: A case study. *European Research Studies Journal, 24*(2B), 23–38.

Saniuk, S., & Grabowska, S. (2021). The concept of cyber-physical networks of small and medium enterprises under personalized manufacturing. *Energies, 14*(17), 5273.

Shafiq, S. I., Sanin, C., Toro, C., & Szczerbicki, E. (2015). Virtual engineering object (VEO): Toward experience-based design and manufacturing for industry 4.0. *Cybernetics and Systems, 46*(1–2), 35–50.

Shamim, S., Cang, S., Yu, H., & Li, Y. (2016). Management approaches for Industry 4.0: A human resource management perspective. In *2016 IEEE Congress on Evolutionary Computation (CEC)* (pp. 5309–5316). IEEE.

Shelzer, R. (2017). What is Industry 5.0 – And how will it affect manufacturers? Retrieved August 18, 2020, from https://blog.gesrepair.com/industry-5-0-will-affect-manufacturers/

Skobelev, P., & Borovik, S. Y. (2017). On the way from Industry 4.0 to Industry 5.0: From digital manufacturing to digital society. *Industry 4.0, 2*, 307–311.

Uhlmann, E., Hohwieler, E., & Geisert, C. (2017). Intelligent production systems in the era of Industrie 4.0–changing mindsets and business models. *Journal of Machine Engineering, 17*, 5–24.

Ustundag, A., & Cevikcan, E. (2018). *Industry 4.0: Managing the digital transformation.* Springer.

Venkatesh, D. N. (2021). *Winning with employees: Leveraging employee experience for a competitive edge.* SAGE Publishing India.

Xu, M., David, J. M., & Kim, S. H. (2018). The fourth industrial revolution: Opportunities and challenges. *International Journal of Financial Research, 9*(2), 90–95.

Yin, Y., Stecke, K. E., & Li, D. (2018). The evolution of production systems from Industry 2.0 through Industry 4.0. *International Journal of Production Research, 56*(1–2), 848–861.

Zafar, M. B. (2019). Theory of human forces in management. *International Journal of Management Concepts and Philosophy*, *12*(3), 329–341.
Zhang, C., & Yang, J. (2020). *A history of mechanical engineering* (pp. 137–195). Springer.
Zhong, R. Y., Xu, X., Klotz, E., & Newman, S. T. (2017). Intelligent manufacturing in the context of Industry 4.0: A review. *Engineering*, 3(5), 616–630.

6 The concept of inclusion and diversity as an accelerator for building Society 5.0 and creating a managed organization in the 5.0 era

Elwira Gross-Gołacka, Teresa Kupczyk, Agnieszka Rzepka, Małgorzata Smolarek, Katarzyna Szczepańska-Woszczyna

Introduction

We are now in a time when innovation that is driven by assistive technologies such as the Internet of Things, artificial intelligence, and robotics are causing significant changes in the economy, society, and management. As part of the new Industrial Revolution 5.0, there are many challenges that must be met by both those responsible for maintaining the security of communication technology and the reliability of production lines but also by those responsible for human resources management. In the age of ubiquitous 5.0, leadership in organizations must remain vigilant to ensure that any innovative competitive strategies are aligned with the existing concept of Society 5.0. The approach that the concept of Society 5.0 promotes is that of a human-centric community that balances economic progress and social responsibility.

With such a dynamic and variable matter as leading and managing people in the organization, it is necessary to explore new or revise the existing approaches to managing employees within the organization. Every day, we observe how theorists and practitioners come up with new models and solutions in this area, but they disappear just as quickly as they appear. Nonetheless, these new management concepts share a departure from the traditional hierarchical management structure, as well as a large delegation of power to employees that leads to an increase in employee involvement and flexibility (Gross-Gołacka, 2022). Keeping that in mind, it is imperative for organizations to increase diversity and establish policies that are inclusive and foster diversity as well as promote the values of acceptance and respect. Research shows that this approach to management produces a wide range of benefits, Studies have shown the benefits of taking this approach to management, ranging from access to a wider pool of talent to an increased level of customer and employee loyalty.

DOI: 10.4324/9781003384311-6

Our goal in this chapter is to identify the areas of human resource management (HRM) that are influencing organizational change. The authors aim to demonstrate how creating businesses that are inclusive and take diversity into account can bring about positive changes that fulfill the assumptions of starting and running a business in the era of 5.0. The main research question relates to which approach to HRM is most effective in initiating and creating changes within an organization in order to transform it into an organization that aligns with Society 5.0. The first supplementary question addresses the role and importance of integrating diversity and inclusiveness into the process of creating an organization to fit with Society 5.0. The supplementary subsidiary question addresses the role and importance of the concept of inclusion in the aforementioned process. And the third supplementary question discusses the role and importance of soft management areas relevant to business development in the 5.0 era. The research method used to achieve the goal and answer the research questions posed included a critical literature review (Gerber, 2021; Hitachi-UTokyo Laboratory, 2020; Keidanren, 2016, 2019; Lasi et al., 2014), as well as an analysis of previous research conducted by the authors of this chapter on the implementation of diversity management policy in the Visegrad Group (V4) countries. In order to achieve the goal at hand and provide further clarification, the notion of diversity and inclusion was presented as one of the approaches that can advance the creation of Society 5.0 in the age of 5.0.

Toward Industry 5.0

Based on the Third Industrial Revolution, the Fourth Industrial Revolution is characterized by a fusion of technologies blurring the lines between the physical, digital, and biological realms. Further, it presented a number of challenges to the business world, including a lack of appropriate skills and capabilities, the security of communication systems, the reliability of manufacturing equipment, and the inability of stakeholders to adapt. The Fourth Industrial Revolution is often referred to as Industry 4.0, and it is defined as an advanced digital transformation of the interpenetrating chains of horizontal and vertical interconnections among people and devices, products, services, and business models, the key elements of which are cyber-physical systems, the Internet of Things, the Internet of services, as well as smart factories (Furmanek, 2018; Siuta-Tokarska, 2021).

The next step in this business revolution is a shift in business structure, business processes, and work culture that leads to a business that – as per digITal first – makes full use of its technological capabilities. Industry 5.0 certainly complements the current Industry 4.0 paradigm, positioning research and innovation at the forefront of the transition to a more sustainable, human-centered, and resilient industry. Industry 5.0 aims to capture the full value of new technologies and ensure prosperity beyond jobs and economic growth while protecting the planet and putting the well-being of workers at the heart of manufacturing. Industry 5.0 proposes a humanizing response to the threat posed by limiting the role of humans in Industry 4.0, as it assumes that humans and machines form a functional whole. In the next industrial revolution, collaborative robots will be at the forefront, facilitating greater human-robot cooperation.

The concept of Society 5.0

Let us go back to Industry 4.0, where the presence of the Internet of Things gave rise to new ideas. As a result of this digital transformation, many countries have created new values and incorporated their principles into industrial policy. As a response to such global trends, Society 5.0 was proposed.

The concept of Society 5.0 was endorsed by the Japanese Cabinet in January 2016 in the 5th Science and Technology Basic Plan and was designated as one of Japan's development strategies. Society 5.0 is also an integral part of the Japanese Investment Strategy for the Future 2017 (Fukuyama, 2018). Industry 5.0 is defined by the Japanese as Society 5.0 and the "human touch" revolution. It is defined as "a human-centered society that balances economic progress with solving social problems through a system that highly integrates cyberspace and physical space" (Keidanren, 2016, p. 17). This phenomenon depicts a society oriented to the future and free of information stagnation (Keidanren, 2019).

It is important to emphasize that Society 5.0, which has its roots in Japan, represents a quiet revolution that places the human at the center of technological and innovative modifications for the benefit of humanity and promises to revolutionize society (Costa, 2018). Society 5.0's main purpose is to improve people's quality of life through the opportunities offered by Industry 4.0 (Ferreira & Serpa, 2018, pp. 26–31). As we examine the history of mankind, it is worthwhile to note the different eras of societies that have successively influenced the construction of present-day concepts (Table 6.1).

Table 6.1 Previous societies' contributions to Society 5.0

Age	*1.0 – hunting and gathering*	*2.0 – agriculture*	*3.0 – industry*	*4.0 – information*
Characteristics	The need for sustainable development	Inclusion	Effectiveness	The power of intelligence (and knowledge)
Society 5.0	Communication and information fully utilized	Citizen-centered integration (inclusive citizens)	The participation of all (rejection of splits and divisions)	Values shared: sustainable development, integration, effectiveness, power of intelligence

Source: Own elaboration.

Society 1.0 is defined as groups of people hunting and gathering in harmony with nature. In Society 2.0 groups were organized around agricultural cultivation, increasing organization, and establishing nations. Society 3.0 represents a society that promotes industrialization through the industrial revolution and thus enables mass production, while Society 4.0 represents the Information Society that is able to generate increased added value by combining intangible assets into information networks (Fukuyama, 2018, pp. 47–50).

The new paradigm known as Society 5.0 is expected to play a dominant role in making society happier, more satisfied, fulfilled, and consequently, more productive. Society 5.0 intends to use the advanced technology provided by Industry 4.0 for the benefit of mankind, enabling people and systems to interact in cyberspace as well as optimize results through artificial intelligence. In this evolution, Society 5.0 represents information. Society 4.0 allows people to access and share information over the Internet, but Society 5.0 is an era in which all technology becomes an integral part of humanity (Yunda, 2019).

Society 5.0 is not only a Japanese phenomenon but a global one as well. As an example, the European Union has launched a number of programs to support the creation of innovative businesses (venture innovation). Employees play a major role in the success of innovative businesses as they are expected to actively and purposefully participate in the continuous process of innovation (Ahuja & Morris Lampert, 2001).

In essence, Society 5.0 envisions a human-centered society that achieves a balance between economic progress and social issues by linking cyberspace and the physical world. With each innovation, the world moves closer to creating a society that is sustainable, inclusive, and super-intelligent (Dinana, 2020).

The approaches outlined above are part of the concept of diversity and inclusion. Because Society 5.0 is linked with greater employee autonomy, it necessitates a focus on increasing flexibility of operation as well as employee involvement. All of this means that the organization must operate in a particular way, with all members being equal, but the group's value comes from its diversity. The most productive workplace is one where everyone can contribute according to their differences/diversity in terms of education, background, skills, interests, etc. Therefore, in the business of 5.0, each employee should be encouraged to develop their authentic role while releasing their creativity to take full advantage of the inherent talents within their societies/organizations/teams. Based on the premise that society 5.0 aims to move from deindividuation to individuation, it should be required that organizations promote diversity and inclusion.

Diversity and inclusion

Diversity

The current growth in diversity in the labor force can be attributed to a number of factors including globalization, easier mobility, anti-discrimination laws, and changes in the demographic structure of societies (Gross-Gołacka, 2018).

According to Drucker (2007), diversity encompasses a wide range of demographic and socioeconomic factors including aging, improved competencies and knowledge of employees, increased immigration, the changing role of women in the workplace, and increasing gender and cultural differences within organizations. Regardless of the reasons for its existence and the importance it holds for the organization, we must better understand the importance of diversity for organizations and how to address it. The literature on the topic offers many descriptions of the dimensions of diversity. It is believed that there are several dozens of dimensions of diversity that can change during a person's lifetime, illustrating the multifaceted nature of this issue (Maier, 2002). The sheer number of the dimensions and the links between them means that there can be no straightforward answer to the question of what diversity means. In a traditional approach, primary and secondary dimensions are considered (Griggs, 1995). The primary dimension of diversity is those differences between people we are born with and/or which have a major impact on our early socialization and how we function as individuals (Litvin 1997, pp. 187–209, 2006, pp. 75–94). They shape our image of the world and have a significant impact on the way we perceive it. This dimension mainly takes biological traits that are visible to the naked eye into account. Essentially, they are innate, cannot be changed, and their significance pervades throughout our lives. It is assumed that there are six dimensions of primary diversity: age, ethnic heritage, gender, physical and mental ability, race, and sexual orientation. The secondary dimensions of diversity tend to be less visible or invisible altogether to the naked eye, might be of less importance to human life, and can be changed. They include education, language, physical appearance, marital status, lifestyle, value system, worldview, mindset, ethics as well as psychosocial aspects, etc. (Carr-Ruffino, 1997; Thomas, 1992; Triandis & Suh, 2002, pp. 133–153). The notion of diversity management, on the other hand, concerns:

- making use of all the talents available in an organization, without referring to ethnocentrism and stereotypes,
- (in relation to a group of employees) implementing diversity policies that contribute to increased innovation and creativity, reducing the shortage of employees with specific skills, and improving the quality of customer service,
- (in relation to the company) continuing to serve the needs of a variety of customers, increasing its market share in the context of individual customers, employees, and stakeholders,
- an approach focused on adapting the organization to its environment through strategic management (Gross-Gołacka, 2018).

Inclusion

In order to reap the benefits of diversity in an organization, it is not only necessary to hire and retain diverse employees but also to ensure that these employees are fully included and are fully integrated into the organization's social fabric (Nishii et al., 2006). Importantly, diversity is a mixture of many loose, unrelated features/factors/components, and inclusion makes these components fit together well and complement one another. Inclusion refers to a cultural and social sense of belonging. Inclusion can be defined as the extent to which employees feel part of the fundamental processes of an organization, including the ability to influence decision-making, participation in critical workgroups, and resource and information accessibility (Mor Barak, 2008, pp. 239–254; Roberson, 2006, pp. 212–236).

To sum up, the feeling of inclusion and acceptance in a group is associated with many positive outcomes such as increased loyalty, cooperation, and trustworthiness (O'Donovan, 2015). Essentially, inclusive cultures make people feel respected and appreciated for who they are as individuals or groups. Employees experience positive and encouraging energy from their coworkers, which makes them more motivated and satisfied with their work. It is imperative to take individual differences into account when creating inclusive jobs and create a working environment where workers feel valued and treated fairly. Generally speaking, diversity and inclusion refer to a group of individuals that get to know each other and get along with each other but who are each completely unique and possess distinct strengths. Such a framework is based on an approach that allows for the acceptance and appreciation of the diversity dimensions that exist within each individual and acknowledges the significance of diversity in society/community and within organizations. It has also been proven that workplaces that prioritize diversity and inclusion are safer, happier, and more productive.

Research results

An empirical approach is a form of interpretive research that is based on the assumption that organizational reality is a social construct (Sułkowski, 2012). The subject of such a study is the benefits an organization can obtain when it becomes inclusive and diverse. The research methodology adopted in this chapter uses phenomenological and idiographical approaches that are based on a targeted sample of 401 employees from companies in the V4 region (Czech Republic, Slovakia, Poland, Hungary). The study surveyed employees (management) and owners of the companies who volunteered to take part in the study. Women comprised 51.20% and men 49.80% of the sample. Age-wise, the largest group of respondents consisted of people aged 40 to 49 (28.90%), followed by those ages 30 to 39 (26.60%) and those under 39 (21%). Respondents aged 40 or over accounted for almost 53% of the sample. The majority of respondents were business owners or co-owners (27.9%) and those with a variety of job titles (31%). About 17% of respondents held the position of a Human Resource specialist, while 11% that of a Human Resource Director. There were fewer people representing the positions of Chair and Vice-Chair (3.3%) and Public Relations Director (11%). Most of the companies participating in the survey were privately owned (80%), 13% were state-owned, and only

Table 6.2 Diversity management advantages (%)

Diversity management advantages	*1*	*2*	*3*	*4*	*5*
1 indicates the weakest contribution diversity management makes, and 5 the strongest					
Improving image of the company	13.2	8.4	30.5	21.9	20.6
Improving employee motivation and performance	10.7	10.8	19.5	40.1	13.3
Improving employee satisfaction	9.0	10.8	24.6	22.2	26.7
Increasing company profits	11.7	12.4	29.1	28.9	11.8
Access to new markets, retaining new customers	11.2	10.4	21.4	31.9	18.6
Recruiting the best staff	8.2	8.9	20.0	36.7	19.0
Retaining the best talents	8.7	8.3	19.7	30.7	25.5
Increasing creativity and innovation through building diverse teams	7.5	9.5	17.6	25.3	31.0
Avoiding any risk of discrimination in the company	8.2	10.5	25.0	28.3	21.4
Boosting customer loyalty	11.9	14.7	21.1	23.6	20.2
Reducing costs	18.4	16.8	24.9	19.4	14.9
No advantages	53.6	8.4	16.7	7.4	9.9

Source: Own study.

1.3% were non-government organizations. Based on the size of the organization, the study included small businesses of 1 to 49 employees (44.53%, which included businesses that employed less than 10 employees – 10.66%, and 10 to 49 employees – 33.87%), medium-sized businesses with 50 to 249 employees (27.79%), and large ones with over 250 employees (27.55%).

Particular manifestations of objectivity in the management of diversity are access to a larger pool of potential talent, as well as increased creativity and innovation. Table 6.2 contains the respondents' answers used to measure these features. Among the benefits resulting from the introduction of the concept of diversity management in an organization (see Table 6.2) that received the highest ratings from the organizations surveyed (scores of 4 and 5) were retaining top talent in the company/reducing employee turnover (56.2%), increasing creativity and innovation by building diverse teams (56.3%), recruiting the best employees (55.7%), increased employee motivation and productivity/decreased absence rates (53.4%). The study results clearly show that implementing the concept of diversity management can help recruit and retain the best employees in the organization and increase their motivation, creativity, and innovation. A smaller number of respondents mentioned benefits stemming from access to new markets and the acquisition of new customers (50.5%), lowering of the risk of discrimination in the workplace/avoiding lawsuits (49.7%), or better employee satisfaction (48.9%).

Slightly fewer positive responses were reported for enhancing customer loyalty/retaining existing customers (43.8%), improving the company's image and reputation (42.6%), increasing the company's profits (40.8%), while the smallest number was reported for reducing costs (acquisition, training, hiring, replacement of employees) (34.3%). A total of 17.8% of respondents confirmed that diversity management was not beneficial. On the other hand, 62% of respondents disagreed with the statement that diversity management provided little to no benefits. In contrast, 35.2% of respondents did not agree that diversity management could contribute to cost reduction (acquisition, training, hiring, replacement of staff), and 26.6% said it did not contribute to boosting customer loyalty/helping retain existing customers. It also turned out that about 30% of the respondents believe that diversity management contributed to a moderate degree to the improvement of the company's image and reputation as well as increased the company's profits.

Essentially, the survey data shows that businesses recognize the advantages that diversity and inclusion activities could bring to an organization regardless of its size and geographic location. Therefore, it is appropriate to conclude that pro-inclusive and pro-diversity practices in HRM have a positive impact on developing organizations that provide space for creativity, and inventiveness, and foster talents and individuality. And it is precisely in the age of 5.0 that is expected to be a platform for people to show their creativity in identifying the diverse needs and challenges in society and the potential solutions, as well as in implementing these solutions using digital technology and data.

Discussion

The new (current) management paradigm seems to revolve around individualization and flexibility in combining technology with human needs. It also revolves around improved communication, integration, collaboration and closer interaction, and partnerships with customers, suppliers, and other stakeholders. It seems appropriate to try to identify the management mechanisms, including those included in HRM, that are useful in monitoring and stimulating these development processes.

When we define reality in this manner, we can see that creating inclusive environments and appreciating and promoting diversity in the workplace (and not only there) should be considered a valuable approach that leads to a new business environment in the 5.0 era. Empirical research also shows that by creating inclusive and diversity-friendly organizations, positive changes can also occur in organizations. Those changes may lead to transformations within the organization toward Society 5.0 (see Figure 6.1).

Our theoretical considerations allow us to see that Society 5.0 will be a society of imagination, in which the digital revolution will be combined with the creativity of diverse people that will lead to *solving problems* and *creating value* that will contribute to sustainable development. It is a concept that can contribute to achieving the Sustainable Development Goals (SDGs) adopted by the UN. Therefore, contrary to how science fiction movies portray the future, digitalization will not make people in organizations obsolete. For example, a human and a machine working together becomes possible if we divide the assembly line into two parts. The use of robots will occur for repetitive and laborious work, but people will still be needed for adaptation-related activities and critical thinking, e.g. thinking outside of the box. The so-defined view of the new era of 5.0, which has a strong reference to Society 5.0, allows us to conclude that diversity and inclusion policies are important for building

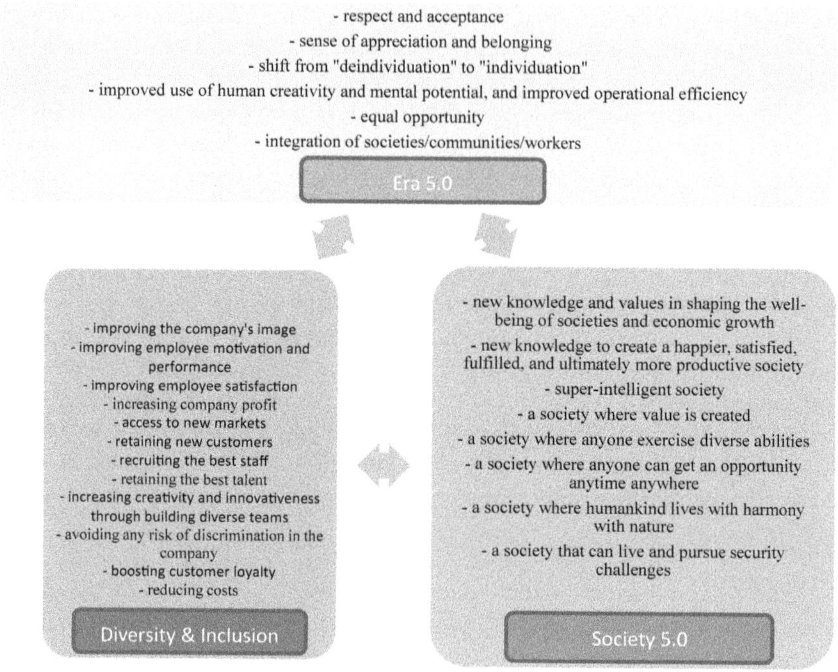

Figure 6.1 Organizations in 5.0.

Source: Own elaboration.

Society 5.0. The value of a society/organization/group is based on the diversity of its members. It is best for the workplace if all members can contribute, regardless of differences in age, gender, education, background, or skills. In addition, research confirms that organizations that focus on creating diverse and inclusive environments benefit from greater creativity, innovativeness, and better use of talent. This, however, requires establishing a safe, inclusive, respectful, and accepting work environment. In this way, HRM in the organization takes on a new meaning. Researchers point out that this process has slowly begun and will systematically move from the logic of Society 4.0 to the logic of Society 5.0, referred to as a human-centered society (Fukuyama, 2018, pp. 47–50; Konno & Schilliaci, 2021, pp. 478–505; Yabanci, 2019, pp. 1–9). Although the discussion of this significant change is relatively new (Ulrich, 2001, pp. 90–97), the approach has been gaining interest from the community (Gueutal & Stone, 2005; Stone et al., 2015).

Conclusions

The notion of Society 5.0 is becoming an objective requirement in increasing the innovation capabilities of organizations in the global market in addition to increasing employee creativity, innovation, and engagement. The idea is based on the understanding of current global trends. Technology, economics, and social change are accelerating, and businesses and communities are attempting to keep pace.

This chapter emphasizes the importance of the idea of Society 5.0 when building Business 5.0. The new paradigm of society 5.0 aims to create a happier, more satisfied, more fulfilled, and hence a more productive society. The purpose of Society 5.0 is to use the advanced technology of Industry 4.0 in the service of and for the pleasure of humanity while facilitating the connection of people and systems in cyberspace using artificial intelligence to optimize results. The implications of such a view on HRM are substantial. The literature and empirical research seem to support this trend. A Society 5.0 organization promotes an environment where all human resources can actively participate regardless of nationality, age, or gender, respond flexibly to various changes in the world, and create new value. Another aspect of HRM that impacts the change occurring in current organizations toward Society 5.0 is the tendency to create a work environment open to diversity and its inclusion through appropriate policies in the company's strategy (inclusion). Thus, it is crucial to further disseminate the concept of promoting diversity of human resources within the organization and integrating that diversity through inclusive policies. The research should also be intensified to determine trends and tendencies for building Society 5.0, of which there are relatively few.

References

Ahuja, G., & Morris Lampert, C. (2001). Entrepreneurship in the large corporation: A longitudinal study of how established firms create breakthrough inventions. *Strategic Management Journal, 22*(6–7), 521–543. https://doi.org/10.1002/smj.176

Carr-Ruffino, N. (1997). *The promotable woman*. Career Press.

Costa, J. (2018). *Sociedade 5.0, o futuro, pelo presente*. Retrieved May 18, 2022, from https://www.dinheirovivo.pt/opiniao/sociedade-50-o-futuro-pelo-presente-12820830.html

Dinana, H. (2020). *Society 5.0 and the future economies*. The Cairo Review of Global Affairs. Retrieved May 24, 2022, from https://www.thecairoreview.com/essays/society-5-0-and-the-future-economies/

Drucker, P. (2007). *Managing in the next society*. Butterworth Heinemann.

Ferreira, C., & Serpa, S. (2018). Society 5.0 and Social Development. https://doi.org/10.20944/preprints201811.0108.v1

Fukuyama, M. (2018). Society 5.0: Aiming for a new human-centered society. *Japan Spotlight, 27*, 47–50.

Furmanek, W. (2018). The most important ideas of the fourth industrial revolution. *Didactics of Computer Science, 13*, 55–63.

Gerber, A. (2021). *Society 5.0*. Springer International Publishing.

Griggs, L. (1995). Valuing diversity: Where from ... where to? In L. B. Griggs & L. L. Louw (Eds.), *Valuing diversity* (pp. 1–14). McGraw-Hill.

Gross-Gołacka, E. (2018). *Diversity management. Towards diversified human resources within the organization*. Difin.

Gross-Gołacka, E. (2022). Accelerating creation of self-managing (teal) organizations through diversity and inclusion. In E. Jędrych, Z. Olesiński, & A. Rzepka (Eds.), *Self-management, entrepreneurial culture, and economy 4.0*. Routledge.
Gueutal, H. G., & Stone, D. L.(Eds.) (2005). *The brave new world of eHR: Human resources management in the digital age*. Jossey Bass.
Hitachi-UTokyo Laboratory (2020). *Society 5.0*. Springer Verlag.
Keidanren (Japan Business Federation). (2016). Toward realization of the new economy and society. Reform of the economy and society by the deepening of "Society 5.0". Retrieved May 18, 2022, from http://www.keidanren.or.jp/en/policy/2016/029_outline.pdf
Keidanren (Japan Business Federation). (2019). *Society 5.0 for SDGs*. Keidanren.
Konno, N., & Schillaci, C. E. (2021). Intellectual capital in society 5.0 by the lens of the knowledge creation theory. *Journal of Intellectual Capital, 22*(3), 478–505. https://doi.org/10.1108/jic-02-2020-0060
Lasi, H., Fettke, P., Kemper, H. G., Feld, T., & Hoffmann, M. (2014) Industry 4.0. *Business & Information Systems Engineering, 6*, 239–242. https://doi.org/10.1007/s12599-014-0334-4
Litvin, D. (1997). The discourse of diversity: From biology to management. *Organization, 4*(2), 187–209. https://doi.org/10.1177/135050849742003
Litvin, D. (2006). Diversity: Making space for a better case. In A. M. Konrad, P. Prasad, & J. K. Pringle (Eds.), *Handbook of workplace diversity* (pp. 75–94). Sage Publications.
Maier, C. (2002). *Leading diversity – A conceptual framework* (pp. 132–134). Institute for Leadership and HR Management.
Mor Barak, M. (2008). Social psychological perspectives of workforce diversity and inclusion in national and global contexts. In R. Patti (Ed.), *Handbook of human service management* (pp. 239–254). Sage Publications.
Nishii, L., Rich, R., & Woods, S. (2006). *Framework of organizational inclusion*. Cornell University ILR.
O'Donovan, D. (2015). *Diversity, inclusion and organizational citizenship behaviors: A study of nurses in the Irish healthcare sector* [Unpublished PhD thesis]. Cork Institute of Technology.
Roberson, Q. M. (2006). Disentangling the meanings of diversity and inclusion in organizations. *Group & Organization Management, 31*(2), 212–236.
Siuta-Tokarska, B. (2021). Przemysł 4.0 i sztuczna inteligencja: Szansa Czy Zagrożenie dla Realizacji Koncepcji zrównoważonego i Trwałego Rozwoju? *Nierówności Społeczne a Wzrost Gospodarczy, 65*(1), 7–26. https://doi.org/10.15584/nsawg.2021.1.1
Stone, D. L., Deadrick, D. L., Lukaszewski, K. M., & Johnson, R. (2015). The influence of technology on the future of human resource management. *Human Resource Management Review, 25*(2), 216–231.
Sułkowski, Ł. (2012). *Epistemology and management methodology*. Polskie Wydawnictwo Ekonomiczne.
Thomas, R. (1992). *Beyond race and gender*. Amacom.
Triandis, H., & Suh, E. (2002). Cultural influences on personality. *Annual Review of Psychology, 53*(1), 133–160. https://doi.org/10.1146/annurev.psych.53.100901.135200
Ulrich, D. (2000). From e-business to e-HR. *Human Resource Planning, 23*(2), 12–21.
Yabanci, O. (2020). From human resource management to intelligent human resource management: A conceptual perspective. *Human-Intelligent Systems Integration, 1*(2–4), 101–109. https://doi.org/10.1007/s42454-020-00007-x
Yunda, N. (2019). Dampak Revolusi Industri 4.0 dan Society 5.0 Menciptakan Kesempatan Baru bagi Indonesia. Retrieved May 18, 2022, from https://www.kompasiana.com/nadyarahma

7 Cyber-physical platforms for monitoring and controlling industrial processes

Krzysztof Król, Tomasz Rymarczyk, Joanna Wyrwisz

Introduction

The purpose of this chapter is to present an intelligent cyber-physical system platform with an open architecture with free configuration and interoperability with external systems for the diagnosis and control of technological processes using the industrial internet of things (IIoT).

This cyber-physical system is a new generation of digital systems that mainly focus on the complex interdependencies and integration between cyberspace and the physical world. A cyber-physical system consists of highly integrated computing, communication, control, and physical components. Related to the issue of a cyber-physical system is Industry 4.0, which has created a revolution in manufacturing processes (He et al., 2017; Kong et al., 2020; Manavalan & Jayakrishna, 2019; Shang et al., 2019) due to the interconnection of elements that allow different worlds (such as physical, human, and digital) to be linked together.

Another of the terms to be mentioned is the internet of things (IoT) and its related IoT services. In its conception to industry, this platform brings some concepts and technologies to the development of industrial devices and device networks (Akhtari et al., 2019; Assawaarayakul et al., 2019; Occhiuzzi et al., 2019; Poor et al., 2019).

Industrial devices consist of sensors, actuators, and industrial robots that are connected through communication lines. Through these connections, the monitoring of analysis, data collection, and changes are possible. As a result of the above capabilities, the values that can be achieved include horizontal integration through value networks that support companies' business strategies, end-to-end engineering by integrating the digital and real worlds throughout the value chain, and vertical integration by networking manufacturing systems.

There can be many benefits to industrial environments by networking smart sensors, e.g. combining information and operational technologies. While operational technologies include hardware and software systems for controlling processes on a shop floor, these have typically not been integrated into a network or larger computer system. Nowadays, this combination

DOI: 10.4324/9781003384311-7

allows the various components of information technology to communicate directly with other machines and central servers, exchanging information through a computer network (Król et al., 2021).

In addition, one can see a reduction in the number of required operations: better efficiency and asset utilization, minimization of asset life cycle costs, faster decision-making, buying and selling products as services, expanding business opportunities, and enabling new business models for manufacturing. Therefore, the requirements for emerging factories that help to form global networks involving assets, storage systems, and manufacturing processes in the form of cyber-physical systems are key themes (Lins & Oliveira, 2020).

Cyber-physical systems are automated distributed systems that integrate physical reality with communication networks and computing infrastructures (Figure 7.1). Unlike traditional embedded systems, their main purpose is to network different devices. Therefore, these consist of control units that are capable of handling sensors that interact with the physical world, processing acquired data, and exchanging it with other systems and/or cloud services through a communication interface. An important feature is their ability to retrieve information and services in real-time regardless of location by implementing Internet access in production machines. In addition to real-time communication, it is necessary to ensure their stability, reliability, performance, and safety in operation. One goal is to provide a high level of security support across all layers of the architecture, which will help protect sensitive information.

Automation and digitization focus on integrating both sensors/instrumentation and algorithms in order to improve how raw data is extracted, analyzed, and transformed into actionable information that can then be used to optimize manufacturing processes. There are tremendous opportunities for change and competitive advantage in many IoT industries; for example, real-time data is collected while a system is running in order to provide insights

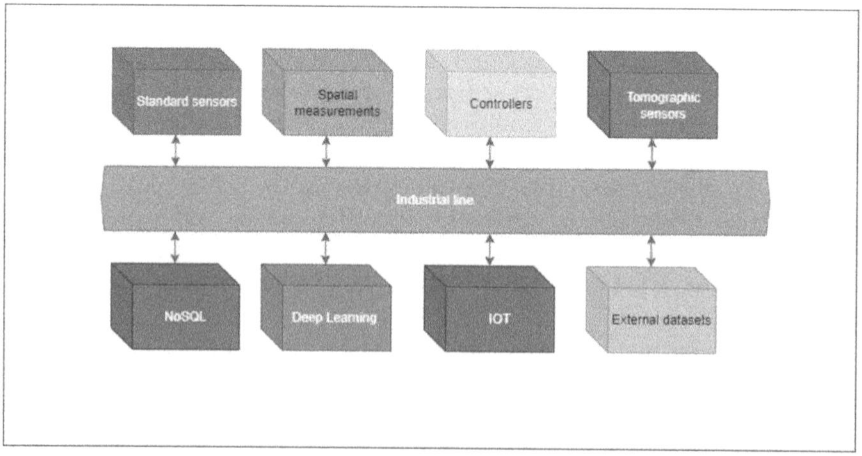

Figure 7.1 Conceptual design and device connections in cyber-physical platform.

Source: Own elaboration.

into system operations and help determine which equipment is working well and where there is any potential downtime (and why). By itself, Industry 4.0 obviously does not have this information; this data must be drawn from many elements that are interconnected. Namely, Industry 4.0 combines standardization, automation, sensors and actuators, smart devices, advanced analytics, and people into a common platform. This ultimately enables automation and digitization in order to enable problem-solving (Saarikko et al., 2017).

Material and methods

Fermentation

For this research, two systems were prepared to simulate those processes that occur in the operations of different production systems. The first studied process was the fermentation process that occurs in biogas plants.

A biogas plant's control system can be built based on any industrial PLC control system when suitably extended with analogue and digital inputs and outputs; these should provide the required parameters for the control, measurement, and management devices that are used in the plant. In most cases, controller, sensor, and actuator manufacturers will ensure that their devices implement basic communication methods. Since biogas plant installations and infrastructures are usually located over quite large areas (from several dozen to several hundred square meters), the applied controllers should enable the distribution of a control and monitoring system and, at the same time, ensure the compatibility of the devices as well as the possibility of communicating among the particular subsystems. When designing such a system, it is also worth considering the possibility of communicating with external systems, e.g. error notification or control/remote control systems.

A measurement method that uses capacitance tomography has been proposed. When using capacitance tomography, it is necessary to consider the possibility of the automatic use of tomographic measurement results when controlling the individual elements of a system.

The process can be monitored noninvasively by using capacitance tomography in the biomass study that is presented in Figure 7.2. Comparing tomographic results with conventional laboratory tests makes it possible to identify features that can indicate problems with the fermentation process. The prerequisites for determining such correlations are preparing an appropriate tomographic probe (or set of probes), using measuring instruments that are suitably sensitive, and applying reconstructive algorithms that allow one to continuously monitor changes in the parameters of the contents of a fermentation reactor and determine the correlations between the measurement results as well as the actual state based on the collected data from laboratory tests. Information about the distribution of the permeability coefficient can be obtained by repeatedly measuring the capacitance of an object's surface when changing the positions of the excitation electrodes. The primary problem is determining the dependence of the permeability distribution on the

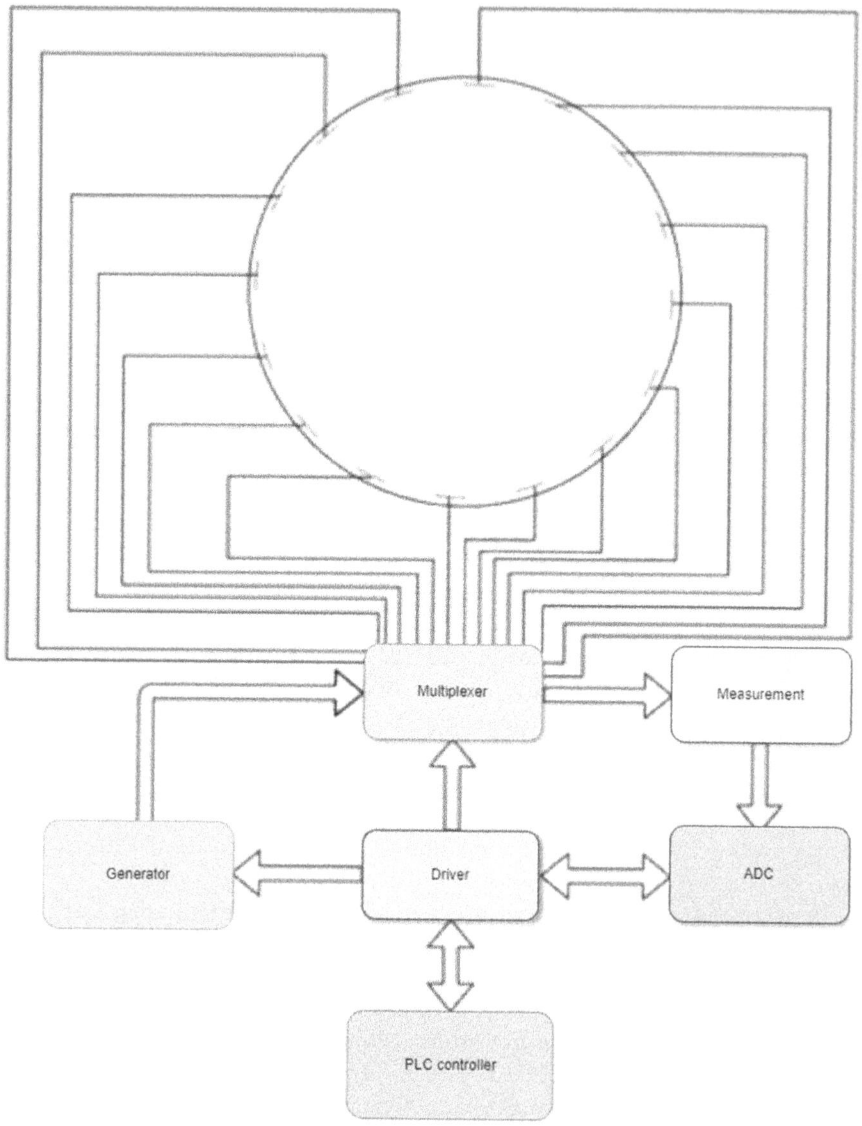

Figure 7.2 Diagram of measurement system in capacitance tomography.

Source: Own elaboration.

known and defined internal structure of the test item through experimentation. The measured capacitances are shown in femtofarads, which requires special measurement techniques.

The measuring system (Figure 7.3) consists of a sensor, special electronics for measuring the capacitance, and a reconstruction system. Currently, the most convenient way is to use a computer for reconstruction. Electrical

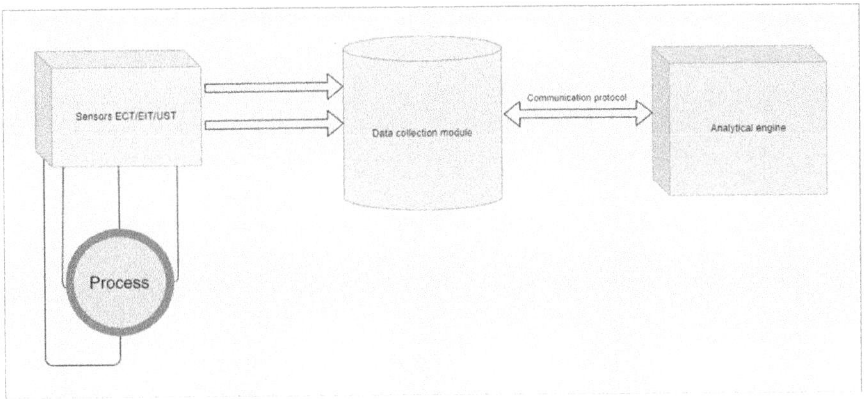

Figure 7.3 Monitoring of crystallization and fermentation processes.

Source: Own elaboration.

capacitance tomography allows us to observe the physical and chemical phenomena without penetrating their interiors. The source of information is the electrical capacitance between those electrodes that are distributed around a sensor circuit. From the collected capacitance measurements, a picture of the electric field strength distribution in the area of the measuring sensor can be obtained by solving the inverse problem for the electric field. An essential feature of measurement in electrical capacitance tomography is that there is no need for physical interaction between a sensor and the test medium (making this method non-invasive); it does not interfere with the current industrial process. Another advantage of this measurement technique is the high speed of the data acquisition. The obtained results are verified by comparing the simulation results with the analytical analysis results from the test data set.

Crystallization

The second process that was studied was the crystallization process. Crystallization is a widely used process in purification and particulate production. In addition, most industrial processes use nucleation-cooled crystallization in which the nucleated crystals of a specific compound are added to a reactor and the supersaturation of a liquid is produced by cooling.

Cooling crystallization is used when the solubility varies significantly regarding temperature and when a compound is thermally stable. Alternatively, supersaturation can be produced by adding an antisolvent (that is, a solvent of much lower solubility) or by a chemical reaction (such as by altering the pH level). One of the goals in the manufacturing process is to control a product's properties; for example, the particle size and particle size distribution, purity, residual solvent content, and crystallinity and polymorphic forms (hydrate or solvate).

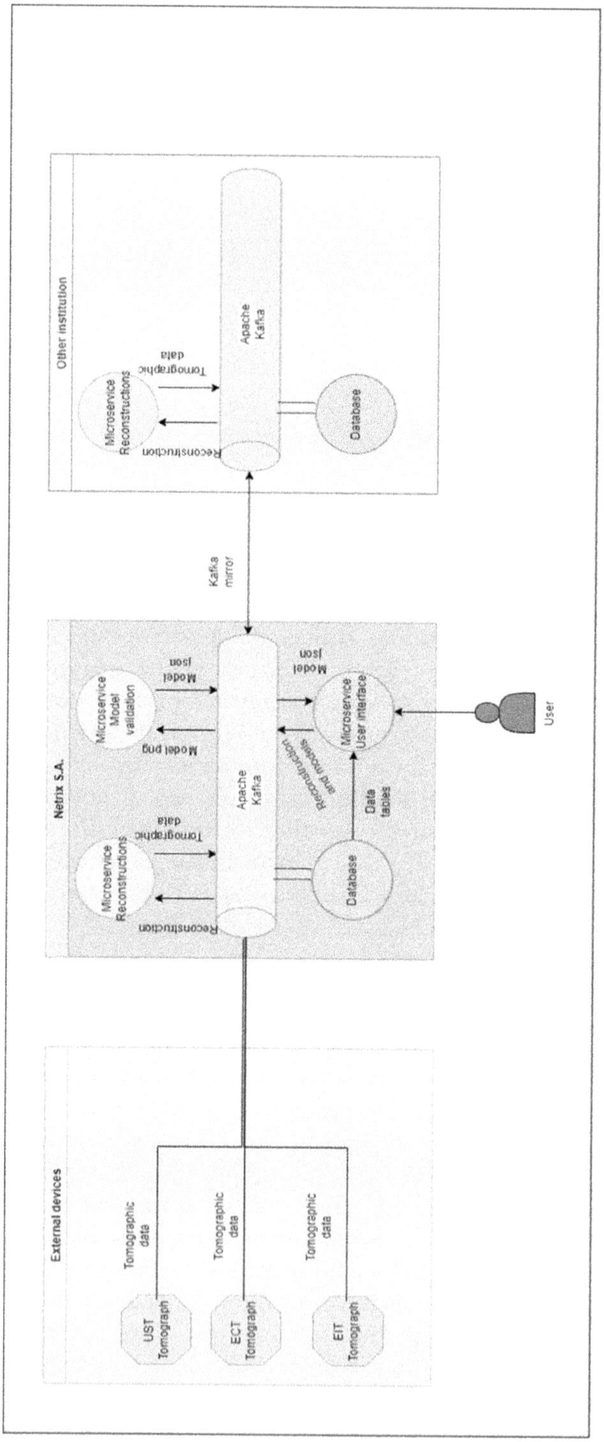

Figure 7.4 Distributed system architecture based on Apache Kafka and MirrorMaker.

Source: Own elaboration.

To some extent, product properties can be manipulated by changing the process parameters. A crystal size distribution that meets any assigned specifications (for example, maximum average particle size, minimum coefficient of variation, etc.) can be obtained by growing the given seed crystals and, for example, by minimizing the nucleation (that is, by keeping the system in an unstable zone, provided that any agglomeration and cracking can also be avoided). The operating conditions for obtaining the desired product properties can be selected by trial and error or model-based process optimization.

Control and advanced automation in manufacturing processes play very important roles in maintaining competitiveness. Even though production lines and expensive equipment are at the heart of production in many industrial processes, it should be mentioned that all control systems and information technologies play key roles. They provide the flexibility to quickly adapt production processes to the changing requirements of potential customers (as well as ensure safety and efficiency at the lowest cost). For this reason, the development and application of advanced process controls are some of the most effective levers for immediate and long-term gross energy savings, improved product quality, increased process safety, and greater production flexibility.

Results

The goal is to achieve the highest possible crystallization efficiency by optimizing the dynamic parameters of the liquid mixing.

The data that is collected can be analyzed in order to look for the maximum crystallization gain. This can be done simply by searching a data set or in a more complex manner. By approximating the data with a mathematical function and then extrapolating beyond the collected data set, we can look for further increments and use this knowledge for planning further measurements. It is possible that the most efficient crystallization can be achieved at variable mixing speeds.

An optimization and preprocessing model has been designed that enables us to optimize the design, logistics, and manufacturing processes. This model enables product lifecycle tracking and provides interoperability with external applications. The system autonomously monitors, controls, measures, and collects the results; the collected data can be easily visualized. Additionally, this data can be used to create a unique knowledge base and support an expert system.

The concept of the IIoT and Industry 4.0 assumes intelligent communication and an analysis of any collected data; this is meant to ensure the improvement of the decision-making processes. An appropriately designed technological line is meant to transmit readings between devices. The data is processed and analyzed in an appropriate IT system that communicates and integrates the individual elements of an intelligent production line. However, this communication is not limited to only those devices that

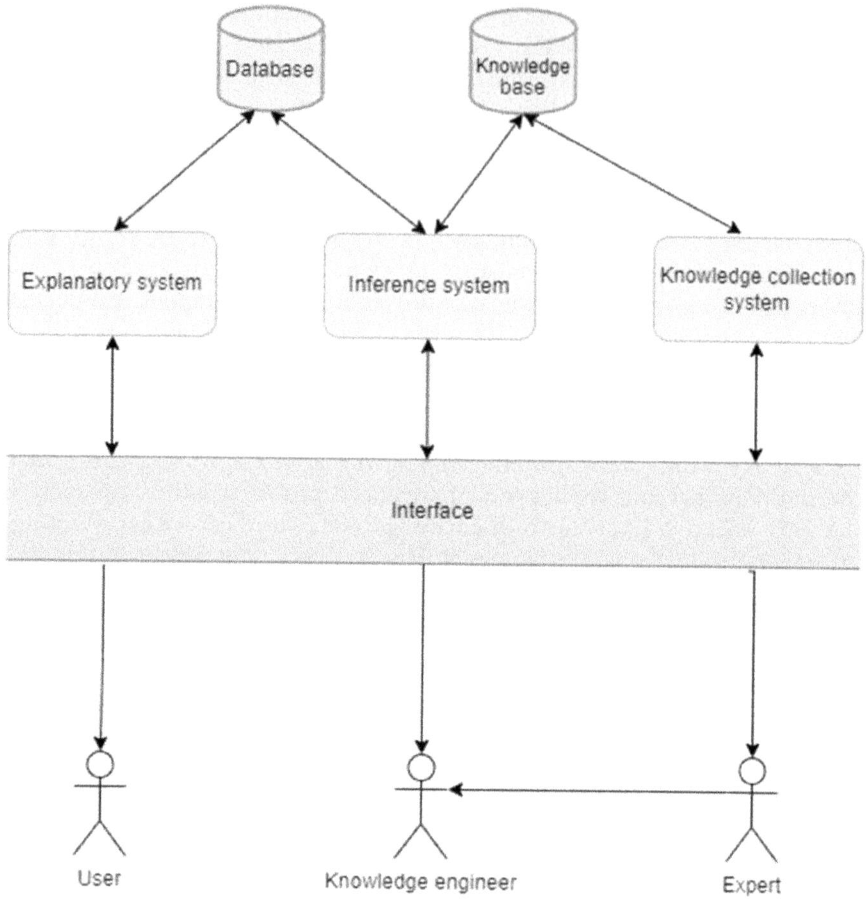

Figure 7.5 General overview of expert system.

Source: Own elaboration.

operate in a company; it should go beyond the internal infrastructure (e.g. by analyzing any data that is received from external suppliers in order to optimize one's production or logistics processes). The production lines consist of workstations or machines that are connected and meant to be used for serial and mass production.

Discussion

Cyber-physical systems enable increased efficiency and productivity in industrial value creation due to the real-time information that is provided about the technical processes. The information that is collected should include personnel knowledge to take full advantage of cyber-physical systems. Often, such knowledge is only available informally and formalizing it is a problem.

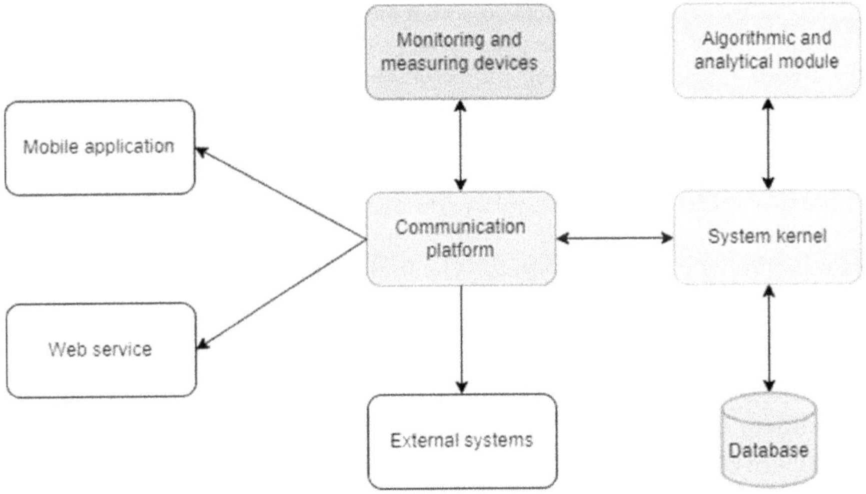

Figure 7.6 Wiring diagram in smart sensor platform.

Source: Own elaboration.

However, methods of systematic recording, categorization, and mapping should be implemented because of the great value of such knowledge. Furthermore, the availability of this knowledge can be used to develop action guidelines that are essential parts of decision support systems.

One example would be repairing a malfunctioning machine. When an error first occurs, the troubleshooting process should be documented so that, when it occurs again, action guidelines are available, and whoever performs the repair can benefit from the experience curve effect. However, systematically recording, categorizing, and mapping tacit knowledge means extra efforts for employees. Therefore, it is necessary to clarify the overall added value based on the availability of action guidelines after developing and implementing a decision support system.

Monitoring and measurement devices (as presented in Figure 7.6) represent intelligent measurement sensors and other components that can be added to these devices. Such additional devices can be cameras that capture images and then send them through an analytics system. They can also be tomographs that are used for non-destructive analysis inside the test objects. As intelligent sensors, they can continuously monitor behavior beyond any established boundaries (failures or imminent equipment failure). The data from monitoring and measuring devices is transmitted to a system kernel, where the algorithmic-analytical module processes it. Additionally, the data from the sensors is stored in a database.

The data-processing results that are created by particular modules are transferred to external systems to control the production and logistic processes. The measured values can be presented on a web service or in a mobile application.

Any information and conclusions that are obtained from intelligent industrial data directly re-enter the production-execution process and form the basis for a wide range of intelligent industrial services. These data-driven services can be internal services for supporting value-creation processes or services that are offered to external customers. For better optimization, raw data must be processed systematically – passing it through various algorithms. In this context, pattern detection should particularly be mentioned, as this method identifies and quantifies causal correlations and makes it possible to predict changes in the state of the system. The importance of the information that is provided by such an analysis depends on the amount of data that is processed.

Despite all of the benefits and advantages of implementing the IIoT and Industry 4.0, this proposal is complex. The large amount of digitization and networking of companies increases the numbers of architectures that are created by different authors, thus resulting in possible problems with network communication and the interoperability of systems.

Cyber-physical systems represent machines, products, customers, service providers, and inventory; these ensure adequate interaction in all of the above areas executed autonomously. Applications of systems can be found in manufacturing, health, renewable energy, smart building, transportation, and agriculture.

In manufacturing, this is used for automatic monitoring, production control, and real-time information exchange. In the health area, it can be used in real time to monitor patients' physical conditions remotely. In the renewable energy sector, sensors enable grid monitoring and control to ensure energy consumption reliability and efficiency. In smart buildings, the interaction among a cyber-physical system and smart devices can reduce energy consumption and increase the protection, safety, and comfort of the occupants. In the transportation area, this technology allows for communication between vehicles and infrastructure, exchanging information such as traffic volume, congestion, and accident locations in order to prevent further accidents or congestion. Finally, information about weather and several resources such as irrigation and moisture data can be collected in the agricultural sector, increasing the precision of agricultural-management systems.

However, there are huge opportunities for changes in the industry and competitive advantages using the IoT. For example, real-time data that is collected during system operation (which provides information on multiple pieces of information such as individual machine performance, maintenance, and repair scheduling) can be combined and used to increase and optimize production efficiency through the use of IoT technologies – including artificial intelligence (AI), machine learning (ML), and deep learning (DL). This is an example of focusing on connectivity and recombination rather than displacement and replacement. In addition, new sensors can provide more precise data with higher resolutions at higher frequencies, which will help develop more accurate algorithms for automation.

Therefore, the industry needs to adapt and find the right balance among differentiation, integration, centralization, and decentralization to reap the benefits of systems like the IoT.

Summary

This article presents a cyber-physical system with an open architecture with the possibility of any configuration and interaction with external systems that is able to diagnose and control technological processes using the IIoT. The system consists of highly integrated computational, communication, control, and physical components. Two systems that simulated the processes in the operations of various production systems were prepared for this research. The first studied process was the fermentation process that takes place in biogas plants, while the second was crystallization, where an optimization and pre-processing model was developed to optimize the design, logistics, and production processes. This enables product cycle tracking and interoperability with external applications. The solution works autonomously by monitoring, controlling, measuring, and collecting results. Cyber-physical systems make it possible to increase efficiency and productivity in creating industrial value thanks to a large amount of information about technical processes that are provided in real-time. The presented approach enables specific personalization that optimizes production and technological processes using cyber-physical systems. Virtual simulations and the testing of products from different angles increase the efficiency of the final product's dynamic modeling and execution. This solution allows companies to manage the intelligent structures of processes, products, simulations, and virtual products by tracking their product cycles.

References

Akhtari, S., Pickhardt, F., Pau, D., Pietro, A., & Tomarchio, G. (2019). Intelligent embedded load detection at the edge on Industry 4.0 powertrains applications. *2019 IEEE 5th International Forum on Research and Technology for Society and Industry (RTSI).* https://doi.org/1b0.1109/rtsi.2019.8895598

Assawaarayakul, C., Srisawat, W., Ayuthaya, S., & Wattanasirichaigoon, S. (2019). *Integrate digital twin to exist production system for Industry 4.0* [Conference session]. 2019 4th Technology Innovation Management and Engineering Science International Conference (TIMES-Icon). https://doi.org/10.1109/times-icon47539.2019.9024430

He, J., Jia, G., Han, G., Wang, H., & Yang, X. (2017). Locality-aware replacement algorithm in flash memory to optimize cloud computing for smart factory of Industry 4.0. *IEEE Access, 5*, 16252–16262. https://doi.org/10.1109/access.2017.2740327

Kong, X., Zhong, R., Zhao, Z., Shao, S., Li, M., & Lin, P. et al. (2020). Cyber physical ecommerce logistics system: An implementation case in Hong Kong. *Computers &Amp; Industrial Engineering, 139*, 106170. https://doi.org/10.1016/j.cie.2019.106170

Król, K., Marciniak, A., Gudowski, J., & Bojanowska, A. (2021). Intelligent sensor platform with open architecture for monitoring and control of Industry 4.0 systems. *European Research Studies Journal, XXIV*(Special Issue 2), 597–606. https://doi.org/10.35808/ersj/2288

Lins, T., & Oliveira, R. (2020). Cyber-physical production systems retrofitting in context of Industry 4.0. *Computers &Amp; Industrial Engineering, 139*, 106193. https://doi.org/10.1016/j.cie.2019.106193

Manavalan, E., & Jayakrishna, K. (2019). A review of internet of things (IoT) embedded sustainable supply chain for Industry 4.0 requirements. *Computers &Amp; Industrial Engineering, 127*, 925–953. https://doi.org/10.1016/j.cie.2018.11.030

Occhiuzzi, C., Amendola, S., Nappi, S., D'Uva, N., & Marrocco, G. (2019). *RFID technology for Industry 4.0: Architectures and challenges* [Conference session]. 2019 IEEE International Conference on RFID Technology and Applications (RFID-TA). https://doi.org/10.1109/rfid-ta.2019.8892049

Poor, P., Basl, J., & Zenisek, D. (2019). *Predictive Maintenance 4.0 as next evolution step in industrial maintenance development* [Conference session]. 2019 International Research Conference on Smart Computing and Systems Engineering (SCSE). https://doi.org/10.23919/scse.2019.8842659

Saarikko, T., Westergren, U., & Blomquist, T. (2017). The internet of things: Are you ready for what's coming? *Business Horizons*, *60*(5), 667–676. https://doi.org/10.1016/j.bushor.2017.05.010

Shang, C., Bao, X., Fu, L., Xia, L., Xu, X., & Xu, C. (2019). A novel key-value based real-time data management framework for ship integrated power cyber-physical system. *2019 IEEE Innovative Smart Grid Technologies – Asia (ISGT Asia)*. https://doi.org/10.1109/isgt-asia.2019.8881124

8 Artificial intelligence in a distributed supply chain control model for the personalization and identification of products in real-time

Łukasz Gołąbek, Damian Pliszczuk, Michał Maj, Sylwester Bogacki, Magdalena Rzemieniak

Introduction

The Fifth Industrial Revolution (Industry 5.0) constitutes the development direction of the present Fourth Industrial Revolution. Using the synergy effect, it allows for better human-machine interaction in order to achieve faster and more effective results. Furthermore, it focuses on personalized customer demand (Javaid & Haleem, 2020).

The development of the Fourth and Fifth Industrial Revolutions is connected with continuous technological progress and the development of methods that are based on AI. The literature is drawing increasing attention to machine-learning methods (T. Rymarczyk et al., 2021), including artificial neural networks (ANN) (Kłosowski et al., 2020), deep-learning algorithms (convolutional neural networks (CNNs)) (Nasir & Sassani, 2021), and long short-term memory networks (LSTMs) (Kłosowski et al., 2020). AI is used to improve the efficiency and accuracy of processes and their automation in order to raise the quality of products and services. Digital technologies with an AI-based system enable us to meet personalization challenges in supply chain control with less human effort. Additionally, these can be run on any device – even a smartphone.

The Fifth Industrial Revolution enables customers to obtain personalized products and services. This revolution allows us to track the correctness of processes by implementing AI. Modern enterprises strive to perform specialized and better work that results from the synergy of human-machine cooperation and technological progress (Özdemir & Hekim, 2018).

Industry 5.0 aims at increasing efficiency and productivity through programmable machines, devices, networks of intelligent sensors, various AI algorithms, and the ability to manage an entire infrastructure in the cloud (Doyle-Kent & Kopacek, 2019). In this case, various information technologies can be used to enable us to optimize the times and costs of tasks. The required business goals are easily achieved with system improvements due to smart digital control of the processes. A rapidly changing business

DOI: 10.4324/9781003384311-8

environment requires us to develop new mechanisms that enable the continuous introduction of new products and services (Geissdoerfer et al., 2018).

With the ever-growing trend of digital solutions, offering flexible digital services that contribute to high customer satisfaction is crucial; therefore, transforming its overall strategy or specific tasks into its digital representation is necessary. Digital architecture favors the rapid integration of new technologies; it drives digital transformation. This is composed of a stack of layers that support and correspond to particular elements of business policy. The basic technological layer provides applications, API management, security, analytics, services, and data integration.

Rapid technological progress has meant that many companies refrain from transferring their software to the cloud, fearing "giving" their data to a cloud service provider. Additionally, they are afraid of a technological deadlock, i.e. dependence on only one cloud service provider. Therefore, hybrid clouds and a model of using several vendors are increasingly important (Asthana et al., 2020; Megahed et al., 2019). According to "The cloud migration forecast: Cloudy with a chance of clouds" – TMT Predictions 2021 Delloitte – a hybrid cloud is the new standard. It has been predicted that more than 90% of global companies will use hybrid clouds by 2023. Another survey shows that 97% of IT managers plan to move tasks among two or more clouds in order to maximize operational flexibility (Stewart et al., 2020).

There are numerous IT solutions for enterprises on the market; unfortunately, many have functional limitations and lack complexity and integration in the logistics area of a network model.

This research is aimed at building a modular platform using AI to flexibly configure and adapt software to work with external systems in the supply chain area. This platform enables managing a company's structure in terms of its processes and products. The new software allows for the optimization and auto-optimization (owing to the implemented computer-intelligence algorithms) of logistics processes. This enables better synergy between people and machines, can be used for prototyping and product version management in the planning, manufacturing, and distribution processes, and enables the more accurate personalization of products within the intelligent Industry 5.0. supply chain. It also allows for tracking a product's life cycle and ensures interoperability with external applications. The system works autonomously, monitoring and collecting results that are sent by sensors and external applications and allowing the collected data to be visualized.

Methods

The ready-made analyses that were implemented in the system that performs individual business issues were built as stored procedures that included Python scripts. The vast majority of the individual analyses were containerized and operated as microservices. Figure 8.1 shows a general scheme of the various proposed algorithms. The data for analysis is retrieved from the

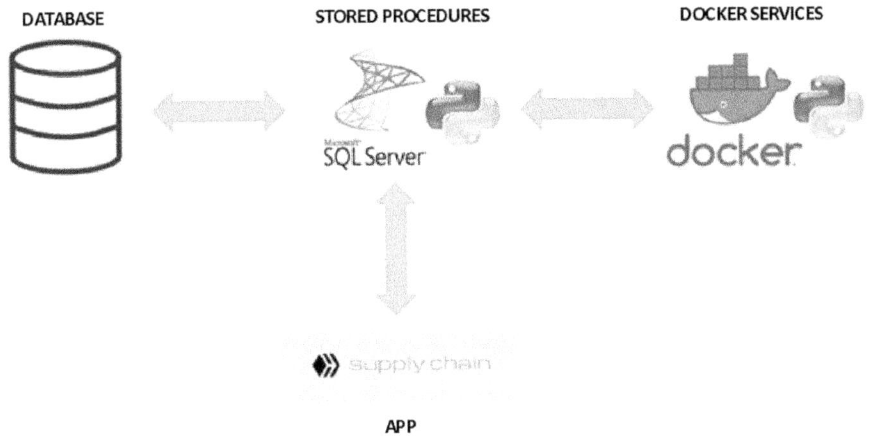

Figure 8.1 Diagram of data exchange and processing in the supply chain system

database and then processed by the stored procedures. Such procedures either carry out certain analyses themselves and add the results to the database or call the appropriate docker services, which send the results back to the procedure after completing the task, saving them to the database. The solutions are displayed directly in the application along with the generation date, enabling one to view the previously generated analyses.

The presented solution uses a tool that allows for the automation and management of business processes presented in digital form as distributed microservices that implement the individual stages of the processes. This approach is driven by the Camunda environment (Camunda Community, 2022), which enables creation and management processes that use various tools and programming languages. The Camunda system allows for recording information about each of the triggered processes, which is important from the point of view of further analyses that concern the operation of the entire supply chain system.

Due to the many limitations of the basic version of Camunda, the Excamad tool was also implemented, enabling observation of individual stages of the application. Moreover, the Prometheus and Grafana (Grafana Labs, n.d.) tools were introduced to monitor the course of the processes and the visualization methods of those indicators that are of interest to the user. The above-mentioned standard solutions ensure the ease of configuring the system to the user's needs.

Artificial machine-learning methods were used to create individual modules, including deep-learning methods for formulating algorithms, i.a., for data analysis and system optimization, visualizing product life stages or monitoring logistic and technological processes, and identification and classification algorithms. Deep-learning methods support the automation of many processes that are related to customer support and product quality, for example. The system was also built using RFID technology, i.a., for traffic and location records and the identification of marked objects.

The system is based on API interfaces that are part of each module; thus, the modules can operate independently, and their implementation can occur at many stages. It is also possible to use some system components.

Results

The main objective of the research was to build a platform for managing the structure of a given company in terms of processes and products using AI. This platform enables the continuous monitoring of the quality and status of a product, the personalization and identification of products in real-time, the management of product versions in the production and distribution process in a flexible and free configuration, and thus adapting the software to cooperate with external systems.

Containerization-based modularity ensures system implementation flexibility and scalability, from the on-premise model through one cloud service provider to the hybrid model. In addition, the proposed system allows for the use of cloud resources and scaling the system in the cloud and storing the data on the local servers of the client if the client only wishes to store certain data "at home".

The system structure with the communication interface, the unique algorithms for data analysis and system optimization, the algorithms for visualizing a product's life stages and monitoring its logistic and technological processes, the algorithms for identifying and classifying products in real-time, and the prototype of the platform that constituted the subject of the project were prepared as part of the research.

The main elements of the solution are as follows:

- System kernel – workflow management, resource monitoring, system message management;
- Integration platform – joining and exchanging data between various systems and communication standards;
- Algorithmic modules – series of subsystems for analyzing and extracting information from obtained data and modules that are responsible for graphic presentation of monitored phenomena and processes;
- User interfaces based on web and mobile technologies;
- IT ecosystem based on so-called containers and microservices.

The created application offers the translation of business logic into a specific software platform that enables, i.a., the implementations of the following functionalities:

- Integrated intelligent enterprise management for processes and products;
- Optimization and auto-optimization of design and logistics processes – implementation of mechanisms that allow both operators and programs themselves to optimize entire processes and individual operations;

- Product lifecycle tracking (from design to sale and even to scrapping/decommissioning);
- Planning, designing, and simulating of products – IT support for design stage by user integrated within one platform with resource planning, technology, and product simulation;
- Cooperation with ERP (Enterprise Resource Planning) /MRP (Material Requirements Planning), CRM (Customer Relationship Management), and MES (Manufacturing Execution System) systems;
- Integration of system functionality in mobile applications;
- Analysis of large datasets – optimization of tasks that are related to data storage and processing in real-time with use of Big Data methods;
- Tracking status of projects and orders at various stages of their implementations.

The presented IT system architecture consists of the two most important layers: presentation (for which the WWW services and mobile applications are responsible) and operational (deep-learning algorithms and ERP systems that are integrated with the B2B platform and are responsible for enterprise management).

The user interface (a web portal) allows an operator to manage the data that is collected in the system and consider customer orders, production orders, deliveries, invoices, settlements, complaints, and product conditions. This element contains interfaces for data exchanges with the systems of customers and suppliers. Sample screens from the web application are shown in Figure 8.2. The information to be presented and the data to be used can be modified depending on a company's needs.

The system works 24 hours a day/7 days a week; it does not require a company's support. Commercial and marketing information is personalized and only visible to specific users. The most important commercial information regarding the introduction of new products, planned promotions, and sales is presented. The information on the state of cooperation is available worldwide owing to the system's cooperation with any external IT system. The system enables analyses of both small and large data sets in batch mode and real time.

As a result of the system's operation, various types of analyses and simulations can be carried out in the supply chain management. These mainly concern the prediction of demand, analyses of returns or complaints, and analyses of the deliveries themselves (e.g. delays in deliveries) as well as the identification of demand.

In addition, the quality control can be automated based on optical-detection algorithms. This allows us, i.a., to detect damage during production (e.g. cracks) and test the color compliance of many elements in order to complete an entire order (comparison with a reference color). The second case may arise due to the aging of products that is caused by long-term storage in warehouses. Therefore, a mobile application that sends a photo to the color-detection module that indicates whether an analyzed element is within

Figure 8.2 Sample data visualizations

the required color spectrum is indispensable for testing color compliance (Figure 8.3).

In addition, RFID technology enables the tracking of the quantities and locations of moving goods (e.g. during the delivery process, in warehouses, or on store shelves), thus optimizing one's resources and processes.

The designed system also allows for conducting the design and monitoring of the process in the form of a pictorial representation of the processes and observations of the implementation of their stages. Monitoring of the process in the Camunda environment using Excamad is shown in Figure 8.4a, while the use of visualization and the Grafana system are presented in Figure 8.4b, showing the statistics on a selected supply chain process.

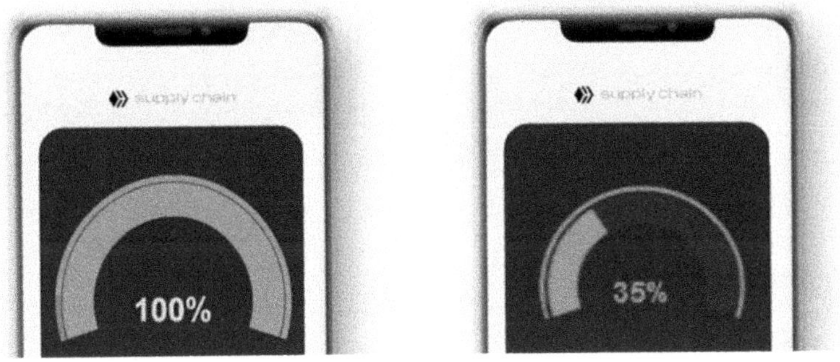

Figure 8.3 Examples of operation of mobile application for determining differences in colors of elements

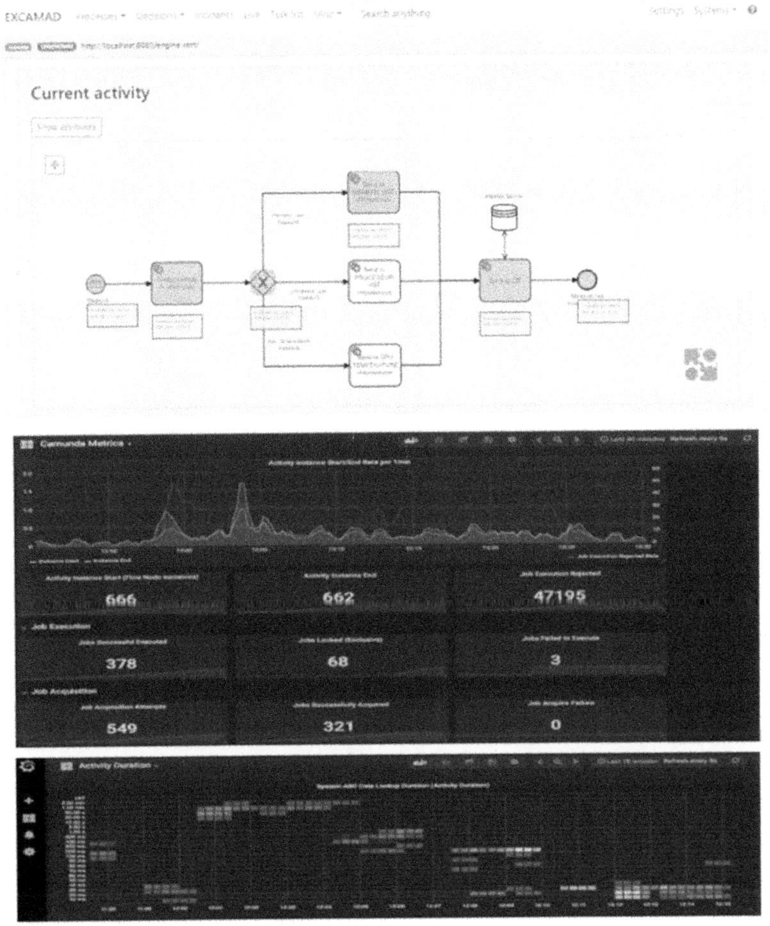

Figure 8.4 Process monitoring performed in Camunda environment with Excamad visualization (a) and Grafana system (b)

Part of the system functionality is available in a mobile application; sample screenshots from the mobile application are shown in Figure 8.5. The set of functionalities in the prototyping phase is legible, compact, and user-editable. Each module can be represented in the mobile application as necessary. The following functionalities were implemented:

- module for automating quality control – analysis of aging of products;
- product search module based on photos – with use of optical-detection algorithms.

Discussion

Traditionally, supply chain processes have been virtually unchanged; however, a supply chain must be dynamically adapted to changing market conditions, e.g. switching suppliers because of closing borders (pandemics) (Kovács et al., 2021), and as a result of continuous technological development and successive industrial revolutions (Alvarez-Aros & Bernal-Torres, 2021).

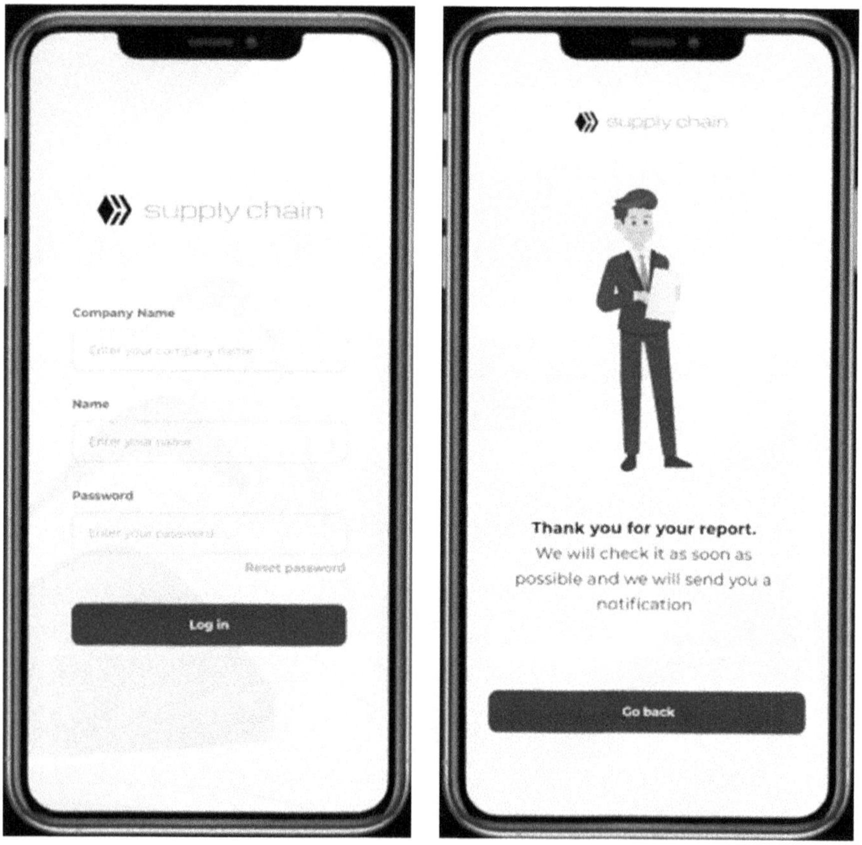

Figure 8.5 Examples of functionalities of mobile application. (*Continued*)

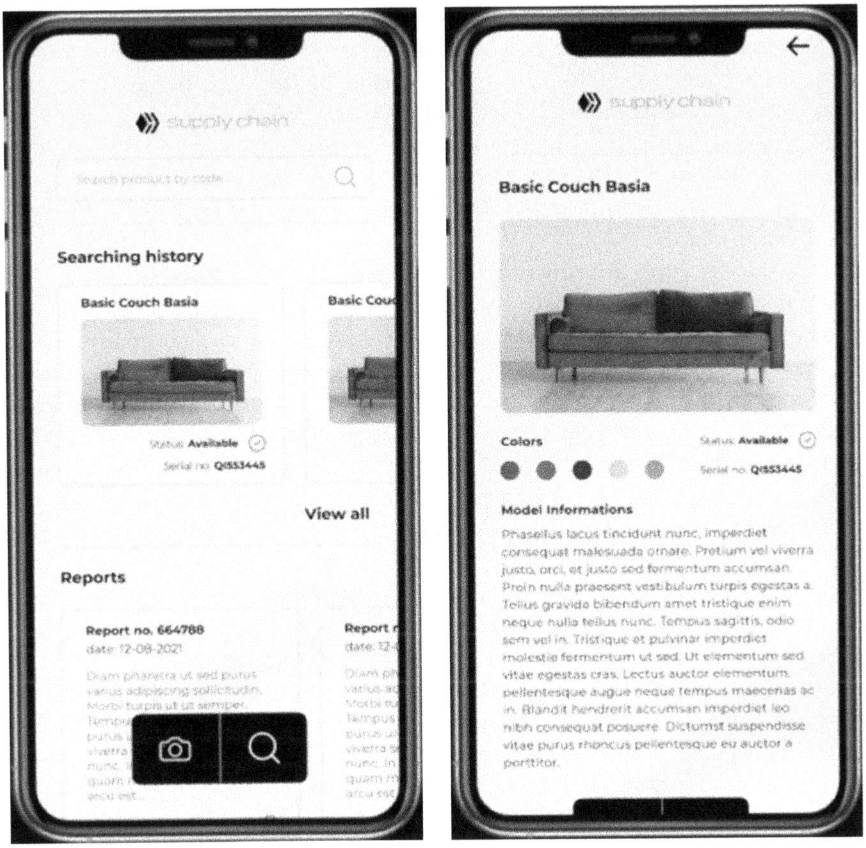

Figure 8.5 (Continued)

Changing processes in an enterprise requires the flexibility of IT systems to reflect business processes in the IT systems naturally (Gomes Barbosa & Maia, 2020). Modularity that is implemented in the form of a distributed IT system based on microservices enables one to expand and adjust the functionality of the IT system.

The evolution of software toward the global integration of functional modules and a multi-faceted approach to computerized support for managing these areas requires the simultaneous consideration of the specificity of manufacturing network products. The model of network logistics includes i.a., companies with their trade (product) brand and using services or distribution that are entirely outsourced. Although there are numerous IT solutions that are available, many have functional limitations – lacking complexity and integration in the approach to the logistics area in the network model.

These solutions do not translate the business logic of such a model of operation into a specific platform that enables, i.a., implementing the aforementioned functionalities. One of these is the integrated management of an intelligent enterprise in terms of processes and products – the currently used IT systems supported by a hardware layer are often not integrated enough with each other to enable the optimization of the logistics processes in a distributed (network) model (Hader et al., 2020; Woźniakowski et al., 2018). The proposed system in a distributed model enables flexible and free configurations, thus adapting the software to cooperate with external systems within the supply chain. Additionally, it is possible to analyze large data sets using Big Data methods.

The system aims to reduce costs and optimize the processes of concluding transactions and automate and modernize the logistic and organizational processes. Various types of predictions that are made in a company regarding sales, returns, or complaints allow for a reduction of the risk of losses and choices of appropriate strategies to increase profits. Demand forecasts form the basis of all supply chain planning (Aamer et al., 2020). An analysis of supplies themselves is extremely important in supply chain management; this enables companies, i.a., to predict which products may not arrive on time; this is associated with both property losses and tarnished reputations (Vakhania & Mamporia, 2020).

Optimizing resources and processes requires information about stock levels and the locations of materials, semi-finished products, etc. RFID technology enables one to track the quantities and locations of moving goods, e.g. in the delivery process, in warehouses, or on store shelves (P. Rymarczyk et al., 2021). The issued packaging can be checked with the use of stationary RFID readers. After a cart that is loaded with packages passes through an RFID gateway, the information about the goods is automatically read from the labels that are attached to the packages. These are further submitted to the IT system, where warehouse documents are issued. RFID technology allows the automatic monitoring of all operations that are related to, i.a., warehouse traffic.

The presented system ensures cooperation with ERP/MRP, CRM, and MES systems, which allows for improving the cooperation of a company with its business partners and solving the following organizational problems:

- ensuring integrated synchronization of product data and documentation;
- eliminating misunderstandings and errors in commercial communication;
- reducing need to print commercial documents;
- improving way commercial transactions are processed;
- reducing mistakes and speeding up reactions to possible problems;
- shortening ordering processes;
- improving logistics planning and tracking flow of goods and all document statuses (with the possibility of filtering and sorting).

An important functionality of the system is the collection of multi-faceted data by imaging the physical condition of the products – currently, there is no technology that is available for ensuring adequate quality at every stage of distribution. The proposed system enables automatic quality control through optical-detection algorithms (damage analysis, analysis of the aging process of products, and product searches). Deep learning methods support the automation of many processes (Kłosowski et al., 2020, 2021). Artificial intelligence (AI) methods allow for synergy in human-machine cooperation and, i.a., customer support during purchases at the stage of searching for the required article, the personalization of products within an intelligent Industry 5.0 supply chain, and production quality control.

The system provides the tools for process management, monitoring the status of projects, and orders at individual stages of their implementation. Providing users with real-time information on order fulfillment and distribution activities is necessary for making optimal operational decisions. The applied solutions increase the efficiency of processes and optimize their duration through insight into the course of subsequent processes, allowing for a better understanding and improving a company's efficiency.

Summary

The AI-based platform allows entrepreneurs to manage the structure of a given company in terms of its processes and products. This enables the optimization and auto-optimization (owing to the implemented computer-intelligence algorithms) of the design and logistics processes. The platform enables tracking a product's life cycle and ensures cooperation with external applications. Separate modules allow results to be directly viewed on a mobile or in a web application. The use of microservices and containers allows for a flexible system in which modules perform clearly defined tasks. The system enables the use of cloud resources, scaling in the cloud, and storing data on private servers. The system is operated autonomously, constantly monitoring and collecting results that are sent by sensors and external applications. Additionally, the data can create a unique knowledge base and support an expert system. The created application allows us to obtain information about orders, the stages of their implementation, a product's life cycle, supported payments, or complaints.

It is possible to indicate certain aspects of the presented solution that prove the novelty and innovative nature of the system:

- Unique technological solution based on AI;
- New algorithms for identification, classification, visualization, and data analysis have been developed, allowing us, i.a., to personalize products as part of Intelligent Industry 5.0. supply chain;
- Integrated supply chain ecosystem owing to integration platform and electronic identification of components and products;
- Continuous quality and status monitoring at every stage of the intelligent supply chain;
- Customize plans and processes in real-time and manage product versions in manufacturing and distribution processes.

The introduction of various AI-based algorithms and analytical methods allows for their optimal and individual selection depending on one's needs.

References

Aamer, A., Eka Yani, L., & Alan Priyatna, I. (2020). Data analytics in the supply chain management: Review of machine learning applications in demand forecasting. *Operations and Supply Chain Management: An International Journal*, 1–13. https://doi.org/10.31387/oscm0440281

Alvarez-Aros, E., & Bernal-Torres, C. (2021). Technological competitiveness and emerging technologies in Industry 4.0 and Industry 5.0. *Anais Da Academia Brasileira De Ciências*, *93*(1). https://doi.org/10.1590/0001-3765202120191290

Asthana, S., Megahed, A., & Iyoob, I. (2020). *A cloud-migration feasibility advisor* [Conference session]. 2020 IEEE 40th International Conference on Distributed Computing Systems (ICDCS). https://doi.org/10.1109/icdcs47774.2020.00126

Camunda Community (2022). *Introduction | docs.camunda.org*. Docs.camunda.org. Retrieved May 27, 2021, from https://docs.camunda.org/manual/7.14/introduction/

Doyle-Kent, M., & Kopacek, P. (2019). Industry 5.0: Is the manufacturing industry on the cusp of a new revolution?. *Lecture Notes in Mechanical Engineering*, 432–441. https://doi.org/10.1007/978-3-030-31343-2_38

Geissdoerfer, M., Vladimirova, D., & Evans, S. (2018). Sustainable business model innovation: A review. *Journal of Cleaner Production*, *198*, 401–416. https://doi.org/10.1016/j.jclepro.2018.06.240

Gomes Barbosa, M., & Maia, P. M. (2020*). Towards identifying microservice candidates from business rules implemented in stored procedures* [Conference session]. 2020 IEEE International Conference on Software Architecture Companion (ICSA-C). https://doi.org/10.1109/icsa-c50368.2020.00015

Grafana Labs (n.d.). Get started with Grafana and Prometheus. Retrieved July 28, 2022, from https://grafana.com/docs/grafana/latest/getting-started/getting-started-prometheus/

Hader, M., Elmhamedi, A., & Abouabdellah, A. (2020). *Notice of removal: Blockchain integrated ERP Fora Bette supply chain management* [Conference session]. 2020 IEEE 7th International Conference on Industrial Engineering and Applications (ICIEA). https://doi.org/10.1109/iciea49774.2020.9102084

Javaid, M., & Haleem, A. (2020). Critical components of Industry 5.0 towards a successful adoption in the field of manufacturing. *Journal of Industrial Integration and Management*, *05*(03), 327–348. https://doi.org/10.1142/s2424862220500141

Kłosowski, G., Kulisz, M., Lipski, J., Maj, M., & Bialek, R. (2021). The use of transfer learning with very deep convolutional neural network in quality management. *European Research Studies Journal*, *XXIV*(Special Issue 2), 253–263. https://doi.org/10.35808/ersj/2222

Kłosowski, G., Rymarczyk, T., Cieplak, T., Niderla, K., & Skowron, Ł. (2020). Quality assessment of the neural algorithms on the example of EIT-UST hybrid tomography. *Sensors*, *20*(11), 3324. https://doi.org/10.3390/s20113324

Kłosowski, G., Rymarczyk, T., Wójcik, D., Skowron, S., Cieplak, T., & Adamkiewicz, P. (2020). The use of time-frequency moments as inputs of LSTM network for ECG signal classification. *Electronics*, *9*(9), 1452. https://doi.org/10.3390/electronics9091452

Kovács, G., & Falagara Sigala, I. (2021). Lessons learned from humanitarian logistics to manage supply chain disruptions. *Journal of Supply Chain Management*, *57*(1), 41–49. https://doi.org/10.1111/jscm.12253

Megahed, A., Nazeem, A., Yin, P., Tata, S., Motahari Nezhad, H., & Nakamura, T. (2019). Optimizing cloud solutioning design. *Future Generation Computer Systems*, *91*, 86–95. https://doi.org/10.1016/j.future.2018.08.005

Nasir, V., & Sassani, F. (2021). A review on deep learning in machining and tool monitoring: Methods, opportunities, and challenges. *The International Journal of Advanced Manufacturing Technology*. https://doi.org/10.1007/s00170-021-07325-7

Özdemir, V., & Hekim, N. (2018). Birth of Industry 5.0: Making sense of big data with artificial intelligence, "the internet of things" and next-generation technology policy. *OMICS: A Journal of Integrative Biology, 22*(1), 65–76. https://doi.org/10.1089/omi.2017.0194

Rymarczyk, P., Malek, A., Nowak, R., & Dziwulski, J. (2021). Optimization of logistics processes of the supply chain using RFID technology. *European Research Studies Journal, XXIV*(Special Issue 2), 637–647. https://doi.org/10.35808/ersj/2292

Rymarczyk, T., Kłosowski, G., Hoła, A., Sikora, J., Wołowiec, T., Tchórzewski, P., & Skowron, S. (2021). Comparison of machine learning methods in electrical tomography for detecting moisture in building walls. *Energies, 14*(10), 2777. https://doi.org/10.3390/en14102777

Stewart, D., Okubo, N., Jehu, P., & Liu, M. (2020). Cloud migration trends and forecast | Deloitte Insights. Retrieved July 28, 2022, from https://www2.deloitte.com/xe/en/insights/industry/technology/technology-media-and-telecom-predictions/2021/cloud-migration-trends-and-forecast.html

Vakhania, N., & Mamporia, B. (2020). Fast algorithms for basic supply chain scheduling problems. *Mathematics, 8*(11), 1919. https://doi.org/10.3390/math8111919

Woźniakowski, T., Jałowiecki, P., Nowakowska, M., & Zmarzłowski, K. (2018). ERP systems and warehouse management by WMS. *Information System in Management*, 7(2), 141–152. https://doi.org/10.22630/isim.2018.7.2.13

9 Supporting modeling and optimization of business processes and consumer behavior by analyzing multi-source data using artificial intelligence methods

Paweł Rymarczyk, Tomasz Cieplak, Przemysław Adamkiewicz, Sylwia Skrzypek-Ahmed, Stanisław Skowron

Introduction

The ongoing changes in the ways that society perceives values make the market a place not only for concluding commercial transactions but also for establishing dialogue, exchanging experiences, and satisfying needs. Previous traditional customer relationship management strategies have focused on cost reduction and more effective management. Currently, customers are a source of information and revenues for a company, which is why it is important to constantly manage and improve these relationships and individualize one's customer-related processes. In addition, the client is a source and creator of values for a company; for example, good reputation, knowledge, and experience (McDonald, 2017; Oblander et al., 2019).

There have also been changes in marketing, i.e. its development and focus on relationship marketing that is centered on consumers, a presupposition toward an individual approach to them, and conducting numerous campaigns that are targeted at specific recipients. This is based on a detailed study of a buyer's behavior, profile, and long-term relationship between a company and its customer. Relationship marketing consists of establishing loyalty programs, encouraging customers to make regular purchases, identifying and analyzing the purchasing behaviors of the best and worst customers based on a marketing database, and integrating all of the business processes in enterprises (Kwiatek et al., 2020). This aims to better identify customers and their preferences and build "one-to-one" relationships (Munandar et al., 2020); it changes the approach of companies from "acquiring" to "acquiring and retaining" customers and making them loyal (Cerchia, 2016).

Reaching the customer (buyer) while analyzing and adapting the possibilities to the market's needs is a company's only chance to attract potential

DOI: 10.4324/9781003384311-9

customers with its offers and gain a competitive advantage; therefore, companies focus on continuously learning their customer's needs and preferences (i.e. the buyer's system of assessments and priorities) (Gordon et al., 2021). Customer satisfaction significantly affects the purchasing behaviors of consumers (Tarczydło, 2016); therefore, measuring satisfaction, loyalty, and customer satisfaction allows a company to determine those indicators that are important for its business results (such as market share or profit size). Thus, it is important to meet the needs and expectations of one's customers (earlier than the competition) from the point of view of a company by adapting products and services that are targeted to them and maintaining the relationships before and after their purchases. In addition, it is important to identify customers' opinions, attitudes, and preferences, as such information allows for defining a customer's profile, maintaining the customer, and ensuring his/her loyalty by improving the quality of the products and services that are offered (Salehan & Kim, 2016).

Due to the development of new technologies and tools for collecting and storing data, it is possible to deepen research areas regarding the analysis of the relationships and interactions between customers and enterprises using artificial intelligence methods. There are more and more solutions in the literature that are based on machine-learning methods (Rymarczyk et al., 2021), neural networks (Kłosowski, Rymarczyks, Cieplak, et al., 2020), LSTM (long short-term memory) (Kłosowski, Rymarczyk, Wójcik, et al., 2020), genetic algorithms (Zhang & Dai, 2019), and semantic networks (Al Madi & Khan, 2015). Using the methods mentioned above, it may be possible to analyze multi-source data that is obtained from sources such as social media, digital media (comments and opinions on the Internet), sales systems, POS (point of service), or loyalty systems.

In addition, a Big Data trend has emerged through the development of the technology, which has changed how data can be collected and stored (including data-storage devices, the data-storage architecture, or the data-access mechanism). Big Data is characterized by the ability to collect, store, and manage large amounts of data with high processing speeds and a large variety of data in order to discover hidden knowledge or information (Malhotra et al., 2017).

It is worth noting that data that is stored and used in some way can build a market advantage. Data and information are becoming essential resources for many organizations. Such data can be used as input data for the modeling and optimization of business processes as well as for the analysis and interpretation of consumer behavior and – furthermore – for the individualization of offered products and services. Based on an analysis that pertains to the history of purchased goods and services as well as the assessment of their credibility, it will be possible to forecast the customer's behavior and predict his/her sequence of purchases (Martínez et al., 2020). Sales forecasting allows companies to act well in advance, including supporting decisions when planning marketing activities and determining the time of introducing and withdrawing individual products from the market.

The main goal of the research was to enable and improve the analysis of multi-source data, human behavior, data mining, business processes, and as a result, the creation and provision of new, improved procedures and solutions using artificial intelligence algorithms. As a result of the research, the algorithms for optimizing business processes have been developed, a methodology for collecting and analyzing information that uses semantic networks and ontologies of information systems has been created, a complete system for profiling customers and potential contractors (including the effective use of time and resources) has been developed, and the necessary tools for measuring the effectiveness of advertising campaigns have been created. The solution's innovation in question consists of using artificial intelligence solutions and novel data analysis for personalizing the products and services that are offered.

Methods

The advanced intelligent information and the analytical system are a combination of applications and technologies that enable the collection, merging, gathering, selection, analysis, and clear presentation of information and business knowledge from various sources for the needs of a specific field of business activity.

The e-platform IT system will consist of the following:

- data-mining algorithms;
- internet agents;
- business-process models;
- input validation procedures based on selected data (and not rigid rules);
- data warehouse;
- adaptive user interface.

The proposed system enables the integration, analysis, and correlation of data that is collected from many sources, including data warehouses (i.a., in ERP systems), sales systems, POS, online stores, loyalty systems (both based on traditional card systems and RFID (radio-frequency identification)) – customer flow in stores, websites, beacons, and others – an indoor navigation system, Facebook (profile likes, posts, etc.), comments and opinions on the Internet, and ad words (tracking website traffic). In order to be able to use this data, it often must be properly adjusted, e.g. categorical data needs to be converted to numeric (binary) data for processing by machine-learning algorithms.

The research included the development of various algorithms that were based on artificial neural networks (LSTM, ANNs (Artificial neural networks), and GRU (Gated Recurrent Units)), stochastic methods (including genetic algorithms), statistical methods, fuzzy set theory, and semantic networks as well as their various connections.

Results

As part of the research, an information and analytical system (e-platform) that allows for analyzing people's behavior and business processes was created through an analysis of multi-source data with the use of artificial intelligence algorithms.

The functionality of the intelligent decision support system and business process modeling consists of managing strategic information (i.e. analyzing information) from the direct and indirect environment of a company, thus influencing its strategic development. The application makes it possible to download data from various sources as operational, tactical, and strategic business processes. As part of the system's operation, support for access procedures to all business information (data warehouse, other unrelated systems, information from websites) has been implemented. Furthermore, an appropriate agent that was based on artificial intelligence algorithms and semantic networks was created in order to collect data from internet resources.

The proposed e-platform includes a data-exchange module, a data analysis and presentation module, interface libraries, a management panel, and a user interface. The main basis of our business processes was created:

- analysis of advertising campaigns;
- analysis of customer profiles;
- route analysis;
- process mining;
- customer traffic map;
- sentiment assessment;
- prediction of customer outflow;
- loyalty systems;
- visualization of manufacturing process;
- human resource management;
- web resources;
- complexity of processes;
- POS (data from last day, week, month);
- expert system (drive train, running gear).

The system enables the optimization and formulation of new processes from the process database and data from the network resources (the use of computer-intelligence algorithms, semantic networks, and hybrid methods) and shows the relationship between the data and the processes. Various methods of computational intelligence have been used to formulate the processes. The tools for the intelligent automation of the decision-making processes can learn rules from the existing data to find relationships between the captured data and the subsequent behavior. A key additional task is to prepare a database of the business processes (which are automatically supplemented based on the new processes that are created).

As a result of the e-platform operation, market analyses can be carried out; these limit the risk that is related to the onset of selling the wrong products or producing their surpluses. The system allows for estimations of when discounts should be introduced, presenting specific items at exhibitions, or creating space for new collections; in addition, it determines which company employees perform repetitive sets of activities in given business situations. Based on the performed analysis, it is possible to distinguish employees' attitudes and behaviors, the duration of the processes, whether they end too early or too late, or why some activities are omitted. The results of several selected business processes from the basis that was discussed above are presented below.

Observing customer behavior

Based on customer behavior, it is possible to determine whether an influential customer will leave in the near future ("customer outflow") so that attempts can be made to retain him/her. Based on historical data, a decision regarding the planning of marketing activities for introducing new products to the market or withdrawing them can be made well in advance.

Such issues can be solved with the help of classification methods. The classifiers that are used for this task are Adaptive Boosting, K-neighbors, and XGBoost. The analyses are accurate due to the number of predictors, i.e. variables that are based on which a decision is made whether a given customer will leave. Figure 9.1 shows the application window in which a customer outflow analysis is generated.

Analysis of advertising campaigns

An analysis of the effectiveness of advertising campaigns is based on the prediction of the success or failure of a given advertising campaign in the future based on its previous behavior. Here, three predictive models were used: Gaussian Naive Bayes, Linear SVC, and the K-neighbors classifier; these are classifiers

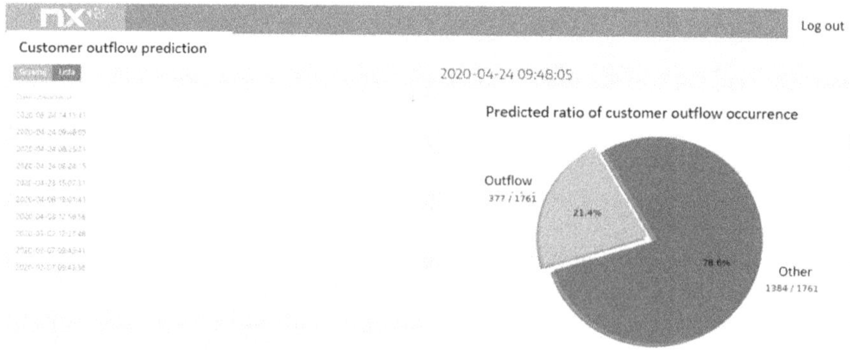

Figure 9.1 Customer outflow prediction window

that place a campaign that is being considered into a group of solutions for which success is predicted or one for which failure is predicted. Graphs that show the fit of models based on the test data are shown in Figure 9.2, while Figure 9.3 shows the results of the application that is responsible for analyzing advertising campaigns.

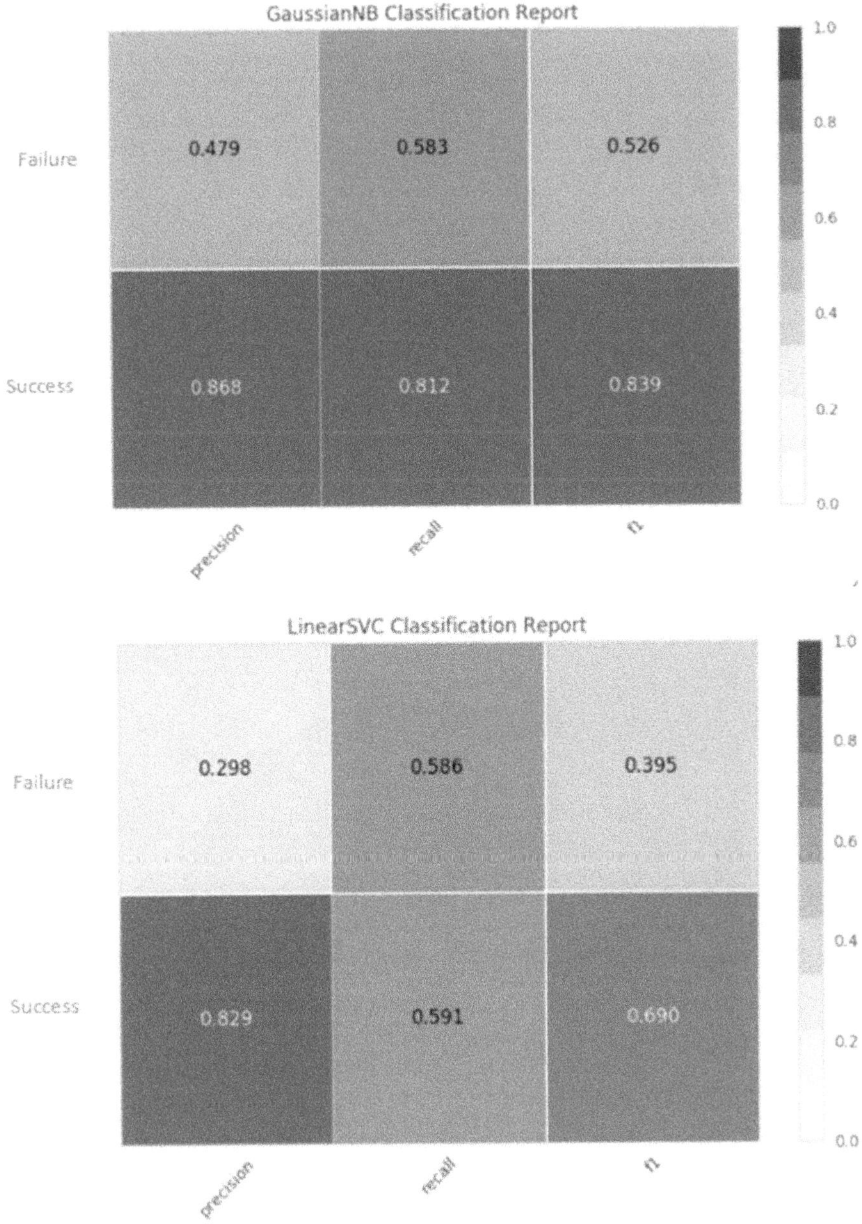

Figure 9.2 Prediction quality with GaussianNB (a), SVC (b), and KNClassifier (c) (*Continued*)

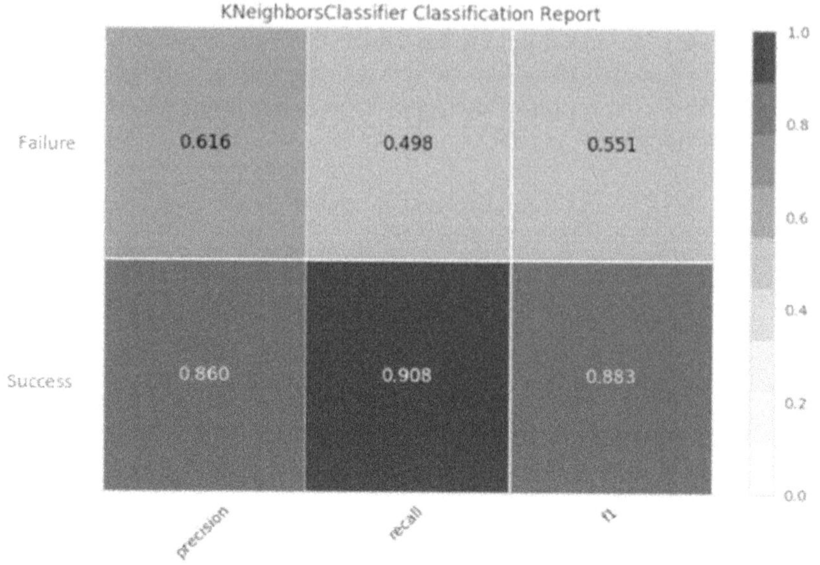

Figure 9.2 (Continued)

Sentiment analysis

With the help of procedures that use natural language processing (NLP) issues, it is possible to calculate customer satisfaction based on their comments on various observed portals. As a result, the appropriate direct or marketing steps can be taken to increase satisfaction with a company's services.

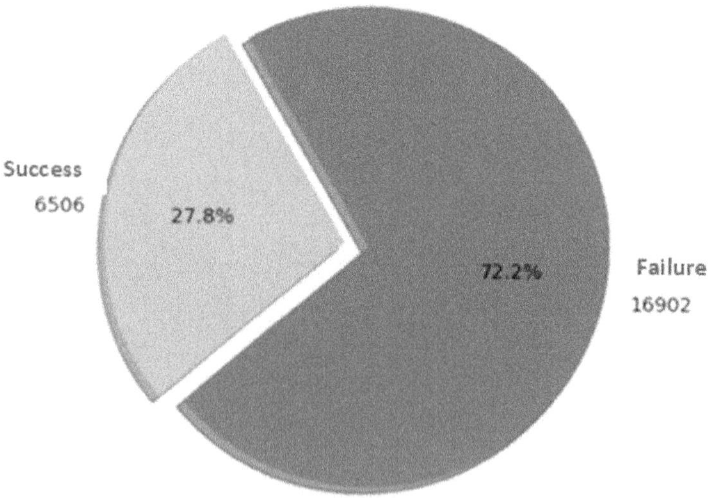

Figure 9.3 (Continued)

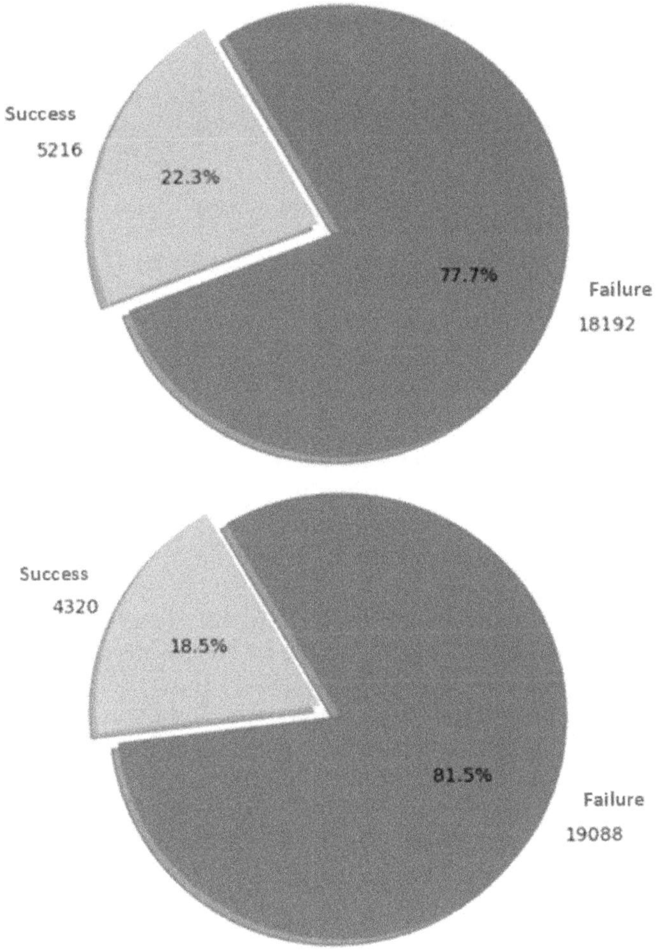

Figure 9.3 Results of advertising campaign analysis application for GaussianNB (a), SVC (b), and KNClassifier (c). *(Continued)*

Sentiment analysis is an NLP-processing problem in which the text is understood, and its intentions are predicted. For example, the algorithm predicts the sentiment of Polish texts as positive, neutral, or negative. Here, the focus was on the use of machine-learning and deep-learning tools. This was done using Python and the Keras deep-learning library. The CBOW and Skip-Gram neural network architecture was used, along with the hierarchical Softmax (hs) and negative sampling (ns) training algorithms.

An exemplary chart that illustrates the obtained sentiment value is shown in Figure 9.4. Here, the sentiment factor's determination can be determined (as in the case of the received data from POS) on three time horizons by analyzing the comments from the previous day, week, and month. As a result, the customer sentiment coefficient is a value that lies within a range

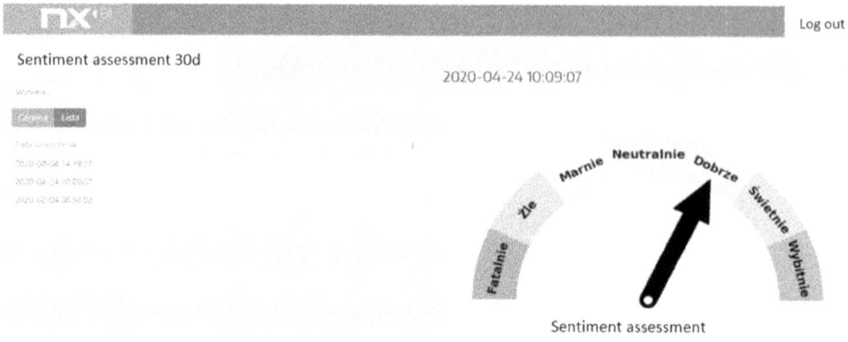

Figure 9.4 Sentiment analysis window

of [−1,1], where negative values represent the negative attitudes of customers toward a company, and positive values indicate positive attitudes.

Loyalty system analysis

An analysis of the implemented loyalty systems allows us to identify their actual impact on sales, making it possible to determine whether it is worth using them. The analyses carried out for this purpose use statistical methods and include, i.a., the average value of purchases and the number of products (depending on whether a customer is a member of the loyalty program or not). In addition, the time between the registration of a product and a first purchase is considered, as it may turn out that many people are issued such cards and use them very rarely. Figure 9.5 shows the sample findings that were obtained as a result of the algorithm.

Customer movement map

Using radio tomography technology, the movement of customers or employees can be monitored with the help of transmitters and receivers that are located in a room, shop, or warehouse in question. Based on the images from the RTI reconstruction (radio tomography), a so-called heat map can be drawn, which shows those places that are visited most often. By default, the procedure that is triggered by starting the application performs an analysis for the last 1000 reconstructions; in this case, however, there was also no problem for the user to select an image set to generate a heat map. Figure 9.6 shows the algorithm's results – a sample customer traffic map.

Route analysis

Route analysis is done through the use of genetic algorithms. Based on the given coordinates of points (cities, shops, etc.), a map finds the shortest

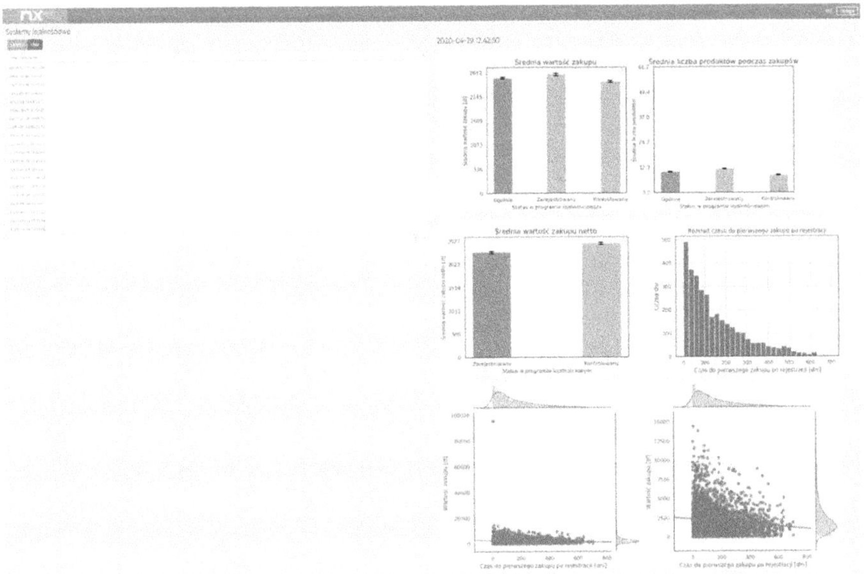

Figure 9.5 Loyalty system analysis window

paths between them; this allows us to optimize working times (e.g. delivery employees or those who are planning deliveries). The issue under consideration is directly related to the so-called traveling salesman problem (TSP).

The flow of the algorithm is as follows: creating a set of possible routes, determining a match, selecting a breeding set (a set of two combined routes to create a new route, which is then used to create the next set of possible

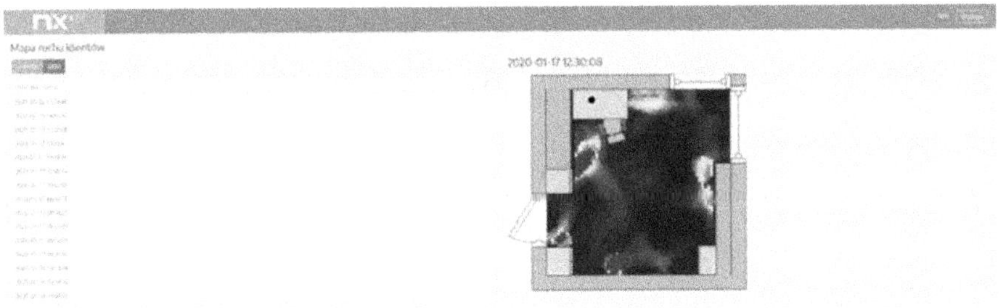

Figure 9.6 Customer traffic map window

Figure 9.7 Example of algorithm-mapping route

routes), propagating routes, mutation (a way of making changes to a population by randomly swapping two cities on a route), and repeating the operation until the results are satisfactory. Figure 9.7 shows the application window with the result of the algorithm – mapping an example route.

Discussion

In today's complex business world, companies need to develop ways of differentiating themselves from other market participants by becoming more cooperative, effective, precise, and flexible. They must be able to react quickly to market needs and changes. Depending on a company's competitive advantage, novelty, price, stellar website content, or social media presence, specific online strategies must be applied in order to reach the desired market. Many companies have noticed that the data that they store and use can build a market advantage. The appearance of new technologies and data-collection tools is now opening up research areas into understanding customer-business relationships and interactions. The effect of using artificial intelligence solutions and novel data analysis translates to the ability to create new business processes and customize (personalize) services and goods to customer requirements.

As a result of an analysis of customer behavior, it is possible to determine whether an influential customer will leave in the near future, thus enabling efforts to retain them. In addition, forecasting such behavior affects the activities of many company areas and supports decision-making in terms of the number of purchases, production planning, or logistics (Katelaris & Themistocleous, 2017).

Reaching a customer (buyer) while analyzing and adapting the possibilities to the market's needs is a company's only chance to attract potential customers with its offers and gain a competitive advantage. Therefore, it seems important to analyze the effectiveness of advertising campaigns; this is based on predicting the success or failure of a given campaign in the future based on its previous behavior. Such analyses also allow for the indirect evaluation of those employees who are responsible for a campaign; combined with other analyses that concern sales, for example, a company can effectively increase its profits by choosing, i.a., the appropriate service lives of subsequent products. Furthermore, trends or key behaviors can also be set by analyzing the behavior of historical campaigns, thus yielding the management information that is needed in order to create a general offer (adjust an offer and services to contractors) and manage possible implementations and sales (Sebastián-Morillas et al., 2020).

Due to the constantly growing importance of customer-relationship management, it is important to analyze customer opinions; this allows the monitoring of the relationships among a company and its customers in real-time and, if necessary, reacting quickly to delays, complaints, and poor product performance. Moreover, an analysis of individual products improves the quality of the products that are offered (Kasturia et al., 2020). In conjunction with sales analysis, this can also show the relationships between the numbers of products sold and any positive comments or even detect whether such comments are credible and do not deliberately tarnish a company's image. The sentiment analysis algorithm performs such an analysis.

In terms of optimizing business processes, it is also important to analyze loyalty systems, i.e. answering questions such as "Does signing up for a loyalty program affect a customer's spending habits?" Owing to this solution, it is possible to determine whether the introduction of a loyalty system in a company will measurably increase its income. This allows it to decide whether maintaining loyalty programs with appropriate discounts that are offered to members is profitable and brings the intended benefits by increasing its number of customers and, thus, its profits (Cheng et al., 2020).

In addition, an analysis of a customer movement map in combination with various data (e.g. regarding sales or a basket analysis) can contribute to the increased sales and work optimization of the employees. The generated map clearly shows those places where people have stayed most often, and it is also easy to see the paths of their most frequent movements. Based on such a map, it can be noticed, i.a., which customers choose places most often. Therefore, additional advertisements or discounts can be placed there; moreover, the store can even be rearranged to increase sales or optimize shopping times – especially during pandemics (Marmol et al., 2020).

The transport service is an important challenge for companies that are involved in planning procurement and distribution in supply chains. Proper route-planning allows them to optimize the working times of delivery employees or people who plan deliveries, for example, reducing transport costs and shortening the times of transport tasks. This will allow for the efficient use of time and resources (Jaiyen & Leksakul, 2020).

The results of the conducted research show that the use of artificial intelligence methods allows a company to optimize and create new business processes and consumer behaviors as well as adapt services and goods to customer requirements. The application learns indirectly by analyzing Big Data. Additionally, so-called hybrid solutions that combine several analyses can be created based on the presented algorithms. The designed algorithms develop methods and concepts for capturing, transmitting, collecting, and extracting information and its appropriate presentation.

Summary

The application objective of the research was to create an IT system that used artificial intelligence methods to analyze consumer behavior as well as optimize and generate innovative business processes through the analysis of multi-source data. Business models were created based on data from external sources, data warehouses, and internet resources. This data was the resource for the operation of the computational intelligence algorithms. As part of the research, new procedures and algorithms in theoretical computer science and numerical mathematics were developed by using the issues of neural networks, genetic algorithms, semantic networks, fuzzy set theory, statistical methods, stochastic methods, and hybrid algorithms.

The proposed system enables integration with a user through a web application that runs on the most popular web browsers, e.g. Chrome or Mozilla Firefox. Furthermore, it enables the performance of original analyses by using the possibility of connecting to various data sources and using ready-made algorithms by providing them with appropriate data.

Through market analyses, the created tool will reduce the risk that is associated with starting the sales of incorrect products or producing their surpluses, making decisions about maintaining loyalty programs, or conducting advertising campaigns. In addition, the system will allow companies to estimate when promotions should be introduced, when to present specific items at exhibitions, or when to create spaces for new collections. This will also enable them to optimize the working times of their employees.

References

Al Madi, N., & Khan, J. (2015). *Is learning by reading a book better than watching a movie? A computational analysis of semantic concept network growth during text and multimedia comprehension* [Conference session]. 2015 International Joint Conference on Neural Networks (IJCNN). https://doi.org/10.1109/ijcnn.2015.7280761

Cerchia, A. (2016). Social media – A strategy in developing customer relationship management. *Procedia Economics and Finance, 39*, 785–790. https://doi.org/10.1016/s2212-5671(16)30266-0

Cheng, F., Wu, C., & Chen, Y. (2020). Creating customer loyalty in online brand communities. *Computers in Human Behavior, 107*, 105752. https://doi.org/10.1016/j.chb.2018.10.018

Gordon, R. F., Jorge, M. O., & Rafael, B. P. (2021). Consumer behavior analysis and the marketing firm: Measures of performance. *Journal of Organizational Behavior Management, 41*(2), 97–123. https://doi.org/10.1080/01608061.2020.1860860

Jaiyen, E., & Leksakul, K. (2020). Application of element decomposing method for solving traveling salesman problems. *Thai Journal of Mathematics, 18*(4), 1715–1731.

Kasturia, V., Sharma, S., & Sharma, S. (2020). *Automatic product saleability prediction using sentiment analysis on user reviews* [Conference session]. 2020 10th International Conference on Cloud Computing, Data Science &Amp; Engineering (Confluence). https://doi.org/10.1109/confluence47617.2020.9058286

Katelaris, L., & Themistocleous, M. (2017). Predicting customer churn: Customer behavior forecasting for subscription-based organizations. In M. Themistocleous & V. Morabito (Eds.), *Information systems*. EMCIS 2017. Lecture notes in Business Information Processing. Springer.

Kłosowski, G., Rymarczyks, T., Cieplak, T., Niderla, K., & Skowron, Ł. (2020). Quality assessment of the neural algorithms on the example of EIT-UST hybrid tomography. *Sensors, 20*(11), 3324. https://doi.org/10.3390/s20113324

Kłosowski, G., Rymarczyk, T., Wójcik, D., Skowron, S., Cieplak, T., & Adamkiewicz, P. (2020). The use of time-frequency moments as inputs of LSTM network for ECG signal classification. *Electronics, 9*(9), 1452. https://doi.org/10.3390/electronics9091452

Kwiatek, P., Morgan, Z., & Thanasi-Boçe, M. (2020). The role of relationship quality and loyalty programs in building customer loyalty. *Journal of Business &Amp; Industrial Marketing, 35*(11), 1645–1657. https://doi.org/10.1108/jbim-02-2019-0093

Malhotra, S., Doja, M., Alam, B., & Alam, M. (2017). *Bigdata analysis and comparison of big data analytic approaches* [Conference session]. 2017 International Conference on Computing, Communication and Automation (ICCCA). https://doi.org/10.1109/ccaa.2017.8229821

Marmol, M., Martins, L., Hatami, S., Juan, A., & Fernandez, V. (2020). Using biased-randomized algorithms for the multi-period product display problem with dynamic attractiveness. *Algorithms, 13*(2), 34. https://doi.org/10.3390/a13020034

Martínez, A., Schmuck, C., Pereverzyev, S., Pirker, C., & Haltmeier, M. (2020). A machine learning framework for customer purchase prediction in the non-contractual setting. *European Journal of Operational Research, 281*(3), 588–596. https://doi.org/10.1016/j.ejor.2018.04.034

McDonald, M. (2017). Book review: The twelve powers of a marketing leader: How to succeed by building customer and company value. *International Journal of Market Research, 59*(2), 263–265. https://doi.org/10.2501/ijmr-2017-018

Munandar, J., Oktaviani, D., & Angraini, Y. (2020). How important is CRM toward customer's loyalty to conventional and Islamic bank marketing strategy? *Journal of Islamic Marketing, 13*(1), 246–263. https://doi.org/10.1108/jima-07-2019-0146

Oblander, E., Gupta, S., Mela, C., Winer, R., & Lehmann, D. (2019). The past, present, and future of customer management. *SSRN Electronic Journal*. https://doi.org/10.2139/ssrn.3445241

Rymarczyk, T., Kłosowski, G., Hoła, A., Sikora, J., Wołowiec, T., Tchórzewski, P., & Skowron, S. (2021). Comparison of machine learning methods in electrical tomography for detecting moisture in building walls. *Energies, 14*(10), 2777. https://doi.org/10.3390/en14102777

Rymarczyk, P., Malek, A., Nowak, R., & Dziwulski, J. (2021). Optimization of logistics processes of the supply chain using RFID technology. *European Research Studies Journal, XXIV*(Special Issue 2), 637–647. https://doi.org/10.35808/ersj/2292

Salehan, M., & Kim, D. (2016). Predicting the performance of online consumer reviews: A sentiment mining approach to big data analytics. *Decision Support Systems, 81*, 30–40. https://doi.org/10.1016/j.dss.2015.10.006

Sebastián-Morillas, A., Muñoz-Sastre, D., & Núñez-Cansado, M. (2020). Relevance of communication strategy and its relationship with insight to achieve advertising effectiveness: The Spanish case. *Cuadernos.info, 46*, 249–280

Tarczydło, B. (2016). Trends in marketing communication for brands – Selected aspects. *Marketing I Zarządzanie, 45*, 381–392. https://doi.org/10.18276/miz.2016.45-34

Zhang, Z., & Dai, Y. (2019). Combination classification method for customer relationship management. *Asia Pacific Journal of Marketing and Logistics, 32*(5), 1004–1022. https://doi.org/10.1108/apjml-03-2019-0125

10 Importance of human capital management in health care institutions

Artur Paździor

The nature and structure of human capital

A modern enterprise's competitive position depends on a number of tangible and intangible factors, both financial and non-financial (cf. Paździor, 2013, pp. 5–25). Financially, they determine growth and profitability (Kumar, 2015, p. 75). The complexity of modern socio-economic systems makes intangible, non-financial resources, such as knowledge, skills, and technological and intellectual resources, increasingly important in generating value (Kateb, 2014, p. 630). While technologies are reflected in the system of financial records and reporting, intellectual resources, although they have always existed (Rzemieniak, 2013, pp. 89–91), have not yet been incorporated into the financial statements of enterprises. In the course of time, this has resulted in a significant gap between the accounting and market values of companies. The need for reliable information was also evident in the area of intellectual capital, as reported by numerous stakeholder groups (cf. Kateb, 2014, p. 630).

The heterogeneity of intellectual capital is one reason for the absence of its inclusion in financial reporting. Essentially, it could be defined as a sum of the impacts of human and structural capital. A company's human capital is intrinsically linked to the experience, knowledge, qualifications, competencies, and capabilities of its workforce. On the other hand, structural capital takes the form of information flow systems, acquired concessions, customer databases, etc. In contrast to human capital, it is owned by a business and can be traded (Bal-Woźniak et al., 2015, p. 51).

Juchnowicz (2014) believes the fundamental principle of managing modern enterprises is the belief that human capital is the most valuable asset of the organization. As a key component of intellectual capital, it contributes to the value of the enterprise by replacing, in a sense, physical and financial capital (Jawor-Joniewicz et al., 2018, p. 33). According to Rzepka (2018, p. 251), the overall value of an organization is influenced by intellectual capital, which consists of human and structural capital, as well as material capital comprised of physical and financial capital.

Proper management of human capital can be seen in the efficient motivation of employees and ensures the survival of enterprises in the long run

DOI: 10.4324/9781003384311-10

(Włodarkiewicz-Klimek, 2018, pp. 34–35). The importance of this is particularly apparent in organizations where labor costs (e.g. salaries, social security contributions, and external services associated with contracts under civil law) account for a large portion of operating costs. Entities in this category include, in particular, professional service companies such as law firms, accounting offices, consulting companies, and hospitals. In a well-run medical institution, the proportion of labor costs should not exceed 60%; in the United States in 2018 the proportion was below 55% (Daly, 2019), but for Poland, in 2015 it reached a level of 70% (Lurka, 2016). Because personnel costs represent such a large portion of operating costs, even a small change in this group of costs can drastically impact an organization's financial performance. Therefore, proper planning and management of personnel costs are essential to the success of Polish hospitals. On the one hand, one should reward the knowledge and commitment of medical staff, who in many cases generate revenue. Reputable, highly trained physicians are sought after by patients who seek high-quality treatment. This is also observed by institutions that establish and operate medical facilities as well as those in management roles who strive to attract the best, and therefore the most expensive, medical professionals to their facilities.

With the increasing importance of intellectual resources in organizations, there is a growing demand for reliable information on how this capital impacts the financial health of the entity (Paździor, 2015, p. 31). This holds true for the medical sector as well. It has not yet been possible to develop a reliable, objective method of measuring this capital (Azad & Mohajeri, 2012, p. 512; Kristandl & Bontis, 2007, p. 1511). This is related not only to the form of ownership of the resources and the challenges in assessing their effectiveness since hospitals utilize a wide variety of forms of employment and cooperation among their medical staff.

Methods for measuring the effectiveness of human capital in a hospital

Efficiency is an ambiguous and multidimensional concept that is most often identified with effectiveness or performance. It is the outcome of the actions taken, measured as the relationship between the results obtained and the cost incurred (Jedliński & Kruszczak, 2020). Some equate efficiency with economic activity that is carried out efficiently, and thus effectively and economically. On the other hand, Winkler points out that efficiency can be thought of as obtaining a result that is similar to the one planned, or as a relation between the Value of the result achieved and expenditure incurred (Winkler, 2010, pp. 105–106). Efficiency is similarly defined by Poskart (2014, p. 180), according to whom it can be expressed as the ratio between the results achieved and the expenditure required for achieving the objectives.

The concept of economic efficiency is hard to apply to medical entities. The concept of organizational and social efficiency may be relevant to this sector. The former is described as the ability of an organization to adapt to changes occurring in the environment as well as the ability to productively utilize its resources to achieve specific goals. The efficiency of management and non-economic efficiency are included in this category (Szymańska, 2010, p. 156). In the context of medical entities, social efficiency can be seen as an effort to ensure society's health and security. The goal is to ensure that patients receive the necessary care in the shortest amount of time. This includes diagnosis, time spent waiting for an appointment with a specialist, hospitalization, rehabilitation wait times, etc. This type of efficiency also includes accuracy, measured by the number of incorrect diagnoses and post-operative complications.

The analysis of human capital efficiency is a special type of analysis that aims to complement information about an organization's efficiency. Efficiency in the use of human resources can be measured by a number of indicators which include, among others, productivity, cost-effectiveness, labor profitability, and indicators related to the operating cost structure, labor, etc. The efficiency of human resources can also be measured through indicators of added value and return on investment in human capital (Janik, 2017, p. 110; Mentel et al., 2014, pp. 398–406). Generally, the efficiency of human resources can be measured by the amount of revenue per employee. It is primarily determined by the prices charged and the structure of medical services provided. As a result, critical information about the use of human capital can be obtained not only by comparing indicators over individual time periods but also by comparing the efficiency of other entities (Zagórowski, 2018).

An analysis of the hospital's characteristics

The hospital under consideration is located in Poland, in the northern part of the Lublin Voivodeship. The hospital was founded by the District Office (Starostwo Powiatowe). The hospital's main function is to provide health care to the residents of the Lublin Voivodeship.

The hospital is a separate organizational unit with its own personnel and assets dedicated to providing comprehensive medical services regarding health promotion, preventive health care, health maintenance and improvement, as well as rehabilitation. A hospital's main purpose is to provide comprehensive health services to citizens of Poland, citizens of EU member states, and other foreigners. The hospital provides specialized in-patient and out-patient health services at hospital wards as well as a network of specialized clinics. The organizational structure of the hospital consists of ten wards, seventeen specialized clinics, a physiotherapy and rehabilitation center, four diagnostic laboratories, and a childbirth school.

There are not too many hospitals in the immediate vicinity of the hospital. Theoretically, it should facilitate exposing the hospital's strengths and limiting the weaknesses in its operation (see Table 10.1).

Table 10.1 Strengths and weaknesses of the hospital under analysis

Strengths	*Weaknesses*
• Location – all organizational units of the hospital are located in one geographical area • New and modernized technical infrastructure adequate to the current requirements of providing health care • Modern medical equipment enabling the implementation of health services at a high-quality level • A helicopter pad • A broad and comprehensive range of health services provided by the hospital • Experienced and qualified administrative and technical staff • Well-trained medical and nursing staff • An efficient IT system • A strong bond between the nursing staff and the hospital (employment agreements) • A flexible remuneration system (contract agreements)	• Lack of modern ventilation or air conditioning systems • Outdated hospital beds • Lack of magnetic resonance imaging laboratory • Bed occupancy rates are low in some wards • A small number of births in the department of obstetrics and gynecology • A relatively low percentage of planned hospitalizations • Few planned diagnostic procedures in the computed tomography lab • The coordination of work between specialized clinics and hospital wards is insufficient • The hospital does not have a surgical clinic • Medical and nursing staff shortages • Medical staff labor costs are high and difficult to plan • Various professional groups make numerous and often unjustified claims regarding wages

Source: Own study based on hospital data and an interview conducted with the hospital management.

The hospital's financial situation

Despite the hospital's relative competitive advantage and its numerous strengths, its financial condition during the study period was less than ideal. Upon analysis of the entity's economic and financial position, the following conclusions are drawn:

- in the 2018 to 2020 period, the value of the hospital's balance sheet total decreased from PLN 24.4 million to PLN 21.3 million. The decrease was caused by a drop in property, plant, and equipment, the value of which fell from PLN 15.8 million to PLN 11.7 million over the period. These numbers do not speak well of the way entity's development policy is being implemented;
- during this period, the property portfolio was mostly made up of fixed assets whose proportion ranged from 60.2% to approx. 65.3%. Over the years studied, the share of current assets increased from 34.7% to 39.8%;
- The hospital would finance approximately two-thirds to three-fourths of its assets with external funding every year. However, this seemingly unfavorable scenario should not be interpreted negatively, considering

the fact that approximately 60% of the value of the hospital's foreign capital in the period studied represented EU subsidy accruals. If the debt ratio had been estimated by taking only repayable foreign capital into account, its value would have been no higher than 33%;

- A positive development occurred with the increase in sales revenues observed from 2018 to 2020. Sales revenues increased from PLN 34 million to almost PLN 42 million (an increase of almost PLN 8 million). Despite a 23% increase, operating expenses increased by 28% mainly due to personnel costs; in 2020, operating expenses were over PLN 10 million higher than in 2018. As a consequence, sales losses increased from PLN 3.0 million in 2018 to PLN 5.7 million in 2020, and net profit declined from PLN 33.5 thousand gain in 2018 to a loss of over PLN 2.2 million in 2020. Losses from operational activities, gross and net, would have been much higher if it had not been for the relatively large amount of subsidies, which were included in other operating income.
- In 2018, the hospital had a positive cash flow from operating activities of PLN 977,000, allowing it to partially finance investment projects with its own funds. Yet, a large portion of the investments was still financed by external capital (mainly EU subsidies), as indicated by high revenues from financial activities. The situation attested to the strong commitment of the hospital's management toward continued development with non-refundable EU funding.
- It is concerning to see how cash flows had been structured in 2019–2020 when operational activities were in the red. Still, the hospital continued with its investment program, albeit on a small scale (investment expenses were lower than depreciation costs). This negative trend resulted in a drop in the value of assets, which in the long run may lead to a decrease in the utility value of medical equipment and consequently will have a negative impact on the lump-sum tax.
- The hospital's method of financing its assets over the examined period was moderately conservative. This is evidenced by the value of the debt-return ratio, which was below 33% in the reviewed years. For each examined year, less than 1/3 of the hospital's assets were financed with foreign capital that needed to be repaid. Non-refundable EU grants financed the hospital's assets in large part.
- The hospital failed to adhere to the golden rule of company finance over the analyzed period. The golden rule of finance was followed in 2018 and 2019, but only as of 31 December 2020, it was not, which stemmed mainly from a decrease in equity value due to the net loss generated by the entity. Nevertheless, in 2018–2019, the hospital's fixed assets were entirely (and at the end of 2020 almost entirely) financed with fixed capital. As a consequence, as of 31 December 2020, there was a moderate level of financial risk associated with the hospital's property and capital structure.
- A deteriorating property and capital structure are resulting in declining values of the indicator of the general financial situation. Given the

favorable structure of foreign capital, it can be concluded that as of 31 December 2020, there are no serious issues related to the hospital's financial stability.

- For each examined year, most of the ROS and ROE ratios were negative. 2018 was the most favorable year since the hospital recorded positive values across most return indicators. In previous years, almost all indicators recorded negative values due to the hospital's losses. There was one positive exception to this rule – the EBITDA indicator that included operating profit plus depreciation and amortization. Especially noteworthy is how rapidly the deficit has deepened at the hospital in recent years. Based on this, it can be concluded that without the implementation of corrective measures, the examined entity may soon be in need of recapitalization.

Based on the assessment, it appears that the financial situation of the hospital deteriorated significantly over that time period. As personnel costs make up a large portion of operating and overall costs, it seems appropriate to investigate changes in the most important items included in the balance sheet or profit and loss account in order to analyze the dynamics of profitability and deficit of the hospital.

Reasons for changes in the hospital's financial condition

In order to determine the factors contributing to the deteriorating financial condition of the hospital, an analysis of the most significant elements of its financial statements is presented below. It shows that there was a decline in the hospital's assets between 2018 and 2020. The decline can be seen in a fall in the value of fixed assets (primarily the value of machines and equipment, and medical equipment). This does not speak well of the entity's economic and medical potential. During the period under consideration, there was also a clear decrease in the book value (equity) of the hospital, which was the result of a net loss. It is noteworthy, however, that its sales revenues increased by nearly 23%. Since the value of fixed assets decreased during that period, it can be concluded that the increase in sales may have been caused by a higher valuation of medical procedures by the insurer, i.e. NFZ (the National Health Fund), rather than the hospital providing more services. A second factor that might have contributed to increased revenues is a better organization of the hospital's operations. An analysis of administrative and medical statistics shows that during the period the hospital bed count did not increase and patient stay length decreased. Neither the hours nor conditions of work were altered. Thus, those facts support the hypothesis regarding the positive effect of the NFZ's procedure valuation change on the value of sales at the hospital.

With such favorable conditions, it is reasonable to ask about the causes of the deteriorating financial condition that occurred without radical measures such as large expenditures on the reconstruction and modernization of fixed assets (which, when combined with an increase in revenues, should have improved rather than deteriorated the hospital's financial result). Based on changes to profit and loss account items, it seems reasonable to put forward a claim concerning the hospital's human resources management negatively affecting its economic efficiency (see Table 10.2).

Based on the financial data above, it can be concluded that the primary cause behind the deteriorating financial situation of the hospital is a lack of control over costs associated with personnel. It can be seen both in costs related to salaries and social security (salaried employees) and external service costs (employees paid for by contract and those paid on a fee-for-task basis). This is evident when we compare the change in sales revenue (22.6%) with the change in the aforementioned costs associated with personnel (23.38% and 35.62%, respectively). The comparison shows that hospital employees (mainly physicians on contract) were paid salaries unrelated to the hospital's revenues from medical procedures. In order to better understand the impact of human capital on the hospital's financial condition, a detailed assessment of the effectiveness of human resource management in the hospital is presented below.

Assessment of the efficiency of the hospital's human resources

During the years of 2018–2020, the entity employed over 330 people (see Table 10.3).

As shown in Table 10.3, the hospital uses a variety of employment forms. Contractual agreements dominated when it comes to the employment of physicians throughout the study period, as did employment agreements for other professions. Fee-for-task agreements were used less frequently. Having such diverse forms of employment makes it difficult to analyze the primary factor that affects profitability/deficit in medical entities, namely labor resources. The analysis that was carried out for the hospital's reorganization and for the purposes of this chapter was designed to take all available information into account so that it could provide reliable and useful results and recommendations to the hospital's board of directors. Table 10.4 shows the synthetic results of this analysis.

Based on the presented indicators, it was possible to observe an unfavorable trend characterized by a change in the cost intensity of human resources that outpaced their productivity during the period studied. Specifically, this applies to the cost-effectiveness of contractual employees. Considering the fact that most of these employees were physicians, it can be argued that the system of their remuneration in the analyzed hospital was unjustified from an economic standpoint. In light of the fact that total labor costs in the studied years accounted for over 90% of operating costs, it can be argued that without any measures designed to regulate the salaries of medical staff, any increases

Table 10.2 Dynamics of the hospital's selected financial data

No	Description	2018	2019	2020	Change in PLN			Change in %
					2018–2020	2018–2019	2019–2020	2018–2020
IV.	**Data for calculation**							
1.	Total assets	24,402,195	22,501,384	21,319,493	−3,082,701	−1,900,810	−1,181,891	−12.63%
2.	Assets	15,930,730	14,301,521	12,834,903	−3,095,827	−1,629,209	−1,466,618	−19.43%
3.	Current assets	8,471,465	8,199,863	8,484,590	13,126	−271,602	284,727	0.15%
4.	Equity	8,462,850	7,276,508	5,055,327	−3,407,523	−1,186,341	−2,221,182	−40.26%
5.	Liabilities	15,939,345	15,224,876	16,264,167	324,822	−714,469	1,039,291	2.04%
6.	Sales revenue	33,858,118	38,656,398	41,510,491	7,652,372	4,798,280	2,854,092	22.60%
7.	Operating expenses	36,872,786	42,528,819	47,170,738	10,297,952	5,656,033	4,641,919	27.93%
8.	Total labor costs	30,946,986	35,513,274	39,504,455	8,557,469	4,566,288	3,991,182	27.65%
9.	Costs of external services related to salaries	10,799,849	12,810,253	14,646,826	3,846,977	2,010,404	1,836,573	35.62%
10.	Costs associated with salaries and social security	20,147,137	22,703,021	24,857,629	4,710,493	2,555,884	2,154,609	23.38%
11.	Salaries	16,787,638	18,975,419	20,668,482	3,880,844	2,187,780	1,693,064	23.12%
12.	Profit from sales	−3,014,668	−3,872,421	−5,660,248	−2,645,579	−857,753	−1,787,827	–
13.	Operating profit	−15,690	−1,221,035	−2,229,014	−2,213,324	−1,205,345	−1,007,979	–
14.	Gross profit	33,482	−1,184,839	−2,221,182	−2,254,664	−1,218,322	−1,036,342	−6733.90%
15.	Net profit	33,482	−1,186,341	−2,221,182	−2,254,664	−1,219,824	−1,034,840	−6733.90%

Source: Own elaboration based on the hospital's financial statements.

Table 10.3 Structure of employment at the hospital

Profession	*2018*	*2019*	*2020*
Physicians	14.14	14.66	15.27
Additionally – contracts	*71*	*65*	*85*
Additionally – fee-for-task agreements	*8*	*13*	*8*
Pharmacists	1	1	1
Other senior staff	26.18	26.64	27.33
Additionally – contracts	*1*	*2*	*3*
Additionally – fee-for-task agreements	*2*	*2*	*2*
Administration staff	25.33	26.25	25.75
Total mid-level staff, including:	217.34	221.87	223.67
Additionally – fee-for-task agreements	*7*	*0*	*0*
Nurses	143.16	138.13	139.66
Additionally – fee-for-task agreements	*6*	*7*	*6*
Midwives	23.75	25	24
Medical technicians	16	15.66	15.48
Additionally – fee-for-task agreements	*1*	*1*	*1*
Other mid-level staff	34.33	43.08	44.51
Additionally – contracts	*0*	*0*	*2*
Lower rank staff	13.91	13.86	13.98
Maintenance staff	34.33	33.49	31.66
Additionally – fee-for-task agreements	*2*	*2*	*1*
Total (FTEs)	**332.23**	**337.77**	**338.66**
Total (contracts)	72	67	90
Total (fee-for-task agreements)	26	25	18

Source: Own elaboration based on hospital data and an interview conducted with the Financial and Accounting Department of the hospital.

in revenues will result in a deeper operating loss, which will result in lower returns on human capital.

Summary and conclusions

The aim of the chapter was to identify key factors in the area of human resources, affecting the economic and financial condition of medical entities by studying one of the hospitals in Lublin Province (Voivodeship), Poland. The goal was achieved via an in-depth review of the literature and an analysis of the hospital's financial statements along with other documents.

The analysis shows that from 2018 to 2020 there was a decline in the financial condition of the hospital. This can be seen, among other things, in the growing loss as well as in a lack of development or replacement investments. It is puzzling that this trend coincided with a 22.6% increase in sales revenues resulting mainly from independent factors such as a more favorable valuation of medical procedures by the insurer (NFZ). Since the value of total labor costs increased by approximately 28% and the costs of external services under contracts increased by nearly 36% over the same period, it can be concluded that medical personnel (mainly contract physicians) earned

Table 10.4 Human resources analysis results

No	*Description*	*Formula for calculation*	*2018*	*2019*	*2020*	*Change (%)*
1.	Human resource productivity	Revenues/total number of employees/12	6558	7496	7745	18.09
2.	Total cost-effectiveness of human resources	Total labor costs/total number of employees/12	5994	6886	7370	22.96
3.	Cost-effectiveness of outsourced human resources	External services related to salaries/number of non-permanent employees/12	9184	11,603	11,302	23.06
4.	Cost-effectiveness of own human resources	Costs associated with salaries and social security/number of full-time employees/12	5054	5601	6117	21.04
5.	Labor sales profitability	Sales profit/total number of employees/12	−583.9	−750.9	−1056.0	80.85
6.	Operational labor profitability	Operating profit/total number of employees/12	−3.0	−236.8	−415.9	13,583.96
7.	Net profitability of labor	Net profit/total number of employees/12	6.5	−230.0	−414.4	−6489.88
8.	Human Capital Return on Investment (HCROI)	(Revenue – operating costs excluding total labor costs)/total labor costs	90.3%	89.1%	85.7%	−5.08
9.	Human Capital Value Added (HCVA)	(Revenue – operating expenses excluding total labor costs)/total number of employees	5410	6135	6314	16.71

Note: Total labor costs include salary costs, social security costs, and salaries-related external costs.

Source: Own elaboration based on the hospital's financial statements and an interview with the Financial and Accounting Department and the HR and Payroll Department of the hospital.

salaries that were not reflective of the increase in medical procedures. The analysis of the dynamics of the most important items included in the balance sheet or profit and loss account clearly shows that the main factor in the deteriorating financial condition of the hospital was a lack of control over personnel costs.

A detailed analysis of human resources showed that in the 2018–2020 period there were distinct discrepancies between the productivity of these resources (an increase of about 18%) and their cost-effectiveness (an increase of nearly 23%). These negative phenomena were also reflected in deteriorating values of Human Capital Return on Investment and in the increase in the Human Capital Value Added that was significantly lower than the change in the levels of total cost-effectiveness of human resources, the cost-effectiveness of outsourced human resources, and the cost-effectiveness of own human resources.

Based on all the analyses carried out for the purposes of hospital reorganization and for the purposes of this chapter, it can be concluded that the primary factor affecting medical entities' financial health is the efficient control over the employment and compensation of medical workers (primarily physicians). Without proper supervision over human resources management, even increasing valuations of medical procedures by the insurer will not be able to improve profitability (deficit reduction), nor will the hospital be able to afford to take care of its infrastructure (new medical equipment). Therefore, there is an urgent need to find a compromise that takes into account the interests of medical personnel (wage pressures), the needs and goals of the management boards and other stakeholders (stable financial condition, control of costs), and patients whose needs and goals are often neglected and for whom medical institutions exist.

References

Azad, N., & Mohajeri, L. (2012). The effects of intellectual capital on financial performance: A case study of petrochemical and pharmaceutical firms. *Management Science Letters*, *2*(2), 511–516. https://doi.org/10.5267/j.msl.2011.12.022

Bal-Woźniak, M., Firszt, D., Jabłoński, Ł., Soczyńska, E., & Woźniak, G. (2015). *Human capital in the development of innovative economy and management of enterprise innovation*. Polskie Wydawnictwo Ekonomiczne.

Daly, R. (2019). *Hospitals innovate to control labor costs*. hfma. Retrieved June 14, 2021, from https://www.hfma.org/topics/hfm/2019/october/hospitals-innovate-to-control-labor-costs.html

Janik, W. (2017). *Management of labour resources in an enterprise*. Lublin University of Technology.

Jawor-Joniewicz, A., Warwas, I., & Wiktorowicz, J. (2018). *Human capital and management of many generations in the organization*. Wydawnictwo Uniwersytetu Łódzkiego.

Jedliński, P., & Kruszczak, K. (2020). *Efektywność*. Encyklopedia Zarządzania. Retrieved June 14, 2021, from https://mfiles.pl/pl/index.php/Efektywno%C5%9B%C4%87

Juchnowicz, M. (Ed.) (2014). *Zarządzanie kapitałem ludzkim*. Wydawnictwo PWE.

Kateb, I. (2014). The determinants of intellectual capital disclosure: Evidence from French stock exchange. *International Journal of Accounting and Financial Reporting, 4*(2). https://doi.org/10.5296/ijafr.v4i2.6579

Kristandl, G., & Bontis, N. (2007). Constructing a definition for intangibles using the resource based view of the firm. *Management Decision, 45*(9), 1510–1524. https://doi.org/10.1108/00251740710828744

Kumar, R. (2015). Determinants of value creation: An empirical examination from UAE market. *International Journal of Economics and Financial Issues, 5*(1), 75–85.

Lurka, K. (2016). *Eksperci przeanalizowali finanse SPZOZ-ów*. Termedia.pl. Retrieved June 14, 2022, from https://www.termedia.pl/mz/Eksperci-przeanalizowali-finanse-SPZOZ-ow,23655.html

Mentel, G., Migała-Warchoł, A., & Sobolewski, M. (2014). Wpływ kapitału ludzkiego na wyniki finansowe organizacji. *Zeszyty Naukowe - Uniwersytet Szczeciński*, 66, 395–408, from Wpływ kapitału ludzkiego na wyniki finansowe organizacji - Mentel Grzegorz | Polona.

Paździor, A. (2013). *Valuation of the value of the company in the conditions of destabilization of financial markets*. Difin.

Paździor, A. (2015). *Value management of a modern enterprise*. Lublin University of Technology.

Poskart, R. (2014). A definition of the concept of economic effectiveness. *Central and Eastern European Journal of Management and Economics, 2*(3), 179–187.

Rzemieniak, M. (2013). *Management of intangible assets of enterprises*. Dom Organizatora.

Rzepka, A. (2018). Intellectual capital in inter-regional cooperation. Studia i Prace WNEiZ, 51, 249–259. https://doi.org/10.18276/sip.2018.51/2-21

Szymańska, E. (2010). Effectiveness of enterprises – defining and measuring. *Roczniki Nauk Rolniczych*, Seria G, *97*, notebook 2.

Winkler, R. (2010). Effectiveness – an attempt to conceptualize the concept. *Zeszyty Naukowe Uniwersytetu Ekonomicznego w Krakowie*, 820.

Włodarkiewicz-Klimek, H. (2018). *Human capital in shaping the agility of knowledge-based enterprises*. Poznań University of Technology Publishing House.

Zagórowski, J. (2018). Effectiveness of using human resources in the IT industry on the example of a selected enterprise. *Scientific Papers of Silesian University of Technology. Organization and Management Series, 2018*(120), 245–255. https://doi.org/10.29119/1641-3466.2018.120.20

11 Innovations in management education about sustainable development in Industry 5.0

Barbara Mazur, Anna Walczyna

Introduction

In today's world, innovative education is one of the most important factors determining the success or failure of companies as innovation is "the lifeblood of every organization" (DeLoach, 2019). In recent years, innovation has been increasingly discussed in the management literature as it has become increasingly important (Ciumara, 2013). In addition to managerial skills and their effective practical application, innovation in management involves determination and courage in taking responsibility for implementing changes that lead to growth.

Educating managers in innovative ways is equally important. In managerial education, any efforts to introduce innovative changes in a specific context are considered innovative. A pedagogical approach such as this aims to provide students with more thorough preparation for the role of future managers who will make interactive decisions on behalf of the organization (Béchard, 2005). In order to make such changes, the curriculum and teaching methods must be reorganized. They can be an innovative act and, as a result of the increasing commercialization of education, are necessary for the postmodern educational system (Manea, 2015).

The development of each country is associated with and dependent on high-quality education (Kar & Lillian, 2018). For more than two decades, education has been recognized as playing a critical role in transforming society to become more sustainable (UNESCO, 2005; United Nations, 2012). The importance of fulfilling this role has been confirmed by the research conducted by Swedish students, which demonstrated that learning about sustainability improves knowledge, skills, and competencies in this field (Pauw et al., 2015). The higher education system is also considered to be an integral part of the global community's efforts to implement sustainable development principles (Mazur et al., 2021). In light of the fact that universities are one of the most important education hubs, incorporating the principles of sustainable development into curriculums can provide students with the skills and knowledge to change systemic structures and demands of a new and more sustainable paradigm in social and business development (Setó-Pamies & Papaoikonomou, 2015). The need for this is further increased by the fact

DOI: 10.4324/9781003384311-11

that deficiencies in this area of education still exist (Brundiers & Wiek, 2017; Molera et al., 2021).

According to sustainable development experts, in order for universities to fulfill their role in this area of education well, teaching paradigms must change. Such a change should be of an epistemological nature that leads to a balance based on holism, subjectivity, and systems thinking (Sterling, 2004). The implementation of education aimed at sustainable development poses a challenge that requires reformulating curriculums and educational models in a way that enables students to be seen as actors who work in the interests of society. An example of such a comprehensive approach is available at Spanish universities (Molera et al., 2021).

In the field of sustainable development, university education aims to promote and shape competencies that allow students to reflect on their own actions broadly. The reflection should take into account the social, economic, environmental, and cultural impacts of these actions, past and present, as well as how they are assessed from a local and global perspective, recognizing that the ultimate aim of these actions is to promote sustainable societies (UNESCO, 2017). In order for the social transition toward a more sustainable world to be long-lasting, education should be creative, innovative, constructive, culturally relevant, and action-oriented (Tilbury & Wortman, 2004).

In its traditional form, education in management focuses on business skills (marketing, accounting, etc.) and the acquisition of professional competencies (strategic planning, operational management, etc.), preserving existing development concepts. To become future-oriented, it must incorporate innovation and combine traditional business skills training with creative thinking skills and the ability to synthesize knowledge. Managers should be aware of the influences of social, political, economic, technological, and ecological factors on their decisions. They must also understand and be able to assess the impact of their management practices and planning choices on local communities and the environment. As sustainability requires a cross-sectoral and interdisciplinary approach, "sustainable managers" should have a long-term outlook while meeting short-term objectives (Hailey, 1998).

Education in management should encourage an innovative approach to day-to-day operations while incorporating sustainable development principles. However, attempts to incorporate sustainability into a university management program are challenging. The aim is to integrate the environmental, economic, organizational, and individual dimensions of sustainability into the curriculum to the best of our ability. Such a course should address issues surrounding sustainable development, give managers an in-depth understanding of this field, and equip them with a complete set of competencies to implement its principles (Hailey, 1998).

Sustainable development competence can be defined as the ability to shape future scenarios by active participation in the modeling and transforming society toward sustainable practices (Barth et al., 2007). One of the most frequently cited sets of competencies in this area available in the literature is de

Haan's concept of Gestaltungskompetenz (de Haan, 2006, 2010). According to the author, the competency set includes

- ability to think and act in a forward-looking manner,
- ability to work in an interdisciplinary manner,
- ability to demonstrate openness, understanding, and intercultural collaboration competency,
- participatory competencies,
- ability to plan and implement a plan practically,
- the ability to feel empathy, sympathy, and solidarity,
- the ability to motivate oneself and others, and
- the ability to analyze one's own behavior and its cultural determinants.

A similar catalogue of competencies has been presented by López-Alcarria et al. (2019), Wiek et al. (2011), and Cebrián et al. (2019). Based on these concepts, a set of eight competencies was adopted, as shown in Figure 11.1.

Developing these competencies in students is of particular importance in improving their sustainability abilities (Stibbe, 2012). Through them, students can become agents of positive change in the workplace (Sipos et al., 2008), which is extremely important in creating innovative work environments.

Sustainable development education has taken on a special significance in the era of Industry 5.0. This relatively new concept has its roots in the concept of Industry 4.0, which focused on digitization and technologies that increase production efficiency. The concept of Industry 5.0, on the other hand, highlights the importance of research and innovation in supporting

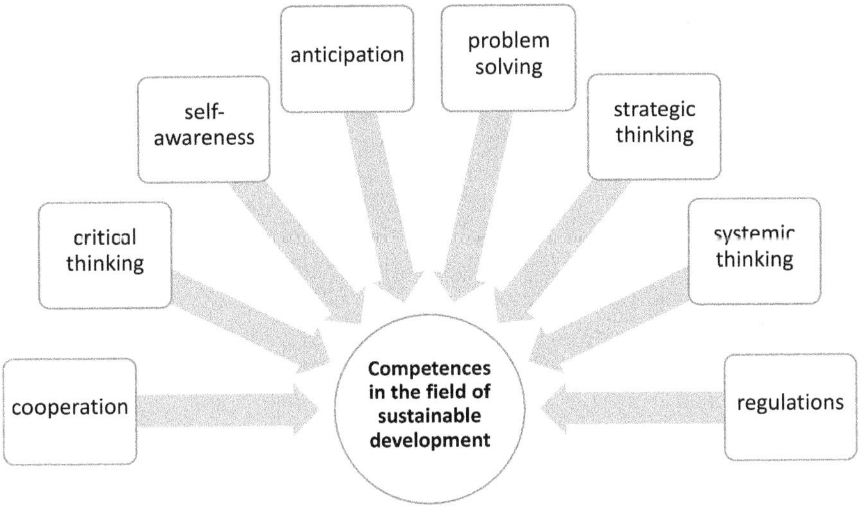

Figure 11.1 Sustainability competencies.

Source: Own elaboration.

the industry in its long-term service to humanity. The concept calls for a fundamental shift in the paradigm of development for the society and economy, which includes elements such as a human-centered approach and sustainable development. To meet this task, changes and financial investments in innovation and education are needed (Breque et al., 2021). These will facilitate the development of competencies that will be important both in the context of sustainable development and Industry 5.0, such as critical thinking (Maddikunta et al., 2022; Mendonça et al., 2020).

Methodology

Based on the concept of competencies in the field of sustainable development formulated above (see Figure 11.1), we developed a self-assessment tool that allows for assessing these skills. Each competency was diagnosed based on five statements (items). Responses were categorized according to the following scale: (5) strongly agree, (4) agree, (3) neither agree nor disagree, (2) disagree, and (1) strongly disagree. Moreover, a section of the questionnaire contained questions about participants' gender, major, and course level (Mazur et al., 2021). Before the research began, a pilot study was conducted. In the final version of the questionnaire, the following statements were included (Table 11.1).

The tool presented above is universal in nature. It can be used by students themselves to assess the competency level of a group of students in order to monitor the progress in the acquisition of competencies throughout a course. It can also be used to diagnose the level of competence of students from other faculties at the same or other universities. Consequently, it is innovative and can be viewed as an example of innovation in education.

Research and results

The study conducted over the course of January and February 2021 involved a group of 184 students in first-cycle degree programs in management at the Lublin University of Technology. They were part of a larger research group that included students from other faculties at the university. Considering that the course curriculum is the same for all students enrolled in the course, socio-demographic variables were not considered.

Having re-coded the reverse-scale questions, the responses allowed us to create sets of aggregated data under the following categories: collaboration competency, critical thinking, self-awareness, anticipatory thinking, problem-solving, strategic thinking, systems thinking, and normative competence. A variable created this way could have a value between 5 and 25. The Cronbach's alpha coefficient for aggregated data is 0.82 and 0.87 when it comes to raw data. To determine the degree of individual competencies in the self-assessment, the Student's t-test was used. The Statistica TIBCO statistical package was used for statistical analyses.

According to the data obtained, the surveyed management students rated their competencies in sustainable development quite favorably (see Table 11.2).

Table 11.1 Self-assessment questionnaire for sustainability competencies

Competence in the scope of	*Statements*
Collaboration competency	1 I'm eager to learn from others 2 I am always open to understanding and respecting the opinions of others 3 I like to work as part of group 4 I am eager to participate in joint problem-solving 5 As an active individual, I am willing to take part in a variety of initiatives
Critical thinking	1 I always express my disagreement with someone openly 2 When I disagree with social norms, I have the courage to question them 3 I can act in opposition to common practices 4 I analyze and am able to critically evaluate my own actions and their motivations 5 I am capable of admitting my mistakes
Self-awareness	1 I'm thinking about my role in the local community 2 I am aware of my impact on the natural environment 3 I am aware that my actions can have a global impact 4 I recognize my own emotions and feelings 5 I deal better with my fears when I recognize their cause
Anticipatory thinking	1 I plan my future 2 In considering my future, I consider different scenarios 3 I always analyze the consequences of my decisions before making them 4 There is always a "plan B" in my mind 5 I am open to change
Problem-solving	1 Whenever possible, I choose environmentally friendly solutions (e.g. reusable bags). 2 When making decisions, including purchases, I am primarily guided by the costs (e.g. the price of goods)* 3 When making decisions, I think about their effects on the people around me (the common good) 4 When making decisions, I take future generations' needs into consideration 5 I believe that when solving important problems (e.g. the problem of extracting natural resources in Poland), it is important to consider solutions that take social, economic, and ecological factors into account.
Strategic thinking	1 When planning my actions, I take into account their global impact (e.g. reducing water consumption or plastic waste) 2 When planning my actions, I pay close attention to local conditions and needs 3 As I solve problems, I analyze their immediate effects* 4 I see that many of today's problems have their roots in the past 5 I consider the effects of my solutions when solving problems

(*Continued*)

Table 11.1 Self-assessment questionnaire for sustainability competencies (*Continued*)

Competence in the scope of	*Statements*
Systems thinking	1 I see the complexity/multifacetedness of the modern world's problems
	2 I see the connections among phenomena and processes in the near and distant environment
	3 I see the world as a whole as a network of interconnected vessels
	4 When considering development around the world, I am able to recognize and combine its ecological, economic, and social dimensions.
	5 I believe that solving problems related to sustainable development requires an interdisciplinary approach (as well as applying a variety of viewpoints and tools)
Normative competence	1 I understand the assumptions behind sustainable development
	2 I believe that nature should be protected at all costs*
	3 My relationships with other people are guided by the principle of social solidarity (i.e. the common good; i.e. I wear a protective mask to avoid endangering others)
	4 It is my belief that ethical principles should guide the economic development of the world
	5 Societies should develop harmoniously and in a balanced manner

Source: Questionnaire prepared by employees of the Faculty of Management of the Lublin University of Technology (Mazur et al., 2021).

* Questions with inverted scale.

The response that was most frequently chosen by the surveyed students was 4 (I agree). Additionally, it is apparent that the competencies assessed could be divided into two categories. Among them are collaboration competency, critical thinking, self-awareness, and anticipatory thinking. Respondents assessed their competencies in systems thinking, normative competencies, strategic thinking, and problem-solving as a little worse. The Student's t-test indicates that some of the differences are statistically significant (Table 11.3).

Table 11.2 Self-assessment of sustainability competencies – descriptive statistics

Variable	*N of valid responses*	*Average*	*Median*	*Minimum*	*Maximum*	*Standard deviation*
Collaboration competency	184	19.7	20	12	25	2.4
Critical thinking	184	19.6	19	15	25	2.2
Self-awareness	184	19.6	20	13	25	2.6
Anticipatory thinking	184	19.5	19	12	25	2.7
Problem-solving	184	18.7	19	11	25	2.8
Strategic thinking	184	18.9	19	12	25	2.4
Systemic thinking	184	19.1	19	12	25	2.6
Normative competence	184	19.0	19	11	25	2.4

Source: Own research.

Table 11.3 Differences in self-assessment of competencies related to sustainability

Competence 1 vs. competence 2	*Average Group 1*	*Average Group 2*	*t*	*p*
Collaboration competency vs. problem-solving	19.7	18.7	3.8891	0.0001
Collaboration competency vs. strategic thinking	19.7	18.9	3.4083	0.0007
Collaboration competency vs. systemic thinking	19.7	19.1	2.3881	0.0174
Collaboration competency vs. normative competence	19.7	19.0	2.6356	0.0088
Critical thinking vs. problem-solving	19.6	18.7	3.7446	0.0002
Critical thinking vs. strategic thinking	19.6	18.9	3.2466	0.0013
Critical thinking vs. systems thinking	19.6	19.1	2.2071	0.0279
Critical thinking vs. normative competence	19.6	19.0	2.4555	0.0145
Self-awareness vs. problem-solving	19.6	18.7	3.4298	0.0007
Self-awareness vs. strategic thinking	19.6	18.9	2.9229	0.0037
Self-awareness vs. systems thinking	19.6	19.1	1.9781	0.0487
Self-awareness vs. normative competence	19.6	19.0	2.1942	0.0289
Anticipatory thinking vs. problem-solving	19.5	18.7	2.8083	0.0052
Anticipatory thinking vs. strategic thinking	19.5	18.9	2.2591	0.0245

Source: Own research.

Table 11.2 shows that the first four competencies were assessed as more important by the respondents, which is also confirmed by the statistical analyses carried out. The averages of competencies in collaboration competency, critical thinking, and self-awareness are higher (a statistically significant difference) than all four competencies found in the second group. In the case of collaboration competency, these differences are statistically significant in comparison to problem-solving competence and strategic thinking.

Discussion

Taking sustainability into account in management programs became apparent at the end of the 20th century. Evidence of this can be found in a study of management curricula that was commissioned by the Roosevelt Foundation in 1993. The goal was to create an MBA program that would address the issue of sustainability and meet the needs of managers from the public, private, and non-profit sectors. The analysis revealed that either three key elements were missing or little attention was given to them in management courses at the time. The first missing element was a lack of explanation for operational differences between short- and long-term goals and their implications for sustainability. The second one addressed soft factors related to developing interpersonal skills, intercultural sensitivity, and understanding oneself were not considered as important as hard practical skills such as financial planning. A third issue was that most modern management programs did not address the role of culture and values in managerial decisions and tended to favor western values.

Using the aforementioned tool for the self-assessment of competencies in sustainable development can deliver information on whether the above-mentioned key elements have been included or excluded from a curriculum of an educational program. Nevertheless, it cannot be the only basis for assessing competence in sustainable development. Despite its undeniable advantages, self-assessment also has some limitations as a way to measure competence. It appears that the greatest danger is contamination with the individual's subjective viewpoint. As a result, if it is to be used for designing educational programs, it should be supported by an assessment that is carried out by academic teachers responsible for implementing educational programs. This requires the development of an additional diagnostic tool. For a proper determination of deficiencies in competencies, it is necessary to consider both the student's self-assessment and the teacher's assessment.

Education in sustainability aims to teach management students that curricula are designed to help them understand the critical importance of sustainability at work and in the decisions they make, as well as to meet the practical needs of modern managers. In this regard, self-assessment can be one of the most effective methods for shaping awareness. This is what the tool presented aims to accomplish. The use of this tool made it possible for respondents to assess their competence in the field of sustainable development, which they did relatively favorably, even though the level of proficiency in individual competencies varied. This may serve as a starting point for adjusting the curriculum contents and didactic methods used in the educational process to ensure that the competencies that were found to be inadequate are taken into account and strengthened.

All this indicates that both the development of competencies in sustainable development and the assessment of the degree to which they have been mastered is a process that should be continually monitored and improved. In this regard, a good practice example is a comprehensive and innovative approach used in the Economics Degree of the Faculty of Economics and Business of the University of Murcia. It is based on the sustainable development competence (SCM) map, on the basis of which learning outcomes are linked to the sustainable development goals. Separate contents for each of the components used in the SCM (economic, social, environmental, and holistic) were also developed and the professional development needs for teachers in this area were diagnosed. Extending this approach to include student self-assessment makes the proposed concept more comprehensive.

The results of the survey presented above could also be used by businesses. Values such as empathy, solidarity, transparency, and altruism can be the basis for developing business strategies that are beneficial to the various stakeholder groups within the company. As has already been emphasized, students of today will become decision-makers in enterprises in the future. Their sustainability competencies will make them strong advocates for sustainable management strategies that include social, economic, and environmental aspects. It will also contribute to addressing Industry 5.0 challenges (Severino-González et al., 2021).

References

Barth, M., Godemann, J., Rieckmann, M., & Stoltenberg, U. (2007). Developing key competencies for sustainable development in higher education. *International Journal of Sustainability in Higher Education*, *8*(4), 416–430. https://doi.org/10.1108/14676370710823582

Béchard, J. (2005). L'enseignement supérieur et les innovations pédagogiques: une recension des écrits. *Articles*, *27*(2), 257–281. https://doi.org/10.7202/009933ar

Breque, M., De Nul, L., & Petridis, A. (2021). *Industry 5.0: Towards a sustainable, human-centric and resilient European industry*. Publications Office

Brundiers, K., & Wiek, A. (2017). Beyond interpersonal competence: Teaching and learning professional skills in sustainability. *Education Sciences*, 7(1), 39. https://doi.org/10.3390/educsci7010039

Cebrián, G., Segalás, J., & Hernández, À (2019). Assessment of sustainability competencies: A literature review and future pathways for ESD research and practice. *Central European Review of Economics and Management*, *3*(3), 19–44.

Ciumara, T. (2013). Explorarea functiilor economice ale consultantei in practicile inovative de management in conditiile dezvoltarii economice durabile, Bucharest: Institutul National de Cercetari Economice "Costin C. Kiritescu".

de Haan, G. (2006). The BLK 21 programme in Germany: A "Gestaltungskompetenz"-based model for education for sustainable development. *Environmental Education Research*, *12*(1), 19–32.

de Haan, G. (2010). The development of ESD-related competencies in supportive institutional frameworks. *International Review of Education*, *56*(2–3), 315–328. https://doi.org/10.1007/s11159-010-9157-9

DeLoach, J. (2019). *Innovation: The organization's lifeblood*. Corporate Compliance Insights. Retrieved July 9, 2022, from https://www.corporatecomplianceinsights.com/innovation-the-organizations-lifeblood/

Hailey, J. (1998). Management education for sustainable development. *Sustainable Development*, *6*(1), 40–48. https://doi.org/10.1002/(sici)1099-1719(199803)6:1<40::aid-sd80>3.0.co;2-q

Kar, S., & Lillian, M. (2018). Towards sustainability: Required competencies of management graduates. *Organization & Management Scientific Quarterly*, *4*(44), 93–105.

López-Alcarria, A., Olivares-Vicente, A., & Poza-Vilches, F. (2019). A systematic review of the use of agile methodologies in education to foster sustainability competencies. *Sustainability*, *11*(10), 2915. https://doi.org/10.3390/su11102915

Maddikunta, P., Pham, Q., Prabadevi, B., Deepa, N., Dev, K., & Gadekallu, T. et al. (2022). Industry 5.0: A survey on enabling technologies and potential applications. *Journal of Industrial Information Integration*, *26*, 100257. https://doi.org/10.1016/j.jii.2021.100257

Manea, A. (2015). Innovation in the management of educational institutions. *Procedia – Social and Behavioral Sciences*, *209*, 310–315. https://doi.org/10.1016/j.sbspro.2015.11.239

Mazur, B., Walczyna, A., & Bojar, M. (2021). Structure of competencies of Lublin university of technology students in the field of sustainable development. *European Research Studies Journal*, *XXIV*(Special Issue 2), 394–404. https://doi.org/10.35808/ersj/2271

Mendonça, J., Pinto, C., & Babo, L. (2020). Industry 5.0 expectations of engineering critical thinking. In Gómez Chova, L., López Martínez, A., & Candel Torres I. (Eds.), *EDULEARN20 Proceedings. 12th International Conference on Education and New Learning Technologies*. Online Conference (pp. 8518–8529). 7/6/2020–7/8/2020, IATED.

Molera, L., Sánchez-Alcázar, E., Faura-Martínez, Ú, Lafuente-Lechuga, M., Llinares-Ciscar, J., Marín-Rives, J. et al. (2021). Embedding sustainability in the economics degree of the faculty of economics and business of the University of Murcia: A methodological approach. *Sustainability*, *13*(16), 8844. https://doi.org/10.3390/su13168844

Pauw, J., Gericke, N., Olsson, D., & Berglund, T. (2015). The effectiveness of education for sustainable development. *Sustainability*, 7(11), 15693–15717. https://doi.org/10.3390/su71115693

López-Alcarria, A., Poza-Vilches, F., & Mazuecos-Ciarra, N. (2019). A professional competencies' diagnosis in education for sustainability: A case study from the standpoint of the education guidance service (EGS) in the Spanish context. *Sustainability, 11*(6), 1568. https://doi.org/10.3390/su11061568

Setó-Pamies, D., & Papaoikonomou, E. (2015). A multi-level perspective for the integration of ethics, corporate social responsibility and sustainability (ECSRS) in management education. *Journal of Business Ethics, 136*(3), 523–538. https://doi.org/10.1007/s10551-014-2535-7

Severino-González, P., Villalobos-Antunez, J., Vergara-Gómez, J., & Yáñez-Venegas, M. (2021). Percepción sobre la responsabilidad social corporativa de los estudiantes de educación superior de Chile. *Formación Universitaria, 14*(4), 39–48. https://doi.org/10.4067/s0718-50062021000400039

Sipos, Y., Battisti, B., & Grimm, K. (2008). Achieving transformative sustainability learning: Engaging head, hands and heart. *International Journal of Sustainability in Higher Education, 9*(1), 68–86. https://doi.org/10.1108/14676370810842193

Sterling, S. (2004). Higher education, sustainability, and the role of systemic learning. In P. Corcoran & A. Wals (Eds.), *Higher education and the challenge of sustainability. Problematics, promise, and practice* (1st ed., pp. 49–70). Kluwer Academic Publishers.

Stibbe, A. (2012). *The handbook of sustainability literacy.* Green Books.

Tilbury, D., & Wortman, D. (2004). *Engaging people in sustainability.* UICN Commission on Education and Communication – The World Conservation Union.

UNESCO (2005).The UN Decade of Education for Sustainable Development (DESD 2005–2014), International Implementation Scheme, Paris. Retrieved June 24, 2022, from https://www.bibb.de/dokumente/pdf/a33_unesco_international_implementation_scheme.pdf

UNESCO (2017). Education for sustainable development goals, learning objectives, Paris. Retrieved June 24, 2022, from http://unesdoc.unesco.org/images/0024/002474/247444e.pdf

United Nations (2012). *The Future We Want, Outcome document of the United Nations Conference on Sustainable Development* [Conference session]. RIO+20 United Nations Conference on Sustainable Development, June 20–22, Rio de Janeiro, Brazil.

Wiek, A., Withycombe, L., & Redman, C. (2011). Key competencies in sustainability: A reference framework for academic program development. *Sustainability Science, 6*(2), 203–218. https://doi.org/10.1007/s11625-011-0132-6

12 Integration of intellectual capital, sustainable development, and Business 5.0

Elwira Gross-Gołacka, Teresa Kupczyk, Barbara Siuta-Tokarska, Joanna Dzieńdziora

Introduction

In the last decade, concepts such as sustainability, intellectual capital, and innovation have established themselves as immanent and become integral to the most important directions of economies and businesses. The aim behind most of them is not only to foster economic growth or development but also to promote sustainable development and increase the level of innovation, especially in the development of technologies that are environmentally friendly. With the advancement of technology, information technology, and processes within companies, this trend is becoming more evident, demonstrating that success in the market is less and less determined by the tangible assets within a company. It is common knowledge that such factors as knowledge and skills of employees, organizational culture, relationships with customers, and IT resources (i.e. intangible factors) play an increasingly important role in gaining competitive advantage. In a unanimous view held by many scholars and practicing entrepreneurs (e.g. P. Drucker, M. Bratnicki, G. Hamel, C. K. Prahalad, I. Nonaka, H. Takeuchi, K. Obłój, B. Wawrzyniak, J. Penc, T. A. Steward, L. Edvinsson, W. J. Hudson, W. R. Bukowitz, R. L. Williams, and others) all this will play a critical role in the current and future economies. This is especially true for smart knowledge-based companies that by managing information and know-how effectively gain a competitive advantage.

The purpose of the chapter is to identify organizational management aspects that affect the changes occurring in businesses today. In this paper, the authors aim to demonstrate how building and utilizing intellectual capital can lead to positive changes within an organization. The research aims to bridge the basic theoretical concepts of intellectual capital, sustainability, and Society 5.0 from the perspective of managing them as a whole ecosystem. This chapter aims to develop a conceptual framework by reviewing the literature and presenting selected empirical studies (both our own and those of other researchers). This approach seeks to present the existing concepts or phenomena in a new way by combining them with the phenomena that previously seemed unrelated or incompatible. The key research question relates to whether intellectual capital contributes to the creation of the sustainable

DOI: 10.4324/9781003384311-12

development concept and the transformation within organizations toward becoming organizations of the 5.0 era.

The first auxiliary research question relates to the importance attributed to intellectual capital in the process of developing organizations according to the principles of sustainable development. The second one addresses the role of intellectual capital in establishing Society 5.0. Reaching these goals requires clarification and discussion of the idea of intellectual capital as one of the resources of modern organizations that foster and perhaps accelerate the building of an organization that operates in line with the assumptions of Society 5.0.

Literature review

Intellectual capital and company performance

According to Roos and Roos, intellectual capital is defined as a set of intangible assets (resources, capabilities, and competitiveness) that influence organizational performance and value creation (Roos & Roos, 1997). In the literature, intellectual capital is classified in a variety of ways. The most widely used concept for the allocation of intellectual capital is the model developed in the early 1990s by Edvinsson and Malone (1997) or Stewart (2001). According to some definitions, intellectual capital is divided into three categories: human capital, structural capital, and relational capital.

Using this approach, human capital includes employees' knowledge, skills, and experience, all of which drive the growth of the company. In addition, it may also include such characteristics of an employee as intelligence, creativity, ability to share knowledge, and ability to learn (Patalas-Maliszewska, 2010). Structural capital, on the other hand, is defined as a company's organizational capacity to support employee productivity. Edvinsson (Edvinsson & Malone, 2001) describes it as "an embodiment, empowerment of human capital". This means that in this model human capital is a dominant category of intellectual capital as it serves as the basis of a firm's structural capital. The capital consists of customer capital as well as organizational capital. The former is the organization's relationship with the environment (i.e. relationships with suppliers, customer loyalty, and the company's reputation in the market). Organizational capital, on the other hand, includes the systems and tools used to improve the exchange of knowledge within an organization and is divided into process capital and innovation capital. Process capital includes working processes, procedures, standards (e.g. ISO 9000), and employee programs designed to improve the efficiency of manufacturing or service provision. Innovation capital refers to an organization's ability to renew itself through intellectual property and other intangible assets that are used to create new products and services and quickly launch them on the market. In contrast to human capital, structural capital can be owned by a company and resold. These elements are interconnected and characterized by a feedback loop. A combination of these three elements is necessary to create value from a manager's standpoint. In this context, intellectual capital is a phenomenon of interaction, transformation, and interdependence. Therefore, the efficiency of one resource can be increased by making investments in other resources.

Thus, a company's value that is derived from intellectual capital depends on the interaction of all its subcomponents. As a result, intellectual capital needs to be properly managed in companies, in a way that includes its identification, measurement, development, and protection. According to the above classification system, intellectual capital has the following characteristics (Kaczmarek, 2005):

- it can be permanent (fixed), e.g. patents, or it can be variable, e.g. employee skills;
- can be an instrument for the value creation process or an end product of the knowledge transformation process; and
- is created through the interplay of the knowledge transformation process.

When it comes to the definition of intellectual capital, even though some authors have slightly different interpretations, we still see that most of these definitions overlap in several ways. There is a consensus among the authors regarding the importance of intellectual capital. There are publications in the literature that discuss intellectual capital's role in business development. These empirical studies demonstrate that intellectual capital significantly affects the financial performance of firms regardless of their line of business, size, or market sector. In their research, Sardo and Serrasqueiro (2017) have found that intellectual capital plays a dominant role in increasing the wealth of European firms. Research from other countries (Singapore, India, and China) has also confirmed this discourse (Tan et al., 2007; Tiwari & Vidyarthi, 2018). And so, researchers on every continent conclude that intellectual capital has a positive impact on financial results and that companies with higher levels of intellectual capital are more likely to generate more profit in the future, as has been confirmed by numerous researchers (Basuki & Kusumawardhani, 2012; Kamath, 2008; Mehralian et al., 2012; Ozkan et al., 2016; Ramezan, 2011). In general, the concept of intellectual capital is used to help develop the potential of an organizational structure and society to be more advanced or outside the group (Jaya, 2019). Intellectual capital also has an impact on the company's innovation capability and performance (Yu et al., 2011). Companies that have more innovative capabilities are considered to be more successful in adapting to external changes. In addition, it can increase their competitiveness (Hariyono & Tjahjadi, 2021). Researchers have shown that intellectual capital has a positive effect on innovation (Wang & Chen, 2013). The key factor of this creative performance is intellectual capital, considered one of the most critical capital but also one of the most important strategic assets that an organization can possess (Gogan et al., 2016).

Intellectual capital vs. sustainability development

Intellectual capital represents those intangible resources that are not measured or expressed in a company's financial statements (Bhasin et al., 2011; Martın de Castro et al., 2004; Mavridis, 2004) but have a critical role in creating long-term value (Zhou & Fink, 2003). While human capital is a contributing factor to creativity and leads to the generation of new ideas, relational capital contributes to establishing a company's reputation and allows the company to communicate with its external environment and stakeholders. These issues become relevant in the face of growing demand for an integrated approach to address complex economic, social, environmental, and institutional challenges (Alvino et al., 2021). The aspects of building and operating an organization in accordance with the philosophy of sustainable development that was adopted by the United Nations (Xu & Wang, 2018) and according to the sustainability model (The Global Risks Report, 2019) – which emphasizes that the fundamental goal is the economic development and well-being of societies – is becoming increasingly sought after, also among stakeholders (de Villiers & Sharma, 2017). This means that companies need to disclose information about the environmental and social impacts of their operations. The Global Reporting Initiatives (GRI) have created a fairly clear and transparent system for documenting sustainability issues. It describes non-financial data related to the flow of intellectual, social, and environmental capital. With this in mind, large companies have made new commitments to change their business model and contribute to meeting the SDGs (Sustainable Development Goals) (Barth et al., 2017).

According to researchers, in order for organizations to contribute to sustainable development, every type of capital must be utilized more effectively, including intellectual capital management, which is one of the most sensitive areas (de Leaniz & del Bosque, 2013). In addition, presenting non-financial data that goes beyond financial statements provides an opportunity to pay attention to non-traditional capital, strategy, and business models and can increase future-oriented thinking. Researchers point out that in addition to acquiring new knowledge, the ability of organizations to meet the sustainability challenge determines their profits and survival in the market (Alves et al., 2021; Hahn et al., 2007; Lubin & Esty, 2010). Companies that master the implementation of intangible investments will have an advantage over their competitors. New research uses sector-level data and the results of a new survey of more than 860 executives that reveal that "top growers" – companies in the top quartile for growth in gross value added, a measure of economic growth-invest 2.6 times more in intangibles than low growers, companies in the bottom two quartiles (Hazan et al., 2021). Over the past 25 years, the investment share of intangibles has increased by 29%. These trends reveal the importance of intellectual capital as a long-term source of productivity, organizational competitiveness, and sustainability (Vătămănescu et al., 2019).

Research results

The theoretical considerations in this chapter are enriched by the results of empirical studies on the intellectual capital of enterprises in Poland. The survey was conducted in 2019 using CATI and CAWI on a representative sample of 1067 companies operating in Poland with an assumed confidence level of 0.95 and an estimation error of 3%. The study employed a proportionate sampling of companies by geographical region and company size as measured by the number of employees. In addition, the sample structure assumed differentiation of enterprises by type of activity (the number of interviews conducted as part of the study was proportional to the percentage of enterprises in each section of the Polish Classification of Activity PKD). Notably high recognition of this area has been observed by large enterprises, employing from 250 to 999 employees (82% indications). In the case of small and medium enterprises, a positive answer has been given by 67% and 68% of respondents, respectively. The assessment of the impact of the elements of intellectual capital on the sustainable development of enterprises was carried out through its division into three components of intellectual capital, among which the following were specified:

1 human capital: H1 – employee knowledge, H2 – employee skills, H3 – creativity and innovativeness of employees, H4 – employee motivation, H5 – employee experience, H6 – employee integrity, H7 – employee honesty, H8 – ability to work in a team, H9 – ability and willingness of employees to share knowledge and information, H10 – employee satisfaction, H11 – employee involvement, H12 – employee well-being, H13 – health;
2 structural capital: S1-technical infrastructure, S2-information resources/systems and databases, S3 – intellectual property (patents, licenses, trademarks), S4 – organizational culture, S5 – processes and management methods; and
3 relational capital: R1 – customer loyalty and satisfaction, R2 – customer participation in creating products/services, R3 – investor relations, R4 – relations with science and research units, R5 – relations with suppliers, R6 – reputation and image of the enterprise on the market.

Analyzing the structure of intellectual capital, factors associated with human capital play a significant role in the sustainable development of enterprises in Poland (Table 12.1). In the case of small enterprises, employing 10–49 employees, the following factors have been identified as extremely relevant: employee honesty (69% indications), reliability of employees (65% indications), skills of employees (63% indications), knowledge of employees (58% indications), engagement of employees (53% indications), and health (51% indications). The following factors have been identified as relevant for this group of enterprises: ability and readiness of employees to share knowledge and information

Table 12.1 The impact of human capital factors on the sustainable development of small enterprises – research results (%)

Human capital elements	*Definitely insignificant*	*Insignificant*	*Difficult to say*	*Significant*	*Very significant*
H1	1	4	4	33	58
H2	1	2	2	32	63
H3	1	7	8	43	41
H4	1	2	4	44	49
H5	1	3	7	44	45
H6	1	1	1	32	65
H7	1	0	1	29	69
H8	0	3	7	50	40
H9	0	4	6	52	38
H10	1	2	5	49	43
H11	0	1	2	44	53
H12	0	4	8	52	36
H13	1	2	4	42	51

Source: Own elaboration.

(52% indications), the well-being of employees (52% indications), teamwork skills (50% indications), the satisfaction of employees (49% indications), and creativity and innovativeness of employees (43% indications).

Medium enterprises (Table 12.2), which employ around 50–249 employees, have indicated the following factors tied to human capital, as extremely relevant for their sustainable development: employee honesty (63% indications), their abilities (63% indications), knowledge (60% indications), and reliability (56% indications). A relevant impact for these enterprises is made by:

Table 12.2 The impact of human capital factors on the sustainable development of medium enterprises – research results (%)

Human capital elements	*Definitely insignificant*	*Insignificant*	*Difficult to say*	*Significant*	*Very significant*
H1	0	3	4	33	60
H2	0	2	1	34	63
H3	0	8	11	39	42
H4	0	1	6	46	47
H5	0	6	9	50	35
H6	0	0	2	42	56
H7	0	0	3	34	63
H8	0	5	6	47	42
H9	0	4	12	52	32
H10	0	1	5	56	38
H11	0	0	5	50	45
H12	0	5	9	54	32
H13	0	2	3	52	43

Source: Own elaboration.

Table 12.3 The impact of human capital factors on the sustainable development of large enterprises – research results (%)

Human capital elements	*Definitely insignificant*	*Insignificant*	*Difficult to say*	*Significant*	*Very significant*
H1	0	5	0	18	77
H2	0	5	0	22	73
H3	0	5	0	63	32
H4	5	0	0	45	50
H5	5	0	9	59	27
H6	0	0	0	68	32
H7	0	0	5	40	55
H8	0	5	5	68	22
H9	0	5	9	45	41
H10	5	9	5	49	32
H11	0	0	0	50	50
H12	0	9	18	46	27
H13	0	9	9	50	32

Source: Own elaboration.

employee satisfaction (56% indications), the well-being of employees (54% indications), their ability and readiness to share knowledge and information (52% indications), health (52% indications), experience (50% indications), and engagement (50% indications), whereas over 10% of enterprises from this group were unable to indicate the importance of factors such as the ability and readiness of employees to share knowledge and information (12% indications) and creativity and innovativeness of employees (11% indications).

Large enterprises (Table 12.3) view the following factors as extremely relevant for human capital: knowledge of employees (77% indications), their skills (73% indications), honesty (55% indications), motivation (50% indications), and engagement (50% indications). These enterprises have indicated the following as relevant: reliability of employees (68% indications), teamwork skills (68% of indications), creativity and innovativeness of employees (63% indications), their experience (59%), engagement (50% indications), and health (50% indications).

Whereas organizational capital factors are to a major degree relevant for small enterprises and include: organizational culture (59 indications), technical infrastructure (54 indications), and management processes and methods (53 indications). Intellectual property is perceived as relevant by 37 respondents, whereas according to 24 of small enterprises, it is irrelevant to their development (Table 12.4).

In the case of medium enterprises there is a similar perception of elements of organizational capital as with small enterprises (Table 12.5). This group has indicated the following factors as relevant: technical infrastructure (54 indications), processes and management methods (54 indications), and organizational culture (51 indications). Intellectual property has been indicated as a relevant factor for 36 companies, whereas according to 25, it is extremely relevant.

Table 12.4 The impact of structural capital factors on the sustainable development of small enterprises – research results (%)

Structural capital elements	*Definitely insignificant*	*Insignificant*	*Difficult to say*	*Significant*	*Very significant*
S1	1	6	8	54	31
S2	1	12	9	46	32
S3	5	24	15	37	19
S4	1	6	9	59	25
S5	1	7	9	53	30

Source: Own elaboration.

Table 12.5 The impact of structural capital factors on the sustainable development of medium enterprises – research results (%)

Structural capital elements	*Definitely insignificant*	*Insignificant*	*Difficult to say*	*Significant*	*Very significant*
S1	0	4	5	54	37
S2	0	11	6	47	36
S3	2	24	13	36	25
S4	0	6	10	51	33
S5	0	6	6	54	34

Source: Own elaboration.

Large enterprises (Table 12.6) have indicated the following organizational capital factors as extremely relevant for the sustainable development of their activity: management processes and methods (50 indications) and organizational culture (45 indications). The following factors have been as relevant: technical infrastructure (72 indications), and information resources/systems and databases (63 indications). The following organizational capital factors have been indicated by 14 enterprises as irrelevant to their sustainable development: intellectual property and management processes and methods.

In the scope of relational capital, the following factors have been indicated as extremely relevant for the sustainable development of small enterprises:

Table 12.6 The impact of structural capital factors on the sustainable development of large enterprises – research results (%)

Structural capital elements	*Definitely insignificant*	*Insignificant*	*Difficult to say*	*Significant*	*Very significant*
S1	0	5	0	72	23
S2	0	5	0	63	32
S3	0	14	32	36	18
S4	0	9	5	41	45
S5	0	14	0	36	50

Source: Own elaboration.

Table 12.7 The impact of relational capital factors on the sustainable development of small enterprises – research results (%)

Relational capital elements	*Definitely insignificant*	*Insignificant*	*Difficult to say*	*Significant*	*Very significant*
R1	1	1	3	34	61
R2	4	20	17	39	20
R3	8	19	11	35	27
R4	15	35	16	25	9
R5	3	6	4	46	41
R6	1	1	2	28	69

Source: Own elaboration.

reputation and image of the enterprise on the market (69 indications) and loyalty and satisfaction of clients (61 indications). The following have been indicated as relevant: supplier relations (46 indications), participation of clients in developing products/services (39 indications), and investor relations (35 indications) (Table 12.7). According to 35 enterprises, relations with research and science units are irrelevant.

Medium enterprises (Table 12.8), similarly to small enterprises, perceived the role of particular factors of relational capital for the sustainable development of their activity. The following factors have also been indicated as extremely relevant: reputation and image of the enterprise on the market (68 indications), loyalty, and client satisfaction (56 indications). A relevant meaning is associated with investor relations (44 indications), participation of clients in developing products and services (40 indications), and investor relations (35 indications). Similarly to small enterprises, according to 31 of the respondents, relations with research and science units have been identified as irrelevant.

For large enterprises (Table 12.9), the reputation and image of the enterprise on the market have been identified as extremely relevant (50 indications). Whereas loyalty and satisfaction of clients (50 indications), participation of clients in developing products and services (50 indications), supplier relations

Table 12.8 The impact of relational capital factors on the sustainable development of medium enterprises – research results (%)

Relational capital elements	*Definitely insignificant*	*Insignificant*	*Difficult to say*	*Significant*	*Very significant*
R1	1	3	4	36	56
R2	1	18	15	40	26
R3	6	15	10	35	34
R4	11	31	15	28	15
R5	0	9	8	44	39
R6	0	1	3	28	68

Source: Own elaboration.

Table 12.9 The impact of relational capital factors on the sustainable development of large enterprises – research results (%)

Relational capital elements	*Definitely insignificant*	*Insignificant*	*Difficult to say*	*Significant*	*Very significant*
R1	0	9	5	50	36
R2	0	14	22	50	14
R3	5	14	23	40	18
R4	5	27	32	23	13
R5	0	5	23	45	27
R6	0	5	5	40	50

Source: Own elaboration.

(45 indications), and investor relations (40 indications) are factors that have been identified as relevant for sustainable development of this group of enterprises. Relations with research and science units are irrelevant for 27, whereas 32 were unable to determine their role in the sustainable development of their activity.

Discussion

Historically, we were Society 1.0, a group of people hunting and gathering in harmony with nature. We then moved to the Society 2.0 level, where groups were formed based on farming, better organization, and nation-building. The next transformation of our society was the Society 3.0 stage which refers to a society that encouraged industrialization through the Industrial Revolution, making mass production possible. Society 4.0, on the other hand, is a concept radically different from the previous stages as it is the era of the so-called information society, which generates increased added value by combining intangibles into information networks (Fukuyama, 2018). Currently, we are embracing the idea of Society 5.0. This model (or super-smart society) is inherently based on super-innovative companies and societies.

Introduced in Japan, the concept of Society 5.0 is human-centered and meant to improve social life (Fukuda, 2020). The approach goes beyond the traditional organizational context as it addresses both economic development and solving social problems by integrating the intellectual capital system in cyberspace (virtual space) and physical space (real space) in Society 5.0 (Konno & Schillaci, 2021). The main goal of Society 5.0 is to improve people's quality of life by making use of the capabilities made available by Industry 4.0 (Ferreira & Serpa, 2018). As part of the 5th Science and Technology Basic Plan, the Japanese government proposed Society 5.0, which focused on shifting attention from industry to society (Fukuyama, 2018; Konno & Schillaci, 2021). In contrast to repeatedly expressed concerns and fears that at some point artificial intelligence and robotics are going to replace humans – if not completely – the concept of Society 5.0 can be seen as one that is definitely human-centric.

As a result of these considerations, it is important to remember that along with technological advancements, knowledge drives economic growth at the moment. In today's knowledge-based economy, the creation and use of knowledge play a central role in the process of creating wealth. In light of such a debate, intellectual capital serves as a strategic resource for knowledge-based societies, economies, and organizations today. The development of these structures will depend on knowledge components, their unique character, as well as our capability to generate them, and the degree to which we use them. Also, innovation is a knowledge-based process and a product of knowledge and intellectual capital (Gross-Gołacka et al., 2019, 2020).

There is now a growing awareness that the human element is of vital importance in the present-day world; for example, the previously mentioned concept of Society 5.0 as a human-centered approach. However, it is worth mentioning that today, for businesses and managers, employees are quite often considered "resources" (human resources), and customers are described in business plans as "consumers" rather than living people. This approach continues to be uncomfortable. On the other hand, managers strive to incorporate a human dimension to their management in an economy based on people and society, through the use of the sustainable development concept, for instance.

So what should the practical approach entail? Isn't it time to change our viewpoint so we can see things from a different perspective? Doesn't the challenge lie precisely in finding a way we can see things from a different angle? The emerging era of 5.0, which includes the Society 5.0 approach, places people at the center of change along with economic growth, technological development, and sustainability. This rather novel approach to shaping society is based on the fact that humanity is embarking on the fifth social revolution at the same time as developing sustainable technologies without compromising our well-being.

Conclusions

To conclude, when it comes to Society 5.0, artificial intelligence, big data, automation, or digitization are merely means while humans become central actors. In the traditional approach that has been around for years, innovation has been frequently driven by technology, which results in social development. With Society 5.0, we are encouraged to turn our thinking on its head in order to build a society that makes us happy and makes us feel valued. At the same time, this approach is expected to contribute to eliminating regional inequalities or disparities based on age, gender, origin, and language, for example. At the same time, it is intended to facilitate the delivery of products and services tailored to people's diverse individual needs and hidden needs. By using this approach, we hope to create a society that promotes economic development and finds solutions to social problems. Therefore, taking the previous theoretical considerations and selected results of empirical studies into account, it is possible to see intangible assets as business drivers that create lasting value for companies and move toward being smart and in line with the concept of sustainable development. Sustainability also calls for rethinking how we do business and developing new capabilities and innovations within the organization through knowledge management and learning to ensure appropriate and implementable practices, attitudes, and behaviors. Therefore, it can be said that the intellectual capital of the organization can contribute to the concept of sustainable development, transforming the organization toward becoming one of the organizations of era 5.0. Intellectual capital can be considered one of the resources of contemporary organizations that promote and perhaps accelerate an organization's evolution to operate and fulfill the assumptions of the concept of Society 5.0. As a result, having innovation capabilities in organizational management requires a combination of concepts and approaches that transcend existing corporate boundaries. And by devising an ecosystem of diverse ideas and approaches, it is possible to build a sustainable environment for the 5.0 age.

References

Alves, H., Cepeda-Carrion, I., Ortega-Gutierrez, J., & Edvardsson, B. (2021). The role of intellectual capital in fostering SD-orientation and firm performance. *Journal of Intellectual Capital, 22*(1), 57–75.

Alvino, F., Di Vaio, A., Hassan, R., & Palladino, R. (2021). Intellectual capital and sustainable development: A systematic literature review. *Journal of Intellectual Capital, 22*(1), 76–94.

Barth, H., Ulvenblad, P. O., & Ulvenblad, P. (2017). Towards a conceptual framework of sustainable business model innovation in the agri-food sector: A systematic literature review. *Sustainability, 9*(9), 1620.

Basuki, B., & Kusumawardhani, T. (2012). Intellectual capital, financial profitability, and productivity: An exploratory study of the Indonesian pharmaceutical industry. *Asian Journal of Business and Accounting, 5*(2), 41–68.

Bhasin, M. L., Shaikh, D., & Hanif, J. M. (2011). Intellectual capital disclosures in the annual reports: A comparative study of the Indian and Australian IT-corporations. *International Journal of Managerial and Financial Accounting, 3*(4), 1–24.

de Leaniz, P., & del Bosque, I. (2013). Intellectual capital and relational capital: The role of sustainability in developing corporate reputation. *Intangible Capital, 9*(1), 262–280.

de Villiers, C., & Sharma, U. (2017). A critical reflection on the future of financial, intellectual capital, sustainability and integrated reporting. *Critical Perspectives on Accounting, 70,* 101999, https://doi.org/10.1016/j.cpa.2017.05.003

Edvinsson, L., & Malone, M. (1997). *Intellectual capital: Realising your company's true value by finding its hidden brainpower.* Harper Collins.

Edvinsson, L., & Malone, M. S. (2001). *Intellectual capital.* PWN.

Ferreira, C., & Serpa, S. (2018). Society 5.0 and social development: Contributions to a discussion. *Sciedu Press*, 2018, *5*, 26–31.

Fukuda, K. (2020). Science, technology and innovation ecosystem transformation toward society 5.0. *International Journal of Production Economics*, *220*(C), 55–71.

Fukuyama, M. (2018). Society 5.0: Aiming for a new human-centered society. *Japan Spotlight, 27*, 47–50.

Gogan, L. M., Artene, A., Sarca, I., & Draghici, A. (2016). The impact of intellectual capital on organizational performance. *Procedia – Social and Behavioral Sciences, 221*(0), 194–202.

Gross-Gołacka, E., Jefmański, B., & Spałek, P. (2019). *Kapitał intelektualny przedsiębiorstw w Polsce. Wybrane aspekty teoretyczne i praktyczne*, Polskie Wydawnictwo Ekonomiczne.

Gross-Gołacka, E., Kusterka-Jefmańska, M., & Bartłomiej, J. (2020). Can elements of intellectual capital improve business sustainability? The perspective of managers of SMEs in Poland. *Sustainability, 12*(1545), 1–23.

Hahn, T., Figge, F., & Barkemeyer, R. (2007). Sustainable value creation among companies in the manufacturing sector. *International Journal of Environmental Technology and Management*, 7(5/6), 496. https://doi.org/10.1504/ijetm.2007.015627

Hariyono, A., & Tjahjadi, B. (2021). The role of intellectual capital in the development of financial technology in the new normal period in Indonesia. *Journal of Asian Finance, Economics and Business, 8*(1), 217–224. https://doi.org/10.13106/jafeb.2021.vol8.no1.217

Jaya, I. (2019). The impact of financial inclusion on public financial services education through financial technology in Sleman Regency, Indonesia. *Esensi: Jurnal Bisnis Dan Manajemen, 9*(2), 155–174. https://doi.org/10.15408/ess.v9i2.13576

Kaczmarek, B. (2005). Intellectual capital (knowledge) and creating company's vision. In M. G. Woźniak (Ed.), *Social inequalities and economic growth. Human and intellectual capital, part. 2*, Notebook No. 7. University of Rzeszow, Department of Economic Theory.

Kamath, G. B. (2008). Intellectual capital and corporate performance in Indian pharmaceutical industry. *Journal of Intellectual Capital, 9*(4), 684–704.

Konno, N., & Schillaci, C. E. (2021). Intellectual capital in society 5.0 by the lens of the knowledge creation theory. *Journal of Intellectual Capital, 22*(3), 478–505.

Lubin, D., & Esty, D. (2010). The sustainability imperative, *Harvard Business Review*, 88.

Martın de Castro, G., Lopez Saez, P., & Emilio Navas Lopez, J. (2004). The role of corporate reputation in developing relational capital. *Journal of Intellectual Capital, 5*(4), 575–585.

Mavridis, D. G. (2004). The intellectual capital performance of the Japanese banking sector. *Journal of Intellectual Capital, 5*(1), 92–115.

McKinsey Global Institute (2021). Getting tangible about intangibles: The future of growth and productivity?

Hazan, E., Smit, S., Woetzel, J., Cvetanovski, B., Krishnan, M., Gregg, B., Perrey, J., & Hjartar, K. (2021, July 30). *Getting tangible about intangibles: The future of growth and productivity?* McKinsey & Company. Retrieved December 21, 2022, from https://www.mckinsey.com/capabilities/growth-marketing-and-sales/our-insights/getting-tangible-about-intangibles-the-future-of-growth-and-productivity

Mehralian, G., Rajabzadeh, A., Sadeh, M. R., & Rasekh, H. R. (2012). Intellectual capital and corporate performance in Iranian pharmaceutical industry. *Journal of Intellectual Capital, 13*(1), 138–58.

Ozkan, N., Cakan, S., & Kayacan, M. (2016). Intellectual capital and financial performance: A study of the Turkish banking sector. *Borsa Istanbul Review, 17*(3), 190–198.

Patalas-Maliszewska, J. (2010). Nowe spojrzenie na strategiczne zarzadzanie zasobami ludzkimi. *E-mentor,* 4(36), 17–22, www.e-mentor.edu.pl. Retrieved December 21, 2018, from e-mentor: Archiwum

Ramezan, M. (2011). Intellectual capital and organizational organic structure in knowledge society: How are these concepts related? *International Journal of Information Management, 31*(1), 88–95.

Roos, G., & Roos, J. (1997). Measuring your company's intellectual performance. *Long Range Planning, 30*(3), 413–426.

Sardo, F., & Serrasqueiro, Z. (2017). A European empirical study of the relationship between firms' intellectual capital, financial performance and market value. *Journal of Intellectual Capital, 18*(4), 771–788.

Stewart, T. A. (2001). *The wealth of knowledge. Intellectual capital and the twenty-first century organization*. Nicholas Brealey Publishing.

Tan, H. P., Plowman, D., & Hancock, P. (2007). Intellectual capital and financial returns of companies. *Journal of Intellectual Capital, 8*(1), 76–95.

World Economic Forum. (2019). The Global Risks Report. Retrieved December 21, 2022, from https://www3.weforum.org/docs/WEF_GRR18_Report.pdf

Tiwari, R., & Vidyarthi, H. (2018). Intellectual capital and corporate performance: A case of Indian banks. *Journal of Accounting in Emerging Economies, 8*(1), 84–105.

Vătămănescu, E., Gorgos, E., Ghigiu, A., & Pătruţ, M. (2019). Bridging intellectual capital and SMEs internationalization through the Lens of sustainable competitive advantage: A systematic literature review. *Sustainability, 11*(9), 2510. https://doi.org/10.3390/su11092510

Wang, D., & Chen, S. (2013). Does intellectual capital matter? High-performance work systems and bilateral innovative capabilities. *International Journal of Manpower, 34*(8), 861–879.

Xu, J., & Wang, B. (2018). Intellectual capital, financial performance and companies' sustainable growth: Evidence from the Korean manufacturing industry. *Sustainability, 10*(12), 4651.

Yu, H.-C., Wang, W.-Y., & Chang, C. (2011). The pricing of intellectual capital in the IT industry. *SSRN Electronic Journal*. http://dx.doi.org/10.2139/ssrn.1327668

Zhou, A. Z., & Fink, D. (2003). The intellectual capital web: A systematic linking of intellectual capital and knowledge management. *Journal of Intellectual Capital, 4*(1), 3. https://doi.org/10.1108/14691930310455379

13 Developing economic activity zones

A case study of Cracow

Magadalena Rzemieniak, Zbigniew Makieła, Janusz Michałek, Radosław Miśkiewicz

The message of the concept of sustainable development that is contained in the 1987 Report of the World Commission on Environment and Development indicates that the common future of future generations should be strongly correlated with resource management (Rudewicz, 2019). The rational management of resources determines and influences sustainable development in which the needs of the current generation can be met without limiting the chances of future generations to meet them (MRiT, 2022). In Poland, the principle of sustainable development is regulated in the Constitution of the Republic of Poland.

The definition of sustainable development that was adopted in Polish terminology differs from the terminology that is used in the EU and UN. The word "sustainable" is not really used to refer to development as we understand it in Polish. "Sustainable" is a translation of the English word "sustainable," a verbal adjective from "sustain". It is not really a question of a development that is in some kind of equilibrium but one that can be sustained indefinitely – lasting, but not necessarily stable (Stodolak, 2020).

When studying the literature on sustainable development, we often notice the thesis that societies and nature are hostile forces. We live at the expense of nature, we overexploit its resources and lead to their exploitation, and we degrade resources, without which it is not possible to continue living without conflicts at the local and global levels. As a consequence, it will be impossible to continue mindlessly satisfying the growing unlimited needs of an ever-growing population, and we will reach the limits of growth – beyond which would have catastrophic consequences. Has this moment supposedly already happened (as evidenced by climate change and limited access to resources in many regions)?

Krakow functional area (KrOF)

Functional areas have been outlined in the city's Concept of Country Development 2030 (KKZK 2030) as an appendix to Resolution No. 239 of the Council of Ministers of December 13, 2011). According to KKZK 2030, an urban functional area is a compact spatial layout that consists of functionally located areas and is characterized by common conditions and reliable

DOI: 10.4324/9781003384311-13

anticipated development goals (Koncepcja Przestrzennego Zagospodarowania Kraju 2030, 2012).

Functional areas are open to all Polish voivodship cities, including metropolises; Krakow is classified as such an area. At this point, it should be mentioned that the Krakow Metropolitan Area (Krakowski Obszar Metropolitarny – KOM) incorporated in the Voivodship Development Plan of the Malopolska region is slightly wider than KrOF. However, the boundaries of KrOF roughly coincide with the inner zone of KOM (Noworól, 2014).

Those factors that influence the proper functioning of these areas include financial, infrastructural, legal, administrative, planning, information and marketing, and institutional instruments (Markowska-Bzducha, 2013).

The KOM has established a metropolitan function. A function such as this is the main part of the system that was adopted for evaluation; its indicators include the extent of the development of international tourism, the size of the city's budget, and the extent of territorial development and cohesion (Noworól, 2013).

KrOF consists of the city of Krakow as well as ten rural and four urban-rural communes. These are the communes of Krakow (11) and Wieliczka counties (3). The areas of the studied communes are characterized by a rich natural environment; they lie within the area of the Krakow-Częstochowa Jura. KrOF is characterized by a high ability to create economic growth in the region due to its economic and social values (increased access to a wide range of public services, high earnings, low levels of unemployment, and very good transport accessibility) and is a magnet that attracts human resources from other areas of the province (Malopolska Regional Operational Program ...). The Krakow Functional Area covers 1275 km^2, and the population amounted to 1,027,492 people at the end of 2014 (including 265,619 people living in suburban areas, i.e. primarily rural areas). The population density of all of KrOF is 805.9 people/km^2; in Krakow, this number is 2330 people/km^2, while in the suburban zone, it is 280.2 people/km^2 (Harańczyk, 2020).

The development of entrepreneurship in KrOM is characterized by high intensity. The number of business entities is gradually increasing from year to year. An important element of the transformation of the KrOF economy is building an economy that is based on the development of creative sectors. The largest labor markets outside Krakow are municipalities: Zabierzów, Skawina, Wieliczka, and Niepołomice. By far, the highest level of entrepreneurship development is characterized by Krakow and its neighboring municipalities (e.g. Zabierzów, Niepołomice, and Wieliczka). Krakow's dominance results from the fact that the city is distinguished by a concentration of scientific and research and development functions as well as a concentration of innovative industries.

Economic activity zone

The concept of an economic activity zone (SAG) that functions in the literature and in the environment that is related to the management of local governments and local economies seems to be not fully specified (in contrast to special economic zones – the definition and framework of which are defined by Polish legislation). This topic is overlooked; during an era of intensified competition among regions, it is paramount for multifunctional rural development. Thanks to SAG, it may be possible to achieve the synergy effect with additional mutual benefits – both for the local communities and investors. SAGs stimulate the development of investments by contributing to the location of innovative enterprises that not only contribute to the creation of new jobs but, above all, inspire the modernization of the branch structure of industry and services and create new networks of cooperative connections; as a result of the diffusion process, the multiplier effect of the local economy is strengthened. The development of a SAG is also the development of vocational education, which helps launch market-oriented programs.

Bearing in mind the above processes of economic growth and the activation of the entrepreneurship of residents, it is necessary to consider what local SAGs are, what functions they perform, what they will become in the near future, and what role they will play in the development of local communities and economies (Stanienda, 2011).

SAGs are "dedicated and investment-ready areas tailored to the needs of potential investors, most often created by local governments" (*Zarządzanie strefami aktywności gospodarczej. Podręcznik dobrych praktyk,* 2015). Therefore, these constitute distinct (dedicated) parts of Poland's territory that are supposed to perform the functions of investment areas. These should be characterized by readiness on multiple fronts to carry out their roles. Local government units have a wide range of options to influence the development of entrepreneurship.

These zones are of key importance to increasing the levels of commercial investments, significantly increasing the investment attractiveness of a region, developing entrepreneurship, and creating new jobs. Recognizing the advantages of such zones, municipalities merge new areas, build technical infrastructure, and change the purpose of an area in a local spatial development plan; thanks to this, the number of zones of economic activity constantly increases.

Economic activity zones are created and function on the basis of the Act on Special Economic Zones, regulations of the Council of Ministers on the creation of individual zones, and regulations of zones and plans for their development.

Entrepreneurs are able to invest favorably in such zones with low or no taxes, and in areas that have been properly prepared. Today, the zones differ in size, infrastructure, and development approach. Over time, special economic zones will be transformed into economic activity zones.

The first SAGs were created in the mid-90s – primarily in undeveloped communal areas. SAGs are of key importance for increasing levels of commercial investment, increasing the investment attractiveness of a region, developing entrepreneurship, and contributing to the creation of new jobs.

The most important tools and activities that attract investors to SAGs include the following (Wojtyra, 2014):

- infrastructure development of an area with basic utilities integrated into local, regional, and national transport, communication, water and sewage, energy networks, etc.;
- financial benefits resulting from tax incentives, competitive land prices, and competitive lease prices;
- intensive marketing activities of areas intended for economic activity;
- logistical assistance to investors regarding investment, administrative, and employment processes;
- legal regulations governing land that facilitate and accelerate investment processes; and
- a friendly sociocultural climate among local communities.

Determinants of development of economic activity zones

The development of SAG is a process that is regulated by formal, legal, and institutional conditions; these are important to the process of preparing investment areas and servicing investors. We can divide these into conditions that are related to agricultural real estate trading and land ownership, conditions that result from the provisions of construction law, and conditions that are directly and indirectly related to the investment process.[1]

In the investment process, it is important to obtain the appropriate administrative decisions that are part of the investment process; the main actor in this process is the municipality. The concept of creating SAGs was based on the assumption of the more effective use of a municipality's resources; this results in better investment decisions. In this context, the ownership of investment land is an important aspect. In many cases, the owner of such land is a municipality, while investors do everything possible to secure the right to develop it.

The basic legal instrument that shapes the space at the commune level is the local spatial development plan (MPZG) that is adopted by a municipality on the basis of previously adopted studies of the conditions and directions of the spatial development (SUiKZP). The basic legal act that regulates the spatial planning issues in municipalities is the Act on Spatial Planning and Development of March 27, 2003. If the investment process takes the development of the area that is covered by the MPZP into account, an investor may apply for a building permit. If, on the other hand, an area is not covered by the MPZP, a decision on the conditions of development and land development may be issued. It is worth mentioning that the location of commercial facilities with areas of more than 2000 m^2 can only take place on the basis of a local spatial development plan.

Pro-investment attitudes of local authorities play an important role in attracting investors. As the supply of potential investment areas increases, municipalities must seek investors, strive to facilitate any formal issues that are related to the investment, and conduct active activities in the field of economic promotion.

Among the directions that facilitate the investment process are activities that are primarily aimed at improving access to information, integrating registration systems (the so-called one-window principle, according to which registry courts and offices cooperate in the field of sharing data on entities that apply for registration under the Act on the National Court Register amended in 2014), and improving communications with investors (including communication via the use of electronic channels).

In Malopolska, the activity in the field of supporting investment activities and economic promotions at the local and regional levels is carried out by the Investor Service Center (COI), Malopolska Regional Development Agency (MARR), Krakow Technology Park (KTP), Krakow Nowa Huta Przyszłości S.A. (KNHP), and Malopolska Regional Development Observatory (MORR) (Table 13.1).

Impact of metropolises on functioning of Krakow functional area

Metropolises tend not to restrict their influence to the administrative boundaries of the city; however, their influence extends spatially, economically, and socially (sometimes very far beyond the city boundaries to areas that lie in other municipalities). On the other hand, the metropolitan area includes a zone with a significant direct range of permanent impact and areas of potential development opportunities. A metropolitan area is the main multifunctional center of a given region in which higher-order functions are concentrated: economic, scientific, and cultural. "A metropolitan area (OM) consists of a center in the form of a single city or urban agglomeration and neighboring municipalities; i.e., the environment from which a significant proportion of economically active residents commute to the center on a daily basis. An OM is therefore almost identical to the concept of an employment catchment area or a functional urban region based on daily trips to work in the center within the limits of a max. one hour isochrone. This also takes into account the importance of the fact of the mutual dependence of the center and the environment for shaping and strengthening the development of the entire system that is defined as an OM" (Lendzion, 2004).

Metropolitan centers are places for the production of goods, services, and information (Ustawa z dnia 27 marca 2003 r. o planowaniu i zagospodarowaniu przestrzennym [Act of March 27, 2003, on spatial planning and development], 2003). Metropolises are also important spaces on the map for generating knowledge, technology, and innovation. They have a huge development potential, which is used by their respective metropolises themselves in large part. Looking for development opportunities, metropolises strive

Table 13.1 Institutions operating in KrOM that deal with acquisitions of investors

Lp	*Support institutions*	*Scope of activity*
1	**Centrum Obsługi Inwestora (COI) [Investor Service Center]**	Centrum Obsługi Inwestora is an entity that was established to serve investors in Krakow (it operates within the structure of the city of Krakow). COI's activity is addressed to all of those who are interested in business development in Krakow. The scope of COI's activities is wide and includes providing services to foreign and domestic investors, monitoring the investment process of COI clients, advising investment recipients, maintaining databases of municipal investment offers, and acting to promote the city's investment offer in Poland and abroad. COI is supported by so-called coordinators, i.e. designated employees working in departments and municipal units that partake in the investment process.
2	**Malopolska Agencja Rozwoju Regionalnego (MARR) [Malopolska Regional Development Agency]**	The Malopolska Regional Development Agency deals primarily with providing services to enterprises (particularly consulting, assisting in obtaining EU funds, and investing). MARR's offer also includes loans for micro, small and medium-sized enterprises. MARR also offers a "Capital Investments" fund for companies, which invests in newly created companies that use and implement innovative solutions. The fund invests financial resources into ideas at the early stages of their development and is actively involved in the process of their market commercialization. It offers personalized service and expert assistance to its customers. Preferred industries are healthcare and medical engineering technologies, pharmacy, renewable energy sources, and environmental protection (*Inwestycje Kapitałowe*, n.d.). The institution also organizes training sessions, seminars, and conferences that are aimed at helping entrepreneurs establish business contacts and run businesses. Examples of such projects are *Zielone światło*, *Projekt szwajcarski*, and *Malopolskie Forum Finansowe*. The agency also offers land for rent ("MARR Business Park"); this is an offer for companies that are looking for warehouse space, production parks, and logistics centers. MARR Business Park is nearly 50 ha of real estate in Krakow that has been made available to entrepreneurs – a large shopping center and a business park formed by two property complexes.
3	**Krakowski Park Technologiczny (KTP) [Krakow Technology Park]**	Krakow Technology Park strives to have an integrated and comprehensive impact on the regional economy; its main objectives are the technological development of the voivodship, the development of entrepreneurship, and the promotion of innovation and new technologies. KTP manages the Krakow Special Economic zone, which consists of 32 subzones that are located in 30 municipalities. It currently covers an area of more than 866 hectares and is located in the Malopolskie, Podkarpackie, and Świętokrzyskie voivodeships. KTP offers investors primarily areas of a greenfield type. Their offer also includes office space that is located in attractive places: the Czyżyny business center, the Pychowice business center, and Krakow Business Park in Zabierzów (*Specjalna Strefa Ekonomiczna*, n.d.).

Table 13.1 Institutions operating in KrOM that deal with acquisitions of investors (*Continued*)

Lp	*Support institutions*	*Scope of activity*
4	**Spółka Krakow Nowa Huta Przyszłości S.A. (KNHP)**	KNHP is a company that was established in 2014 by the Municipality of Krakow and the Malopolska Region in order to implement a project under the name of "Krakow–Nowa Huta Przyszłości". The key task of the company is to undertake effective actions that are aimed at accelerating the economic development of the eastern part of Krakow at the infrastructural, functional, and social levels. Specifically, this will be accomplished by developing the area in such a way that increases the attractiveness of Nowa Huta to investors, the community of the city and municipality of Krakow, the entire region, and tourists (*O Projekcie – Kraków Nowa Huta Przyszłości S.A.*, n.d.).
5	**Malopolska Malopolskie Obserwatorium Rozwoju Regionalnego (MORR) [Regional Development Observatory]**	The Malopolska Regional Development Observatory is a unit of the Marshal's Office of the Malopolska Region and operates as part of the Department of Regional Policy. The observatory's activities support improvements in the region's management system through the conducting of research and introducing the results of that work into the circulation of a broad public debate. The objectives of MORR include implementing research and analysis, obtaining and providing data and information, providing recommendations and forecasts, establishing and deepening cooperation with research institutions as well as with other regions of Poland and Europe, promoting good practices and disseminating developed knowledge, developing and deepening cooperation with public institutions, official statistics institutions, research institutions, universities, and private companies that deal with social and economic research issues, evaluating public policies, and providing economic advice (*O nas – MORR*, n.d.).

Source: Own study based *on Multidisciplinary Study on Economic Activity Zones (SAG)*; Krakow Metropolis Association, Warsaw, October 2016.

to increase competitiveness by increasing investment attractiveness (creating preferential conditions for investors, developing technical infrastructure, making transport accessible, and promoting sustainable development, tourism, etc.). Attracting investors is one of the main ways to stimulate a market of goods and services while also increasing the prestige of a metropolis. Global corporations that decide to establish their headquarters in a metropolis envelop the world with a network of their economic, scientific (research), transport, and information connections. This process is accompanied by the transformation of urban spaces by changing the relationship between a central city and its immediate outskirts, for example (Kudłacz, 2009).

When determining the impact of metropolises, reference should be made to the assumptions of sustainable development that indicate the strong link between a city and its region – emphasizing their coexistence and harmonious development. The relationship between a metropolis and its regional environment is shaped by regional and local development.

Key economic phenomena

A key phenomenon that could be observed in KrOF in recent years was an increase in its economic activity; this is reflected in the increase in business entities registered with REGON per 10,000 residents. From 2016 to 2018, the median for this analyzed indicator increased from 1201 to 1279. During the years of 2014–2018, an increase in the entities that entered the register per 1000 working-age individuals was observed in the Krakow metropolis. Over the analyzed period, the largest increase was recorded in Krakow as well as in the municipalities of Zabierzów and Michałowice.

Another indicator of increased economic activity and economic development in the Krakow metropolis was the total number of newly registered business entities during the years of 2014–2018.

Those municipalities that were characterized by the highest relative growth of registered business entities in the Krakow metropolis during the period 2016–2019 were Krakow, Wielka Wieś, Skawina, Kocmyrzów-Luborzyca, and Zielonki. A decrease in newly established business entities (as compared to 2016) was only observed in the municipality of Zabierzów over this time period.

Throughout the Krakow metropolis, there was an increase of 1080 newly registered business entities between 2014 and 2019. In 2019, approximately 78% of all newly registered business entities in the Krakow metropolis were located in Krakow. Among the municipalities surrounding Krakow, Wieliczka and Skawina recorded the largest increase in newly registered business entities in 2019. In both of them, the number of newly registered business entities in 2019 exceeded 450.

Technology transfer

KrOF is an important center for modern business services. At the beginning of 2019, there existed 217 BPO, SSC/GBS, IT, and R&D service centers in Krakow and Zabierzów that provided services in foreign languages. Today, Krakow's centers employ a total of about 70,000 people. As many as 18 of the companies that were located in Krakow were entities that employed more than 1000 employees. From the first quarter of 2018 to the first quarter of 2019, KrOF centers created around 6500 new jobs (Table 13.2).

There are nearly 600 entities that conduct research and development activities in the region, which gives Malopolska the third ranking in the country (second in terms of population). In addition, there are about 15 cluster initiatives, including the LifeScience Krakow Cluster and the Sustainable Infrastructure Cluster (which have the status of Key National Clusters). Companies such as ABB, Aptiv, Motorola, CH2MHill, and Ericpol have chosen Krakow as a location for the development of R&D activities.

Conclusions and recommendations

Metropolitan areas are characterized by formed relationships between the center (metropolis) and their regional environment; this results in an impact on the functioning and transformation of the regional structures. Strengthening

Table 13.2 Share of newly registered businesses in the creative sector in total number of newly registered entities in KrOF in 2014–2019 (in %)

Municipality	*2014*	*2015*	*2016*	*2017*	*2018*	*2019*	*2014 (= 100%)*
Biskupice	4.35	3.70	0.00	10.00	7.41	9.43	116.78%
Czernichów	5.34	6.96	6.25	3.23	5.30	5.84	9.36%
Igołomia-Wawrzeńczyce	6.38	0.00	2.86	11.63	6.67	8.06	26.33%
Kocmyrzów-Luborzyca	6.62	4.55	5.94	9.09	6.12	7.87	18.88%
Krakow	9.56	9.55	9.00	9.66	9.40	9.98	4.39%
Liszki	6.62	6.67	5.44	5.49	6.90	4.46	−32.63%
Michałowice	14.17	7.07	12.21	12.17	8.72	7.28	−48.62%
Mogilany	10.40	3.23	5.84	7.87	10.99	6.38	−38.65%
Niepołomice	6.74	9.72	5.64	8.41	8.42	5.23	−22.40%
Skawina	3.83	7.47	4.92	8.00	5.10	6.58	71.80%
Świątniki Górne	2.34	5.49	3.19	5.50	5.69	7.32	212.82%
Wieliczka	6.70	6.35	6.53	8.00	9.85	8.51	27.01%
Wielka Wieś	2.92	11.86	13.27	10.97	6.96	10.00	242.47%
Zabierzów	7.17	7.47	5.60	9.41	10.53	9.90	38.08%
Zielonki	7.07	10.16	6.11	6.69	7.55	8.31	17.54%

Source: Extracted from Local Data Bank; retrieved September 28, 2020, from https://bdl.stat.gov.pl

the relationship of a metropolis with its surroundings translates into a wealth of economic, social, and environmental advantages for the metropolis and the suburban area realized by strengthening development planning at the local and regional levels (Markowski & Marszał, 2006).

Fully developed metropolitan centers have their own metropolitan areas – especially when we assume that a metropolis is formed from agglomerations (a large city with outskirts and conurbation). The transfer of urban functions (residential, commercial, and production) and their expansion beyond the formal boundaries of a city is a natural and very old process that accompanies urbanization. A metropolitan area (the surroundings of a metropolis) consists of areas that are connected with the center, perform urban functions, and where parts of the metropolitan's facilities and functions are located in the vicinity of the city center. However, the key partner for a metropolis in terms of cooperation (network-wise) remains not its own facilities (which support the competition, but which are not an equal partner) but rather other metropolises (Markowski & Marszał, 2006).

An important element of a local government's functional structure is its metropolises and metropolitan areas. These are becoming increasingly important as local economic centers (SAGs) emerge from the effective use of local resources, thus allowing a municipality to gain a competitive advantage. An increase in interregional competition emphasizes the need for multifunctional rural development. Thanks to SAGs, a synergistic effect is created, generating benefits for local communities and stakeholders such as investors. SAGs stimulate the development of investments by contributing to the establishment of innovative enterprises that not only contribute to the creation of new jobs but, above all, inspire the modernization of the industry structure of an economy, and inspire new networks of cooperative connections. As a result of the diffusion process, the multiplier effect strengthens the local economy.

Note

1 The Act on Shaping the Agricultural System of 11 April 2003 and its amendment of 6 July 2016 increasing the role of the Agricultural Property Agency in the right of pre-emption of agricultural real estate, the Act on the suspension of the sale of real estate of the Agricultural Property Stock of the State Treasury of 14 April 2016, the Act of 7 July 1994 Construction Law, the Act of 27 March 2003 on spatial planning and development, Act of 27 April 2001 Environmental Protection Law, Act of 23 July 2003 on the Protection of Monuments and Care of Monuments, Act of 29 January 2004 Public Procurement Law, Act of 17 May 1989 Geodetic and Cartographic Law, Act of 10 April 1997 Energy Law, Act of 9 June 2011 Geological and Mining Law.

References

Harańczyk, A. (2020). Procesy suburbanizacji w Krakowskim Obszarze Funkcjonalnym. *Studia Miejskie, 18*, 131–146. https://doi.org/10.25167/sm.2439

Inwestycje Kapitałowe. (n.d.). Małopolska Agencja Rozwoju Regionalnego: MARR. Retrieved June 22, 2022, from https://www.marr.pl/ik/

Koncepcja Przestrzennego Zagospodarowania Kraju 2030. (2012). Monitor Polski, Dziennik Urzędowy RP z 27 kwietnia 2012, Warszawa.

Kudłacz, M. (2009). Rola metropolii w rozwoju regionów w świetle programów rozwoju szczebla regionalnego na przykładzie województw: małopolskiego, mazowieckiego i dolnośląskiego. *Zarządzanie Publiczne, 4*(10), 53–72

Lendzion, J. (2004). *Znaczenie obszarów metropolitalnych i ich otoczenia oraz współczesnych procesów metropolizacyjnych w kształtowaniu polityki regionalnej Państwa.* Ekspertyza na zamówienie Dep. Polityki Regionalnej MGiP dla potrzeb tworzenia Narodowej Strategii Rozwoju Regionalnego.

Markowska-Bzducha, E. (2013). Rola samorządu terytorialnego we wspieraniu lokalnej przedsiębiorczości. *Finanse Komunalne, 9*, 5–23.

Markowski, T., & Marszał, T. (2006). *Metropolie, obszary metropolitalne, metropolizacja.* KPZK PAN.

MRiT. (2022). *Zrównoważony rozwój.* Retrieved June 22, 2022, from https://www.gov.pl/web/rozwoj/zrownowazony-rozwoj

Noworól, A. (2013). *Diagnoza obszaru strategicznego "Kraków Metropolitalny" opracowana w procesie aktualizacji Strategii Rozwoju Krakowa.* Bip.krakow.pl. Retrieved June 22, 2022, from http://www.bip.krakow.pl/zalaczniki/dokumenty/n/113569/karta

Noworól, A. (2014). *Strategia Zintegrowanych Inwestycji Terytorialnych dla Krakowskiego Obszaru Funkcjonalnego.* Metropoliakrakowska.pl. Retrieved June 22, 2022, from https://metropoliakrakowska.pl/wp-content/uploads/2018/11/Strategia-ZIT-KrOF.pdf

O nas – MORR. (n.d.). MORR. Retrieved June 22, 2022, from http://www.obserwatorium.malopolska.pl/o-nas/

O Projekcie – Kraków Nowa Huta Przyszłości S.A. (n.d.). Knhp.com.pl. Retrieved June 22, 2022, from http://knhp.com.pl/oprojekcie

Rudewicz, J. (2019). *Rozwój zrównoważony wielkich miast w Polsce.* Wydawnictwo Naukowe Uniwersytetu Szczecińskiego.

Siuta-Tokarska, B., Borowiecki, R., & Kusio, T. (2018). Innowacyjne przedsiębiorstwo. In Z. Makieła & M. Stuss (Eds.), *Przedsiębiorczość i zarządzanie innowacjami. Wiedza, technologia, konkurencja, przedsiębiorstwo*. Wydawnictwo C. H. Beck.

Specjalna Strefa Ekonomiczna. (n.d.). Krakowski Park Technologiczny. Retrieved September 28, 2020, from http://www.kpt.krakow.pl//

Stanienda, J. (2011). Determinanty rozwoju stref aktywności gospodarczej. *Zeszyty Naukowe MWSE w Tarnowie*, *1*(17).

Stodolak, S. (2020). *Tylko niezrównoważony rozwój może nas uratować. Przyrodę także*. Forsal.pl. Retrieved June 22, 2022, from https://forsal.pl/gospodarka/aktualnosci/artykuly/7838054,tylko-niezrownowazony-rozwoj-moze-nas-uratowac-przyrode-takze.html

Ustawa z dnia 27 marca 2003 r. o planowaniu i zagospodarowaniu przestrzennym [Act of March 27, 2003 on spatial planning and development]. Isap.sejm.gov.pl. (2003). Retrieved June 22, 2020, from https://isap.sejm.gov.pl/isap.nsf/DocDetails.xsp?id=wdu20030800717

Wojtyra, B. (2014). Strefy aktywności gospodarczej w teoriach rozwoju lokalnego/The economic activity zones in the theories of the local development. *Rozwój Regionalny i Polityka Regionalna*, *28*, 25–36.

Zarządzanie strefami aktywności gospodarczej. Podręcznik dobrych praktyk. (2015). Małopolskie Obserwatorium Rozwoju Gospodarczego, Departament Polityki Regionalnej, Urząd Marszałkowski Województwa Małopolskiego, Kraków, p. 22. Retrieved June 22, 2020, from https://www.obserwatorium.malopolska.pl/wp-content/uploads/2016/05/Zarz%C4%85dzanie-Strefami-Aktywno%C5%9Bci-Gospodarczej.-Podr%C4%99cznik-Dobrych-Praktyk.pdf

14 Business productivity assessment

Concepts and methods

Jakub Bis, Borys Burkynskyi, Aleksander Prokopiuk, Valeriy Goryachuk, Oleksandr Laiko

Introduction and review of the literature

Topic of the article is important because business planning and management of the enterprise should be carried out on the basis of an objective assessment of the results of its activities. An inadequate assessment can disorient management and lead to subjectivity in making management decisions, significantly reduce management efficiency, and lead to negative consequences. In modern conditions, the availability of scientifically based methods and tools for assessing the performance of entrepreneurial activities is of high value, both from a research and management point of view. The originality of the article, comparing to previous researches, is that there is no generally accepted theoretical and methodological approach to the analysis and assessment of the productivity of entrepreneurial activity. In this regard, the development of new conceptual and methodological foundations for assessing the productivity of entrepreneurial activity is characterized by scientific novelty and practical importance.

Speaking of the productivity of entrepreneurial activity, we mean the productivity of certain economic entities and legal entities engaged in entrepreneurial activity. The productivity of entrepreneurial activity depends on the combination of factors, among which the main ones are natural resources, the quality of human labor (intensity and dexterity), the volume and quality of means of production (fixed assets, technologies, etc.), intangible assets (patents, information technologies), the organization of production, the state of the business environment (regulatory policy of the state). Growing productivity allows businesses to produce more goods and offer greater service. This creates higher wages, supports economic growth, holds back inflation, and increases tax revenues.

Entrepreneurial activity is a very expanded concept that is characterized by a set of interrelated indicators of labor that reflect its effectiveness, economy, quality, profitability, productivity, innovation, and quality of working life. According to Article 42 of the Economic Code of Ukraine, entrepreneurial activity (entrepreneurship) is an independent, proactive, systematic, at-their-own-risk economic activity aimed to achieve economic and social results and make a profit

DOI: 10.4324/9781003384311-14

(Verkhovna Rada of Ukraine, 2003). In domestic economics, the most complete concept of entrepreneurship was outlined by Varnalii: "Entrepreneurship as an economic category is a special type of management, where the main subject is an entrepreneur who rationally mixes (combines) the factors of production on an innovative basis and responsibility, organizes and manages production in order to obtain entrepreneurial income" (*Entrepreneurship – Wikipedia*, 2022). The definitions of other authors of the concept of "entrepreneurial activity" are quite similar (Asaul et al., 2004). For example, in the textbook "Entrepreneurship" this economic category is defined as a free economic management in various fields of activity (except those prohibited by law), carried out by market participants to meet the needs of specific consumers and society in goods (works and services) and get profit (income), necessary for self-development of own business (enterprise) and provision of financial obligations to budgets and other business entities (Almodóvar-González et al., 2020; Baumol, 1996; Johnston & Stewart, 2019; Kusumastuti et al., 2016; Sobel, 2008).

The productivity of entrepreneurial activity is a determining factor in the socio-economic development of the state at the micro level. We consider its relationship with indicators that characterize the level of socio-economic development at the regional and national levels. At the national level, this main indicator is gross domestic product, which is the aggregate of gross value added created by various types of economic activity (agriculture, industry, construction, trade, transport, etc.). The same applies to the regions, namely the gross regional product. But at the enterprise level, the situation is completely different. Traditionally, when assessing the productivity of an enterprise, the main indicators that are used are not the "gross value added" indicator and other, but the "output", "sales volume", and "profit" indicators. But they have significant disadvantages.

The "output" indicator consists of gross value added and intermediate consumption. The latter is the cost of material resources and services that were purchased from other enterprises and fully consumed during the production process. That is, the "output" indicator depends both on the result of the enterprise itself and on the results of the activity of other enterprises. At the same time, the external contribution can be decisive. It buys the engine, fuel system, electrical equipment, transmission, cooling system, bodywork, suspension, steering, braking system, wheels, tires, and so on from other companies. In this case, the main contribution to the production of the car in its cost, belongs to the supplier enterprises. That is, an increase in output may not be the result of an increase in the efficiency of the enterprise but a consequence of an increase in the volume of goods and services consumed. In this case, there is an increase in output without an increase in gross value added created by the enterprise. At the same time, the further the enterprise is in the technological chain, the greater the output and the less it reflects the real labor productivity at the enterprise. Therefore, it is proposed to estimate labor productivity at the enterprise as the gross value added per employee. It is this view that reflects the real productivity of labor at the enterprise.

Another key indicator of enterprises performance is the "profit" indicator. From a business point of view, this is probably the most important indicator. When focused on it, remuneration, social security financing, and employee training are expenses of the enterprise. With this approach, the lower these costs, the greater the profit of the enterprise. But in modern conditions, to ensure the sustainable economic development of an individual enterprise and the country as a whole, it is important to consider that the employees are not a set of individuals who can be changed at least every day without significant losses in the efficiency of the production process, but a team of interconnected employees who are the bearer of human capital. The loss or reduction of this capital may result in more significant losses than the loss of physical and financial capital. In modern conditions, the role of employees in shaping the final results of enterprises activities is growing, and human and social ones occupy a central place in the system of social reproduction. Profit is only a part of gross value added. The latter consists of the profit that the owners of the enterprise receive, remuneration for employees, and taxes to the state.

Thus, the "output" and "profit" indicators do not give an adequate idea of the results of enterprises activities. In contrast, the "gross value added" indicator is purely the result of the enterprise activities. It does not include the performance of other enterprises and therefore reflects the real contribution of the enterprise to the creation of specific goods and services that it produces or provides. Given this, it is advisable to change the benchmark, namely the use of gross value added as the main indicator of the enterprise's performance. It is on the basis of this indicator that the main result of economic activity of the country (gross domestic product) and regions (gross regional product) is determined. This approach will provide a single conceptual framework for evaluating economic performance at the micro, meso, and macro levels.

The expediency of using the "gross value added" indicator to assess the enterprise productivity is indicated by many researchers, namely Cobbold (2003), Johnston and Stewart (2019), Kalchenko et al. (2018), Lieberman and Kang (2008), Ndubisi and Nair (2009), Neto et al. (2014), OECD (2001), Schreyer and Pilat (2001), and Vlasiuk et al. (2018). It is necessary to highlight two aspects:

- enterprises with high gross value added can be considered potential growth points, which is very important from the point of view of determining the country's ability to ensure high economic growth rates. To this we can add that the human potential of an enterprise and the amount of gross value added that it creates are directly proportional; that is, the higher the human potential, the greater the share of gross value added in the gross income of the enterprise and
- gross value added is a very important indicator for increasing the interest of business entities in creating, producing, and using innovations, since it is a source of funds that are used to meet the needs of all interested parties in the enterprise performance.

Choosing the "gross value added" indicator as the main indicator for evaluating the enterprise performance will allow to consider the interests of all economic entities:

- employees and their interest in the salary,
- business owners and their interest in profit and business development, and
- state and its interest in tax revenues to the budget (Figure 14.1).

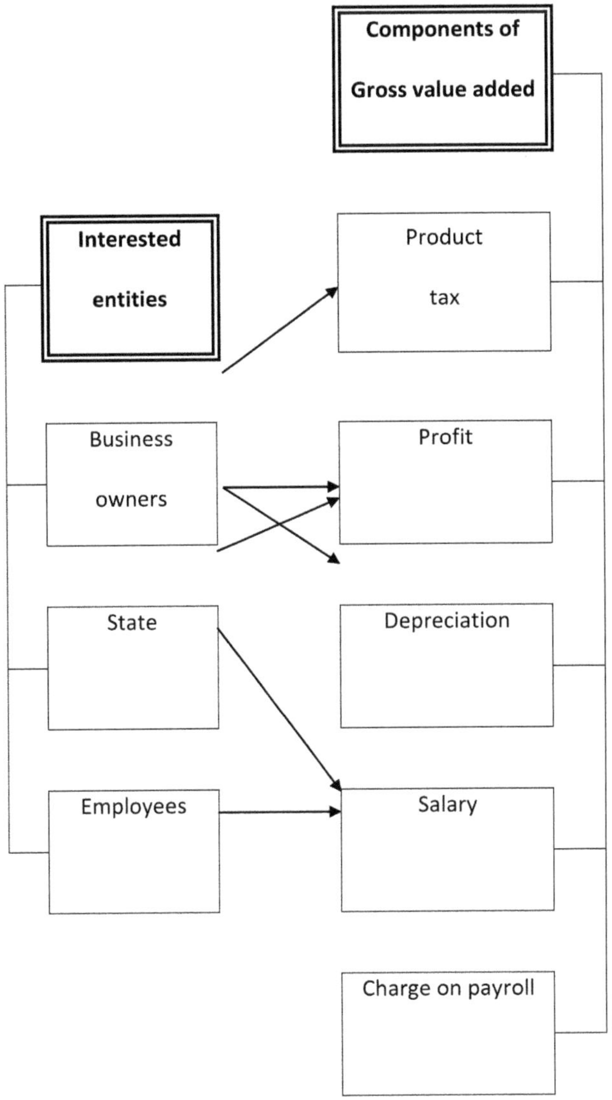

Figure 14.1 Structure of gross value added and distribution of its components among interested economic entities.

Source: Own elaboration.

Today, at the enterprise level, gross value added is not calculated or used. Even the calculation of value-added tax does not provide for determining the amount of gross value added, but an indirect method of calculating the tax is used. At the same time, the main macroeconomic indicator of the country and regions performance is GDP and GRP, respectively. According to the 2008 system of national accounts (SNA-2008), the idea that underlies the concept of GDP is that it should measure the total gross value added of all institutional units that are residents of a given country (Organization of United Nations, 2009).

The existing discrepancy, when at the enterprise level the main indicator of performance is profit, and at the regional and national levels – gross value added, is due to the presence of a contradiction between the interests of society and the owners of enterprises. If the enterprise is interested in increasing gross value added, then the owners of the enterprises are interested in increasing profits. Given that the enterprise profit is a part of gross value added, it can be increased in two ways: firstly, by introducing new technologies, increasing the level of organization of the production process that meets the interests of society, and secondly, by reducing salaries and tax evasion. In the latter case, gross value added does not increase, but only its redistribution is carried out in favor of business, which does not meet the interests of society.

Separately, it should be noted that the accumulation of fixed capital in the country is carried out at the expense of the share of gross value added that remains after consumption. In other words, gross value added determines the potential of countries, regions, and enterprises to accumulate capital. The greater the gross value added is and the greater its share goes to the accumulation of fixed capital, the greater the amount of fixed capital accumulated.

In terms of gross value added as an indicator for assessing the productivity of enterprises, it should be noted that it is more justified to use the "net value added" indicator; that is, it is necessary to exclude the consumption of fixed capital (depreciation) from gross value added, which from an economic point of view is also intermediate consumption. But depreciation in accounting is usually calculated based on the initial cost of fixed assets, which usually does not correspond to their real value. In addition, the depreciation can be calculated on the basis of accelerated depreciation methods, which does not correspond to real economic processes. All this has led to the fact that statistics mainly use the "gross value added" indicator but not the "net value added" indicator.

Results and discussion

The study of the literature indicates the use of various indicators of value added to assess the enterprises performance. "Economic value added" (EVA) indicator is widely recognized. It is calculated as the difference between net operating profit after tax and capital raising costs. That is, EVA is the profit remaining after the payment of capital, which is determined by multiplying the weighted average cost of capital (WACC) by the amount of involved capital (Dierks & Patel, 1997; Maditinos et al., 2007; Shil, 2009).

$$EVA = NOPAT - WACC \star CAPITAL, \tag{14.1}$$

where NOPAT – net operating profit after tax; WACC – weighted average cost of capital; CAPITAL – involved capital.

EVA can also be calculated by multiplying the invested capital by the difference between return on equity and WACC.

$$EVA = CAPITAL \star (ROC - WACC), \tag{14.2}$$

where ROC – return on capital invested in an enterprise.

These two formulas are equivalent and allow us to consider EVA from different points of view.

Many large consulting companies offer their own EVA-based analysis systems, using additional indicators that refine EVA. For example, there are EVA models from KPMG, PWC, Accenture, and A.T. Kearney. EVA founder Stern, Stewart & Co. publishes ratings in which companies are ranked according to the standardized indicator "Stern & Stewart Performance 1000".

All EVA models assume that to create value in the first year, one of the following conditions must be met:

1 company's net operating profit after tax (NOPAT) must exceed the fee for equity and borrowed capital

$$NOPAT > WACC \star CAPITAL, \tag{14.3}$$

and the company's net profit (EAT – Earnings after Tax) must exceed the equity.

2 the return on capital invested to the company must exceed the cost of capital

$$ROC > WACCL, \tag{14.4}$$

The difference (ROC – WACC) is called the performance spread and is a key indicator of company ranking.

A positive EVA value indicates efficient use of capital, and vice versa: a negative EVA value indicates inefficient use of capital. An EVA value of zero characterizes the acceptability of maintaining such a business in the market, as the investors receive an income which compensates them for the risk of investment.

The advantages of EVA include the following:

- EVA can serve as a good base for calculating managers' remuneration. It is this indicator that encourages them to make managerial decisions that will bring economic benefits,

- EVA allows you to see the possibility of increasing the value of a business not only by influencing profit but also by reducing the capital involved.

The disadvantages of EVA include the following:

- future cash flows are not considered when calculating this indicator. This, in turn, can lead managers to accept investment projects with quick payback. Consequently, projects that require large investments and a long period of development time will not be implemented by the company,
- EVA is calculated as an absolute indicator, which is inconvenient when comparing different companies. In this regard, it is advisable to use relative EVA indicators, for example, per unit of capital raised,
- the name of this indicator, which causes an association with added value, is not good enough. A more reasonable name would be "economic profit" or another, but with the word "profit" preserved in the name, since EVA is calculated based on net operating profit,
- EVA focuses on profit, that is, solely on the interests of the owners of the enterprise, and not on society. This may encourage managers to reduce the company's employees' salaries and avoid taxes.

Shareholder value added (SVA)

The SVA indicator was proposed by Alfred Rappaport in 1986. SVA means the change in the company shareholder value over the period. Rappaport's methodology for determining SVA is based on the concept of residual income and cash flow discounting models. SVA is defined as the difference between the cost of equity after a certain transaction and the cost of the same capital before that transaction (Cheremushkin, 2017). Often a slightly different interpretation is given: SVA is the difference between the estimated value of share capital and its book value. Despite the significant differences between these two approaches, they have something in common: to evaluate SVA, it is necessary to determine the estimated value of share capital. For this purpose, well-known methods of estimating the value of a company by discounting cash flows are used.

SVA is calculated according to the following formula

$$SVA = CF - SC, \tag{14.5}$$

where CF is the net present value of future cash flows discounted on capital raising costs (cost of capital), SC (share capital) is the book value of share capital.

The main disadvantage of SVA is the complexity of calculations and complexity associated with forecasting cash flows.

There is a relationship between EVA and SVA indicators. If the company pays dividends and their volume is equal to the price of equity, then

$$CF = PV(EVA), \tag{14.6}$$

where PV (EVA) is the present value of future EVA discounted at capital raising costs (cost of capital).

According to Equations 14.5 and 14.6, we have that

$$SVA = PV(EVA) - SC, \tag{14.7}$$

Market Value Added (MVA). The MVA indicator focuses on the market capitalization of the enterprise, which is more significant for open joint-stock companies whose shares are listed on stock exchanges. The share price determines the well-being of shareholders more precisely than the profit. In general terms, MVA is the difference between the market value of capital achieved over a certain period and the cost of capital according to the balance sheet (Atril, 2003).

MVA is calculated using the following formula:

$$MVA = MV - IC, \tag{14.8}$$

where MV (Market Value) – the market value of an enterprise, IC (Investment Capital) – the cost of invested capital of an enterprise according to accounting.

In Ukraine, in an undeveloped stock market, the use of the MVA indicator is limited.

Atrill (2003) indicates a relationship between MVA and EVA. As a justification, he cites the following. The value of the business (VB) is equal to the present value of the expected future EVA flow plus the amount of capital invested. Therefore:

$$VB = IC + PV(EVA), \tag{14.9}$$

This equation can be rewritten as follows:

$$PV(EVA) = VB - IC, \tag{14.10}$$

MVA is defined as the difference between the value of a business and the capital invested. Therefore

$$MVA = VB - IC, \tag{14.11}$$

Comparing Equations 14.10 and 14.11 we can write the following:

$$PV(EVA) = MVA, \tag{14.12}$$

In our opinion, this justification for the relationship between MVA and EVA is erroneous, because in Equation 14.10, the value of a business is defined on the basis of the discounted flow of EVA, and in Formula 14.11 the value of a business is defined on the basis of the value of an enterprise's shares. In other words, we are talking about different estimates of business value. The first is determined within the framework of the revenue approach, and the second is determined on the basis of the market approach. In practice, these estimates can vary significantly.

The lack of a well-defined relationship between EVA and MVA can be explained by the fact that EVA reflects the real capitalization, and MVA is a fictitious capitalization of the enterprise. The share price is determined not only by internal factors of the enterprise (profit, volume of equity and debt capital, etc.) but also by external factors (industry, global, psychological and behavioral). If the influence of the first group of factors on the stock price is decisive, then we can talk about a significant correlation between EVA and MVA indicators. If the influence of external factors, especially psychological and behavioral factors, is decisive, then we cannot talk about the correlation of EVA and MVA indicators.

Based on the results of the analysis of the above-mentioned indicators, the following conclusions can be drawn:

- in their names, the phrase "value added" is unreasonably used, because EVA is determined on the basis of the net operating profit of the enterprise, SVA – on the basis of the present value of future cash flows and the book value of share capital, MVA – on the basis of the market value of the enterprise and the invested capital in the enterprise according to accounting,
- in contrast to the "gross value added" indicator, they reflect the interests of only business owners, and not society as a whole.

Indicators for assessing the enterprises productivity based on gross value added

Based on the above-mentioned, it is advisable to use the "gross value added" indicator to assess the productivity of enterprises, along with the traditional "output", "sales volume", and "profit" indicators.

It is also proposed to use derived indicators to assess the enterprises productivity:

1 labor productivity at value added (PVA), as the volume of gross value added per employee at an enterprise

$$P_{VA} = GVA / N_{/}, \tag{14.13}$$

where GVA – annual gross value added of the enterprise, N – average annual number of employees at the enterprise.

2 return on sales at value added (ROS_{VA}), as the ratio of gross value added of an enterprise to the volume of products sold by it,

$$ROS_{VA} = (GVA/S) \star 100\%_{/}, \tag{14.14}$$

where GVA – annual gross value added of the enterprise, S – annual volume of sales of products by the enterprise;

3 return on fixed assets at value added (ROC_{VA}), as the ratio of gross value added to fixed assets of the enterprise:

$$ROC_{VA} = (GVA/C) \star 100\%_{/}, \tag{14.15}$$

where GVA – annual gross value added of the enterprise, C – average annual cost of fixed assets of the enterprise.

This indicator reflects the efficiency of using fixed assets of the enterprise in terms of generating gross value added and determines the gross value added that the enterprise receives from each hryvnia of fixed assets.

4 return on assets at value added (ROA_{VA}) indicator, as the ratio of gross value added to the assets of the enterprise:

$$ROA_{VA} = (GVA/A) \star 100\%_{/}, \tag{14.16}$$

where GVA – annual gross value added of the enterprise, A – average annual value of the enterprise's assets.

This indicator reflects the efficiency of using the enterprise assets in terms of generating gross value added and determines the gross value added that the enterprise receives from each hryvnia of assets.

The above-mentioned indicators are proposed to be used both for enterprises and for certain types of economic activity (industry, agriculture, construction, trade, transport, etc.).

It makes sense to correlate the profitability of sales, equity, and assets only between enterprises in one industry, as well as in the factor analysis of the enterprise or in the analysis of changes in the value of this indicator over a period of time.

There is a direct relationship between the "labor productivity at value added", "return on sales at value added", "fund return", and "capital-labor ratio" indicators. This is easy to see if the "labor productivity at value added" indicator is presented in the form of a three-factor model, as a return on sales at value-added, fund return, and capital-labor ratio.

$$P_{VA} = (GVA/S) \star (S/C) \star (C/N) = ROS_{VA} \star FB \star FO_{/}, \tag{14.17}$$

where P_{VA} – labor productivity by value added; GVA – gross value added; S – sales volume; C – cost of fixed assets; N – number of employees; ROS_{VA} – return on sales by value added; FB – fund return; FO – capital-labor ratio.

Results and discussion

Valuation of the productivity of enterprises based on the "profit" indicator

The main indicator of valuation of the enterprise performance, from the point of view of their owners, is profit, as well as indicators derived from it – return on sales and return on assets (equity). The financial result (profit/loss) of enterprises in Ukraine in 2012–2019 was very volatile. In 2014–2016, this indicator was negative and in 2014 losses amounted to 523.6 billion UAH. In the future, the situation changed and in 2017–2019 this indicator was positive and in 2019 it reached 664.8 billion UAH (State Statistics Service of Ukraine, 2018, 2019b). In 2012–2019, the dynamics of the financial result of enterprises significantly differed by type of economic activity. Thus, in agriculture, this indicator was positive throughout this period and reached a maximum of 103.1 billion UAH in 2015. Conversely, in the construction and transport sectors, it was negative for most of this period. The largest decline occurred in industry and trade in 2014–2015, where losses averaged about 180 billion UAH and 130 billion UAH, respectively (Figure 14.2).

This situation may indicate, on the one hand, the crisis phenomena in the country's economy and, on the other hand, the concealment of profits and evasion of income tax. According to the results of the first quarter of 2016, the total number of income tax payers was about 270,000 UAH. Income tax revenues totaled 113.8 billion UAH, of which 11.3 billion UAH, or 80%, was paid by only 1086 payers (0.4% of the total number of taxpayers). Analysis of this category of payers shows that these are usually companies with foreign

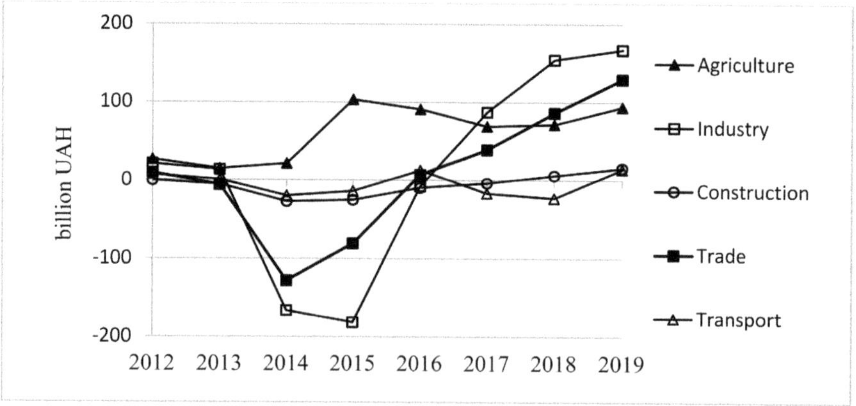

Figure 14.2 Financial result of Ukrainian enterprises by type of economic activity in 2012–2019 in actual prices.

Source: Calculated by the authors.

Table 14.1 Sales volume of Ukrainian enterprises by type of economic activity in 2012–2019 (in billion UAH)

	2012	*2013*	*2014*	*2015*	*2016*	*2017*	*2018*	*2019*	*2019/ 2012*
Total	4307.1	4153.1	4319.9	5319.0	6387.9	7862.7	9388.1	9841.1	2.28
Agriculture	162.6	161.1	213.9	362.3	403.6	454.4	525.1	556.3	3.42
Industry	1498.9	1473.1	1546.6	1887.5	2305.7	2817.8	3248.4	3230.0	2.15
Construction	155.8	141.1	150.5	142.9	169.7	221.4	302.7	370.8	2.38
Trade	1623.6	1612.1	1629.7	1953.3	2385.7	3061.7	3764.4	3958.4	2.44
Transport	212.3	207.1	203.6	294.0	365.3	437.2	502.2	543.0	2.56

Source: Calculated by the authors.

investments and state-owned enterprises. At the same time, 8000 payers who are unprofitable (the amount of accumulated losses is 1 trillion 68 billion UAH), for the 1st quarter of 2016, 13.6 billion UAH were withdrawn from Ukraine (Taptunova, 2016). Thus, the "profit" indicator does not give an idea of the real productivity of enterprises, since in the conditions of existing legislation it is quite easy to "optimize" (reduce) it.

Valuation of the productivity of enterprises based on the "sales volume" indicator. According to this indicator, the productivity of the country's enterprises in 2012–2019 in actual prices increased by 2.28 times, but it was mainly due to the influence of inflation (Table 14.1).

The largest increase occurred in agriculture – by 3.42 times, and the smallest in industry – by 2.15 times. Above the average level in the country, there was an increase in construction, trade, and transport by 2.38 times, 2.44 times, and 2.56 times, respectively.

A completely different picture takes place if we estimate the volume of sales by Ukrainian enterprises at constant prices in 2012. This indicator in 2012–2019 in the country as a whole decreased by 20.4%, in industry by 29%, in trade by almost 20%, and in construction and transport by 8.7% and 1.4%, respectively. Only in agriculture was there an increase, which amounted to 30.0% (Table 14.2).

Table 14.2 Sales volume of Ukrainian enterprises by type of economic activity in 2012–2019 in 2012 prices (in billion UAH)

	2012	*2013*	*2014*	*2015*	*2016*	*2017*	*2018*	*2019*	*2019/ 2012*
Total	4307.1	4091.7	3628.4	3204.8	3312.3	3394.7	3509.3	3429.3	0.796
Agriculture	162.6	155.7	170.1	187.5	189.0	187.4	195.1	210.6	1.295
Industry	1498.9	1472.4	1278.6	1110.5	1126.7	1127.8	1128.3	1064.5	0.710
Construction	155.8	133.1	116.3	83.4	91.3	110.8	125.4	142.3	0.913
Trade	1623.6	1605.7	1254.4	1053.6	1145.9	1185.0	1323.3	1301.1	0.801
Transport	212.3	204.3	184.9	190.5	212.0	213.7	208.1	209.4	0.986

Source: Calculated by the authors.

Table 14.3 Labor productivity at Ukrainian enterprises in terms of sales by type of economic activity in 2012–2019 in 2012 prices (in thousand UAH)

	2012	*2013*	*2014*	*2015*	*2016*	*2017*	*2018*	*2019*	*2019/ 2012*
Total	560.8	552.4	576.1	544.1	571.0	584.0	588.9	535.2	0.954
Agriculture	228.4	226.5	270.5	313.7	307.7	316.1	335.8	371.6	1.627
Industry	495.3	503.4	526.3	493.1	517.5	524.2	534.7	517.6	1.045
Construction	379.0	358.2	406.4	336.3	369.8	429.6	460.5	472.4	1.246
Trade	1 360.5	1 389.0	1 235.6	1 138.1	1 235.1	1 197.7	1 281.8	1197.0	0.880
Transport	226.5	224.1	242.5	245.4	277.0	279.7	273.0	276.2	1.219

Source: Calculated by the authors.

About 70% of sales are accounted for by industrial and commercial enterprises. Since 2016, the sales volume in trade exceeds the sales volume in industry, the difference is growing, and in 2019 the excess was 22.2%. Enterprises of other types of economic activity are significantly inferior in terms of sales.

At the same time, labor productivity in terms of sales (sales per 1 employee) at the country's enterprises in 2012–2019 in 2012 prices decreased by 4.6%. The largest growth was in agricultural enterprises – by 62.7%, while a larger than 20.0% growth was observed in enterprises in construction and transport, a 4.5% increase was observed in industry. There was a decrease by 12.0% in trade enterprises (Table 14.3).

The highest level of labor productivity in terms of sales in 2012–2019 took place at trade enterprises – 1100–1400 thousand UAH per 1 employee, which is 2 times more than the national average, 4.83 times more than at agricultural enterprises, 2.44 times more than at industrial enterprises, 3.12 times more than at construction enterprises, 4.91 times more than at transport enterprises. This situation is largely due to the high level of intermediate costs at trade enterprises, which accounts for about 85% of sales, while at transport and agricultural enterprises it is about 50%.

Thus, the "sales volume" indicator does not give an idea of the real productivity of enterprises, since this indicator is the results of the activities of a set of enterprises, the enterprise itself, and its suppliers. At the same time, the further the enterprise is in the technological chain, the greater the sales volume and the less this indicator reflects the real labor productivity at the enterprise.

Valuation of the productivity of Ukrainian enterprises based on the "gross value added" indicator

In 2012–2019, the volume of gross value added at the country's enterprises increased by 2.70 times. This growth is mainly due to the high level of inflation. Above the average level in the country, there was growth at enterprises in agriculture by 2.76 times, in construction by almost 5.0 times, in trade

Table 14.4 Gross value added of Ukrainian enterprises by type of economic activity in 2012–2019 (in billion UAH)

	2012	*2013*	*2014*	*2015*	*2016*	*2017*	*2018*	*2019*	*2019/ 2012*
Total	1015.5	977.1	1234.1	1329.3	1702.7	2099.5	2310.6	2744.3	2.70
Agriculture	74.4	69.7	125.5	183.9	186.9	195.4	201.9	205.4	2.76
Industry	422.2	377.8	465.4	488.3	651.9	812.5	868.1	988.4	2.34
Construction	24.1	41.4	51.3	37.1	48.3	58.5	71.2	120.2	4.99
Trade	187.8	198.9	302.8	299.5	334.4	455.3	524.7	587.1	3.13
Transport	105.4	103.3	108.7	144.8	186.5	211.4	220.7	260.5	2.47

Source: Calculated by the authors.

by 3.13 times, below the average level in the country was at enterprises in transport by 2.47 times and in industry by 2.34 times (State Statistics Service of Ukraine, 2018, 2019a) (Table 14.4).

A completely different picture takes place if we estimate the gross value added of Ukrainian enterprises at constant prices in 2012. Its volume in 2012–2019 decreased by 9.8%, and in transport by 8.2%. The situation is particularly negative in industry, where the decline was by 35.2%, which indicates a further process of deindustrialization of the country's economy. Against this background, the growth of gross value added of enterprises in construction by 104.4%, looks like a contrast. The growth of gross value added of agriculture and trade enterprises amounted to 6.4% and 0.9%, respectively (Table 14.5).

From 2012 to 2019, the main source of gross value added was industrial enterprises, whose share together with trade enterprises was about 60% (Figure 14.3).

As a result of the deindustrialization of the country's economy, the share of industry decreased from 41.6% in 2012 to 36.0% in 2019, while the share of trade, on the contrary, increased from 18.5% to 21.4%. The share of agriculture

Table 14.5 Gross value added of Ukrainian enterprises by type of economic activity in 2012–2019 in 2012 prices (in billion UAH)

	2012	*2013*	*2014*	*2015*	*2016*	*2017*	*2018*	*2019*	*2019/ 2012*
Total	1015.5	936.9	1020.9	791.7	866.0	874.5	834.0	915.5	0.902
Agriculture	74.4	67.1	98.8	93.1	86.3	81.0	76.1	79.2	1.064
Industry	422.2	363.2	362.2	268.0	282.1	279.0	255.9	273.6	0.648
Construction	24.1	38.8	38.6	21.6	26.5	29.7	31.1	49.2	2.044
Trade	187.8	188.8	224.6	160.1	160.6	174.1	182.3	189.6	1.009
Transport	105.4	98.1	96.2	93.4	106.9	103.5	91.9	96.7	0.918

Source: Calculated by the authors; gross domestic product using the production method and gross value added by type of economic activity. Retrieved from http://www.ukrstat.gov.ua/operativ/operativ2008/vvp/vvp_ric/xls/vtr_u_xls.zip

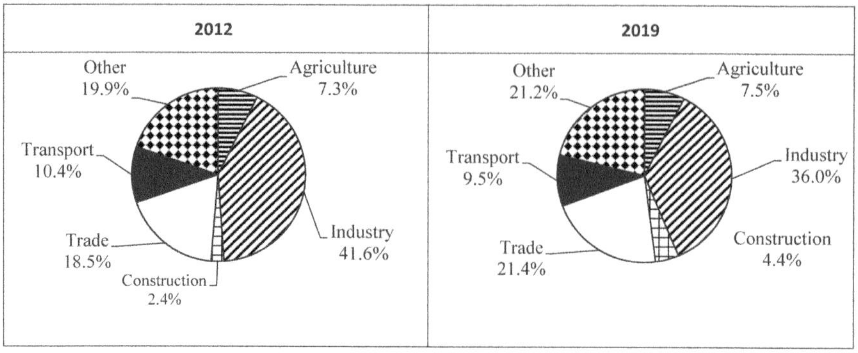

Figure 14.3 Structure of gross value added of Ukrainian enterprises by type of economic activity in Ukraine in 2012 and 2019.

Source: Calculated by the authors.

also increased from 7.3% to 7.5%, and construction from 2.4% to 4.4%, while transport decreased from 10.4% to 9.5%.

Labor productivity in terms of gross value added at the country's enterprises (the volume of gross value added per 1 employee) in 2012–2019; in 2012 prices increased by 8.1%. The largest growth was in enterprises in construction – almost by 2.8 times, in agriculture by 33.7%, in trade and transport by 10.8% and 13.4%, respectively, and in industry there was a decrease by 4.6% (Table 14.6).

Thus, labor productivity in terms of gross value added at the country's enterprises as a whole and by main types of economic activity increased in 2012 prices, with the exception of industry.

The highest level of labor productivity in terms of gross value added in 2012–2019 in 2012 prices was at trade enterprises – on average about 175,000 UAH, the lowest in construction and transport – about 110,000 UAH and 125,000 UAH, respectively. The average level of labor productivity in terms of added value in the country in 2012–2019 was 142.2 thousand UAH.

Table 14.6 Labor productivity by gross added value at Ukrainian enterprises by type of economic activity in 2012–2019 in 2012 prices (in thousand UAH)

	2012	*2013*	*2014*	*2015*	*2016*	*2017*	*2018*	*2019*	*2018/ 2012*
Total	132.2	126.5	162.1	134.4	149.3	150.4	139.9	142.9	1.081
Agriculture	104.5	97.7	157.1	155.8	140.4	136.7	131.0	139.7	1.337
Industry	139.5	124.2	149.1	119.0	129.6	129.7	121.3	133.1	0.954
Construction	58.6	104.3	134.9	86.9	107.3	115.3	114.3	163.3	2.789
Trade	157.4	163.3	221.2	172.9	173.1	175.9	176.6	174.4	1.108
Transport	112.4	107.7	126.2	120.3	139.7	135.5	120.6	127.5	1.134

Source: Calculated by the authors.

Table 14.7 Profitability by value added of Ukrainian enterprises by type of economic activity in 2012–2019 (in %)

	2012	*2013*	*2014*	*2015*	*2016*	*2017*	*2018*	*2019*	*Average*
Total	23.6	23.5	28.6	25.0	26.7	26.7	24.6	27.9	25.8
Agriculture	45.8	43.2	58.6	50.8	46.3	43.0	38.5	36.9	45.4
Industry	28.2	25.6	30.1	25.9	28.3	28.8	26.7	30.6	28.0
Construction	15.5	29.4	34.1	25.9	28.4	26.4	23.5	32.4	27.0
Trade	11.6	12.3	18.6	15.3	14.0	14.9	13.9	14.8	14.4
Transport	49.6	49.9	53.4	49.3	51.1	48.4	44.0	48.0	49.2

Source: Calculated by the authors.

The profitability of enterprises in terms of gross value added (the ratio of gross value added to sales) differs significantly by type of activity, which is mainly due to their place in the chain of creation of gross value added and, accordingly, the difference in the required volumes of intermediate costs. The average level of profitability of enterprises in terms of value added in the country in 2012–2019 was 25.8%, the highest level was at transport and enterprises – 49.2% and 45.4%, respectively, and the lowest level was at trade enterprises – 14.4% (Table 14.7).

In 2014, there was a sharp increase in the profitability of enterprises in terms of value added in the country as a whole and in the main types of economic activity. In agriculture, it reached the level of almost 60%, but later there was a gradual decline to 36.9% in 2019. The same process occurred in other economic activities, but not so clearly: in construction – a drop from 34.1% to 32.4%, in trade – from 18.6% to 14.8%, in transport – from 53.4% to 48.0%, and in the country as a whole – from 28.6% to 27.9%. This indicates a decline in the efficiency of business activities in Ukraine after 2014.

Conclusions

Profit as an indicator of the productivity of enterprises has significant disadvantages. Firstly, under the current legislation, it is quite easy to "optimize" (reduce) it and accordingly it does not give a real idea of the productivity of enterprises; secondly, an increase in profit by reducing wages, financing social security and training of employees can lead to a decrease in human capital, and this in turn leads to more significant losses than with the loss of physical and financial capital, and thirdly, this indicator reflects only the interests of the owners of enterprises, and not society as a whole.

The "sales volume" indicator reflects the labor productivity not of an individual enterprise, but of a set of enterprises, namely the enterprise and its suppliers. At the same time, the further the enterprise is in the technological chain, the greater the sales volume and the less it reflects the real labor productivity at the enterprise.

The "economic value added" (EVA), "shareholder value added" (SVA), and "market value added" (MVA) indicators, in contrast to the "gross value added" indicator, reflect the interests of only the owners of enterprises, and not the company as a whole.

The "gross value added" indicator has a greater analytical value than the "sales volume" and "profit" indicators, since it: gives a more realistic idea of the productivity of enterprises; determines the potential of the enterprise to accumulate capital; provides a single conceptual framework for evaluating the results of economic activity at the micro, meso, and macro levels. It is proposed to use the "gross value added" indicator in statistical and accounting as the main indicator of the productivity of enterprises.

Evaluation of the productivity of enterprises based on the "profit" indicator showed a very high level of its volatility. The profitability of the country's enterprises fell from 2.4% in 2012 to a negative value of 12.1% in 2014; the largest drop occurred in construction and industry to negative values of 18.1% and 10.1%. In 2015–2019, the profitability grew and in 2019 it became positive for almost all major economic activities.

The highest level of labor productivity in terms of sales volume in 2012–2019 in 2012 prices took place at trade enterprises – 1100–1400 thousand UAH per 1 employee, which is 4.83 times more than at agricultural enterprises, 2.44 times more than at industrial enterprises, 3.12 times more than at construction enterprises, 4.91 times more than at transport enterprises. This situation is largely due to the high level of intermediate costs at retail enterprises, which accounts for about 85% of sales. At industrial and construction enterprises, intermediate costs account for about 73%, at transport and agricultural enterprises – about 50%.

Labor productivity in terms of value added (gross value added per 1 employee) in 2012–2019 at the country's enterprises as a whole and by main types of economic activity in 2012 prices increased, with the exception of industry. In the whole country, it increased by 8.1%. The largest growth was in construction enterprises – almost by 2.8 times, agriculture by 33.7%, and trade and transport by 10.8% and 13.4%, respectively, and in industry there was a decrease by 4.6%.

The profitability of enterprises in terms of gross value added differs significantly by type of activity, which is mainly due to their place in the chain of creation of gross value added and, accordingly, the difference in the required volumes of intermediate costs. The average level of profitability of enterprises in terms of value added in the country in 2012–2019 was 25.5%, the highest level was at transport and agricultural enterprises – almost 50% and 47%, respectively, and the lowest level was at trade enterprises – 14.4%. In 2014, there was a sharp increase in the profitability of enterprises in terms of value added in the country as a whole and in the main types of economic activity. In agriculture, it reached the level of almost 60%, but later there was a gradual decline to 36.9% in 2019. The same process occurred in other economic activities, but not so rapidly. This indicates a decline in the efficiency of business activities in Ukraine after 2014.

References

Almodóvar-González, M., Fernández-Portillo, A., & CarlosDíaz-Casero, J. (2020). Entrepreneurial activity and economic growth. A multi-country analysis. *European Research on Management and Business Economics, 26*(1), 9–17. https://doi.org/10.1016/j.iedeen.2019.12.004

Asaul, A., Voinarenko, M., & Erofeev, P. (2004). Organization of business activities. SPb: Humanistika.

Atrill, P. (2003). *Financial management for non-specialists.* Financial Times Prentice Hall.

Baumol, W. (1996). Entrepreneurship: Productive, unproductive, and destructive. *Journal of Business Venturing, 11*(1), 3–22. https://doi.org/10.1016/0883-9026(94)00014-X

Cheremushkin, S. (2017). Evaluation of the company's value based on the Alfred Rappaport model.

Cobbold, T. (2003). A comparison of gross output and value-added methods of productivity estimation, Productivity Commission Research Memorandum, Canberra. https://www.pc.gov.au/research/supporting/comparison-gross-output-value-added-methods/cgovam.pdf

Dierks, P., & Patel, A. (1997). What is EVA, and how can it help your company? Management Accounting (November): 52–58. https://maaw.info/ArticleSummaries/ArtSumDierksPatel97.htm

Entrepreneurship – Wikipedia. (2022). Retrieved June 22, 2022, from https://en.wikipedia.org/wiki/Entrepreneurship.

Johnston, R., & Stewart, S. (2019). Understanding productivity in Northern Ireland Ulster University. https://www.ulster.ac.uk/__data/assets/pdf_file/0005/414662/Understanding-Productivity-in-NI-May-2019.pdf

Kalchenko, S., Trusova, N., Hrybova, D., & Serhii, B. (2018). The small and large business interaction within national economy's gross added value reproduction in Ukraine. *Oeconomia Copernicana, 9*(3), 403–417. https://doi.org/10.24136/oc.2018.020. http://economic-research.pl/Journals/index.php/oc/article/view/1047/1001

Kusumastuti, D., Narimawati, U., & Pujihartanti, E. (2016). Developing entrepreneurship competency and economic added value among the graduates (study at private universities in Indonesia). *International Journal of Economic Research, 13*(8), 3551–3569. https://www.scopus.com/record/display.uri?eid=2-s2.0-85013648686&origin=inward&txGid=7526695c12b2193aa0c8855a8b0de937

Lieberman, M., & Kang, J. (2008). How to measure company productivity using value-added: A focus on Pohang Steel (POSCO). *Asia Pacific Journal of Management, 25*(2), 209–224. https://doi.org/10.1007/s10490-007-9081-0. https://www.researchgate.net/publication/5143705_How_to_Measure_Company_Productivity_Using_Value-Added_A_Focus_on_Pohang_Steel_POSCO

Maditinos, D., Šević, Ž, & Theriou, N. (2007). Economic value added (EVA). Is it really the best performance measure? A review of the theoretical and empirical literature. The case of Athens stock exchange (ASE). *Review of Economic Sciences*, 1–25. http://abd.teikav.edu.gr/articles/Review%20of%20Economic%20Sciences,%202006_EVA%20(2).pdf

Ndubisi, N., & Nair, S. (2009). Green entrepreneurship (GE) and green value added (GVA): A conceptual framework (Article). *International Journal of Entrepreneurship, 13*(special issue), 21–34. https://www.scopus.com/record/display.uri?eid=2-s2.0-77953473850&origin=inward&txGid=d3359bf3cb9043336df7f004566eca2d

Neto, P., Santos, A., & Serrano, M. (2014). Public policies supporting local networks for entrepreneurship and innovation: Effectiveness and added value analysis of LEADER program in the Alentejo region of Portugal. *International Journal of Entrepreneurship and Small Business, 21*(3), 406–435. https://doi.org/10.1504/IJESB.2014.060900

OECD (2001). Measuring productivity. Measurement of aggregate and industry-level productivity growth OECD. http://www.pollen-conseil.fr/wp-content/uploads/2019/05/Measuring-productivity-manual-guide-OCDE.pdf

Organization of United Nations (2009). *System of national accounts of 2008*. https://unstats.un.org/unsd/nationalaccount/docs/sna2008.pdf

Schreyer, P., & Pilat, D. (2001). Measuring productivity OECD. *Economic Studies*, 33. https://doi.org/10.1787/eco_studies-v2001-art13-en. https://www.oecd.org/global-forum-productivity/library/1959006.pdf

Shil, N. (2009). Performance measures: An application of economic value added (2009). *International Journal of Business and Management*, *4*(3), 169–177. https://doi.org/10.5539/ijbm.v4n3p169

Sobel, R. (2008). Testing Baumol: Institutional quality and the productivity of entrepreneurship. *Journal of Business Venturing, 23*, 641–655. http://www.appstate.edu/~perritj/Sobel.pdf

State Statistics Service of Ukraine (2018). *Activity of business entities*. http://www.ukrstat.gov.ua/druk/publicat/kat_u/2018/zb/11/zd_2018.pdf

State Statistics Service of Ukraine (2019a). *Activity of business entities*. http://www.ukrstat.gov.ua/druk/publicat/kat_u/2019/zb/11/zb_dsg_2018.pdf

State Statistics Service of Ukraine (2019b). Gross domestic product by production method and gross value added by type of economic activity. http://www.ukrstat.gov.ua/operativ/operativ2008/vvp/vvp_ric/xls/vtr_u_xls.zip

Taptunova, I. (2016). Transformation of corporate income tax in tax on withdrawn capital (Policy Paper)/European Information and Research Center. http://euinfocenter.rada.gov.ua/uploads/documents/28909.pdf

Verkhovna Rada of Ukraine. (2003). Economic code of Ukraine. https://zakon.rada.gov.ua/laws/show/436-15#Text

Vlasiuk, Y., Tebenko, V., Hrybova, D., & Biliaiev, S. (2018). The influence of small business spreading on the dynamics of the labor costs share in value added generated by leading industries of Ukrainian economy. *Financial and Credit Activity: Problems of Theory and Practice, 3*(26), 123–132. https://doi.org/10.18371/fcaptp.v3i26.116123

15 Theoretical and practical aspects of entrepreneurship

A case study of Poland

Jacek Witkowski, Barbara Siuta-Tokarska, Agnieszka Thier, Zdzisława Dacko-Pikiewicz

Introduction

Management and economics are part of social science that is concerned with the involvement of individuals in economic processes, i.e. those that are carried out under conditions of basically unlimited needs and limited opportunities, in regard to goods and their availability. As Wilkin (2016) rightly points out, an object of management can be as diverse as the time that an individual has, the space in which he operates, or the skills that he possesses. In this light, both the management objectives and the ways in which human beings act in a management context have always been related to the concept of entrepreneurship.

Based on the literature, we can identify two concepts underlying entrepreneurship that are conducive to the development of its scientific dimension. The first one is the humanistic-social dimension of entrepreneurship which encompasses the actual establishment of a company or the implementation of a project, while the second dimension describes optimal, possibly universal processes. While the humanistic-social approach focuses on the traits, characteristics, and values of the individual (questions about what motivates our actions), in the management-economic approach the focus is on the processes and mechanisms related to it (questions about the consequences/effects of our actions) (Kurczewska, 2014). Entrepreneurship is therefore a phenomenon characterized by great complexity and multidimensionality, making it impossible for a single theory to be formulated, let alone one that is universally valid. Nevertheless, entrepreneurship is the source of economic potential that is considered to be one of the significant factors of socio-economic development and whose high level can ensure the so-called material-cultural-educational well-being.

The purpose of this research chapter is to try to combine the theoretical, methodical, and practical dimensions of entrepreneurship and to provide answers to the following research questions:

1 what is the theory's view of entrepreneurship and its resulting functions?
2 what entrepreneurship measurement models can be applied in practice?
3 did Poland's economic conditions between 2017 and 2020 affect entrepreneurship in a positive way?

DOI: 10.4324/9781003384311-15

Entrepreneurship – theoretical context

Entrepreneurship is an issue that is characteristic of socio-economic sciences, including management sciences, but also psychology, philosophy, or political science. Interest in this issue is related, among other things, to the effects of dynamic phenomena that are taking place in the world economy as a result of permanent changes in the socioeconomic environment. It is worth pointing out that economics understand entrepreneurship as the result of one's work, involvement, and market behavior, as well as the actions that translate into economic results in an economic unit; in the field of management science, it is recognized as a process and a characteristic of one's actions that is reflected in management efficiency (Targalski, 2014, p. 18). This multidimensionality of interpretations arises from the varying perceptions of human activity in the social sciences, which include both economics and management science.[1]

The term *entrepreneurship* is not clear-cut and the ambiguity exists both in everyday language and science. In terms of research, entrepreneurship is characterized not only by its interdisciplinary character (which entails studying it at the meeting point between at least two scientific disciplines) but also by multidisciplinarity, i.e. studying it separately in different scientific disciplines (Wach, 2015, p. 25). Hence, entrepreneurship is expressed in the multifaceted and multilayered nature of the research that is being undertaken. In colloquial terms, it is treated as a synonym for initiative and resourcefulness, cunning, as well as dynamism (Safin, 2002, p. 13) associated with a spirit of initiative that is ultimately expressed in the ability to be entrepreneurial (Szymczak, 1988, p. 968). The embodiment of entrepreneurship is a person (group of people) that – from an economic viewpoint – is referred to as an entrepreneur. According to this view, entrepreneurship is understood as the ability to select production resources and employ them in one's business activities that are conducted under conditions of uncertainty so as to assure that the entrepreneur or a group of entrepreneurs achieves desired results. Moreover, entrepreneurship is also seen as one of the main factors of production apart from land, labor, and capital. However, this approach has been criticized because, as M. Blaug (1994, p. 466) points out, entrepreneurship is a function that does not meet the necessary conditions to be defined as a factor of production due to the fact that neither it is simultaneously and infinitely divisible nor strictly homogeneous. However, at this point, it is worthwhile to ask if the primary factors of production in the modern economy actually meet such defined criteria. One need only look at capital and how its concept, understanding, and forms in the economy have clearly evolved since the classical economics era.

When it comes to the practical aspect of conducting business, entrepreneurship can take two forms:

1 the entrepreneur (i.e. an individual or a group) who is synonymous with an innovator who manufactures and sells new products that either satisfy customer needs better than other products on the market or introduce

new needs, and who implements new methods of production and sales, finds new markets for supply and sale, and introduces new management techniques;
2 the reallocation of resources from activities with relatively low efficiency to those where there are more significant benefits to be gained, i.e. executing tasks typical of a person with sufficient decision-making authority, rationalizing management of the resources available to him/her.

The two types of entrepreneurship can be observable in the market and determine the market's dynamics; attribute-based entrepreneurship demonstrates characteristics that describe human efforts and activities, whereas entrepreneurship in its functional form corresponds with an entrepreneurial's activity and his/her involvement in the market. So it should be acknowledged, as R. W. Griffin (1999, pp. 730–731) observes, that entrepreneurship is regarded, on the one hand, as a set of characteristics that describe an individual, teams, or even entire institutions or the economy act, while, on the other hand, as a process of creating and building new things using ideas and resources that others cannot see.

Compared to the colloquial understanding of entrepreneurship, academic literature offers relatively broad and clearly more criterion-oriented interpretations of the concept in which a distinction between four underlying reference points is made, i.e. entrepreneurship's function as

- a personality trait,
- the individual entrepreneur,
- managerial activities,
- a market phenomenon (Wach, 2015, p. 26).

Figure 15.1 shows the aforementioned dimensions of entrepreneurship.

The first dimension of entrepreneurship deals with personality. In this context, entrepreneurship can be conceptualized as an inherent and creationist personality trait but also as a set of personal traits that are manifested in various social and professional roles of a person, as well as a relatively stable set of behaviors that are conditioned by personality, culture, society, and situation (Mrozowicz, 2010; Thier, 2020). Thus, the personality function of entrepreneurship consists of a person's image and includes his or her intelligence and temperament traits that are determined genetically to a significant extent, as well as traits acquired in the process of ontogenetic development, including character, personality, motivation to act, and the set of values adopted by the individual, and which together affect the individual's perceptual processes as well as his or her abilities.

The second dimension applies to entrepreneurs as individuals. De facto, it does not refer to an individual but rather a particular role, activity, or task that is performed by an individual. It is referred to as market-based

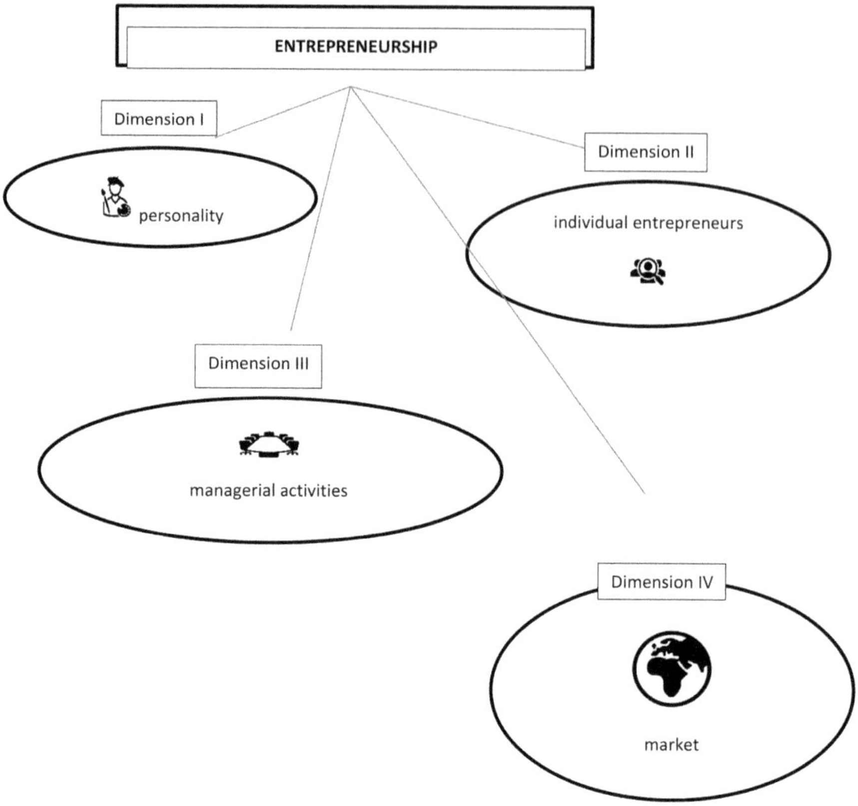

Figure 15.1 Dimensions of entrepreneurship in the literature.

Source: Own elaboration.

entrepreneurial functions, which are conducted with the following factors in mind:

- the entrepreneur is the person who assumes the risk (as pointed out by Cantillon, Say, or Knight),
- the entrepreneur is an organizer and coordinator of limited economic resources (Say),
- the entrepreneur is an allocator and accumulator of capital (Smith, Ricardo, Marshall),
- the entrepreneur constantly looks for opportunities and maximizes the chances to get the intended effects of his activities (Mises, Kirzner).

An entrepreneur expresses his or her entrepreneurial spirit through a need to create that is linked to his or her ability to do so (in the context of new, creative solutions), i.e. creativity, along with seeing the positives in a given business venture, i.e. optimism.

The third dimension of entrepreneurship is related to managerial activities, which are expressed by the exploration and explanation of managerial behavior (Wach, 2015, p. 27) that are focused on choosing appropriate strategies, creating structures (in an effort to create flexible structures), promoting innovation, independence, and initiative in addition to avoiding bureaucracy as well as finding effective ways to lead and develop an organization in a competitive and highly unpredictable environment (Marjanski, 2013, p. 5). A review of the literature identifies two main areas of research in this field:

- entrepreneurship as a process of creating new ventures and
- entrepreneurship as a process of discovering and seizing opportunities (Landström, 2010, pp. 18–19).

It is important to note that the two branches of research are interconnected. The managers who create new ventures often discover new, previously unknown business areas or take advantage of emerging market opportunities.

Entrepreneurship's fourth dimension is its relationship with the market. This economic view of entrepreneurship can be illustrated specifically by looking at demand-supply relationships. As Hébert and Link (1989, p. 4) point out, the degree of entrepreneurship in an economy depends on three important conditions:

1 free market and open economy, which are guarantors of equal access to entrepreneurial opportunities,
2 a guarantee of private property, and
3 stability of the institution, which is necessary to reinforce the two conditions indicated above.

However, one must not forget that the free market, and its model, in particular, is a certain simplification of the economic reality. And such reality, in turn, appears to possess much greater complexity and cannot be reduced to mere supply and demand curves or utility maximization in the process of achieving tasks, functions, and goals that guide an individual entrepreneur or group of entrepreneurs.

Measuring entrepreneurship – an overview

Measuring entrepreneurship and the selection of methods associated with it is a challenging undertaking (Siuta-Tokarska, 2013, p. 91). In practice, two main aspects are emphasized (Raczyk, 2009):

1 measuring the so-called entrepreneurial spirit, studies of which (on the creation of new businesses, for instance) generally involve the surveying of selected groups, and
2 measuring the effects of entrepreneurship, usually based on data or indicators related to the number of different types of enterprises, e.g. in relation to demographics or the total number of economic entities.

Furthermore, many formulas and models of entrepreneurship exist, which, as practice indicates, can be discussed according to (Janczewski, 2005, p. 115):

- a dynamic (cause-and-effect) perspective,
- a static (i.e. outcome) perspective, and
- a systemic perspective.

There is also the possibility of using multivariate studies of organizational entrepreneurship in the context of operational activities. The following topics are covered, among others:

- innovation, proactivity, and risk-taking – e.g. the questionnaire developed by Covin and Slevin, based on the concept of Miller (Covin & Wales, 2012),
- in addition to the above-mentioned issues, competitive aggression and autonomy are also included – a questionnaire developed by Hughes and Morgan (2007),
- using knowledge and social capital building to develop organizations – Yamada (2004, pp. 289–320),
- the context of social entrepreneurship – Weerawardena and Mort (2006, pp. 21–35),
- the context of information society development – Strojny and Stankiewicz (2009, pp. 117–132),
- the concept of entrepreneurial intensity developed by Morris (1998), where the dimensions are arranged sequentially.

As a result, a multidimensional model of organizational entrepreneurship can be proposed using at least three of its dimensions, namely: the definitional, the cause-and-effect, and the process-related.

In addition to various national and international studies assessing entrepreneurship, its level, and dynamics, such as Ahmad and Hoffman (2007), Bacigalupo et al. (2016), Klapper et al. (2007), there is also the Global Entrepreneurship Monitor (GEM) research program. In addition to providing an assessment of entrepreneurship in individual countries, GEM's research also provides a comparative analysis of about 50 countries surveyed. GEM incorporates both quantitative and qualitative methods into its research which serves three primary purposes:

1 to provide a measurement of differences in entrepreneurial attitudes, activities, and aspirations between individual countries,
2 to identify the factors that determine the nature and level of entrepreneurial activity;
3 to draw conclusions applicable to socio-economic policy, including the promotion of entrepreneurship.

Research conducted by GEM is based on theoretical models, including a conceptual model in which the following elements are considered:

- the social, cultural, political, and economic contexts that influence entrepreneurship, with a focus on basic requirements, efficiency enhancers, innovation, and business sophistication,
- outcome affecting broadly understood socio-economic development, including entrepreneurial output that is expressed, among other things, by new jobs or new value added, as well as specific aspects of entrepreneurial activity which have a direct impact on these outputs. This includes businesses (their number) according to their development phase, type of business (by the impact), or the type of entrepreneurship practiced (self-employment – the TEA index, intrapreneurship – the EEA index).

Thus, one can conclude that the proposed GEM methodology takes into account the complex web of relationships between factors affecting entrepreneurship, the individual qualities of the entrepreneur, the nature of emerging enterprises, and the effects of entrepreneurship and their impact on social and economic development. For these reasons, we examined data and information on entrepreneurship in Poland based on the GEM methodology and conducted a descriptive analysis.

Entrepreneurship in Poland in the era of the COVID-19 pandemic

It is necessary to take into account the constant changes in the economic environment when implementing business activities. In its 2021 report, The Global Risk identified nine global risks comprising economic, environmental, geopolitical, social, and technological threats that may or already threaten humanity in coming years (World Economic Forum, 2021, p. 13).

A characteristic of contemporary reality is the occurrence of crises in the world economy. The current crisis associated with the SARS-CoV-2 virus causing acute respiratory illness has spread worldwide and will be felt for quite some time. On March 11, 2020, as a result of the spread of the virus as an infectious disease, the World Health Organization (WHO) declared that COVID-19 had reached a global pandemic status, resulting in as much as 90% of the world's population being affected by the associated measures which included travel restrictions, prohibitions of public gatherings, and the stay-at-home policy (Czech et al., 2020). The current pandemic, referred to as a Black Swan, refers not only to an economic crisis but also to a social as well as an environmental one. As Taleb (2008, p. XXII) points out, a Black Swan event has three main attributes:

- is unexpected, unusual, unpredictable, and highly unlikely,
- when they occur, they have a tremendous impact on the economy and society,
- after they occur, some people claim that they could have been predicted.

A closer look at the causes of economic crises, including the current one, allows us to point out at least some of their basic features, including a reduction in economic growth (a slowdown or even sharp declines), declining real wages, a significant drop in investment, and a decline in consumption. Further consequences of a crisis could include an increase in unemployment and rising inflation, along with a rise in public debt and budget deficits. Some analysts of this issue point to broader implications such as increasing income and opportunity disparities, growing instability in the financial sector, and deterioration of social capital, including moral capital (Horodecka, 2017, pp. 211–238).

Economic and social data collected in the European Union confirm the significant impact of the pandemic on outcomes. According to the European Commission's forecasts, the EU economy was to return to growth and achieve economic growth of 4.2% in 2021, recovering from −6.1% in 2020 (ZBP, 2021, p. 7). Poland performed quite well in this respect compared to other EU countries as the average annual economic growth rate in 2019 was 4.7%, and was followed by a −2.7% rate the following year; however, this was one of the slightest declines among EU countries. Undoubtedly, 2020 brought an economic slowdown to the Polish economy, which, as experts point out, had a dual character; on the one hand, the natural process of the so-called cyclical slowdown began after the high level of economic activity in 2017–2019, and on the other hand, the global shock caused by the COVID-19 pandemic that weighed heavily on the economy. Together, these two processes have left their imprint on macroeconomic results, most notably GDP growth.

According to forecasts at the time, the Polish economy was expected to achieve economic growth of 4% in 2021 and 5.4% in 2022 (*ZBP*, 2021, p. 4). The data and forecasts for the unemployment rate were fairly stable and ranged from 3.3% in 2019, 3.2% in 2020, 3.5% in 2021 and 3.3% in 2022. The problem, however, lies in rising inflation, which went up from 2.1% in 2019 to 3.7% in 2020, although forecasts for the next few years predicted it would decline to 3.4% in 2021 and 2.9% in 2022, which was still one of the highest levels in the EU, second only to Hungary (ZBP, 2021, p. 9; European Commission, 2021). As far as the budget deficit is concerned, its increase was visible, which had its specific rationale in the context of implemented aid programs but at the same time, the public debt value reflected it. According to forecasts, public debt in the EU in 2022 could reach 92.9% of GDP, and 55.1% in Poland.

According to the World Bank (World Bank, 2021), the Polish economy is quite well diversified despite the difficult period and is among the least affected by the COVID-19 pandemic compared to other countries in Europe. These results were also evident in the entrepreneurship undertaken during that period and in the results entrepreneurs achieved. Based on reports from non-financial firms, the corporate sector in Poland showed a high degree of flexibility and resilience to the COVID-19 pandemic crisis (*NBP*, 2021, p. 2). There was a slight decline in sales revenue in 2020 compared with the

Table 15.1 Financial results of enterprises in Poland in January–June 2019–2021

Specification	*January–July 2019*	*January–July 2020*	*January–July 2021*
Total revenues [PLN million]	1,809,167.70	1,714,579.70	2,033,287.20
Dynamics [% y/y]		[94.8]	[118.6]
Total costs [PLN million]	1,717,352.60	1,638,416.10	1,890,865.50
Dynamics [% y/y]		[95.4]	[115.4]
Net profit [million PLN]	94,434.10	95,271.50	140,627.90
Dynamics [% y/y]		[100,9]	[147.6]
Net loss [million PLN]	17,521.50	32,953.10	20,428.90
Dynamics [% y/y]		[188.1]	[62.0]
Commitments and provisions for liabilities [PLN million]	1,561,072.90	1,689,621.20 [108.2]	1,857,227.30 [110.0]
Dynamics [% y/y]			
Total capital expenditures [million PLN]	69,570.10	65,433.90	72,187.30
Dynamics of investment outlays in constant prices [%]	117.90	93.40	108.30
Gross return on sales [%]	4.60	4.50	5.80
Financial liquidity ratio I [%]	35.4	43.8	45.0

Source: *Financial Results* (2021).

Explanation: The data are for bookkeeping firms with more than nine employees.

previous year, and the financial result did not change drastically thanks to cost rationalization (*Szybki monitoring,* 2021, p. 2), although the number of entities suffering losses increased. The overall performance of the corporate sector improved in the first half of 2021. A summary of these data is presented in Table 15.1.

It is worth noting that in the first three months of 2021 the synthetic index stood close to neutral, and hence analysts saw the COVID-19 pandemic and the resulting restrictions as a source of short-term disturbances in the operation of the business sector in Poland that exacerbated the natural cycle (*NBP,* 2021, p. 4). As evidence of the improvement of the situation, domestic and foreign sales dynamics in 2020 took on the shape of a V, which meant an initially sharp decline but subsequently recovering.

It should not be forgotten, however, that the situation for different industries and classes varied, and the degree of pandemic restrictions experienced by companies had a significant impact on their performance. Therefore, the sectors that were the most affected by the pandemic included hotels and restaurants, culture, sports and tourism, and other service sectors (*NBP,* 2021, pp. 19–20). Additionally, a breakdown by size indicates that small businesses have improved profitability in the past few years, while the profitability of large business entities gradually has declined (*NBP,* 2021, p. 20).

An important measure showing the problems of companies during the pandemic is the high level of ongoing exposure to the risk of bankruptcy that companies experienced between 2019 and 2020 (an increase from over 2%

to about 3%) and the risk's highest peak between 2020 and 2021 (over 9%). The forecasts for the following year were positive as they indicated a decline in this value to below 5% (*NBP*, 2021, p. 24).

The significant percentage of companies with a high risk of bankruptcy in the period under analysis was also demonstrated by the performance of Polish companies in the context of their entrepreneurial activities. Based on its survey of more than 40 countries around the world as part of the Global Entrepreneurship Monitor 2019/2020, we can identify entrepreneurship in these countries, with a focus on early-stage entrepreneurship.

According to the GEM methodology, entrepreneurship is understood as "any attempt at new business or new venture creation, such as self-employment, a new business organization, or the expansion of an existing business, by an individual, a team of individuals, or an established business" (Reynolds et al., 1999). The primary index that is used for this research is total early-stage entrepreneurial activity (TEA), which measures the percentage of working-age adults (aged 18–64) who are involved with starting or operating a new (i.e. less than 3.5-year-old) firm. In the GEM model, total early-stage entrepreneurship includes pre-entrepreneurs and new entrepreneurs. In GEM's methodology, countries are divided into groups based on their per capita national income, including low, middle, and high-income countries. Between 2017 and 2020, Poland was ranked as a high-income country. Data on selected measures and key indicators of entrepreneurship are presented in Table 15.2.

The selected measures and indexes for entrepreneurship in Poland in 2017–2020 presented in Table 15.2 clearly show a worsening of the situation in the last period under analysis. While the first signs of a slowdown in entrepreneurship had already been visible in 2018, it seemed that the following year that ended with some fluctuations in index changes (including increases) could bring improvement. 2020, however, was definitely influenced by the COVID-19 pandemic factor. As a result, all of the primary indexes declined that year in comparison with previous years. Two indexes showed the greatest change:

- TEA, which decreased from 8.9 in 2017 to 3.1 in 2020, including female TEA from 7.7 to 2.4 and male TEA from 10.0 to 3.8, and
- nascent entrepreneurship rate, which decreased from 6.7 to 1.6 during the period.

Also, other indexes such as intrapreneurship (down from 6.0 in 2017 to 2.8 in 2019) established business ownership rate (down from 13.0 in 2018 to 12.2 in 2020), new business ownership rate (down from 2.2 in 2017 to 1.5 in 2020) and discontinuation of business (up from 2.8 in 2017 to 3.4 in 2020) show some deterioration in this regard.

The structure of the activity intensity of young entrepreneurs by market indicates that the share of entrepreneurs active exclusively in the domestic

Table 15.2 Entrepreneurship in Poland in 2017–2020 – selected measures and indexes

Description		*2017*	*2018*	*2019*	*2020*
Nascent entrepreneurship rate		6.7	4.1	3.6	1.6
New business ownership rate		2.2	1.1	1.8	1.5
Early-stage entrepreneurial activity (TEA)		8.9	5.2	5.4	3.1
Established business ownership rate		9.8	13	12.8	12.2
Discontinuation of business		2.8	2.4	3.1	3.4
Female TEA		7.7	4.5	5.1	2.4
Male TEA		10	6.0	5.7	3.8
Motivation to set up and conduct business	Necessity driven (% of TEA)	9	8.4		
	Improvement-driven opportunity (% of TEA)	67.6	55.1	----	
	to make a difference in the world			65.4	22.0
	to build great wealth or very high income	--------		13.3	52.8
	to continue a family tradition			81.6	20.4
	to earn a living because jobs are scarce			15.8	62.0
Structure of activity intensity of young entrepreneurs by market	home market	63.0	82.9	90.9	----
	foreign markets (export activity)	27.0	17.1	9.1	
Intrapreneurship (leadership in organizational entrepreneurship over the past 3 years among employees)		6.0	3.0	2.8	-----
National Entrepreneurship Context Index (NECI) (in pts.)		–	–	4.24	4.24

Source: Own compilation based on *Global Entrepreneurship Monitor Reports*, 2017–2020.

Explanation: The NECI indicator was introduced in the 2019 GEM study.

market clearly increased (from 63% in 2017 to 90.9% in 2019), and the percentage of those undertaking their activity in foreign markets decreased (from 27% to 9.1% in the same period). On the one hand, in a situation of an ongoing pandemic and limited access to external markets, this may be justified, but on the other hand, in the case of reduced internal demand, due to rising inflation, for example, it may turn out to be a negative market risk reduction strategy.

It is also worth pointing out that in terms of the NECI index Poland, with a score of 4.24, ranked 30th among the 44 countries assessed in 2020 and 14th among 18 European countries. This shows that it is necessary to improve the conditions for entrepreneurship to develop, especially since the pandemic period – as revealed by the research – has left a clear mark on entrepreneurial activities in Poland and has slowed down the pace of its development. It is even more alarming because the macroeconomic conditions of the Polish economy during the COVID-19 pandemic were quite positively evaluated (in comparison with other European countries) by international institutions such as the World Bank, which emphasized that Poland belonged among the European countries least harmed by the consequences of the pandemic.

Conclusions and recommendations

As the theory and practice of management demonstrate, entrepreneurship has many names, which is why we can identify many of its manifestations as well as outcomes. Entrepreneurship is not only a characteristic of people who overcome obstacles, take risks, and think outside the box but foremost a process (not a single act) that depends on many factors and is a result of a variety of conditions that depend on both the individual's subjective (internal) predispositions and the external conditions. These can effectively provide positive conditions for the development of this process through the use of appropriate instruments. Therefore, understanding them is an extremely important element of the process of creating an entrepreneurial reality in a given economy.

The presented analysis of selected measures and indexes for entrepreneurship in the Polish economy revealed a decline in its level and a decline in its dynamics. The COVID-19 pandemic and its associated restrictions and limitations, which effectively inhibited the development of economic activity, were cited as the main cause. As evidenced by KPMG's research, 78% of struggling businesses stated that it was the pandemic that adversely affected their economic situation had been (KPMG, 2020, p. 4).

The determinants of entrepreneurship in Poland in 2020 also showed that the factors that weaken entrepreneurship (as shown in Figure 15.2) in Poland have been:

- the tax policy of the government and bureaucracy,
- entrepreneurship-supporting government programs,
- lack of schooling in entrepreneurship,
- transfer of research and development.

The above-mentioned factors that hinder the development of entrepreneurship in Poland can be classified as systemic factors. It should be emphasized that these factors have long been identified as Poland's main barriers to entrepreneurship. Research conducted by Grant Thornton and the National Chamber of Commerce (Krajowa Izba Gospodarcza) in 2013 (Grant Thornton & Krajowa Izba Gospodarcza, 2013) showed that impediments relating to administration and taxes are more bothersome to entrepreneurs than economic uncertainty. Of course, 2020 was an especially difficult year for Polish entrepreneurs due to market conditions associated with the COVID-19 pandemic; however, the barriers to entrepreneurship in Poland inhibit attempts at development, a process that requires both time and capital. While the financial performance of the corporate sector shown in this descriptive analysis was not as bad in the January–June periods of 2019 and 2021 as originally expected, the restrictions put on investment activities because of uncertainty in the market will translate into weaker pro-growth trends in the near future. In addition, tax and administrative obstacles, such as inconsistent interpretation of legal regulations, complicated tax regulations or the

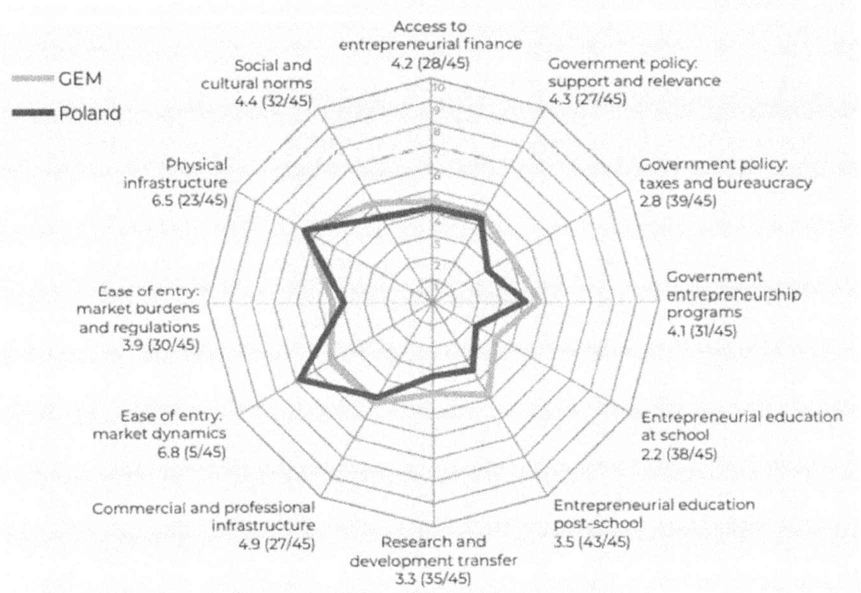

Figure 15.2 The entrepreneurial framework conditions in Poland in 2020.

Explanation: EFCs scale: 0 – Very inadequate insufficient status, 10 – Very adequate sufficient status. Rank out of 45 in brackets.

Source: *Global Entrepreneurship Monitor,* 2020/2021 Global Report (2021, p. 142).

frequency with which they are changing, the complexities of employment law, the need to obtain permits, concessions, licenses, and the time spent on legal proceedings prevent Polish enterprises from working on development initiatives. These negative effects of restrictions affect not only the entrepreneurs directly, their businesses, and their standing in the global economy but also the government's finances due to a reduction in revenue. Therefore, deregulation and the elimination of administrative barriers are pointed to as the necessary solutions to these long-standing, systemic problems. The consistently low level of innovation among Polish enterprises is the result of a lack of reliable systemic solutions to support this activity. The two concepts of entrepreneurship and innovation are strongly related. In order for Polish entrepreneurship to have a qualitative, rather than only a quantitative expression (i.e. a greater number of entrepreneurs), long-term solutions must be found at the national level.

Note

1 We have deliberately used the term *management science* rather than *management sciences* in order to emphasize the notion's status as a single, coherent though relatively young (compared to other branches) science.

References

Ahmad, N., & Hoffman, A. (2007). *A framework for addressing and measuring entrepreneurship*. OECD, Entrepreneurship Indicators Steering Group.

Bacigalupo, M., Kampylis, P., Punie, Y., & Van Den Brande, L. (2016). *EntreComp: The entrepreneurship competence framework*. Publications Office of the European Union.

Blaug, M. (1994). *Economic theory. Ujęcie retrospectivene*. PWN.

Bosma, N., & Kelley, D. (2019). *Global entrepreneurship monitor 2018/2019 global report*. GERA.

Covin, J. G., & Wales, W. J. (2012). *The* measurement of entrepreneurial orientation. *Entrepreneurship Theory and Practice*, *36*(4), 667–702.

Czech, K., Karpio, A., Wielechowski, M., Woźniakowski, T., & Żebrowska-Suchodolska, D. (2020). *The Polish economy in the early stages of the COVID-19 pandemic*. Wydawnictwo SGGW.

Global Entrepreneurship Monitor, 2020/2021 Global Report (2021). The Global Entrepreneurship Research Association, London Business School. Retrieved December 22, 2022, from https://www.gemconsortium.org/file/open?fileId=50691

Grant Thornton, & Krajowa Izba Gospodarcza. (2013). *Bariery rozwoju przedsiębiorstw, czyli co najbardziej hamuje wzrost polskich firm*. rp.pl. Retrieved December 22, 2022, from https://grafik.rp.pl/grafika2/1144116

Griffin, R. W. (1999). *Fundamentals of organizational management*. PWN.

Hébert, R. F., & Link, A. N. (1989). *A history of entrepreneurship*. Routledge.

Horodecka, A. (2017). *Economic* policy in the light of transformations in contemporary economic thought'. Perspektywy polityki gospodarczej. *Prace i Materiały Instytutu Rozwoju Gospodarczego SGH*, No. 90, 211–238.

Hughes, M., & Morgan, R. E. (2007). Deconstructing the relationship between entrepreneurial orientation and business performance at the embryonic stage of firm growth. *Industrial Marketing Management*, *36*, 651–661.

Janczewski, J. (2005). Criteria and measures of small firm entrepreneurship. In Z. Zioło & T. Rachwał (Eds.), *Entrepreneurship and modern civilization challenges*. Pedagogical Academy of the Commission of National Education in Cracow.

Klapper, L., Amit, R., Guillén, M. F., & Quesada, J. M. (2007). *Entrepreneurship and firm formation across countries*. The World Bank Development Research Group.

KMPG. (2020). *Raport: Perspektywy I Nastroje Przedsiębiorców*. Retrieved December 22, 2022, from https://home.kpmg/pl/pl/home/insights/2020/12/raport-perspektywy-i-nastroje-przedsiebiorcow.html

Kurczewska, A. (2014). Entrepreneurship and economics – Separation or integration? *E-Mentor*, *2*(54), 18–22.

Landström, H. (2010). *Pioneers in entrepreneurship and small business research*. Springer.

LePan, N. (2020). A visual history of pandemics. Cologny: World Economic Forum https://weforum.orgagedna/2020//03/a-visual-history-of-pandemics (as of October 23, 2021).

Marjański, A. (Ed.). (2013). *Przedsiębiorczy menadżer przedsiębiorczej organizacji. Nowoczesne tendencje w nauce oraz w praktyce organizacji i zarządzania*, Łódź: Społeczna Akademia Nauk.

Morris, M. (1998). *Entrepreneurial intensity: Sustainable advantages for individuals, organizations and societies*. Westport CT: Quorum Books.

Mrozowicz, K. (2010). Types of entrepreneurial behavior in the light of psychological personality research. *Studies and Materials. Miscellanea Oeconomocae*, *14*(1), 13–23.

NBP. (2021). *Szybki Monitoring NBP - Analiza sytuacji sektora przedsiębiorstw*. www.nbp.pl. Retrieved December 22, 2022, from https://www.nbp.pl/publikacje/koniunktura/raport_4_kw_2021.pdf

Raczyk, A. (2009). Methods for studying entrepreneurship based on the register of national economic entities. In Z. Zioło & T. Rachwał (Eds.), *The role of entrepreneurship in shaping the information society* (pp. 133–146). Department of Entrepreneurship and Spatial Economy of the Institute of Geography of the Pedagogical University in Kraków. New Era Publishing.

Reynolds, P. D., Hay, M., & Camp, S. M. (1999). *Global entrepreneurship monitor 1999 report*. Kauffman Center for Entrepreneurial Leadership, Babson College, London Business School.

Safin, K. (Ed.). (2002). *Uwarunkowania rozwoju przedsiębiorczości w regionach o nomenklaturze przemysłowej*. Published by the O. Lange University of Economics in Wroclaw.

Siuta-Tokarska, B. (2013). Basic aspects of measuring entrepreneurship. *Organization and Management*, *3*(156), 91–106.

European Commission. (2021). European Economic Forecast. Spring 2021. Luxembourg; Publications Office of the European Union.

Strojny, J., & Stankiewicz, B. (2009). Multidimensional analysis of entrepreneurship – Methodology, tools and relevance to the information society. *Entrepreneurship – Education*, *5*, 117–132.

Szymczak, M. (Ed.). (1988). *Slownik Języka Polskiego*. PWN, Warsaw.

Taleb, N. (2008). *The Black Swan. The impact of a highly improbable*. Penguin Books.

Targalski, J. (Ed.). (2014). *Entrepreneurship and management of small and medium enterprises*. Wydawnictwo Difin.

Thier, A. (2020). Directions of family enterprises in the modern economy. *Economic Studies. Economy-Society-Environment*, *1*(5), 27–47.

Wach, K. (2015). Entrepreneurship as a factor in socio-economic development: A literature review. *Entrepreneurship-Education*, *11*, 24–36.

Weerawardena, J., & Mort, G. (2006). Investigating social entrepreneurship: A multidimensional model. *Journal of World Business*, *41*, 21–35.

Wilkin, J. (2016). *Institutional and cultural foundations of management. A humanistic perspective on economics*. Wydawnictwo Scholar.

World Bank. (2021). *Bank Światowy w Polsce*. www.worldbank.org. Retrieved December 22, 2022, from https://www.worldbank.org/pl/country/poland/overview. Status as of October 24, 2021.

World Economic Forum. (2021). *The global risks report 2021*. World Economic Forum. Retrieved December 22, 2022, from https://www.weforum.org/reports/the-global-risks-report-2021/

Yamada, J. (2004). A multi-dimensional view of entrepreneurship: Towards a research agenda on organization emergence. *Journal of Management Development*, *23*(4), 289–320.

ZBP. (2021). *Polska i Europa - Finansowanie Gospodarki. Raport ZBP*. zbp.pl. Retrieved December 22, 2022, from https://zbp.pl/getmedia/27108368-d635-4313-a645-b63a687a31cc/ZBP_Polska_i_Europa_2021_DRUK_maly

16 Innovation in neuromarketing and social media marketing

Agnieszka Bojanowska, Monika Kulisz

Introduction

The 21st century has imposed new marketing activities on all businesses. A solution to such a scenario is neuromarketing (NM) (Brzustewicz, 2014, pp. 2–15). The interest in the topic of "Neuromarketing" (NM) has grown exponentially in recent years and the myriad of different definitions indicates the need for a deep theoretical discussion. The potential of this new discipline has drawn the world's attention, which can be verified through a query on Google Trends (Oliveira & Giraldi, 2017). Google is the world's leading search engine and accounts for about 90% of searches. It serves as a fairly reasonable proxy of interest for a specific topic (Mellon, 2013). NM is the latest and most advanced tool used by marketing researchers to study and understand consumer behavior patterns (Schneider & Woolgar, 2012). NM uses cutting-edge techniques in brain scanning to understand the nuances behind the psychological decision-making process of the customer (Eser et al., 2011). In NM, one can identify the elements of an advertising campaign that create a feel-good effect in the minds and memories of consumers (Fugate, 2007; Ohme & Matukin, 2012; Senior & Lee, 2008). NM is primarily used to identify the preferences of consumers. An important area of focus in marketing is the process of delivery of information about a product and its relevance to the customer (Fisher et al., 2010; Lee et al., 2009). It is a well-established psychological fact in marketing that advertisements create and build trust and recognition through physical and emotional attraction. This in turn will influence the consumers' preferences and purchasing decisions (Solomon, 2018).

Like any of the new techniques and methods, NM has many definitions. One of them was formulated by the authors of a reviewed article that attempted to define this concept, and it read that "neuromarketing is an interdisciplinary field of science that uses various tools traditionally used in medicine, psychiatry, and psychology on neurofeedback, biofeedback, and metabolic processes measures, in conjunction with traditional marketing tools in the search to better understand the most diverse types of emotions, cognitions, physiological reactions, behaviors and thoughts of economic agents, both conscious and unconscious related to typical issues of marketing and its various sub-areas"

DOI: 10.4324/9781003384311-16

(Oliveira & Giraldi, 2017). It seems complete and in line with the theoretical considerations included in this chapter.

The phenomenon of employing NM in analyzing and moderating purchasing processes has been explained by researchers from Oxford University who claim that "the act of seeking and realizing what we desire triggers activity in the reward network of the brain (in a region called the striatum) that is accompanied by the release of a chemical (or a neurotransmitter) which dopamine called reinforces such compulsive behaviors. Most types of the rewards tend to increase the level of dopamine in the brain and if uncontrolled excessive reward and pleasure-seeking may lead to powerful addiction disorders as seen in drug addiction, alcoholism, gambling, and even Wall Street trading" (Khaoui, 2017). We believe neurological connectivity is achieved when a retailer, a brand, or a service creates a strong psychological and emotional response that operates on a subconscious level for the consumer in a way that is typically not readily understood nor recognized by the consumer (Lewis, 2014).

This led to the formulation of the first research question (Q1): Are customers aware of the NM activities companies engage in? Companies like Google, CBS, Frito-Lay, and A&E Television, among others, have used NM research services in knowing consumer thoughts on their advertisements or products (Singh, 2020). The authors of this chapter have also wondered if NM is welcomed by customers, and how it is received. This led to the formulation of the second research question (Q2): How are customers feeling about NM? Research that has been conducted to date focuses on issues such as whether advertising brings happiness to the mind of the consumer, whether online retailers use content to improve customer engagement (Singh, 2020), or what NM is and how it can be used (Harrell, 2019; Touhami et al., 2011).

There are also a number of literature references that discuss ethical issues related to NM (Odekerken, 2018; Thomas, 2017; Wieckowski, 2019; Wilson et al., 2008). Any activities, also in the field of NM, affect a company's market image, which, of course, is reflected in the customer's behavior (Esmaeilpour & Barjoei, 2016; Singh, 2020). Every company wants its actions to be viewed positively by customers and to improve their satisfaction. Customer satisfaction is a term used to describe a customer's feeling and attitude toward a product or service, and is measured by their long-term behavior and serves as an important tool in marketing activities that are based on customer expectations (Bench & Day, 2010). Customer satisfaction can be viewed as a critical tool for companies that aim to create a competitive advantage in today's extraordinarily competitive world (Fonseca, 2009). Thus, it is worthwhile to conduct research that will tell the company what customers expect from the actions the company takes in spreading knowledge about NM and strengthening their positive perceptions. Thus, a third research question (Q3) was formulated: what should the company do, according to customers, to spread knowledge about NM and to strengthen their positive image of the company?

The topic of NM has been frequently addressed in recent years by marketing practitioners and academics alike. This chapter addresses this topic from the perspective of the customer, an approach that is not commonly taken. It is usually NM's impact on marketing activities that is examined. Few researchers survey customers to find out whether they notice these efforts and whether customers are pleased with them. Most often, customers are not questioned as to what the company could do in this regard. This chapter's authors have decided to listen to customers' opinions in this regard. As researchers, we are interested in learning about customer responses to NM activities carried out by companies.

Apple Inc.'s customer group was used for the purpose of this chapter. The aim of this chapter is to show the company's NM activities and determine how they are perceived by the customers of Apple Inc. An additional goal is to present what activities the company should introduce to promote NM knowledge and to strengthen the positive perception of it – based on customer feedback. Given the above review of the literature, the following hypotheses were tested:

H_1: *The feelings of customers who are subjected to NM activities are gender-dependent.*
H_2: *Previous interactions with the company have an impact on customers' thoughts on NM activities that are used by the company.*
H_3: *Customers who can recognize their emotional reactions to NM activities can also articulate their expectations of the company in this regard.*

Methods

Through the use of document analysis, this study examines research on Apple's NM activities. This chapter's authors' observations have also been included. In order to compile the results of the study related to NM in the case study company, we decided to conduct a diagnostic survey based on a proprietary questionnaire. The research sample consisted of 105 users (42 women and 63 men) of Apple Inc. products. A breakdown of the ages of the study group and the duration of their involvement with Apple are shown in Table 16.1.

Table 16.1 Age distribution and length of prior experience with Apple Inc. products according to questionnaire study

	Age			
	6–25	*26–34*	*35–44*	*45 or over*
% of the sample	21%	46%	25%	13%
	Length of experience with the company in years			
	Less than a year	*1 to 3 years*	*3 to 5 years*	*5 years or more*
% of the sample	16%	35%	39%	10%

Source: Own elaboration.

Table 16.2 Questions included in the survey questionnaire

Question symbol	*Question content*	*Response symbol*	*Possible answers*
QQ 1	Did you know that Apple Inc. uses neuromarketing techniques in its marketing efforts?	a	Yes
		b	No
QQ 2	What are your thoughts on the use of neuromarketing?	a	Positive, it doesn't bother me
		b	They illustrate the right approach the company has taken to selling
		c	It doesn't matter to me, products get the most attention
		d	Negative, my outlook can be affected by it
		e	I find it unethical
QQ 3	What should Apple Inc. do to raise awareness about neuromarketing and increase the positive perception it has among customers?	a	Introduce social media campaigns and information campaigns through different media
		b	Use advertisements featuring experts
		c	Provide neuromarketing information on product's packaging
		d	Provide customers with the opportunity to participate in neuromarketing research
		e	Provide information on how neuromarketing can benefit customers
		f	Nothing as customer knowledge is sufficient
		g	Nothing as customers don't need to know about Provide information on Apple's use of neuromarketing tactics

Source: Own elaboration.

The research questionnaire contained three demographic questions about gender, age, and the number of years respondents have been familiar with Apple Inc. The second part of the questionnaire consisted of three questions that were based on research questions Q1, Q2, and Q3, responses to which are presented in Table 16.2. In the case of the last question, two answers were possible.

Results

A review of the documents of Apple Inc. and observation

Based on our observation of activities conducted by Apple Inc. in NM and a review of the company's documents, we were able to draw a number of conclusions that we present below.

In its research on NM, Apple Inc. found that it is necessary to include a "battle" between positive and negative emotions in its advertising campaigns. Therefore, the design of the key emotions model the enterprise adopted says that it is not only about joy, happiness, or fulfillment but also about desire, anger, or sadness that results from not having the product. The idea here is to present a dilemma concerning either fighting a desire or evading it that is viewed in a negative way. These insights came from the specialists who created the advertising campaigns for the iPhone 6 and introduced a sense of danger as a key element that strengthened the desire to buy a particular product. The experts at this enterprise believe that it is conditioned by the evolution of humans and their brain that is able to strive for a sense of happiness and joy when negative emotions are present.

Apple Inc.'s marketing strategy is also created using eye-tracking research. This research defines the direction for shaping the perception of consumers and potential customers and sets out the final design of the company's advertising campaigns, its posters, and other marketing and image enhancement tools. It must be clearly stated at this point that Apple Inc. has approached this issue in a very multifaceted manner. During the development of the sixth-generation iPhone image campaign, the company decided to track the eyeball movements of consumers who tested the product. As a result, marketing experts from Apple Inc. were able to pick out features of the sixth-generation iPhone's interface that were later used in advertising. Using eye-tracking studies, the most effective wallpaper was also identified – one that effectively caught consumers' eye. When exposed to products offered by this company, the brain is stimulated to strengthen spiritual, almost religious experiences.

The company analyzes people's patterns of thought and identifies their desires in order to be able to target these desires by stimulating reward-related brain areas (the brain's striatum). Each campaign conducted by Apple Inc. or the acquisition of their products is designed to be reinforced by a chemical, a neurotransmitter, called dopamine. It is this chemical that is responsible for a feeling of happiness and unique internal experiences of a buyer of the company's products. It is important that Apple Inc.'s subsequent products have only fueled the craving for the prize – dopamine. Hence, when choosing the next Apple product, users are guided primarily by their loyalty to the brand as well as their desire to be rewarded in exchange for previously performed work.

Survey results

Below are the results of a survey that was based on a review of the literature, analysis of documents, and observations. The purpose of the study was to answer the above research questions and to verify research hypotheses. The first question in the survey asked respondents whether they were aware of Apple Inc.'s NM activities. In fact, this question addressed respondents' awareness of how the company's sales environment was devised. To increase the reliability of the survey, the concept of NM was clearly defined in the questionnaire. The data that was collected in the survey clearly indicates that only one in four respondents were aware of Apple Inc. conducting NM activities. As many as 81 participants replied to the contrary.

The follow-up question focused on respondents' feelings about the usage of NM techniques. Participants in the survey were well aware that Apple Inc. was doing so. According to the majority of respondents, their feelings about the usage of NM were rather neutral. This option was selected by 41 individuals, and 23 respondents believed that these measures were good, while 17 rated the answer as "appropriate". Negative feelings about employing NM were expressed by 11 respondents, while 13 opted for "unethical" as their answer to the question.

The third question presented in Table 16.2 was the last one to be asked. The important thing to note is that all respondents chose the "Introduce social media campaigns and information campaigns through different media" response. A significant portion of the research group also pointed out that it is necessary to allow ordinary customers to participate in NM research (35 responses) and to provide information on how NM can benefit customers (34 responses). According to 26 respondents, first and foremost, it is crucial for the company to use advertisements that involve experts. Ten respondents indicated that efforts should be taken to provide customers with information about Apple's use of NM tactics, and that a positive image of these types of practices can be created thanks to the fact that information on the use of NM tactics is placed clearly on the packaging of Apple's products. It is extremely important that none of the respondents indicated that no action was necessary.

To Based on the results received, a statistical analysis was conducted to examine the independence of variables such as age, gender, experience with Apple Inc. products, and answers to the research questionnaire. Dependency analysis was carried out with the help of a χ^2 test. A significance level of $\alpha = 0.05$ was selected. A null hypothesis in the chi-square test has the form of H_0: the X and Y characteristics are independent, against the H_1 hypothesis: the X and Y characteristics are dependent. Table 16.3 shows the results of the Questionnaire Independence Test based on variables such as age, gender, and experience with Apple Inc. products among respondents.

Table 16.3 Variable independence test χ^2 (age, gender, and experience with Apple Inc. products in research trial) and questionnaire questions.

	QQ 1.		*QQ 2.*				*QQ 3.*		
Variable	χ^2	*df/t*	χ^2	*df/t*	*p*	*p*	χ^2	*df/t*	*p*
Age	5.75	4	7.86	12	0.795	0.348	7.86	12	0.795
Sex	0.44	1	2.24	3	0.524	0.000	2.24	3	0.524
Experience with Apple Inc.	0.36	4	15.49	12	0.215	0.087	15.49	12	0.215

Source: Own elaboration.

For questions "Are you aware that Apple Inc. uses neuromarketing in its marketing efforts?" and "What should Apple Inc. do to raise awareness about neuromarketing and increase the positive perception it has among customers?" there is no basis for rejecting the H_0 hypothesis that there is a lack of relationship between responses to these questions and age, gender, and experience with Apple Inc. products variables in a research sample. In the case of the question "What are your thoughts on the use of neuromarketing?", the H_0 hypothesis about a lack of relation between gender and responses to this question should be rejected in favor of hypothesis H_1 ($\chi^2 = 44.51$; $p = 0.000$); as for the other variables – there is no basis for rejecting the H_0 hypothesis. It can therefore be concluded that there is a relationship between gender and the responses to this question but not between respondents' responses and their age or length of experience with Apple Inc. products.

Qualitative data were analyzed using the non-parametric gamma coefficient, which is often used to determine the strength of the correlation between variables. To determine the magnitude of this coefficient's effect, we used the Cohen scale. With a ratio of $\gamma = -0.326$, it can be concluded that the correlation between the gender variable and the responses to "What are your sensations related to neuromarketing use?" is substantial and moderate, which is presented in Table 16.4. It can be concluded that for most women, the feelings associated with the use of NM tended to be neutral, negative, or unethical, while for men, they were neutral, positive, or appropriate.

In the case of the "What are your sensations related to neuromarketing use?" question, a correlation with the sex variable was found, leading to the data being further analyzed by gender.

The next stage of the study was to determine the relationship between each of the questions. Based on the analysis of the chi-square test of answers to questions 1 and 3, it can be concluded that there is no relationship between them ($\chi^2 = 3.55$; $p = 0.313$). An identical conclusion can be drawn by analyzing the responses to questions 1 and 2 for female participants ($\chi^2 = 2.84$; $p = 0.584$). In order to determine the strength of the correlation between the remaining questions, once again the gamma coefficient was used, as shown in Table 16.5.

Based on Table 16.3, a significant and strong correlation can be found between responses to questions 1 and 2 for men ($\gamma = -0.556$) (see Table 16.6). A significant and moderate correlation was observed between responses to

Table 16.4 Gender variable and QQ 2 responses

	QQ 2.				
Sex	*Positive*	*Appropriate*	*Neutral*	*Negative*	*Unethical*
Women	3	2	14	11	12
Men	20	15	27	0	1

Source: Own elaboration.

Table 16.5 Test for independence of responses to selected questions

		QQ 1.			QQ 3.		
	Statistic	χ^2	*df/t*	*p*	χ^2	*df/t*	*p*
QQ 2.		*Women*			*Women*		
	χ^2	2.84	4	0.584	24.16	12	0.019
	Gamma	0.193			0.464		
		Men			*Men*		
	χ^2	9.16	3	0.027	21.66	9	0.010
	Gamma	0.556			0.235		

Source: Own elaboration.

questions 2 and 3 for women ($\gamma = 0.464$), and a significant and weak correlation was observed for men ($\gamma = -0.235$) (Table 16.7).

Discussion

Nowadays, NM activities are highly popular in attempts to enhance a company's market position. The concept of using discoveries in neuroscience to develop marketing campaigns still raises controversy but has real implications for competitiveness.

Among other things, NM is used to improve a company's existing strategy and to create advertising campaigns that will accurately target specific parts of the consumer's brain responsible for making purchasing decisions. This

Table 16.6 Answers to questions 1 and 2

	QQ 2.			
QQ 1.	*Positive*	*Appropriate*	*Neutral*	*Unethical*
No	17	9	24	0
Yes	3	6	3	1

Source: Own elaboration.

Table 16.7 Answers to questions 2 and 3 for women and men

	QQ 2.								
	Women					*Men*			
QQ 3.	*Positive*	*Positive*	*Appropriate*	*Neutral*	*Unethical*	*Appropriate*	*Neutral*	*Negative*	*Unethical*
b	0	4	5	5	0	0	3	3	6
c	1	6	0	2	0	0	0	1	0
d	2	2	9	8	1	2	2	4	5
e	0	8	1	12	0	0	9	3	1

Source: Own elaboration.

chapter examines this subject from the viewpoint of the customer who is influenced by these activities and attempts to find out if customers are aware of NM activities and how they perceive them. A key objective of the chapter was to demonstrate NM activities and assess customer perception using a case study of Apple Inc.

Our study confirmed that Apple Inc. indeed used NM tactics that made it possible for the company to optimize its advertising messages. Apple Inc. utilizes NM to create campaigns based on eye-tracking research, among other things. This company is not the only one to use NM solutions. Other companies that engage in such activities include Yahoo, Hyundai, Microsoft, Facebook, Coca-Cola, and Budweiser, to name only some (Solomon, 2018, pp. 9136–9146). Companies benefit from neuroscience marketing since using these methods allows them to better understand their customers' brains, decipher their decision-making processes, analyze consumer behavior, and optimize the targeting of the company's marketing activities.

According to the study, only one in four respondents was aware that Apple Inc. engaged in NM activities. This means that the activities carried out by Apple Inc. have been subtle and their customers are not entirely aware of them. Consumers are often unaware that companies conduct such research, which is also confirmed by Kumar's research (Kumar, 2018).

Through a review of the literature, we also aimed to find out if there are statistically significant differences between men and women in terms of NM assessment (Stefko et al., 2021; Uva et al., 2015). The study shows that almost 40% of respondents were rather indifferent to the use of NM. It may be noted that there are statistically significant differences between male and female consumers in other responses, confirming the H_1 hypothesis. Negative attitudes are more common among women, while positive attitudes are more common among men. Additionally, based on Table 16.6, it can be concluded that men who are unaware that Apple Inc. uses NM in its marketing activities and have either indifferent or positive attitudes toward associated with the use of NM. Additionally, according to the survey, there is no rationale relating respondents' responses to their experience with Apple Inc. products, so the H_2 hypothesis is rejected.

What is more, this chapter examines what is being done by Apple Inc. in order to spread knowledge about NM and strengthen a positive perception of it. Each respondent indicated that they would do so via social media campaigns and information campaigns in different media. It means that the public expects, in the first place, comprehensive campaigns aimed at providing objective and reliable information about NM activities. Such a view was also presented by Stefko et al. in their research (2021).

When analyzing Apple's efforts with regard to feelings about the use of NM, Table 16.7 shows that the men who reported a positive response described it as recommended that customer benefits resulting from NM activities should be communicated and information about them should be placed on the product packaging. Women who reported negative feelings associated with using NM propose that the company use advertisements featuring experts and allow ordinary customers to participate in NM research. As a result of the above, Hypothesis 3 can be confirmed. This probably has to do with generally different perceptions of marketing activities by women and men, as noted, for example, authors such as Karjaluoto et al. (2008, pp. 242–259) or Moss (2017). It could therefore be an opportunity for Apple Inc. to take steps to promote NM and to reinforce the positive way customers perceive it. Additionally, such actions can be taken by similar market actors.

Conclusions

To conclude, NM plays an important role in the functioning of enterprises primarily due to the fact that it draws attention to the development of marketing activities that involve interaction with the brain. Customers' perceptions of brands are currently dominated by their feelings and emotional states. As a result of marketing research, enterprises are well aware that feelings are produced by information and that it has an impact on the final marketing message. As far as organizations are concerned, the most important step is to identify key values, marketing slogans, metaphors, and a brand's advertising message structure, and then put it into action.

Often, consumers don't have full awareness of the fact that companies conduct such research, which was also confirmed by the study among users of Apple products. Furthermore, there are statistically significant differences in how NM is perceived among male and female consumers. The company's customers suggested what actions should be taken to spread awareness about NM and to strengthen the positive way customers perceive it, which could be useful for the company as well as other market players.

References

Bench, S., & Day, T. (2010). *Customer satisfaction: Improving quality and access to services and supports in vulnerable neighborhoods*. Center for the study of social policy.

Brzustewicz, P. (2014). Marketing 3.0 – nowe podejście do tworzenia wartości. *Marketing and Market*, *2*, 2–15.

Eser, Z., Isin, F., & Tolon, M. (2011). Perceptions of marketing academics, neurologists, and marketing professionals about neuromarketing. *Journal of Marketing Management*, *27*(7–8), 854–868. https://doi.org/10.1080/02672571003719070

Esmaeilpour, M., & Barjoei, S. (2016). The effect of corporate image on customer satisfaction through brand equity. *Advances in Management and Applied Economics*, *6*(4), 1–7.

Fisher, C., Chin, L., & Klitzman, R. (2010). Defining neuromarketing: Practices and professional challenges. *Harvard Review of Psychiatry*, *18*(4), 230–237. https://doi.org/10.3109/10673229.2010.496623

Fonseca, J. (2009). Customer satisfaction study via a latent segment model. *Journal of Retailing and Consumer Services*, *16*(5), 352–359. https://doi.org/10.1016/j.jretconser.2009.04.001

Fugate, D. (2007). Neuromarketing: A layman's look at neuroscience and its potential application to marketing practice. *Journal of Consumer Marketing*, *24*(7), 385–394. https://doi.org/10.1108/07363760710834807

Harrell, E. (2019). Neuromarketing: What you need to know. *Harvard Business Review.* https://hbr.org/2019/01/neuromarketing-what-you-need-to-know

Karjaluoto, H., Lehto, H., Leppäniemi, M., & Jayawardena, C. (2008). Exploring gender influence on customer's intention to engage permission-based mobile marketing. *Electronic Markets, 18*(3), 242–259. https://doi.org/10.1080/10196780802265793

Khaoui, A. (2017). The psychology of iPhone: A neuromarketing strategy, or an overdose? https://medium.com/@aminekh/the-psychology-of-iphone-a-neuromarketing-strategy-or-an-overdose-f76583ce6502

Kumar, H. (2018). Consumer's awareness towards emerging integration of neuromarketing in marketing research with particular reference to India. *UNNAYAN: International Bulletin of Management and Economics, IX*, 61–69.

Lee, N., Senior, C., Butler, M., & Fuchs, R. (2009). The feasibility of neuroimaging methods in marketing research. *Nature Precedings.* https://doi.org/10.1038/npre.2009.2836.1

Lewis, R. (2014). How Apple neurologically hooked its customers. *Forbes.* https://www.forbes.com/sites/robinlewis/2014/09/02/how-apple-neurologically-hooked-its-customers/?sh=4b02e0b2ff00

Mellon, J. (2013). Where and when can we use Google Trends to measure issue salience? *PS: Political Science & Politics, 46*(2), 280–290. https://doi.org/10.1017/S1049096513000279

Moss, G. (2017). Gender, design and marketing. https://doi.org/10.4324/9781315254593

Odekerken, M. (2018). Ethics of neuromarketing. *Neurofied Brain & Behaviour Academy.* https://neurofied.com/the-ethics-of-neuromarketing/

Ohme, R., & Matukin, M. (2012). A small frog that makes a big difference: Brain wave testing of TV advertisements. *IEEE Pulse, 3*(3), 28–33.

Oliveira, J., & Giraldi, J. (2017). What is neuromarketing? A proposal for a broader and more accurate definition. *Global Business and Management Research: An International Journal, 9*, 19–29.

Schneider, T., & Woolgar, S. (2012). Technologies of ironic revelation: Enacting consumers in neuromarkets. *Consumption Markets & Culture, 15*(2), 169–189.

Senior, C., & Lee, N. (2008). Editorial: A manifesto for neuromarketing science. *Journal of Consumer Behaviour,* 7(4–5), 263–271.

Singh, S. (2020). Impact of neuromarketing applications on consumers. *Journal of Business and Management, 26*(2), 33–52. https://doi.org/10.6347/JBM.202009_26(2).0002

Solomon, P. (2018). Neuromarketing: Applications, challenges and promises. *Biomedical Journal of Scientific & Technical Research, 12*(2), 9136–9146. https://doi.org/10.26717/BJSTR.2018.12.002230

Stefko, R., Tomkova, A., Kovalova, J., & Ondrijova, I. (2021). Consumer purchasing behaviour and neuromarketing in the context of gender differences. *Journal of Marketing Research and Case Studies*, 1–11. https://doi.org/10.5171/2021.321466

Thomas, A. (2017). *Ethics and neuromarketing.* Springer.

Touhami, Z., Benlafkih, L., Jiddane, M., Cherrah, Y., El Malki, H., & Benomar, A. (2011). Neuromarketing: Where marketing and neuroscience meet. *African Journal of Business Management, 5*(5), 1528–1532. https://doi.org/10.5897/AJBM10.729

Uva, T., de Freitas, C., & Paiva, T. (2015). Neuroscience technologies in marketing: A study of gender and TV advertisements using electroencephalography. *International Journal of Technology Marketing (IJTMKT), 10*(4), 362–380.

Wieckowski, A. (2019). When neuromarketing crosses the line. *Harvard Business Review.* https://hbr.org/2019/01/when-neuromarketing-crosses-the-line

Wilson, R., Gaines, J., & Hill, R. (2008). Neuromarketing and consumer free will. *Journal of Consumer Affairs, 42*(3), 389–410. https://doi.org/10.1111/j.1745-6606.2008.00114.x

17 Moving toward Communication 5.0 in Polish business clusters

Barbara Szymoniuk

Introduction

Until now, no literature has addressed the issue of Communication 5.0 in business clusters. Research in this area appears to be both academically interesting and practically relevant. During the pandemic, the main business-to-business (B2B) communication channels, i.e. face-to-face and personal channels, were closed or paralyzed by pandemic-related restrictions, leading to the need to transfer communication activities to the digital world. The research discussed in the chapter aimed to examine communication processes in business clusters under Society 5.0 and, specifically, to identify the channels and instruments of Communication 5.0 that are used by clusters under pandemic conditions. The research results are presented in the form of conceptual spherical models of communication in clusters.

The research was conducted in September 2021 by conducting in-depth individual interviews with coordinators of 13 key national clusters (Krajowe Klastry Kluczowe) in Poland. Key clusters are the elite of Polish clusters that are industry-specific organizations that successfully implement innovations and expand their activities internationally. They represent the following industries: aviation, information and communications technology (ICT), metal, construction, chemical, life science, medical products and services, waste management, recycling, as well as transport and logistics.

Literature review

In this chapter, Communication 5.0 implemented in business clusters is understood as an element of Marketing 5.0 that is inspired by the concept of Society 5.0. As defined by the Japanese government, Society 5.0 should be one that, through merging between cyberspace and physical space, will be able to balance economic advancement with the resolution of social problems by providing goods and services that address manifold latent needs regardless of locale, age, sex, or language. (Cabinet Office, 2017, p. 2; Hitachi-UTokyo Laboratory (H-UTokyo Lab), 2020, p. 1). Marketing 5.0 is defined as the use of technologies that mimic human behavior by businesses to create,

DOI: 10.4324/9781003384311-17

communicate, deliver, and enhance value in the overall customer experience (Kotler et al., 2021, p. 29). At the core of Marketing 5.0 lies what we call *next tech* – a group of technologies that aim to replicate the capabilities of human marketers. These include, for example, artificial intelligence (AI), natural language processing (NLP), sensors, robotics, augmented reality (AR), virtual reality (VR), internet of things (IoT), and blockchain (Kotler et al., 2021, p. 20; Polat and Erkollar, 2020).

Marketing communications is the entirety of a company's relationship and contact with the market, resulting in mutual benefits. In the case of Communication 5.0, businesses are able to maintain a continuous connection with each of their customers anywhere, anytime, and nurture an individual relationship with them through the use of digital media (Bajak, 2021, p. 17).

In practice, the development of Industry 4.0, which was the starting point for the development of the notion of Society 5.0, brings numerous benefits to the economy (Kotler et al., 2017; Rzepka, 2019), and the recent pandemic has confirmed these observations. However, Industry 4.0-related processes that use advanced technology such as AI raise many social concerns due to economic and psychological risks (Peraković et al., 2020: 208; Rahman, 2021, pp. 3, 4; Rosenbaum et al., 2021, pp. 3–7). The use of communication should be done with great care and should be in balance with interpersonal communication. This postulate is included in the concepts of Society 5.0, Industry 5.0, and Marketing 5.0 (Peraković et al, 2020, pp. 209–210). It is illustrated with a quote from a book entitled "Marketing 5.0: Technology for Humanity", which states that "machines are cool, but humans are warm" (Kotler et al., 2021, p. 114).

Business clusters are sector-specific economic organizations that combine the flexibility of small businesses with innovation and the global scale of large corporations. They possess an ability to make use of the innovation potential of regional environments and an ability to accumulate and use intellectual capital efficiently. A benchmarking study published in 2020 found that about 25% of cluster members were using Industry 4.0 technologies such as the IoT, Big Data, intelligent industrial robots, data clouds, 3D printing, and automated, robotic, and digitized manufacturing systems (Piotrowski, 2021, p. 69).

Marketing in clusters is primarily done according to a B2B or business-to-government (B2G) model. It refers to the internal marketing activities inside organizations that are managed by institutional coordinators but treat their stakeholders as customers, mainly businesses and their managers. Outside of the cluster, communication is implemented much less frequently according to the business-to-customer (B2C) model. The users of such communication usually include customers of companies that are involved in given clusters, and it is the responsibility of companies to carry out communications rather than burden cluster coordinators with it.

The research conducted in 2017 made it possible to identify the main groups of stakeholders of Polish key national clusters, which were entities responsible for cluster coordination (hereinafter referred to as coordinators or leaders), enterprises affiliated with a cluster, institutions involved in the business environment, universities, research and development centers, and local authorities (Szymoniuk 2017, pp. 170–179), which will be included in the spherical communication diagrams discussed later in this chapter.

A 2018 study found that the communication activities undertaken by cluster coordinators go far beyond the stereotypical communication tasks involving providing information and knowledge as well as providing basic motivation. According to the study, communication is also a part of the process of achieving the cluster's mission, building its image, and harmonizing the organization's activities as a whole. A condition that is necessary to ensure the efficiency of communication in clusters is a synergy between direct (personal) and indirect (media) communication processes adapted to the circumstances and the nature of cluster participants' activities (Szymoniuk, 2019, p. 242). There are not many publications in the literature on how to implement communication activities in the 5.0 era, which is furthermore symptomatic of the pandemic-induced exclusion of the real world.

Another challenge for Communication 5.0 is the varied behavior of customers from different generations, each with varying levels of technical skills when it comes to modern technology (Sawicki, 2021, p. 31). This means, among other things, that from the standpoint of enterprises, as well as clusters, it is necessary to tailor marketing messages and channels specifically to different generations. People born during these time periods make up these generations:

Baby Boomers – 1946 to 1964
Generation X – 1965 to 1980
Generation Y – 1981 to 1996
Generation Z – 1997 to 2009
Generation Alpha – 2010 to 2025

The two youngest generations will act as the catalysts for the development of modern marketing. Those companies that gain the trust of Generation Z and Generation Alpha will gain market advantage in the 5.0 era (Kotler et al., 2021, pp. 32–47). This is also true for business clusters.

Materials and methodology

The picture of Communication 5.0 in clusters presented in this chapter is based on (1) a critical literature review and logical inference and (2) qualitative research conducted in 2021 in thirteen Polish key national clusters comprising a total of more than 2400 enterprises. Based on these results, we developed conceptual models illustrating marketing communication processes in the 5.0 era with three diagrams. A paper published by Polska Agencja Rozwoju Przedsiębiorczości entitled "Benchmarking of Clusters in Poland" (Piotrowski, 2021) was used to conduct the initial secondary research used to develop the assumptions of the qualitative study.

The primary research was conducted using a qualitative, interpretive approach. Due to the nature of the research problem and the purpose and scope of the study, a direct survey was chosen to conduct the study, and among the techniques that it offers researchers, we opted for an in-depth interview with individuals. The interviews were semi-structured, i.e. they were conducted according to a predetermined format that included the most relevant topics in order to allow respondents to express themselves freely.

Interviews were conducted with the individuals responsible for the marketing communications processes of thirteen key national clusters that had similar status during the 2017 and 2018 surveys. In order to present the communication processes in clusters conceptually, a proprietary model for marketing communication, a spherical one, has been devised. It sheds light on the characteristics of marketing communications in clusters in the 5.0 era and facilitates the identification of directions for building resilience to the exclusion of communication channels operating in the real world (e.g. due to pandemic restrictions) or virtual world (e.g. during periods of Internet outages).

The research questions were as follows:

1. How has the pandemic affected the innovation processes in communications in the clusters?
2. What has been the experience of clusters in implementing Communication 5.0 and what are their plans for the future?
3. Have the clusters had a Communication 5.0-specific problem of intergenerational differences among participants who received messages from coordinators? If so, does the problem make it necessary to tailor messages to different audiences or use different communication channels?
4. What communication model can ensure a cluster's resilience to communication channel exclusions, real or virtual, in the 5.0 age?

Results

The findings presented below will be discussed successively by presenting aggregated respondents' responses to the research questions.

Impact of the pandemic on communication innovation processes in the studied clusters

The COVID-19 pandemic has become a major challenge for communications in clusters. Cluster coordinators worried that companies would terminate memberships en masse after the lockdown was announced. This would result in a loss of dues that are a significant portion of revenue to coordinating entities, which would lead to a double crisis for clusters: a communication crisis and a financial crisis. During the first months of the pandemic, both clusters and coordinating units had to deal with the new situation in which there was a complete lack of face-to-face, direct communication.

According to respondents, the basic forms of communication with cluster participants in daily work during the pandemic were not significantly different from those they practiced before the pandemic. These included sending emails and newsletters, making phone calls, posting news on the website, being active on social media (primarily LinkedIn and Facebook), and sharing and processing data through cloud storage. In addition, face-to-face meetings were still held but their frequency was drastically reduced and the manner in which they would be held depended on the pandemic restrictions imposed at the time. All respondents confirmed that they had tested various communication platforms and their usefulness for specific communication projects. And so, Zoom's paid version was most often used when organizing large meetings, sessions, and voting sessions; the GoTo Meeting and Webex platforms were indicated as the most useful when organizing webinars that took the form of lectures; for teamwork in projects that involved meetings, document collaboration, and a database containing documents, the best solution was the Microsoft Teams paid version; when organizing short meetings and consultations, the Google Meet service was identified as the most useful.

Having mobile devices at their disposal, respondents were also keen to make use of group messaging services on WhatsApp, Messenger, and Viber. The messaging service that clusters refused to use was Skype.

As for communication, innovation processes mainly took place for two categories of activities: (1) networking, workshops, and conferences organized by the cluster and (2) internal meetings within clusters.

When it comes to networking meetings, workshops, and conferences, clusters have efficiently used webinars by taking advantage of the platforms that were commonly used. This decision had the following positive effects: (a) it was possible to invite more participants, including those from other clusters and foreign partners, (b) more convenient access to debates, sessions, and discussion panels for participants, (c) less time and expense for organizers (no catering, no need to rent or clean venues, no need to arrange and pay for hotels for the speakers, etc.), and (d) more effective time management during debates and panel discussions.

When it comes to internal meetings within clusters, they required technological and organizational innovations that allowed hybrid and remote meetings to be conducted. The major challenges for the coordinators were to develop new, flexible guidelines for communicating with companies and facilitating their participation in meetings that could have been adapted to the pandemic situation at the time, and the technical capacity of the participants, as well as to meet the standards for voting validity and confidentiality.

Weekly online meetings organized by the Polish Cluster Employers Association provided significant assistance to cluster coordinators. They offered a very important channel for the exchange of information on how the pandemic was progressing and on market conditions and enabled clusters to present their offers during meetings, increasing cooperation between clusters and mutual assistance. Support meetings for cluster coordinators were also organized by European Cluster Alliance, an international organization, and were held several times a week. The clusters that participated in the study took part in those meetings selectively depending on topics of interest to them.

Due to the deficiencies of existing online communication platforms, all clusters in the ICT industry have developed their own innovative platforms that are much more comprehensive than the existing ones. Some of these services will serve a specific cluster exclusively, while others will be available for sale to other clusters or organization networks.

During the study period, volunteer efforts were made by cluster members to help the underprivileged in preventing and combating the pandemic. It was an opportunity to promote their cluster and one that provided a basis for numerous publications. Thanks to it, the cluster coordinator and members were more frequently featured in the media, mainly in broadcasts whose focus was pandemic prevention.

Communication 5.0 implementation experiences in clusters

In addition to the aforementioned communication activities involving digital technologies, some clusters developed or implemented solutions that embodied Communication 5.0 and that were tailored to their industries. They include, for instance

1 a web-based app to manage the energy-efficient building that houses the cluster and a KNX system to monitor it. The use of building automation facilitates efficient energy management as well as enhances the safety and comfort of rooms in an environment that provides access to the visually impaired and the disabled;
2 automation of cluster administration, including automated invoicing;
3 autonomous and semi-autonomous systems used in land vehicles and maritime administration;
4 AI and chatbots that were used to implement services provided by companies participating in ICT clusters.

We are in the design phase of incorporating chatbots into cluster websites. Message content could be personalized with chatbots according to audience information needs and age. Unfortunately, currently, chatbot implementations in cluster communications are too expensive compared to their benefits and therefore have not proved to be cost-effective during the study period. Similarly, the same applies when ICT clusters create their own tools based on the latest technologies e.g. blockchain, AI, VR, AR, and machine learning. The cost of their development and implementation exceeds the funds available to cluster participants as part of alternative investment funds (1 million PLN).

When discussing the activities of clusters on social media, respondents stressed the need for their ongoing, disciplined response to reactive communications, i.e. reading incoming inquiries and responding promptly.

Intergenerational differences among communication recipients in clusters

Respondents' statements about intergenerational differences among cluster participants showed a correlation with the industries represented by the clusters. These differences are either non-existent or negligible in the aviation and construction industries because participants are of similar age (mainly Baby Boomers and Generation X). Coordinators can communicate with them via a unified channel by sending unified or differentiated messages. In this case, the variation is caused by the fact that the message recipients belong to different industry groups, rather than their age. It is true that there are significant age differences in ICT clusters (from Baby Boomers to Generation Z), but generational barriers to communication are being bridged. Older participants have no problem using social media or online communication platforms and are familiar with Communication 5.0 tools. In other clusters, generational differences exist and coordinators use different channels to reach these generations as well as tailor messages accordingly. In these clusters, there is a segment of small or medium-sized business owners from the Baby Boomers generation who are tied to long-standing traditions of communicating in their cluster and do not use online communication platforms or social media. Coordinators contact them by phone or in person. Respondents gave examples of ways to adapt communication to the preferences of the Generation Z audience. The first of those was hiring influencers who are active on social media to run conferences and industry events instead of famous actors or journalists, as was the case in the past. The second was to recruit students to run promotional campaigns. For example, when arranging apprenticeships with cluster members, students used social media in which messages were tailored depending on whether they were directed to students (Generation Z) or their parents (Generation X).

Proposed model of Communication 5.0 in clusters to ensure resilience to exclusion of communication channels in the real or virtual world

Taking into account the experience of the pandemic era, respondents were in agreement on the most effective form of communication in the future – hybrid. The online mode of communication that became a necessity in the pandemic environment was not conducive to building relationships in the cluster. It will not be possible to improve the situation by implementing only the technological solutions associated with the Communication 5.0 model. According to respondents, creating the so-called cluster family and community spirit takes time and effort and takes place mainly during traditional meetings, both formal and informal. The use of friendly gestures, such as shaking hands or patting on the back, is only possible during a face-to-face conversation. For this reason, during the pandemic, clusters developed the concept of hybrid communication on a very flexible basis that would be determined jointly by cluster coordinators and participants. In most clusters, internal communications within the office are conducted directly, while external communication with cluster members and stakeholders is done via digital platforms. As for the trade shows and conferences, sessions and exchanges of ideas generally took place remotely. The presentations of cluster booths, networking meetings, gala luncheons and dinners were generally held face-to-face, within the limits of pandemic regulations.

Respondents commented on their vision regarding communication in their cluster in the event of possible outages or failures of digital telecommunications networks, including the Internet. Such situations are cited by futurologists and trend researchers as potential threats to the global community. There is only one instance where the cluster would have to stop working because the work in the cluster is entirely remote, data is stored in the cloud, and documents are shared. If the Internet were to be shut down, it would be a disaster not only in terms of communication but also in the day-to-day operation of this cluster. For the remaining clusters, functioning without the Internet would be possible but difficult. Data transfer, in particular, would be hindered, but this problem can be dealt with through traditional forms of communication. Ethernet local area networks could be efficiently deployed in the ICT clusters and then the remaining clusters. In clusters located over a small territory, such as science and technology parks, efficient direct communication would be possible. During the pre-pandemic period, some clusters would hold joint business breakfasts for participants every two to four weeks, which respondents said they would like to return to. Moreover, communication by traditional mail, telephone (analog), and face-to-face individual meetings are still practiced in clusters. Respondents stated that the collapse of the digital world (which could take the form of a failure of the Internet or mobile networks, would be a boost toward offline communication innovation, just like the COVID-19 pandemic was to online communication.

Discussion

The clusters that took part in the study viewed the pandemic-induced situation and the problems associated with the pandemic as a challenge rather than a barrier to development. As organizations that flexibly adapt to changes in their environment and as self-learning structures, they have dynamically moved their communications to digital channels while seeking every opportunity to use personal and face-to-face channels as pandemic restrictions weakened. The conditions created by the pandemic became a driving force behind the digitization of the participating companies and the whole sectors involved. They necessitated a number of innovative activities for the clusters, which were:

1 implementing and investigating the capabilities of remote communication platforms in a variety of configurations and for different purposes in order to make their future use more rational;
2 the purchase and use of new equipment, such as cameras and specialist microphones, to ensure high-quality transmission;

3 improving the management of distributed teams and increasing efficiency of work in teams – thanks to collaborative work on files in the cloud and increasing the effectiveness of online meetings.

Communication processes in clusters under the exclusion of the real world and face-to-face communication, typical of pandemic conditions, can be represented conceptually using a spherical diagram (Figure 17.1a). Participants and key cluster stakeholders make up the cluster communication sphere. Communication is primarily carried out through digital and analog means. Personal channels that are represented by curved arrows on the surface of the sphere are completely or partially disabled. Maintaining such a situation for a long time threatens to deteriorate the cluster's cooperative atmosphere, lowering the level of mutual trust and, as a result, resulting in weakened relationships and disintegration of the cluster. The quality of the communication channels and their level of technical sophistication are of paramount importance here. The instruments used in Communication 5.0 that provide the best representation of reality at acceptable prices tend to be used by clusters most often.

In the case of the possible absence of digital telecommunication devices, including the Internet, other forms of communication are likely to be overloaded. Clusters will be able to operate primarily through traditional forms of face-to-face (individual) contact such as analog phone lines, face-to-face meetings, traditional mail, and perhaps Ethernet networks. The greater the concentration of cluster participants in a given area, the more efficient, faster, and cheaper the communication will be. A conceptual diagram of such communication, i.e. excluding digital mass media, is shown in Figure 17.1b. Communication 5.0 using technical digital devices will be crippled unless innovations emerge that allow them to work without access to the Internet and mobile networks.

The next model (Figure 17.2) shows the secure hybrid communication model postulated by the respondents: both media-based and face-to-face communication. Ongoing attention to both channels, i.e. media and personal, ensures that clusters are resilient to the possible exclusion of communications from the real world (for example, during pandemic periods) and the virtual world (during periods of Internet shutdowns). As Communication 5.0 instruments become more diverse and independent of the global network, the more resilient the communication system in the cluster will be to exclusion.

Conclusions and recommendations

The research results showed that communication in marketing is an important factor in the growth and integration of cluster organizations. Internal communication, carried out mainly by cluster coordinators, is of key importance to their functioning. Interpersonal, face-to-face communication is crucial to cluster members as it is the best way to build relationships and mutual trust, fostering confidence, willingness, and motivation to carry out common tasks among collaborating companies. For this reason, the geographical and social

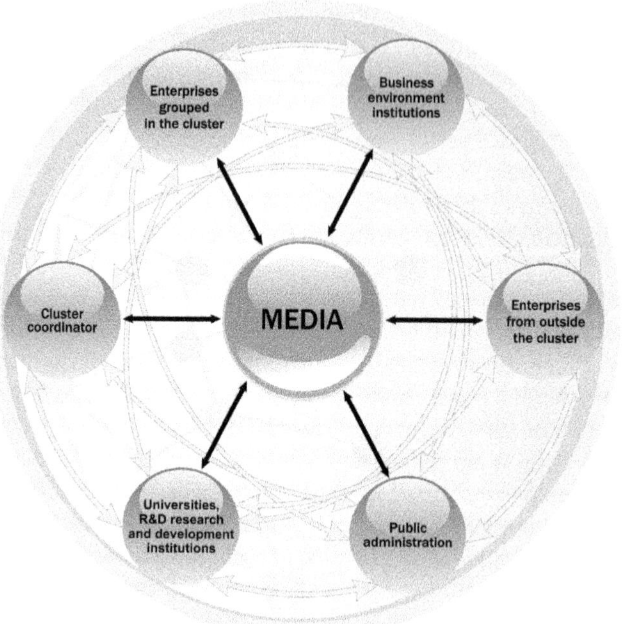

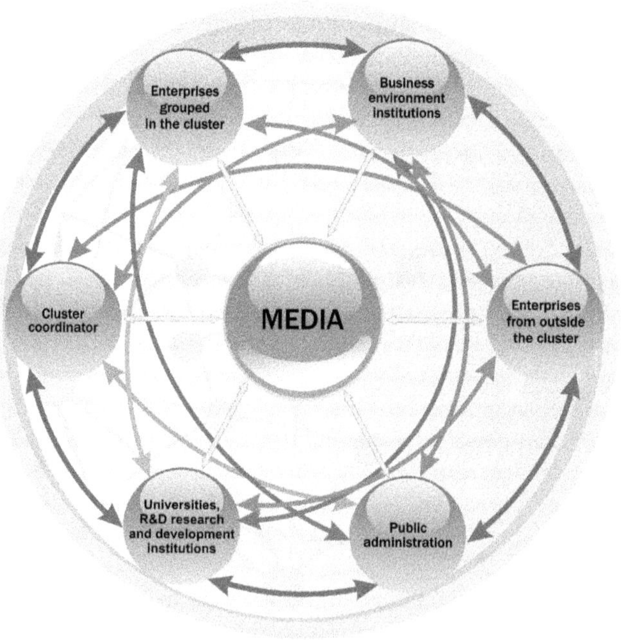

Figure 17.1 Conceptual model of communication in a cluster, in the case of a lack of: (a) direct communication in pandemic conditions (exclusions of the offline world), (b) communication via the internet and other media typical for Communication 5. 0 in the case of unavailability of the online world.

Source: Own study based on research, based on the concept of a spherical model of communication in clusters (Szymoniuk, 2019, p. 238).

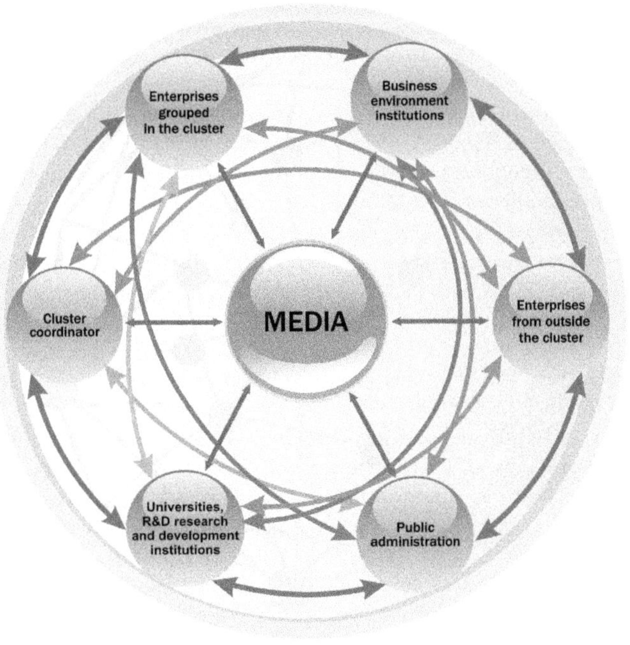

Figure 17.2 A conceptual diagram of hybrid communication in a cluster, providing resilience to possible exclusions from the internet and other digital media, and to real-world paralysis.

Source: Own study based on research, based on the concept of sphere model of communication in clusters (Szymoniuk, 2019, p. 238).

proximity of cluster stakeholders is important as it contributes to efficient and low-cost direct contact. Regardless of traditional face-to-face communication, clusters are developing Communication 5.0 processes based on new technologies. Considering the rapid development of new forms and instruments of communication, it becomes necessary to hire a professional knowledgeable of efficient communication in the digital era and in cyber security.

In clusters, it is also necessary to consider changes in the current communication systems due to the "revolution" associated with the arrival of Generation Z into the labor market. It is necessary to create a foundation for the adaptation of strategies, procedures, and marketing communication instruments to build relationships across generations. The experience of clusters shows that their older members have almost no problem with integrating into the world of the young (i.e. the world of social media, virtual communication, and Communication 5.0 devices). It may be more difficult for the younger generation, or Generation Z, to establish good, lasting relationships based on trust in the world of direct interpersonal contacts.

Future research may focus on identifying Communication 5.0 processes from the perspective of companies that belong to such clusters and, as a result, contribute to the improvement of these processes. With technological progress accelerating, tests of this kind should be periodically repeated.

References

Bajak, M. (2021). *Wykorzystanie beaconów w komunikacji marketingowej*. Polskie Wydawnictwo Ekonomiczne.

Cabinet Office (Council for Science, Technology and Innovation). (2017). Comprehensive Strategy on Science, Technology and Innovation (STI) for 2017. Retrieved July 19, 2022, from https://www8.cao.go.jp/cstp//english/doc/2017stistrategy_summary.pdf

Hitachi-UTokyo Laboratory (H-UTokyo Lab). (2020). *Society 5.0: A people-centric super-smart society*. SpringerOpen. https://doi.org/10.1007/978-981-15-2989-4

Kotler, P., Kartajaya, H., & Setiawan, I. (2017). *Marketing 4.0*. John Wiley&Sons.

Kotler, P., Kartajaya, H., & Setiawan, I. (2021). *Marketing 5.0: Technology for humanity*. Wiley.

Peraković, D., Periša, M., Cvitić, I., & Zorić, P. (2020). Information and communication technologies for the Society 5.0 environment, XXVIII Simpozijum o novim tehnologijama u poštanskom i telekomunikacionom saobraćaju – PosTel 2020, Beograd. https://doi.org/10.37528/FTTE/9788673954318/POSTEL.2020.020

Piotrowski, M. (2021). Benchmarking klastrów w Polsce – edycja 2020. Raport ogólny. Polska Agencja Rozwoju Przedsiębiorczości. Retrieved July 19, 2022, from https://www.parp.gov.pl/storage/publications/pdf/2021.06.04-Raport-oglny-PL-dostpny_13082021.pdf

Polat, L., & Erkollar, A. (2020). Industry 4.0 vs. Society 5.0. *Lecture Notes in Mechanical Engineering*, 333–345. https://doi.org/10.1007/978-3-030-62784-3_28

Rahman, M. (2021). Should I be scared of artificial intelligence? *Academia Letters*. https://doi.org/10.20935/al2536

Rosenbaum, M., Walters, G., Edwards, K., Gonzalez, C., & Contreras Ramírez, G. (2021). Play, chat, date, learn, and suffer? Merton's law of unintended consequences and digital technology failures. *Academia Letters*. https://doi.org/10.20935/al3426

Rzepka, A. (2019). *Przemysł 4.0*. Wydawnictwo Silva Rerum.

Sawicki, A. (2021). Marketing 5.0. Rozważania nad koncepcją. In H. Mruk & A. Sawicki (Eds.), *Marketing. Koncepcje i doświadczenia* (pp. 29–40). Wydawnictwo Bernardinum.

Szymoniuk, B. (2017). Klaster jako sieć interesariuszy według założeń Marketingu 3.0. *Zeszyty Naukowe Szkoły Głównej Gospodarstwa Wiejskiego w Warszawie: Polityki Europejskie, Finanse i Marketing*, *17*(66), 170–179.

Szymoniuk, B. (2019). *Komunikacja marketingowa w klastrach i uwarunkowania jej skuteczności*. Wydawnictwo Politechniki Lubelskiej.

18 Using startup ecosystems as accelerators of innovation

Jakub Bis, Anna Żelazna, Matylda Bojar, Ewa Bojar, Adam Kiersztyn

Introduction

Today, startups play an increasingly important role in the creation of innovation and implementation of modern economic solutions. Among the characteristics associated with startups, in addition to their high ability to innovate, startups are said to have limited financial resources, problems with team management and human resources, a lack of managerial and business expertise, and an above-average high risk of failure. As research shows, statistically, 60% of them fail within the first period of existence across the globe (Mukti et al., 2019; Wen-Hsiang & Lin, 2015). It is important to remember, however, that startup entrepreneurs do not operate in a vacuum. Extended networks of relationships, which often take the form of strategic alliances or virtual organizations, result in a new type of entrepreneurial ecosystem with regional, national, and even global reach. These ecosystems are composed of various actors including customers, suppliers, direct competitors, as well as public administration, industry institutions, business environment institutions, and, most importantly, relationships between startups (Moore, 1993, pp. 75–86). It is assumed that the success of a startup in a given market is highly dependent on the quality of such an ecosystem. Support networks devoted to ventures based on innovation take on particular importance in the context of Industrial Revolution 4.0. Currently, we are witnessing an increasingly passionate discussion about the weaknesses of Industry 4.0 and a trend to focus on the elements of Industry 5.0, which are closely linked to the concept of Society 5.0.

The aim of this chapter is an attempt to evaluate the functioning of selected startup platforms that operate in Eastern Poland by answering the question of how the support provided by such platforms affects the companies using them. Among other things, the chapter presents the results of a survey conducted among startups using the support of two regional platforms – Unicorn from Lublin and Eastern Business Accelerator from Puławy. The chapter proposes two hypotheses. The first hypothesis holds that startups can raise a variety of external financing sources more effectively after being incubated in startup platforms. The second research hypothesis is

DOI: 10.4324/9781003384311-18

that incubation in startup platforms affects the implementation of CSR and sustainability principles for stakeholders. Research conducted in this study provides an answer to the question about the effectiveness of startup platforms established through the support of EU funding for achieving the goals set for businesses in the 5.0 era.

Literature review

Startup ecosystems in the context of Industry 5.0

Business ecosystems are dynamic systems that include not only the firm's value chain but also firms in other industries that produce complementary goods or equipment, outsourcing companies, regulatory agencies, financial institutes, research institutes, media, universities, and even competitors (Baghbadorani & Harandi, 2012; Iansiti & Levien, 2002; Li, 2009; Moore, 1993; Yu et al., 2011).

In addition to value chain elements, Moore (1993, pp. 75–86) included other stakeholders and organizations, such as government, industry institutions, and customers, as major players in the business ecosystem, also taking the interactions between them into account. According to this concept, the performance of organizations that make up business ecosystems depends not only on their own competencies but also on their interactions with other actors and the condition of the ecosystem as a whole (Håkansson & Ford, 2002, pp. 133–139). Entrepreneurial ecosystems are composed of elements that operate in a systematic manner in the entrepreneurial ecosystem and are made up of interrelated entrepreneurial actors (organizations, institutions, and processes) "formally and informally combine to mediate and manage performance in the local entrepreneurial environment" (Mason & Brown, 2014).

Hence, the concept of an "entrepreneurial ecosystem" is holistic and interactive, evoking concepts such as clusters, industrial districts, local innovation systems, and learning regions that shape local economic development policies. Common to all these approaches is the belief that business performance depends not only on the internal behavior of firms (e.g. workforce skills, amount of investment in innovation, marketing and internationalization strategies, etc.) but also on the quantity and quality of interactions with external stakeholders (i.e. firms, investors, the public), industry organizations, universities, research institutes, etc., and the manner in which such interactions take place. What distinguishes the entrepreneurial ecosystem from other concepts is that it puts the entrepreneur in the spotlight. Hence, the capacity of the local environment is analyzed not in the context of innovation in general or economic development in a broad sense, but rather by the support given to entrepreneurs. Entrepreneurs in the ecosystem are seen as key players who generate and maintain it (OECD, 2013).

Håkansson and Ford (2002) emphasized the long-term, complex nature of relationships among ecosystem participants that result from their experience of interacting with each other. The concept of a business ecosystem is not precisely and comprehensively defined in the literature. Lipinski (2018), however, draws references from other researchers (Heikkilä & Kuivaniemi, 2012, pp. 18–24; Iansiti & Levien, 2004, p. 46; Moore, 1993, pp. 75–86; Peltoniemi, 2005, pp. 1–2) and points to the characteristics shared across all business ecosystems, which have been referenced in different concepts:

- a large number of organizations that make up the ecosystem,
- the interrelationship between elements,
- the sharing of knowledge (and other resources) and the cooperation of actors while maintaining high levels of competitiveness (coopetition),
- the execution of specific roles and positions by entities that are part of an ecosystem, such that changing (the position of) one element has an impact on others,
- the multi-directional and complex influence exerted by external forces (including politics, technology, markets, human resources, especially customers, etc.) on firms operating within an ecosystem,
- a dynamic structure, an ability of an entire ecosystem to evolve and grow,
- an ability to compete with other ecosystems.

Emphasizing the local character of entrepreneurial ecosystems, Mason and Brown (2014) offered a typology of policy approaches that are relevant to ecosystem development:

- entrepreneurial actors – business accelerators, incubators, recruiting talent, time-limited support,
- entrepreneurial organizations – business angels, venture capital, banks, service providers, universities,
- entrepreneurial connections – public-private partnerships and alliances, peer-to-peer learning, local and global pipelines,
- entrepreneurial orientation – entrepreneurship education, role models, peer-to-peer networks, entrepreneurial recycling.

A number of ongoing studies of startups confirm that firms collaborate with different actors at different stages because knowledge and resource networks play a key role in supporting the evolution and success of new firms (Passaro et al., 2020). The way to increase the survival chances of actors in the market is to build a set of collaborative relationships with different actors in the business ecosystem (e.g. venture capitalists and business angels, education system actors, innovation agencies, science parks, external partners, suppliers, etc.) through which they can fill knowledge and resource gaps and successfully overcome various challenges (Passaro et al., 2020).

The network of collaborative relationships can be considered in the context of a holistic approach to the entrepreneurial ecosystem where a set of interconnected actors rooted in the entrepreneurial community support new entrepreneurs formally and informally. The definition of an entrepreneurial ecosystem, based on a synthesis of definitions found in the literature, reads that it is "a set of interconnected entrepreneurial actors (both potential and existing), entrepreneurial organisations (e.g. firms, venture capitalists, business angels, banks), institutions (universities, public sector agencies, financial bodies) and entrepreneurial processes (e.g. the business birth rate, numbers of high growth firms, levels of 'blockbuster entrepreneurship', number of serial entrepreneurs, degree of sell-out mentality within firms and levels of entrepreneurial ambition) which formally and informally coalesce to connect, mediate and govern the performance within the local entrepreneurial environment" (Mason & Brown, 2014).

Support networks for innovative ventures take on particular importance when it comes to the next industrial revolution. Nowadays, there is a burgeoning debate on the weaknesses of Industry 4.0 and a trend to focus on the elements of Industry 5.0 related to the concept of Society 5.0. This approach seeks to balance economic development with addressing social and environmental issues. It is not limited to the manufacturing sector but addresses larger societal challenges through the integration of physical and virtual spaces. Society 5.0 is a society in which advanced information technologies, the internet of things (IoT), robotics, artificial intelligence (AI), and augmented reality (AR) are incorporated into daily life, industry, health care, and other areas of activity, not primarily for economic gain but for the benefit and convenience of every citizen (European Commission, 2021). Industry can become a provider of true prosperity, and the definition of its true purpose must include social, environmental, and societal issues. This includes responsible innovation that is not solely or primarily aimed at cutting costs or maximizing profit but also at increasing the well-being of all parties involved, including investors, employees, consumers, society, and the environment. These broader industry goals are based on human-centricity, sustainability, and resilience.

Technologies based on AI or tools used in virtual and AR can be used to manage employees to perform more specialized tasks that would otherwise require specialized knowledge and training. The digitization of industrial processes allows for remote work, allowing people from remote regions to join the workforce, as well as increasing the resilience of manufacturing itself. The World Manufacturing Forum has identified the ten most important skills that will be needed in the manufacturing of the future, four of which relate to digital skills: "digital literacy, AI and data analytics", "working with new technologies", "cybersecurity", and "data-mindfulness" (European Commission, 2021). The PricewaterhouseCoopers report entitled "Millennials at work – Reshaping the workplace in financial services" indicates that corporate social values become more important to Millenials when choosing an employer once their basic needs, such as reasonable pay and favorable working conditions, have been met. The report points out that "Millenials want their work to have a purpose, to contribute something to the world, and they want to be proud of their employer" (PWC, 2012, p. 13). Intelligent mass production seems to be the goal of Industry 4.0, while sustainability is part of Industry 5.0. However, sustainability and mass production are not mutually exclusive, and the industry's efforts can be directed toward "*sustainable smart production*" (Demir & Cicibaş, 2017). Demir and Cicibas indicate that the next industrial revolution – whatever its name and definition will be – should include the following technologies and research areas (Demir & Cicibaş, 2017): IoT, cloud computing, robotics and AI, Big Data, sustainability and environmental protection, bioeconomy, waste prevention, business administration, and organizational research.

Platforms as an example of a startup ecosystem

By looking at the actions taken by European Startup Network together with the German Startup Association or European Commission one can notice a general commitment to strengthen startup ecosystems across the EU. An interesting document in this context is the EU Startup Monitor report produced between 2016 and 2018 as part of an initiative undertaken by the European Commission to improve the conditions of startups, both economically and legally. Startup founders and managers were invited to contribute to the survey through grassroots initiatives in the creation of a European startup ecosystem. The purpose of the EU Startup Monitor is to collect and analyze input data to help monitor the startup environment, differences among countries, and shared challenges within the startup landscape (Startup Monitor, 2019). The analyses that were undertaken to pinpoint the essential elements of the startup ecosystem led to the identification of eight major components (Tripathi et al., 2018), which included financing, demographics, market, education, human capital, technology, entrepreneurs, and supporting factors. These factors impact startups directly or indirectly. Eight important elements that influence the establishment of startups (with particular emphasis on software products) were identified, and they were entrepreneurs, financing, market, technology, human capital, education, demographics, and supporting factors.

As for *supportive factors*, it should be noted that incubators and accelerators are important to budding entrepreneurs because they provide the right support to refine ideas for businesses and turn them into viable business plans. These programs operate in co-working spaces where the interested parties can collaborate and build networks of contacts to help startups grow. Another important element is *financing*, which is required at all stages of product and customer development. Funding may be possible through investors such as business angels, established companies, venture capital, banks, governments, and crowdfunding. *The demographics of the region* also have an impact on the startup ecosystem. Demographics include the region's culture and language, geographic location, history, and the number of foreigners. Another element is the *market*, which can be local or global, and is influenced by customers and the type of business the startup is involved in. Another element of the ecosystem is *education*, which is important because of the nurturing of young talents in educational institutions where they receive the instruction they need to start a startup. Educational institutions, accelerators, incubators, experience, and the media all play a role in creating an educational environment. *Human capital* is one more element influenced by accelerators and incubators, education, experience, government, policy, and young talent. The last two elements are technology and entrepreneurs (Tripathi et al., 2018).

Platforms in Eastern Poland

The Startup Platforms Program has been implemented by Polska Agencja Rozwoju Przedsiębiorczości as an intermediary under Measure 1.1, Startup platforms for new ideas, Sub-measure 1.1.1 Startup platforms for new ideas, and Sub-measure 1.1.2 Development of startups in Eastern Poland under Operational Programme Eastern Poland 2014–2020, priority axis I: Entrepreneurial Eastern Poland [*Journal of Laws* 2016, item 217; OJ. 2015, item 1007]. The Eastern Poland Programme is co-financed by the European Regional Development Fund (ERDF). It serves the development of innovation capabilities and competitiveness of five provinces – Lubelskie, Podlaskie, Podkarpackie, Świętokrzyskie, and Warmińsko-Mazurskie.

The first of these instruments assumed the creation of a support program in the macroregion of Eastern Poland, which was aimed at transforming innovative business ideas into products and services and making them market-ready according to the adopted methodology (e.g. Customer Development, Lean Startup, or Design Thinking) and developing viable business models. Then, startups that were ready to enter the market with the product prepared during incubation could apply for a grant to develop their business in the macroregion under Sub-measure 1.1.2.

The first phase of the project was implemented between 2015 and 2017 via selecting three Startup Platform Animators by competitive selection from among the applications submitted by innovation centers (i.e. science and technology parks, science parks, technology parks, and technology incubators). Animators would build partnerships that included important actors in innovative entrepreneurship, creating startup ecosystems called Startup Platforms. Above all, the purpose of the pilot study was to test the program's assumptions and correct them, if necessary, so that further improvement could be achieved in subsequent editions of the program. It is important to stress that the pilot study showed that this type of support should be continued since, first, it filled a gap in support for early-stage enterprises, and second, the support provided was beneficial, and the introduction of several improvements could only contribute to a better implementation of the program's assumptions. As a result of the pilot study, the European Commission approved the project in November 2017.

In 2018, twelve applications were submitted to a competition for new startup platforms, of which six were chosen and signed contracts in Q4 2018 and Q1 2019:

- "Startup Heroes" startup platform in Olsztyn, where the leader of the project is the Olsztyn Municipality – Olsztyn Science and Technology Park. Industries: ICT, food production, eco energetics.
- "Hub of Talents 2" startup platform in Bialystok, where the leader of the project is the City of Bialystok – Bialystok Science and Technology Park. Industries: metal/machinery, processing metal and machine manufacturing, IT/ICT, and horizontal specialization.
- "Wschodni Akcelerator Biznesu" startup platform in Puławy, where the leader of the project is the Puławy Science and Technology Park. Industries: ecology, food and agricultural products, ICT.
- "Unicorn Hub" startup platform in Lublin, where the leader of the project is the Polska Fundacja Ośrodków Wspomagania Rozwoju Gospodarczego "OIC Poland". Industries: IT/ICT, Smart City/transportation and automotive, medical/public health.
- "IDEALIST" startup platform, where the leader of the project is Park Naukowo-Technologiczny Energii Sp. z o.o. Industries: ICT, energy, medicine/tourism/health.
- "Start in Podkarpackie" startup platform in Rzeszów, where the leader of the project is Rzeszowska Agencja Rozwoju Regionalnego S.A. Industries: IT/ICT, aviation, automotive, construction.

Each leader (animator) offers future entrepreneurs an incubation program provided in a broad partnership with universities, research centers, VC funds, business angels, and small, medium, and large specialized companies, among others (see Figure 18.1). Throughout the entire process of turning an innovative idea into a profitable business, each startup is guided by experienced managers, business experts, and mentors. The recruitment of startups to the platforms is scheduled to end on 31 October 2022.

For the purpose of this paper, the authors have examined two startup platforms – Unicorn Hub and Wschodni Akcelerator Biznesu.

The leader of the first of them was Polska Fundacja Ośrodków Wspomagania Rozwoju Gospodarczego "OIC Poland" in Lublin. Partner entities in this ecosystem include a total of 12 entities:

- University of Economy and Innovation in Lublin,
- INNOventure Sp. z o.o. from Cracow,
- Findustry Sp. z o.o. from Cracow,
- Centrum Medyczne Sanitas Sp. z o.o. from Lublin,
- Powiatowe Centrum Zdrowia Sp. z o.o. from Opole Lubelskie,
- Miejskie Zakład Komunalny Sp. z o.o. from Stalowa Wola,

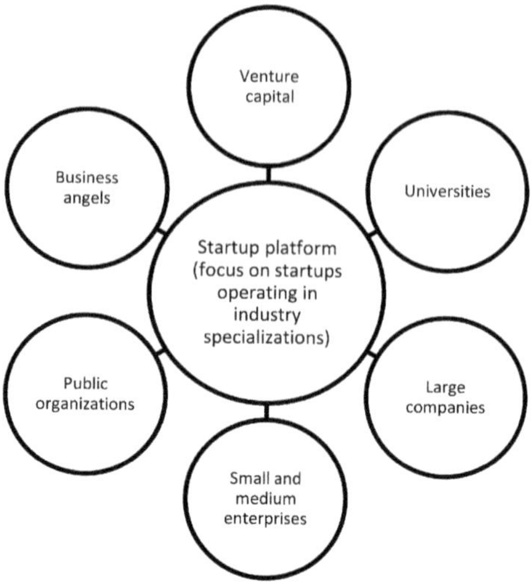

Figure 18.1 Functioning diagram of startup platforms in Eastern Poland.

Source: Own elaboration.

- Vena Art. Sp. z o.o. from Lublin,
- KLS Partners Sp. z o.o. from Warsaw,
- Krakowski Park Technologiczny Sp. z o.o. based in Kraków,
- Pracodawcy Lubelszczyzny "LEWIATAN" based in Lublin,
- Summer Agency sp. z o.o. based in Kraków,
- Sentinel Innovation Sp. Z o.o. with its registered office in Kraków.

The leader of the second platform under consideration is the Puławy Science and Technology Park Sp. z o.o., called, which implements a project with the support of the following partners:

- Grupa Azoty Zakłady Azotowe "Puławy" S.A. with registered office in Puławy,
- Innofin Sp. z o.o. with registered office in Warsaw,
- Instytut Nowych Syntez Chemicznych from Puławy,
- Netrix Group Sp. z o.o. with registered office in Lublin,
- Netrix Ventures Sp z o.o. with registered office in Lublin,
- Rebels Valley Sp. z o.o. with registered office in Warsaw,
- Maria Curie-Skłodowska University in Lublin.

Materials and methods

The research method used was a diagnostic survey conducted with a questionnaire as a research tool. A pilot study was conducted among a group of ten experts to verify the validity of the questionnaire. In the first quarter of 2021, the survey was conducted via Google Forms, and a link to the survey was sent to startups in the Lublin area. The survey was designed to broadly analyze startups in terms of their development stage, sources of business funding, business models used, and the problems that they encountered following the outbreak of the COVID-19 pandemic. For this study, some of the results obtained from startups that operated within startup platforms (46 entities) and outside startup platforms (67 entities) were used. The research questions were as follows:

1 What are the differences between startup platforms and entities operating outside of them?
2 Are platform-based startups more likely to use a variety of funding sources?
3 In which startups are sustainable behaviors more likely to be observed?

Results

Through the statistical analysis, we were able to verify the two research hypotheses (outlined in the introduction). At the beginning of the statistical analysis, the correlations between the different questions were checked and the linear correlation matrix was determined (cf. Figure 18.2). An analysis

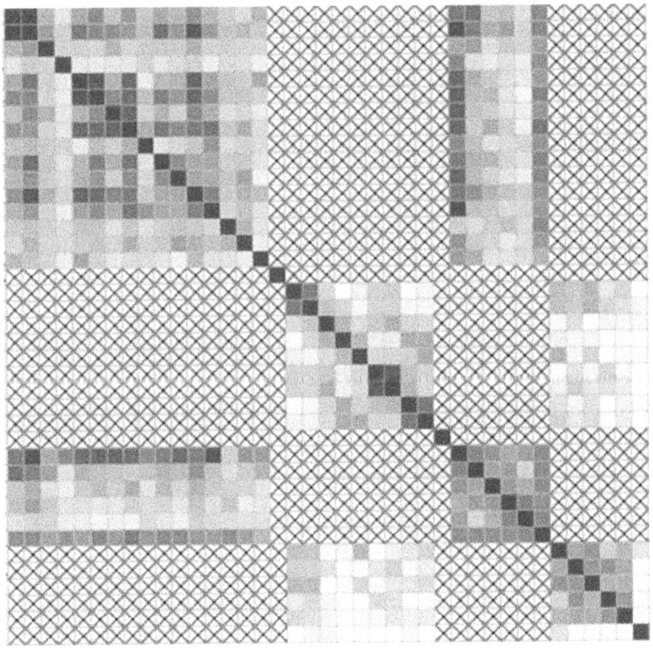

Figure 18.2 Visualization of linear correlation matrix.

Source: Own elaboration based on conducted research.

of the results presented in Figure 18.2 suggests that there are some groups of questions for which there was a relatively high positive (blue) as well as negative (red) linear correlation. It is therefore advisable to conduct additional analyses to identify more precise links among different questions.

In order to verify the research hypotheses, we applied a classical approach to conducting relevant χ^2 tests and analyzing the distributions of individual characteristics. For the first research hypothesis, data from the survey was used and a series of independent χ^2tests were conducted, which tested the independence of the variable indicating participation in a startup platform, while the corresponding item from the survey was sequentially selected as the second variable. The data was also analyzed using KNIME, a specialized analytics platform. For example, an analysis of the relationship between the affiliation of a startup platform and its business model is presented in Figure 18.3. It can be seen that there is a strong correlation between belonging to a platform and having a business model. The differences between the observed and predicted state are at a significant level, which directly translates into the value of χ^2

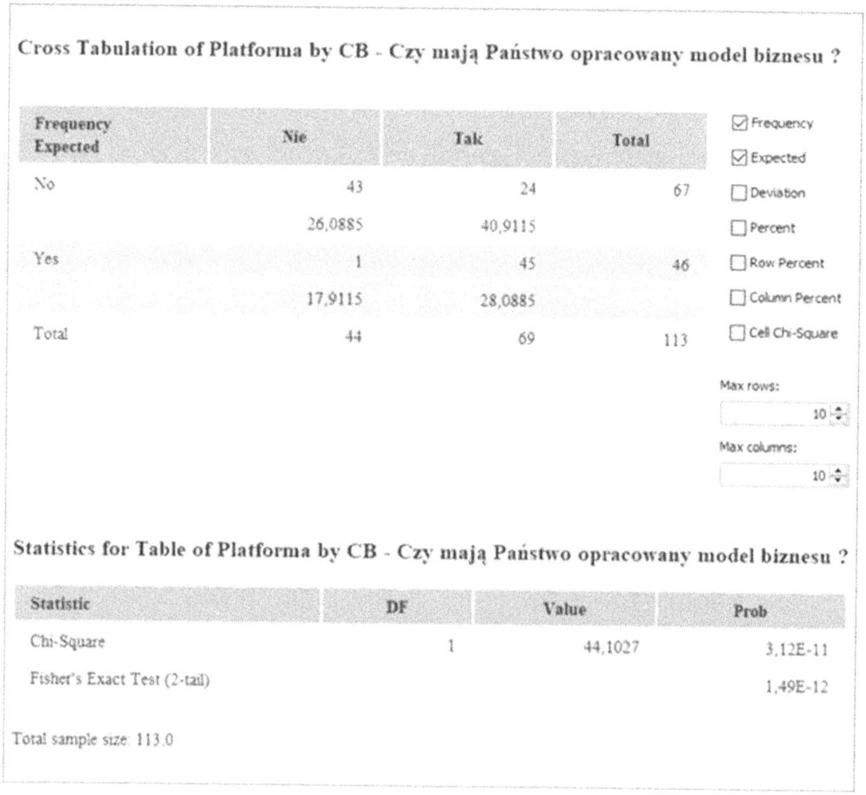

Cross Tabulation of Platforma by CB - Czy mają Państwo opracowany model biznesu ?

Frequency Expected	Nie	Tak	Total
No	43	24	67
	26,0885	40,9115	
Yes	1	45	46
	17,9115	28,0885	
Total	44	69	113

Statistics for Table of Platforma by CB - Czy mają Państwo opracowany model biznesu ?

Statistic	DF	Value	Prob
Chi-Square	1	44,1027	3,12E-11
Fisher's Exact Test (2-tail)			1,49E-12

Total sample size: 113.0

Figure 18.3 Example of result analysis using the test χ^2.

Source: Own elaboration based on conducted research.

statistics. The significance level calculated by the software (with and without Fisher's correction) suggests that the independent variables hypothesis should be rejected.

The significance level values for the remaining tests determined by the analysis of the first and second research hypotheses are presented in Table 18.1. Based on the results presented in this table, we can confirm the research hypothesis that companies incubated within platforms are able to raise financing from non-traditional sources. Only when obtaining financing through a loan from a local financial institution (funds, foundations, development agencies) is there no statistically significant difference among them.

Table 18.1 Significance level obtained in the χ^2 test when analyzing the relationship between startup incubation and the given questions

Survey question	*Significance*
What sources of business funding has your startup used, is currently using, or plans to use? [Own funds (bootstrapping)]	8.15E-04
What sources of business funding has your startup used, is currently using, or plans to use? [Loan from friends, family]	0.110463
What sources of business financing has your startup used, is currently using, or plans to use? [Domestic (national) venture capital]	3.39E-07
What sources of business financing has your startup used, is currently using, or plans to use? [Foreign venture capital]	2.32E-07
What sources of business funding has your startup used, is currently using, or plans to use? [Domestic (national) business angel]	1.25E-07
What sources of business funding has your startup used, is currently using, or plans to use? [Foreign business angel]	1.26E-05
What sources of business financing has your startup used, is currently using, or plans to use? [Loan from bank]	0.023559
What sources of business funding has your startup used, is currently using, or plans to use? [Domestic (national) accelerator]	3.07E-10
What sources of business funding has your startup used, is currently using, or plans to use? [Foreign Accelerator]	3.51E-05
What sources of financing did your startup use, is currently using, or is planning to use? [PARP, NCBR]	1.83E-13
What sources of business funding has your startup used, is currently using, or plans to use? [Crowdfunding]	7.24E-05
What sources of business financing has your startup used, is currently using, or plans to use? [Loans from local financial market institutions (funds, foundations, development agencies)]	0.078619
What sources of business funding has your startup used, is currently using, or plans to use? [European Commission (e.g. Horizon, Framework Programme)]	0.001213
Did you use the following methods when developing your startup?	1.05E-07
Do you have a business model?	3.12E-11
Does your startup incorporate activities around the concept of corporate social responsibility?	6.17E-05
Does your startup's activity meet the requirements of equal opportunity?	1.77E-06
Does your startup's activity have a positive impact on sustainability?	0.022085

Source: Own work on the basis of the survey.

In addition, it should be noted that there is a statistically significant relationship between incubation with a startup platform and the application of methodologies, the development of a business model, the implementation of activities related to the concept of corporate social responsibility, or the application of sustainability principles. An in-depth analysis of the obtained results suggests that companies incubated within platforms apply the abovementioned activities significantly more frequently.

Discussion

According to the literature review we conducted, the majority of startups fail, while others grow exponentially (Cooper, 1993; Spiegel et al., 2015). Research also shows that a company's business model affects its performance (Foss & Saebi, 2017; Lambert & Davidson, 2013; Massa et al., 2017; Weking et al., 2019). As a result of our research, we have found that startups that receive support from startup platforms in Eastern Poland have a business model and follow at least one of three startup methodologies (Lean Startup, Customer Development, Design Thinking) and, at the same time, are more successful in the market. The situation is quite different among startups that are developing independently and do not have easy access to the latest structured management knowledge through courses or expert mentoring.

Being a part of a startup platform also positively affects the ability to secure external funding sources. Startups operating within platforms use or plan to use venture capital or business angels' support more frequently than other entities. However, it should be noted that venture capital is not a common source of financing for startups in Eastern Poland. We came to similar conclusions when we surveyed technology startups in four developing countries – Cambodia, India, Thailand, and Vietnam (Vandenberg et al., 2020). Entities that produce products that require long-term support through design, testing, prototyping, and certification stages suffer from a lack of "patient capital". Meanwhile, companies in growth-oriented sectors had little trouble raising funds from influential investors and international development agencies. The results of the research support hypothesis one, according to which incubation in startup platforms positively influences the ability of startups to obtain various sources of external funding.

Policy makers in developing countries increasingly recognize science, technology, and innovation (STI) as a pathway to achieving sustainable development. An analysis of the performance of STI-based incubators in India shows that the objectives of government-funded incubators are consistent with sustainable development goals. They primarily create employment among the socially excluded, build sustainable infrastructure, and support innovation (Surana et al., 2020). Of course, it is worth adding at this point that appropriate mechanisms and incentives should be created to strengthen the links between actors and encourage them to cooperate in order to achieve sustainable development (Shkabatura et al., 2021). Similar conclusions can be formulated as a result of our research – companies incubated in startup platforms are significantly more likely to carry out activities consistent with the concept of corporate social responsibility, meet the requirements of the principle of equal opportunities and willingly implement the principles of sustainable development in comparison with companies from outside. Therefore, it can be concluded that the second hypothesis that incubation in startup platforms influences the application of CSR and sustainability among stakeholders has also been verified positively.

A study that focused on the impact of startup accelerator on venture capital funding, conducted in metropolitan areas of the US (Fehder et al., 2014), highlighted the regional impact of accelerators on the entrepreneurial ecosystem. A greater number of startups were observed in regions that had accelerators, and those without accelerators also benefited from them (access to venture capital, mentoring, demo day). The threat the researchers pointed out, however, involved shifting investment funds from other regions to regions with accelerators, negatively affecting other regions. There has also been criticism of the region's artificial retention and support of businesses by local policymakers and founders of accelerators. Similarly to the US, startup platforms in Eastern Poland attract startups from other regions, with the difference that the area we examined is a typically underdeveloped region (GDP per capita at about 50% less than the EU average). However, thanks to the EU funding aimed at incubating startups and due to the possibility of receiving up to PLN 1,000,000 grants for the development of the best startups, the least developed region in Poland in which the two platforms – Unicorn and WAB – operate attracts innovative entrepreneurs from all over the country. Therefore, our research team intends to continue its research on the effects of startup platforms on businesses in the underdeveloped region. Another extremely interesting line of research seems to be the impact of the business model schemes that are used by individual startups for surviving and succeeding in the market.

References

Act of 11 July 2014 on the principles for the implementation of cohesion policy programmes financed in the financial perspective 2014–2020 (Journal of Laws 2016, item 217).

Baghbadorani, M. F., & Harandi, A. (2012). A conceptual model for business ecosystem and implications for future research. doi:10.7763/IPEDR. 2012. V52. 17.

Cooper, A. (1993). Challenges in predicting new firm performance. *Journal of Business Venturing*, *8*(3), 241–253.

Demir, K. A., & Cicibaş, H. (2017, October 17–20). *Industry 5.0 and a Critique of Industry 4.0*. 4th International Management Information Systems Conference "Industry 4.0", İstanbul University, İstanbul, Turkey.

European Commission (2021). Industry 5.0. *Towards a sustainable, human-centric and resilient European industry*. Manuscript completed in January 2021. First edition. https://op.europa.eu/en/publication-detail/-/publication/468a892a-5097-11eb-b59f-01aa75ed71a1/

Evaluation of the pilot of Measure 1.1 of the Operational Programme Development of Eastern Poland 2014–2020 "Start-up platforms for new ideas". (2018). STAGE II – ex-post evaluation of the Pilot Startup Platforms Foundation for Entrepreneurship and Regional Development, Warsaw.

Fehder, Daniel C., & Hochberg, Yael V. (2014, September 19). Accelerators and the regional supply of venture capital investment. https://ssrn.com/abstract=2518668 or http://dx.doi.org/10.2139/ssrn.2518668

Foss, N. J., & Saebi, T. (2017). Fifteen years of research on business model innovation: How far have we come, and where should we go? *Journal of Management, 43*(1), 200–227.

Håkansson, H., & Ford, D. (2002). How should companies interact in business networks. *Journal of Business Research, 55*(2), 133–139.

Heikkilä, M., & Kuivaniemi, L. (2012). Ecosystem under construction: An action research study on entrepreneurship in a business ecosystem. *Technology Innovation Management Review, 2*(6), 18–24.

Iansiti, M., & Levien, R. (2002). The new operational dynamics of business ecosystems: Implications for policy, operations and technology strategy. Division of Research, Harvard Business School. Retrieved December 22, 2021, from https://www.hbs.edu/ris/Publication%20Files/03-030_9bfcbb1b-85a1-4e1b-9f73-41bea8f63821.pdf

Iansiti, M., & Levien, R. (2004). *The keystone advantage: What the new dynamics of business ecosystems mean for strategy, innovation and sustainability*. Harvard Business School Press.

Lambert, S. C., & Davidson, R. A. (2013). Applications of the business model in studies of Enterprise success, innovation and classification: An analysis of empirical research from 1996 to 2010. *European Management Journal, 31*(6), 668–681.

Li, Y.-R. (2009). The technological roadmap of Cisco's business ecosystem. *Technovation, 29*(5), 379–386.

Lipinski, A. (2018). Concepts and key drivers of startup ecosystem development. Economic studies. *Zeszyty Naukowe Uniwersytetu Ekonomicznego w Katowicach, 351*, 46–57.

Mason, C., & Brown, R. (2014). Entrepreneurial Ecosystems and Growth Oriented Entrepreneurship. OECD: Background paper prepared for the workshop organized by the OECD LEED Programme and the Dutch Ministry of Economic Affairs on Entrepreneurial Ecosystems and Growth Oriented Entrepreneurship The Hague, Netherlands, 7th November 2013. Retrieved December 22, 2021, from https://www.oecd.org/cfe/leed/entrepreneurial-ecosystems.pdf

Massa, L., Tucci, C. L., & Afuah, A. (2017). A critical assessment of business model research. *Academy of Management Annals, 11*(1), 73–104.

Moore, J. F. (1993). Predators and prey: A new ecology of competition. *Harvard Business Review, 71*(3), 75–86.

Mukti, I. Y., Wibowo, A. P. W., & Galih, S. (2019). Lessons learned to increase the digital startups success rate. *Global Business and Management Research, 11*, 226–234.

OECD. (2013). Entrepreneurial ecosystems and growth-oriented entrepreneurship summary report of an international workshop organized by the OECD and the Netherlands Ministry of Economic Affairs, the Hague, 7 November 2013. www.oecd.org/employment/leed/INTERNATIONAL%20ECOSYSTEM%20WORKSHOP_SUMMARY%20REPORT.pdf

Ordinance of the Minister of Infrastructure and Development of 13 July 2015 on granting financial aid by the Polish Agency for Enterprise Development under Axis I (2015). Entrepreneurial Eastern Poland of the Operational Programme Eastern Poland 2014–2020. *Journal of Laws*, item 1007.

Passaro, R., Quinto, I., Rippa, P., & Thomas, A. (2020). Evolution of collaborative networks supporting startup sustainability: Evidences from digital firms. *Sustainability, 12*, 9437. https://doi.org/10.3390/su12229437

Peltoniemi, M. (2005). Business ecosystem: A conceptual model of an organization population from the perspectives of complexity and evolution. *e-BRC Research Reports, 18*, 1–93.

PWC. (2012). Millennials at work: Reshaping the workplace in financial services. https://www.pwc.com/gx/en/financial-services/publications/assets/pwc-millenials-at-work.pdf

Shkabatura, J., Bar-Elb, R., & Schwartz, D. (2021). Innovation and entrepreneurship for sustainable development: Lessons from Ethiopia. *Progress in Planning*, 16'0, 100599. https://doi.org/10.1016/j.progress.2021.100599

Spiegel, O., Abbassi, P., Zylka Matthäus, P., Schlagwein, D., Fischbach, K., & Schoder, D. (2015). Business model development, founders' social capital and the success of early stage internet start-ups: A mixed-method study. *Information Systems Journal, 26*(5), 421–449.

Startup Monitor. (2019). EU Startup Monitor. Growing Business in Europe. http://startupmonitor.eu/

Surana, K., Singh, A., & Sagar, A. D. (2020, August). Strengthening science, technology, and innovation-based incubators to help achieve Sustainable Development Goals: Lessons from India, 2020. *Technological Forecasting and Social Change, 157*, 120057.

Tripathi, N., Seppanen, P., Boominathan, G., Oivo, M., & Liukkunen, K. (2018). Insights into startup ecosystems through exploration of multi-vocal literature. *Information and Software Technology*. https://doi.org/10.1016/j.infsof.2018.08.005

Vandenberg, P., Hampel-Milagrosa, A., & Helble, M.. (2020). Financing of Tech Startups in Selected Asian Countries. ADBI Working Paper 1115. Tokyo: Asian Development Bank Institute. https://www.adb.org/publications/financing-tech-startups-selected-asiancountries

Weking, J., Böttcher, T. P., Hermes, S., & Hein, A., (2019, June 8–14). "DOES BUSINESS MODEL MATTER FOR STARTUP SUCCESS? A QUANTITATIVE ANALYSIS". Proceedings of the 27th European Conference on Information Systems (ECIS), Stockholm & Uppsala, Sweden. ISBN 978-1-7336325-0-8 Research-in-Progress Papers. https://aisel.aisnet.org/ecis2019_rip/77

Wen-Hsiang, L., & Lin, C. C. (2015). Constructing business incubation service capabilities for tenants at post-entrepreneurial phase. *Journal of Business Research, 68*, 2285–2289.

Yu, J., Li, Y., & Zhao, C. (2011). Analysis on structure and complexity characteristics of electronic business ecosystem. *Procedia Engineering, 15*, 1400–1404.

19 Evolution of motivations and risks associated with IT outsourcing in large organizations in Poland

Jolanta Słoniec

Introduction

Outsourcing is an important management concept that has been developing intensively since the second half of the 20th century. Information technology outsourcing (ITO) is one of the most common functions in modern enterprises requiring a separate discussion. It is no longer a simple means of reducing costs or improving efficiency. It has become an important strategy of the organization, involving the integration of several concepts, some of which are contradictory. It is used to reduce costs (Han & Mithas, 2013), increase efficiency (Salimath et al., 2008; Thouin et al., 2009), and focus on core competencies (Quinn, 1999) at the same time.

The subject of research discussed in this chapter is ITO in large organizations in Poland. In view of the fact that large organizations were the first to use outsourcing (and to the greatest extent) and still do, the state of ITO development in Poland can be determined from the presented research.

The purpose of the research was to identify motivational changes and risks associated with using ITO and to identify mechanisms of changes to motivation and risks.

The research problem was presented as a series of questions:

- How has the motivation of large organizations in Poland using ITO changed over time?
- How have the risks faced by large organizations in Poland using ITO been changed over time?
- What are the mechanisms involved in changing these variables?

The research problem involves important and current aspects since ITO is an important element of the digital economy. In Poland, information technologies are being developed rapidly, but the level of digitization is still below that of more developed countries. On the other hand, Poland has highly qualified staff in IT, which is why outsourcing is becoming an important "export commodity" and a workplace for many qualified employees. Polish companies, which compete in domestic, regional, and global markets, implement business

DOI: 10.4324/9781003384311-19

models that can give them a competitive advantage. Such a model may involve the use of outsourcing, especially in the area of information technology.

ITO has been the subject of research among scientists for several decades. However, longitudinal studies in this area are rare due to the difficulty of conducting them. The only ITO longitudinal study available focused on Spanish companies and covered a period of 12 years (González et al., 2016). However, each country has its own specificity, and research conducted in Spanish enterprises corresponds only to some extent with the research conducted in Polish enterprises. When I undertook the research into changes to motivation and risks, I knew that changes were occurring, but I didn't know how they happened and what the mechanisms were.

Due to the fact that information technology in Poland is developing intensively, it was advisable to conduct research in ITO to identify its specific characteristics of development and outline the change mechanisms.

In the course of the research, the following hypotheses were formulated:

H1: the motivation to use ITO evolves from economic to technological and then strategic;
H2: outsourcing IT is reinforcing the risks; and
H3: mechanisms of changes to motivations and risks associated with ITO are related to outsourcing development phases, digitization processes, and the development of the knowledge-based economy.

To address the hypotheses, I conducted a longitudinal study of large organizations in Poland (the vast majority of which were enterprises) in 2016 and 2021, over a five-year timeframe. The research was quantitative and involved 200 organizations every time. The research method was a diagnostic survey, while the research tool was a questionnaire. I used the CATI (Computer Added Telephone Interview) method to conduct the research.

As a result of the conducted research and analysis, I determined the changes in the motivation and risks associated with ITO in Poland and presented the mechanisms behind these changes. The results of the surveys differ slightly from those published for Spanish companies (longitudinal ITO studies covering 12 years). Each country has its specificity, Poland as well. The specificity of the development of the economy in Poland results especially from the economic history of the country in the second half of the 20th century and its geopolitical location. The mechanisms of changes to motivations and risks associated with ITO in Poland result from the development processes of outsourcing itself, the development of the knowledge-based economy, and changes in the digital economy in Poland and the world.

The presented research broadens the knowledge about motivational changes and risks associated with using ITO because, in addition to identifying changes and indicating their directions, they try to explain the mechanisms of change and the impact of recognized change trends on the development of a new ITO offer by outsourcing providers, suitable for changing demands.

Literature review

ITO has been a subject of research covering a wide range of issues. Cross-sectional studies (Lacity et al., 2009, 2010, 2017) identified many areas of empirical research and presented issues that require further research. A monograph by the author of this article discusses cross-sectional ITO research in Poland and research gaps (Słoniec et al., 2018). Identifying the reasons and risks of ITO is a key issue that has been studied by scientists from many countries for a quarter of a century (Abdullah & Verner, 2012; Bahli & Rivard, 2000; Benoit et al., 2013; González et al., 2010; Harland et al., 2005; Kluk, 2010; Madhuchhanda & Saji, 2009; Nakatsu & Iacovou, 2009; Nassimbeni et al., 2012; Ngwenyama & Sullivan, 2007; Słoniec et al., 2016; Sullivan & Ngwenyama, 2005; Willcocks et al., 1999; Kulu, 2021). It is rare for longitudinal studies on outsourcing to be the subject of scientific consideration. The only existing cross-sectional study of ITO motivations and risks was conducted by González et al. (2007, 2016) on a group of Spanish companies over a 12-year period (i.e. in 2001, 2006, and 2012). In its course, the researchers found that companies followed the trends of outsourcing and evolution. According to their latest study, the most important reasons for using ITO are strategic, followed by technological, and economic reasons are the least important. Furthermore, they showed a great deal of stability in the ranking of outsourcing motivations. Accordingly, the level of risks is equally important in the context of the review period.

By undertaking this research, I knew that changes in motivation follow the evolution of ITO. There is no mention of the mechanisms of motivation and threat changes and their impact on the creation of an adequate ITO offer by suppliers in either of the referenced studies or other publications. Accordingly, this chapter presents research that:

- broadens knowledge about the evolution of changes in ITO motivations and risks, particularly for Polish companies;
- provides an overview of the trends in changes to ITO motivations and risks; and
- examines the impact of identified trends in changes to motivation and risks on the creation of an adequate ITO offer by outsourcing providers.

These are the results that this research brings to science.

The reasons why the research topic undertaken is important and current are varied. First, utilitarian – relates to the development of the IT industry, which is changing dynamically in Poland. Annual growth rate among companies in the IT/ICT industry is 10% and the value of IT/ICT services exports is 5.6 billion euros. The ITO market is also experiencing rapid growth, with new companies providing ITO services and the existing ones expanding their offer. The most important reasons for choosing an ITO provider from Poland include highly skilled developers (ranked third in the world), an insignificant culture gap and good knowledge of English, small time difference (short wait-times for responses), high security standards, and a relatively low price of services (Małysiak, 2018).

Based on official data on the development trends of the IT/ICT industry and ITO (the ICT sector in 2020), it is expected that the use of ITO in Poland will increase. The second reason for taking up the topic, cognitive – the intention is to identify and fill the research gap in the presented area by determining changes in the motivation and risks associated with ITO in Poland, recognizing the mechanisms and tendencies for change, and determining the impact of the changes observed on the creation by suppliers of an offer adequate to the changes. Longitudinal research, as Dibbern points out (Dibbern et al., 2004), brings a new dimension to research that is usually static.

Materials and methods

"Longitudinal data analysis consists of the statistical tools and methods used to analyze data collected on the same group of individuals on multiple occasions over time" (Das 2014). As a method of research in management sciences, longitudinal research involves multiple examinations of the same subjects at predetermined intervals using the same methods and tools. Research in this area is based on the criterion of time and serves to understand the mechanisms of change and factors influencing behavior. The priority of this research is to track changes in the variables under study (Stańczk-Hugiet 2014:48). It is also referred to as prospective studies. The methodology of transverse testing is addressed in a publication by Hedeker and Gibbons (2006), while longitudinal studies in medicine are considered by Fitzmaurice and Ravichandran (2008). According to the classification (Miller & Friesen, 1982), the studies presented are multivariate, long-range, replicable (repeatable) studies. The method used in this study is not often applied to ITO because it is a difficult and expensive study to conduct. Much more often researchers use the case study method (Amiruddin et al., 2013; Svejvig & Pries-Heje, 2011; Vivek et al., 2007) or a quantitative method where the research tool is a survey questionnaire (Ali & Green, 2009; Bahl & Wali, 2014; Yu, 2013). With the last method, it is then possible to build ITO models. The identified longitudinal studies in the IT domain have addressed new product development and innovation (Ciravenga & Maielli, 2011), the reasons and risks of ITO (González et al., 2016), outsourcing recruitment activities (Laumer et al., 2012) and the learning curve in outsourcing using a large Australian company as an example (Fisher et al., 2008).

In this study, ITO was studied from a cross-sectional perspective in order to determine the size of the phenomenon, its characteristics and the relationship between the quantities studied. Each study was quantitative in nature. The research method was a diagnostic survey and the research tool for data collection was a survey questionnaire. The questionnaire included semi-open content questions and a metric. Each study involved 200 large organizations, the vast majority of which were enterprises that used ITO in their day-to-day activities. The selection of the research sample was both purposeful and random. The survey sample represented 14.3% of the total number of large companies that used ITO in 2016, and 19.4% in 2021. The research was conducted using the CATI (Computer Added Telephone Interview) technique between January and February 2016 and January and February 2021. The choice of large organizations for ITO research was based on the fact that these organizations externalize IT activities most often and to the greatest degree (Lee et al., 2016). They are also relatively stable entities, are the earliest adopters of ITO and use different types and forms of outsourcing. On the basis of research of large organizations, the intent was to draw conclusions concerning the evolution of changes to motivation and risks to the use of ITO in Poland.

In light of the fact that the longitudinal study presented in this study focused on the state of development of ITO in large organizations in Poland, it was not possible to study the same enterprises. In both cases, the research sample was numerous (and totaled 200 large organizations), allowing us to examine the dynamics of ITO development in various aspects.

When investigating the reasons and risks associated with ITO, an extended Likert scale was used for answers, ranging from 1 to 7, with 1 representing "completely unimportant" and 7 "very important", and 4 was a neutral answer representing "neither yes/nor important, nor no/nor invalid". The questions about the reasons and risks associated with ITO were semi-open, with the option for respondents' individual answers to be included.

Table 19.1 shows the industry structure of the companies and organizations participating in the 2016 and 2021 surveys.

In terms of the structure of sectors, industrial enterprises and administration accounted for a larger proportion of the branches of the organizations participating in the survey in 2021 than in 2016.

Figure 19.1 presents the percentage share of client organizations and supplier organizations in ITO divided into onshoring and offshoring (onshoring is understood as conduct of ITO activities inside the country, offshoring is understood as conduct of activities outside the country). Shares do not add up to 100% because some organizations used both onshoring and offshoring. In 2021, in comparison with 2016, the share of organizations using onshoring has increased and in those using offshoring has decreased. This is due to the rapid development of the ITO services industry in recent years, the

Table 19.1 Branches of organizations that participated in the research, %

No.	*Sector*	*2016*	*2021*
1	Industry	23.8	45.0
2	Trade	23.8	14.4
3	Services	15.6	12.4
4	Logistics/transport	17.3	4.3
5	Science/research/education	16.0	11.0
6	Administration/organizations/agencies	3.5	12.9

Source: Own elaboration.

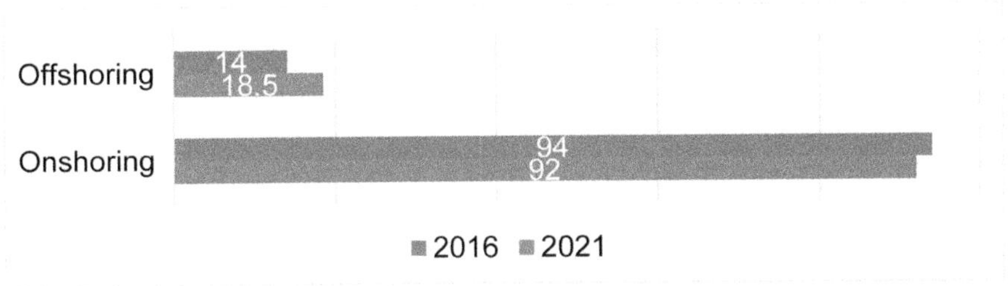

Figure 19.1 Organizations' use of ITO (longitudinal study, %).

Source: Own elaboration.

specialization of services, and the consequent increase in the supply of suppliers. It is common for foreign providers to offer specialized types of ITO services that may not yet be available domestically.

ITO in large organizations in Poland is developing, and its dynamics have increased by several percent.

Results

The reasons for using outsourcing refer to the factors that motivate organizations to use this service. On the other hand, a number of factors prevent organizations from deciding to outsource IT activities, i.e. dangers. If the organization uses ITO, the motivating factors outweigh the risk factors.

Factors responsible for reasons and risks associated with ITO have been listed in order to construct a questionnaire and implement this research on the basis of a literature review, in particular Gupta and Gupta (1992), Lacity and Hirschheim (1993), Grover et al. (1994; 1996), Lacity et al. (1994), Clark et al. (1995), Jurison (1995), McFarlan and Nolan (1995), Smith et al. (1998), Willcocks et al. (1999, 2006), Bahli and Rivard (2000), Bahli (2005), Hayes et al. (2000), Alner (2001), Baldwin et al. (2001), Barthélemy (2001), Claver et al. (2002), Harland et al. (2005), Sullivan and Ngwenyama (2005), Brooks (2006), Ngwenyama and Sullivan (2007), Olson (2007), Yang et al. (2007), Walden and Hoffman (2007), Al-Ghrabi et al. (2009), Cox et al. (2011), Fan et al. (2012), and Gandhi et al. (2012).

Next, reasons and risks were grouped based on Grover's classification (Grover et al., 1994; 1996). Statistical methods such as cluster analysis (k-mean grouping) were used for that purpose. A licensed version of Statistica 13.3 was used for the grouping. To perform other analyses and to illustrate the results, a licensed version of Microsoft Excel 16.53 was used.

In the process, four groups of reasons were distinguished:

- economic: cost savings on personnel and use of technology, cost savings on infrastructure (in 2021);
- technological: minimizing the risk of outdated technology, facilitating access to new technologies, improving the quality of services offered;

- organizational and strategic: increasing the flexibility of IT departments, providing an alternative to internal IT, eliminating routine and problematic tasks, focusing on strategic IT issues; and
- other: adaptation to trends, outsourcing of IT is an irreversible trend, dependence on the mother company (in 2021).

Figures 19.2 and 19.3 show the importance of the reasons for the use of ITO in large organizations in Poland, in 2016 and 2021, respectively, grouped.

In 2016, the top reasons for using ITO were technological, more specifically, improving the quality of services offered and facilitating access to new technologies, and among organizational and strategic reasons, the top reason was increasing the flexibility of the IT department (more than 60% of respondents said these reasons were important). Organizational and strategic reasons and economic reasons were less important, and other reasons related to the current fad were rated least important (only 14.5% of organizations rated them as important).

In 2021, just like in 2016, the most important reasons in the technological group included *the improvement of the quality of services* offered and *facilitating access to new technologies,* whereas in the organizational and strategic reasons these were *increasing the flexibility of the IT* department (over 60% of

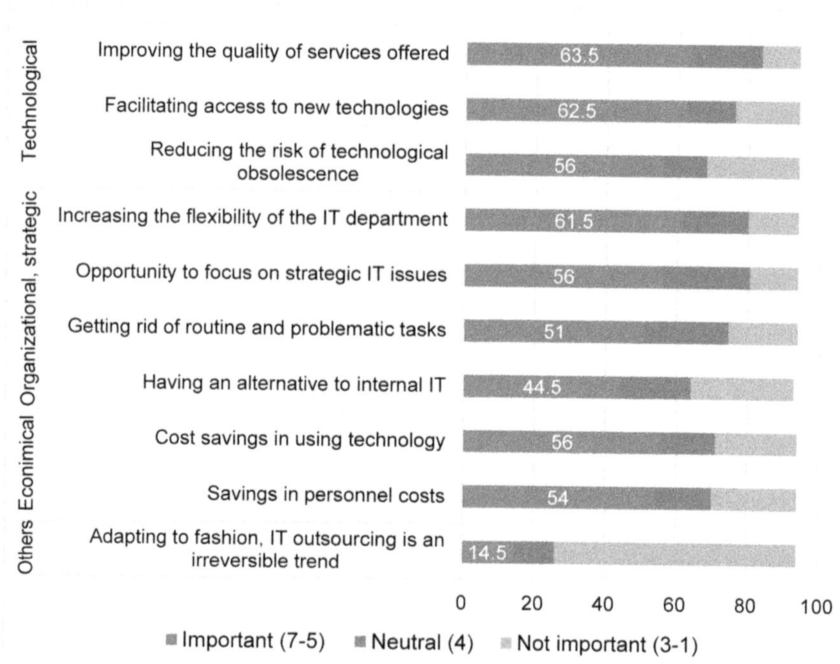

Figure 19.2 Reasons for the use of IT outsourcing in 2016 (in %).

Source: Own elaboration.

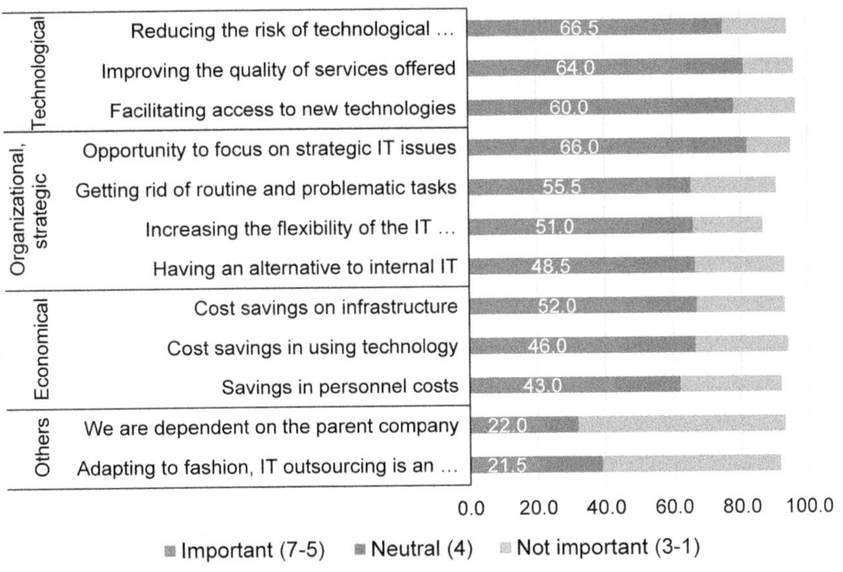

Figure 19.3 Reasons for the use of IT outsourcing in 2021 (in %).

Source: Own elaboration.

respondents said they are important). Similarly to the research 5 years prior, the other organizational and strategic reasons were rated less favorably. There is a noticeable decrease in the importance of economic reasons. The one rated as least important in 2016 was the reason that it was a fad – considered important by only over 20% of organizations. The assessment of the remaining reasons was slightly more favorable than 5 years earlier.

In a similar fashion to the reasons, Figures 19.4 and 19.5 show the risks associated with ITO in 2016 and 2021, compiled into groups.

In 2016, overreliance on the supplier was considered the most important risk (a client-related risk) and was rated as important by 53% of the organizations. The second most important risk comes from security issues (an external risk), rated as important by 52% of the organizations. As for the most important groups of risks, these consisted of external risks. Less important risks related to the supplier, while the least important ones were those related to the customer.

In 2021, risk assessment increased by approximately 20%. The qualifications of the supplier's staff *(a supplier-related risk)* were considered to be *the most important risk recognized as important by 73% of the organizations, followed by exposure to misuse of company's sensitive and confidential data* (a risk concerning the client) assessed as important by 70% of the organizations, and *data* corruption or loss (an external risk) that was assessed as important by 68.5% of the organizations. The most important risk groups were those related to the supplier,

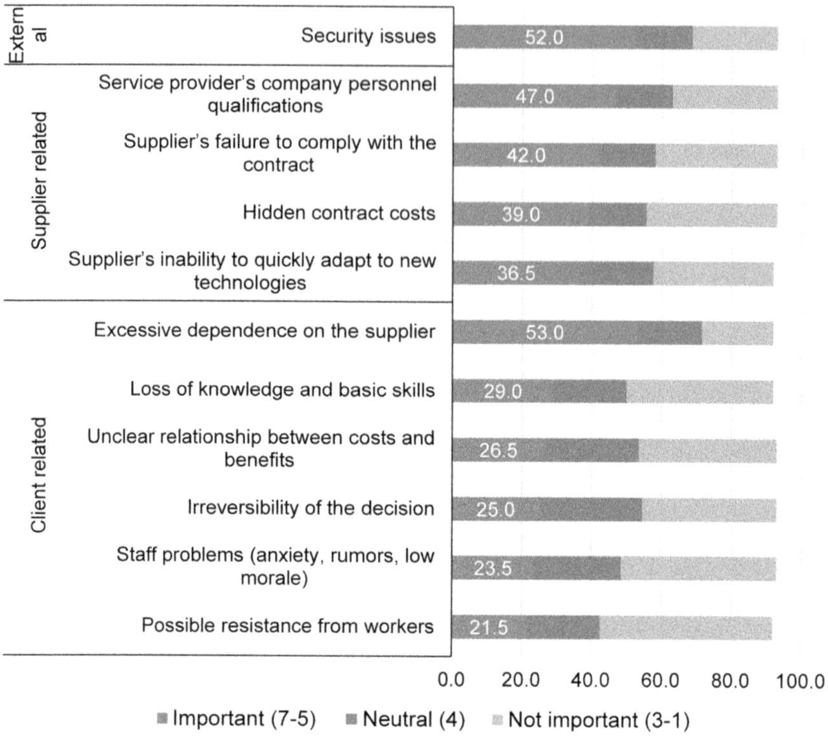

Figure 19.4 Risks of IT outsourcing in 2016 (in %).

Source: Own elaboration.

slightly less important were those related to the customer, and external risks were the least important.

Discussion

Table 19.2 lists the reasons for using ITO in large Polish organizations (assessed as *important* and *unimportant*) in 2016 and 2021, respectively, grouped.

The data in Table 19.2 indicate that during the 5-year period the importance of technological reasons increased by 2.8%, organizational and strategic by 2.0%, and other reasons by 7.3%. In contrast, the importance of economic reasons decreased by 8%. Hypothesis 1 is confirmed by this evidence.

Table 19.3 lists the risks associated with ITO in large Polish organizations (assessed as *important* and *unimportant*) in 2016 and 2021, respectively, grouped into groups.

Based on Table 19.3, it can be concluded that during the 5 year period studied, the importance of all risks increased. The significance of supplier-related risks increased most by 21.4%, while customer-related risks rose by

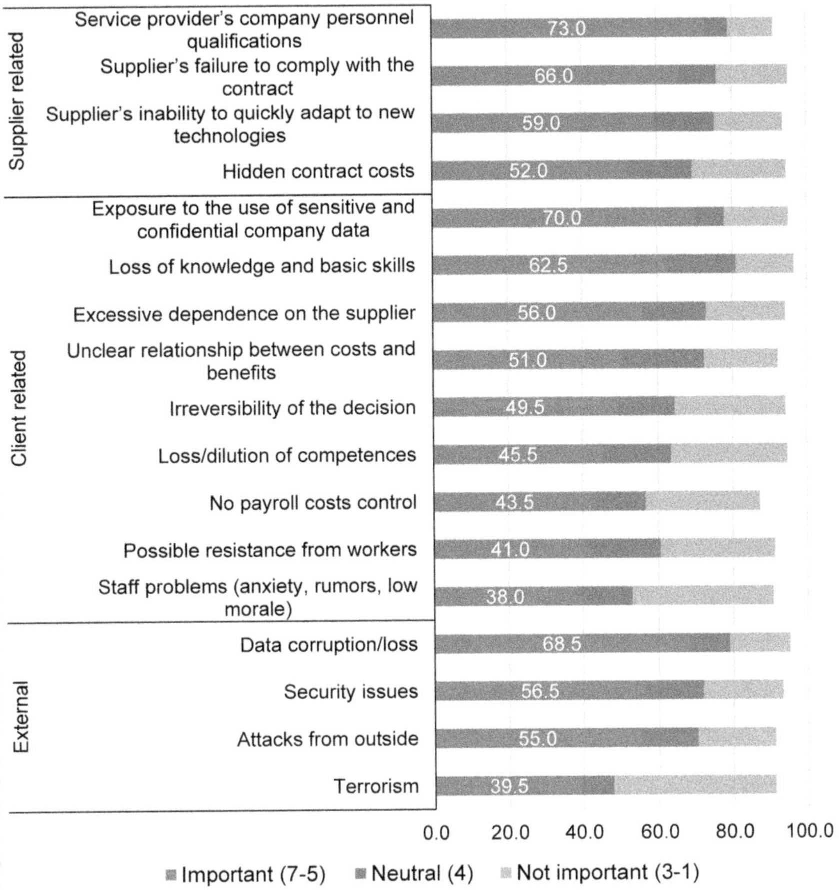

Figure 19.5 Risks of IT outsourcing in 2021 (in %).

Source: Own elaboration.

21.0%. Meanwhile, external factors gained 2.9% importance. Hypothesis 2 is confirmed by this evidence.

As for works of other scientists, it can be concluded that the only longitudinal research on the reasons and risks of ITO can be found in González et al. (2016). Their article contains a ranking of reasons and risks associated with ITO in Spanish companies in 2001, 2006, and 2013 (a 12-year perspective). The authors noted that there is high stability in the ranking of the most important reasons for the use of outsourcing. Spanish companies use outsourcing primarily for strategic reasons to increase the flexibility of departments and achieve higher quality by eliminating routine tasks. Technological reasons occupy a slightly lower position, and economic reasons are the least important.

Table 19.2 Reasons for using IT outsourcing, average, %

		2016		2021	
No.	*Reasons*	*Important*	*Unimportant*	*Important*	*Unimportant*
1	Technological	60.7	18.2	63.5	17.5
2	Organizational-strategic	53.3	19.0	55.3	21.3
3	Economic	55.0	23.5	47.0	27.8
4	Other	14.5	68.0	21.8	56.8

Source: Own elaboration.

Answers 1–3 representing "unimportant", and answers 4–7 "important".

The study conducted on Polish enterprises in 2016 and 2021 shows a slightly different ranking; technological reasons came as the most important ones, followed by organizational and strategic reasons, and economic reasons came as least important. It was also found that the importance of technological and organizational and strategic reasons is increasing while the importance of economic reasons is decreasing. These changes result from the natural development of ITO. This phenomenon consists of three phases, namely: the first – when the motivation is to reduce costs and increase the quality of services – the second – when the most important reason is access to external competencies, resources, and potential – and the third – when activities identified as key competencies are outsourced (Kehal & Singh, 2006). The presented research indicates that Polish enterprises are currently in the second phase of ITO development, in which the importance of economic reasons that were dominant in the first stage of ITO development is decreasing, and the importance of technological, organizational, and strategic reasons is increasing. This is evidenced particularly by the slightly higher growth in the importance of technological rather than organizational and strategic reasons in the last five years (see Table 19.2).

Responding to hypothesis 1, it can be stated that the importance of technological as well as organizational and strategic motivations is increasing, and the importance of economic motivations is decreasing. Figure 19.6 illustrates the mechanisms of motivation changes.

The outsourcing motivation study identified two new reasons that were not addressed in the previous study (they were established through face-to-face

Table 19.3 Risks for using IT outsourcing, average, %

		2016		2021	
No.	*Risk*	*Important*	*Unimportant*	*Important*	*Unimportant*
1	External	52.0	24.5	54.9	25.1
2	Supplier-related	41.1	34.3	62.5	18.5
3	Client-related	29.8	39.1	50.8	25.8

Source: Own elaboration.

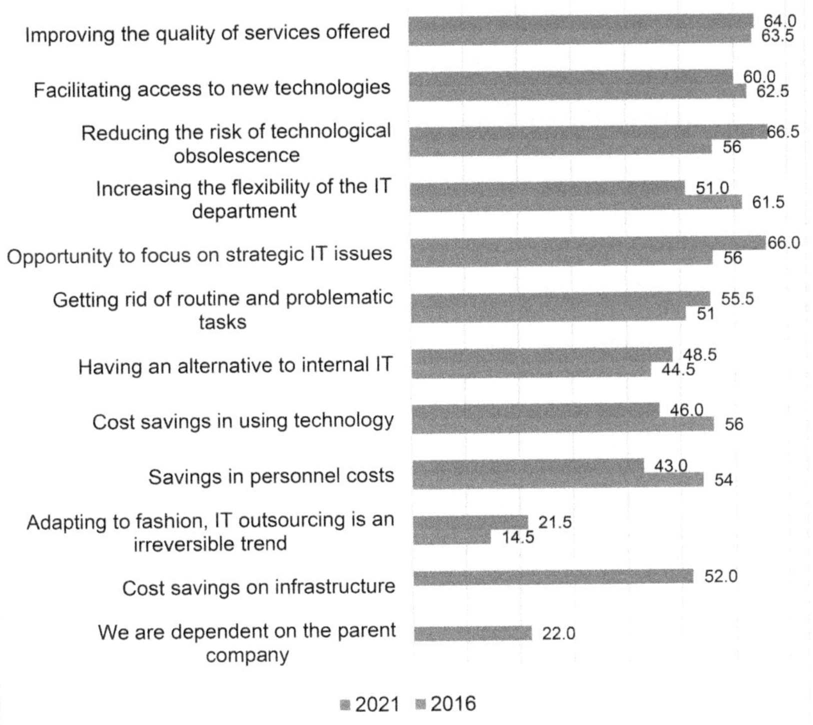

Figure 19.6 Comparison of IT outsourcing motivations in 2016 and 2021 (in %).

Source: own elaboration.

interviews with representatives of companies that served as ITO clients). Since they had not occurred in 2016, changes among them could not be compared.

The most important mechanism contributing to a change in the motivation behind using ITO is the very process of how outsourcing develops. According to the phases of its development in Poland (Kehal & Singh, 2006; Słoniec et al., 2018), we are nearing the end of the first phase in which the most important rationales for making use of outsourcing were economic reasons. Companies are currently going through the second phase in which technological, organizational, and strategic factors prevail. There is also an increase in the importance of factors included in the third phase, in which tasks identified as key competencies are outsourced. An equally important mechanism includes changes occurring in the economy, especially in the digital economy, that involve digitization and networking. They consist of Globalization 4.0, Consumption 4.0, Production 4.0, Market 4.0, and State 4.0 (Śledzińska & Włoch, 2020). Technological changes (e.g. Industrial Internet of Things), organizational changes (e.g. vertical integration, digital leadership) and process-related changes (e.g. agile manufacturing), the emergence of new business models (e.g. personalization and customization of products), digitization of the work environment (e.g. digital agents), and new competencies and skills (e.g. transferable skills) seem to be particularly important here. Based on the above considerations, part of hypothesis 3 can be verified positively.

As far as the study of risk is concerned, longitudinal studies among Spanish companies indicate the continuity of risks, the most important of which are supplier's staff qualifications, over-dependence, and non-compliance with the contract (González et al., 2016).

The basic conclusion of this ITO risk study is that risks have become increasingly important. There is no doubt that this is due to enterprises becoming more aware of the existence of risks. The study among large enterprises in Poland also revealed changes in risks over the period under review. In the last 5 years, suppliers have become the most important risk, while external risks were the most important 5 years ago. Currently, client-related risks are rated the least important, just like five years ago. The risks to Polish enterprises related to the use of ITO are not stable and show high dynamics (see Table 19.3).

Similarly to motivations, in order to determine the mechanisms underlying changes in risks, Figure 19.7 has been created.

In 2021, risks were slightly different than the ones in 2016; the more recent research was expanded to include six new risks not identified in previous studies, which is why changes in these risks could not be identified (new risks were determined based on interviews in ITO client enterprises).

The most important mechanism contributing to altering the risks of ITO seems to be processes related to the development of knowledge-based economies. Today, individuals who decide on the use of outsourcing are aware of potential risks and understand that such risks may arise in their company. The increase in the importance of risks results directly from the development of the digital economy (a greater number of potential risks), in particular from the platformization of production (e.g. distributed systems, Manufacturing-as-a-Service, relocation of production), changes in the work environment (e.g. crowd employment, virtual work, globalization of work), digitization of the work environment (e.g. AI-based automation, datification).

Among the risks whose importance has increased the most are client-related factors. This is again due to the processes related to the development of knowledge-based economies. The importance of economic and security risks has decreased slightly, which corresponds to the mechanisms of motivational changes associated with outsourcing development phases. As a result, part of hypothesis 3 can be positively verified.

To summarize the mechanisms of changes to motivations and risks associated with using ITO in large enterprises in Poland, it can be concluded that they result from:

- processes involved in the development of outsourcing,
- processes involved in the development of the knowledge-based economy, and
- processes that are driving changes in the digital economy in Poland and the world.

The above considerations indicate that hypothesis 3 is correct.

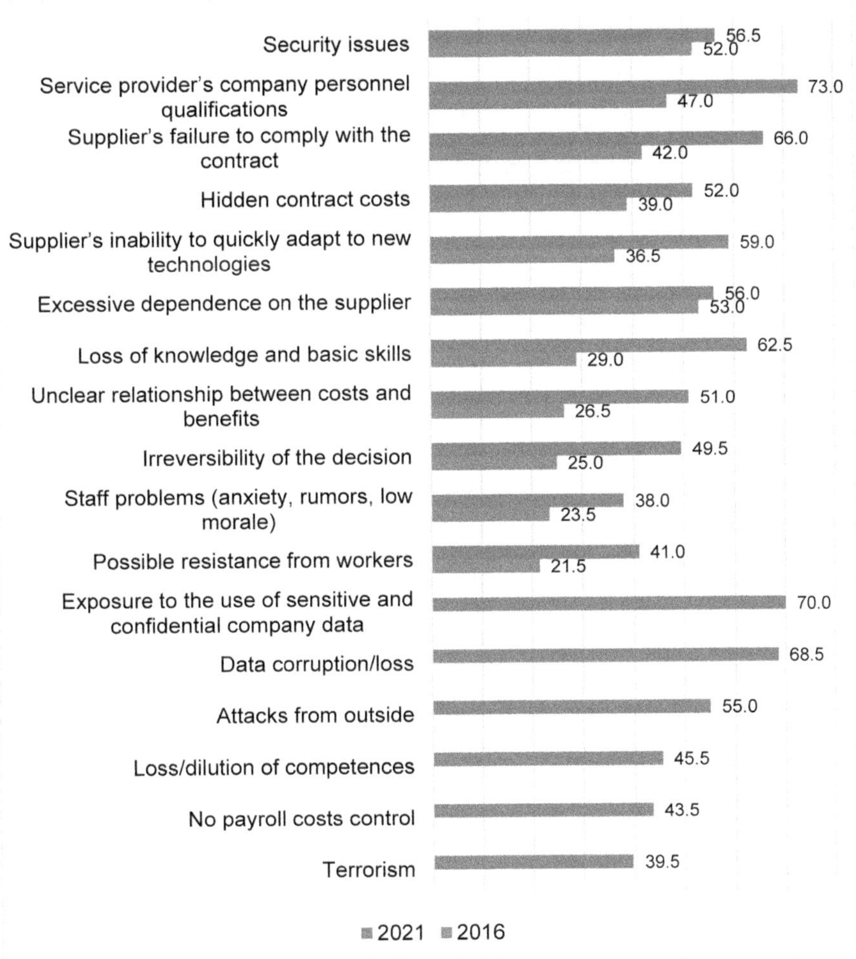

Figure 19.7 Comparison of IT outsourcing risks in 2016 and 2021 (in %).

Source: Own elaboration.

The processes have been described above to explain the mechanisms of changes to motivation and risks associated with ITO.

In conclusion, it can be stated that all hypotheses have been verified positively.

By outlining the directions of changes to motivation, it can be said that the importance of organizational and strategic motivations will increase (following the phases of ITO development). The development of the digital and knowledge-based economies will further increase the importance of risks (increasing the number of risks, increased awareness of risks).

Considering the impact of the trends in changes in ITO motivations and risks on the development of offers addressing these changes by outsourcing providers, it can be concluded that such new offers should address the processes of development of the knowledge-based economy and the processes of changes in the digital economy. In particular, in the author's opinion and based on the available directions of IT development, a new offer of ITO suppliers should take the following aspects into account:

- cloud computing (CC); includes self-service procurement of cloud services (Ragowsky et al., 2014; Schneider & Sunyaev, 2016; Yanosky 2008);
- platformization (expansion of platforms); relies on the use of platforms in a business model (including data collection, processing, and analysis) enabling the benefit of scale and networking (McAfee & Brynjolfsson, 2017; Śledzińska & Włoch, 2020);
- widespread use of systems based on Artificial Intelligence (*machine learning, deep learning*), in particular business AI; allows for optimization, minimization, maximization, and better alignment (Kai-Fu, 2018) and automization of processes;
- robotization, automation, and internetization (*collaborative robots, cobots, cloud robotics*); includes the use of efficient robots in a dynamic environment (ABI Research, Google Cloud), on-demand work involving the use of human resources and freeing them at will (Mayer-Schönberger & Ramge, 2018);
- data and process security, cybersecurity; it is related to access to data, privacy, transparency, and protection against unauthorized use; and
- a growing importance of knowledge-intensive production; it is related to the datification and development of digital products, which involves the use of human resources capable of high levels of expertise (Lee et al., 2016).

This study has several limitations that can be categorized as follows:

- limitations related to the research methodology – the number of companies surveyed, method of surveying, the timing of the survey, and the respondents;
- examination of ITO clients only, without taking the service provider into account; and
- limitations related to the development of the digital economy – there is an acceleration and intensification of processes and changes taking place in outsourcing, in particular ITO. In countries with a higher level of digitalization, ITO is in its third phase of development. Therefore, it is expected that as the digital economy develops in Poland, ITO will enter the third phase of development (i.e. outsourcing tasks related to key competencies). This will involve the development of new forms and types of outsourcing but also new motivations and new risks.

These limitations will serve as the starting point for further research on the development of ITO in Poland – research that will help to explain and understand the processes and mechanisms involved, mitigate risks, and facilitate development so that motivations outweigh the risks and encourage enterprises to use ITO to a greater and wider extent.

References

Abdullah, L., & Verner, J. (2012). Analysis and application of an outsourcing risk framework. *Journal of Systems and Software, 85*(8), 1930–1952. https://doi.org/10.1016/j.jss.2012.02.040

Ali, S., & Green, P. (2009). Effective information technology (IT) governance mechanisms: An IT outsourcing perspective. *Information Systems Frontiers, 14*(2), 179–193. https://doi.org/10.1007/s10796-009-9183-y

Alner, M. (2001). The effects of outsourcing on information security. *Information Systems Security, 10*(2), 1–9. https://doi.org/10.1201/1086/43314.10.2.20010506/31401.6

Amiruddin, R., Aman, A., Hamzah, N., & Maelah, R. (2013). Mitigating risks in a shared service relationship: The case of a Malaysian bank. *Qualitative Research in Accounting &Amp; Management, 10*(1), 78–93. https://doi.org/10.1108/11766091311316202

Bahl, S., & Wali, O. (2014). Perceived significance of information security governance to predict the information security service quality in software service industry. *Information Management &Amp; Computer Security, 22*(1), 2–23. https://doi.org/10.1108/imcs-01-2013-0002

Bahli, B. (2005). Validating measures of information technology outsourcing risk factors. *Omega, 33*(2), 175–187. https://doi.org/10.1016/j.omega.2004.04.003

Bahli, B., & Rivard, S. (2000). *Information technology outsourcing risks: Conceptualization and measurement*. ASAC-IFSAM Conference Proceedings. https://doi.org/10.1080/02683960320001302l4

Baldwin, L., Irani, Z., & Love, P. (2001). Outsourcing information systems: Drawing lessons from a banking case study. *European Journal of Information Systems, 10*(1), 15–24. https://doi.org/10.1057/palgrave.ejis.3000372

Barthélemy, J. (2001). *The hidden costs of IT outsourcing*. MIT Sloan Management Review. Retrieved July 23, 2022, from https://sloanreview.mit.edu/article/the-hidden-costs-of-it-outsourcing/

Benoit, A., Patry, M., & Rivard, S. (2013). *Information systems outsourcing: Enduring themes, emergent patterns and future directions*. Springer.

Brooks, N. (2006). Understanding IT outsourcing and its potential effects on IT workers and their environment. *The Journal of Computer Information Systems, 46*(4), 46–53.

Ciravenga, L., & Maielli, G. (2011). Outsourcing of new product development and the opening of innovation in mature industries: A longitudinal study of fiat during crisis and recovery. *International Journal of Innovation Management, 15*(01), 69–93. https://doi.org/10.1142/s1363919611003088

Clark, T., Zmud, R., & Mccray, G. (1995). The outsourcing of information services: Transforming the nature of business in the information industry. *Journal of Information Technology, 10*(4), 221–237. https://doi.org/10.1177/026839629501000403

Claver, E., González, R., Gascó, J., & Llopis, J. (2002). Information systems outsourcing: Reasons, reservations and success factors. *Logistics Information Management, 15*(4), 294–308. https://doi.org/10.1108/09576050210436138

Cox, M., Roberts, M., & Walton, J. (2011). *Motivations for IT Outsourcing in Public Sector Local Government, Toronto, Canada*. Proceedings of the 2nd International Conference on Information Management and Evaluation. Retrieved March 3, 2021, from www.scopus.com/record/display.uri?eid=2-s2.0-84873432047&origin=inward&txGid=E3C8E9F-D7C6FF29424CAB9C36CD4B018.wsnAw8kcdt7IPYLO0V48gA%3a2

Das, A. (2014). Longitudinal data analysis. In A. Michalos (Ed.), *Encyclopedia of quality of life and well-being research*. Springer.

Dibbern, J., Goles, T., Hirschheim, R., & Jayatilaka, B. (2004). Information systems outsourcing. *ACM SIGMIS Database: The DATABASE for Advances in Information Systems*, *35*(4), 6–102. https://doi.org/10.1145/1035233.1035236

Fan, Z., Suo, W., & Feng, B. (2012). Identifying risk factors of IT outsourcing using interdependent information: An extended DEMATEL method. *Expert Systems with Applications*, *39*(3), 3832–3840. https://doi.org/10.1016/j.eswa.2011.09.092

Fisher, J., Hirschheim, R., & Jacobs, R. (2008). Understanding the outsourcing learning curve: A longitudinal analysis of a large Australian company. *Information Systems Frontiers*, *10*(2), 165–178. https://doi.org/10.1007/s10796-008-9070-y

Fitzmaurice, G., & Ravichandran, C. (2008). A primer in longitudinal data analysis. *Circulation*, *118*(19), 2005–2010. https://doi.org/10.1161/circulationaha.107.714618

Gandhi, S., Gorod, A., & Sauser, B. (2012). Prioritization of outsourcing risks from a systemic perspective. *Strategic Outsourcing: An International Journal*, *5*(1), 39–71. https://doi.org/10.1108/17538291211221951

González, R., Gascó, J., & Llopis, J. (2010). Information systems offshore outsourcing: An exploratory study of motivations and risks in large Spanish firms. *Information Systems Management*, *27*(4), 340–355. https://doi.org/10.1080/10580530903455205

González, R., Gascó, J., & Llopis, J. (2016). Information systems outsourcing reasons and risks: Review and evolution. *Journal of Global Information Technology Management*, *19*(4), 223–249. https://doi.org/10.1080/1097198x.2016.1246932

González, R. M., Gascó, J., & Llopis, J. (2007). El outsourcing de sistemas de información: un estudio descriptivo y longitudinal. *Investigaciones Europeas De Dirección Y Economía De La Empresa*, *14*(1), 117–138. https://doi.org/10.1016/s1135-2523(12)60015-x

Grover, V., Cheon, M., & Teng, J. (1994). A descriptive study on the outsourcing of information systems functions. *Information &Amp; Management*, *27*(1), 33–44. https://doi.org/10.1016/0378-7206(94)90100-7

Grover, V., Cheon, M., & Teng, J. (1996). The effect of service quality and partnership on the outsourcing of information systems functions. *Journal of Management Information Systems*, *12*(4), 89–116. https://doi.org/10.1080/07421222.1996.11518102

Gupta, U., & Gupta, A. (1992). Outsourcing the IS function. *Information Systems Management*, *9*(3), 44–47. https://doi.org/10.1080/10580539208906881

Han, K., & Mithas, S. (2013). Information technology outsourcing and non-IT operating costs: An empirical investigation. *MIS Quarterly*, *37*(1), 315–331. https://doi.org/10.25300/MISQ/2013/37.1.14

Harland, C., Knight, L., Lamming, R., & Walker, H. (2005). Outsourcing: Assessing the risks and benefits for organisations, sectors and nations. *International Journal of Operations &Amp; Production Management*, *25*(9), 831–850. https://doi.org/10.1108/01443570510613929

Hayes, D., Hunton, J., & Reck, J. (2000). Information systems outsourcing announcements: Investigating the impact on the market value of contract-granting firms. *Journal of Information Systems*, *14*(2), 109–125.

Hedeker, D., & Gibbons, R. (2006). *Longitudinal data analysis*. John Wiley & Sons.

Jurison, J. (1995). The role of risk and return in information technology outsourcing decisions. *Journal of Information Technology, 10(*4), 239–247.

Kai-Fu, L. (2018). *AI superpowers: China, Silicon Valley, and the new world order.* Houghton Mifflin Harcourt.

Kehal, H., & Singh, V. (2006). *Outsourcing and offshoring in the 21st century: A socio-economic perspective (pp.* 1–17). Idea Group Publishing. https://doi.org/10.4018/978-1-59140-875-8

Kluk, J., (2010). *Changes of the profile of risk factors associated with requirements management in outsourcing projects.* 16th International Conference on Information and Software Technologies, Kaunas.

Kulu, A. (2021). Risk and benefits of information technology (IT) outsourcing in Nigerian polytechnic libraries. *International Journal of Public Administration and Management Research, 4*(1), 24–30. http://journals.rcmss.com/index.php/ijpamr/article/view/433

Lacity, M., & Hirschheim, R. (1993). The information systems outsourcing bandwagon. *Sloan Management Review, 35*(1), 73–86.

Lacity, M., Hirschheim, R., & Willcocks, L. (1994). Realizing outsourcing expectations. Incredible expectations, credible outcomes. *Information Systems Management, 11*(4), 7–18. https://doi.org/10.1080/07399019408964664

Lacity, M., Khan, S., & Willcocks, L. (2009). A review of the IT outsourcing literature: Insights for practice. *The Journal of Strategic Information Systems, 18*(3), 130–146. https://doi.org/10.1016/j.jsis.2009.06.002

Lacity, M., Khan, S., & Yan, A. (2017). Review of the empirical business services sourcing literature: An update and future directions. *Outsourcing and Offshoring Business Services*, 499–651. https://doi.org/10.1007/978-3-319-52651-5_14

Lacity, M., Khan, S., Yan, A., & Willcocks, L. (2010). A review of the IT outsourcing empirical literature and future research directions. *Journal of Information Technology, 25*(4), 395–433. https://doi.org/10.1057/jit.2010.21

Laumer, S., Blinn, N., & Eckhardt, A. (2012*). Opening the black box of outsourcing knowledge intensive business processes – A longitudinal case study of outsourcing recruiting activities.* 2012 45th Hawaii International Conference on System Sciences. https://doi.org/10.1109/hicss.2012.459

Lee, E., Gerla, M., Pau, G., Lee, U., & Lim, J. (2016). Internet of vehicles: From intelligent grid to autonomous cars and vehicular fogs. *International Journal of Distributed Sensor Networks, 12*(9), 155014771666550. https://doi.org/10.1177/1550147716665500

Madhuchhanda, D., & Saji, K. (2009). Risks in offshore IT outsourcing: A service provider perspective. *European Management Journal, 27*, 418–428.

Małysiak, J. (2018). Top 5 reasons for outsourcing in Poland, Retrieved July 23, 2022, from https://itsg-global.com/top-5-reasons-outsourcing-to-poland/

Mayer-Schönberger, V., & Ramge, T. (2018). *Reinventing capitalism in the age of big data.* Basic Books.

McAfee, A., & Brynjolfsson, E. (2017). *Machine, platform, crowd: Harnessing our digital future.* W.W. Norton & Company.

McFarlan, F., & Nolan, R. (1995). How to manage an IT outsourcing Alliance. *Sloan Management Review, 36*(2), 8–23.

Miller, D., & Friesen, P. (1982). The longitudinal analysis of organizations: A methodological perspective. *Management Science, 28*(9), 1013–1034. https://doi.org/10.1287/mnsc.28.9.1013

Nakatsu, R., & Iacovou, C. (2009). A comparative study of important risks factors involved in offshore and domestic outsourcing of software development projects: A two-panel Delphi study. *Information & Management, 46*(1), 57–68.

Nassimbeni, G., Sartor, M., & Dus, D. (2012). Security risks in service offshoring and outsourcing. *Industrial Management &Amp; Data Systems, 112*(3), 405–440. https://doi.org/10.1108/02635571211210059

Ngwenyama, O., & Sullivan, W. (2007). Outsourcing contracts as instruments of risk management. *Journal of Enterprise Information Management, 20*(6), 615–640. https://doi.org/10.1108/17410390710830691

Olson, D. (2007). Evaluation of ERP outsourcing. *Computers &Amp; Operations Research, 34*(12), 3715–3724. https://doi.org/10.1016/j.cor.2006.01.010

Quinn, J. (1999). Strategic outsourcing: Leveraging knowledge capabilities. *Sloan Management Review, 40*(4), 9–21.

Ragowsky, A., Licker, P., Miller, J., Gefen, D., & Stern, M. (2014). Do not call me chief information officer, but chief integration officer: A summary of the 2011 Detroit CIO roundtable. *Communications of the AIS, 34*(1), 1333–1346.

Salimath, M., Cullen, J., & Umesh, U. (2008). Outsourcing and performance in entrepreneurial firms: Contingent relationships with entrepreneurial configurations. *Decision Sciences, 39*(3), 359–381. https://doi.org/10.1111/j.1540-5915.2008.00196.x

Schneider, S., & Sunyaev, A. (2016). Determinant factors of cloud-sourcing decisions: Reflecting on the IT outsourcing literature in the era of cloud computing. *Journal of Information Technology, 31*(1), 1–31. https://doi.org/10.1057/jit.2014.25

Śledziewska, K., & Włoch, R. (2020). *Gospodarka cyfrowa*. Wydawnictwa Uniwersytetu Warszawskiego.

Słoniec, J., Kaczorowska, A., & Motyka, S. (2016). Risk assessment of IT outsourcing in enterprises depending on their branch. *Zeszyty Naukowe Politechniki Śląskiej Seria Organizacja i Zarządzania, 99*, 473–486.

Słoniec, J., Kaczorowska, A., & Motyka, S. (2018). Generations of the development of IT outsourcing in Poland. *Acta Scientiarum Polonorum. Series: Oeconomia, 17*(4), 141–155.

Smith, M., Mitra, S., & Narasimhan, S. (1998). Information systems outsourcing: A study of pre-event firm characteristics. *Journal of Management Information Systems, 15*(2), 61–93. https://doi.org/10.1080/07421222.1998.11518209

Stańczk-Hugiet, E. (2014). Longitudinal research in management, or how to see regularities in dynamics. *Organization and Management, 2*, 45–56.

Sullivan, W., & Ngwenyama, O. (2005). How are public sector organizations managing IS outsourcing risks? An analysis of outsourcing guidelines from three jurisdictions. *The Journal of Computer Information Systems, 45(3)*, 73–87.

Svejvig, P., & Pries-Heje, J. (2011). Enterprise Systems outsourcing "Behind the Curtain": A case study showing how rational and institutional explanations coexist and complement each other. *International Journal of Enterprise Information Systems, 7(1)*, 1–17. https://doi.org/10.4018/jeis.2011010101.

Thouin, M., Hoffman, J., & Ford, E. (2009). IT outsourcing and firm-level performance: A transaction cost perspective. *Information &Amp; Management, 46*(8), 463–469. https://doi.org/10.1016/j.im.2009.08.006

Vivek, S., Banwet, D., & Shankar, R. (2007). Analysis of interactions among core, transaction and relationship-specific investments: The case of offshoring. *Journal of Operations Management, 26*(2), 180–197. https://doi.org/10.1016/j.jom.2007.02.010

Walden, E., & Hoffman, J. (2007). Organizational form, incentives and the management of information technology: Opening the black box of outsourcing. *Computers &Amp; Operations Research, 34*(12), 3575–3591. https://doi.org/10.1016/j.cor.2006.01.002

Willcocks, L., Feeny, D., & Olson, N. (2006). Implementing core IS capabilities. *European Management Journal, 24*(1), 28–37. https://doi.org/10.1016/j.emj.2005.12.005

Willcocks, L., Lacity, M., & Kern, T. (1999). Risk mitigation in IT outsourcing strategy revisited: Longitudinal case research at LISA. *The Journal of Strategic Information Systems*, *8*(3), 285–314. https://doi.org/10.1016/s0963-8687(00)00022-6

Yang, D., Kim, S., Nam, C., & Min, J. (2007). Developing a decision model for business process outsourcing. *Computers &Amp; Operations Research*, *34*(12), 3769–3778. https://doi.org/10.1016/j.cor.2006.01.012

Yanosky, R. (2008). From users to choosers: The cloud and the changing shape of enterprise authority. In R. N. Katz (Ed.), *The tower and the cloud: Educause e-book, campanile* (pp. 126–136). University of California.

Yu, T. (2013). An empirical study of collaborative partnering among enterprises and government organizations for information system outsourcing. *Applied Economics*, *46*(3), 312–322. https://doi.org/10.1080/00036846.2013.844332

Index

Note: Page references in *italics* denote figure and in **bold** tables.

For Product Safety Concerns and Information please contact our EU
representative GPSR@taylorandfrancis.com
Taylor & Francis Verlag GmbH, Kaufingerstraße 24, 80331 München, Germany

www.ingramcontent.com/pod-product-compliance
Ingram Content Group UK Ltd.
Pitfield, Milton Keynes, MK11 3LW, UK
UKHW020834221026
476832UK00010B/325

9781032470351